To my buddies Joanna and Perri

**To my wife Cheryl,
and to my parents Keith and Bess**

PREFACE

Enthusiasm for economics is proportional to one's appreciation of its usefulness and analytical and predictive power. One method of demonstrating the relevance and implications of economics is to discuss current issues in the classroom.

This book is designed to facilitate the analysis of news stories using economics. It shows that economics has the capacity to explain a wide variety of phenomena, starting with the first day of class. Distinctively, the book guides the student through the analysis of each news story.

As well as enhancing student interest in economics, this book can be used to raise the quality and the effectiveness of the learning process. It affords opportunities for students to think critically, applying theoretical concepts to meaningful real-world situations. It encourages writing, and therefore thinking, about economic principles. It allows students to practice using concepts and the vocabulary of economics which many students regard in the same way as a foreign language. It also provides a means for the instructor to vary the content of class and maintain student attention.

In writing the second edition of *Economics in the News,* our objective was to continue to provide the student and the instructor with a variety of interesting and topical issues for discussion and analysis. Reviewing the issues that were selected for the first edition reminded us of how quickly economic issues change, and, as a result, how exciting and dynamic the study of economics is. For example, impending recession has given way to recovery. Command economies in the eastern bloc are now being transformed into market economies. Consequently, all of the articles in the second edition are new.

How to Use This Book

As in the first edition, this book comprises four units:
(1) Introduction;
(2) Microeconomics;
(3) Macroeconomics; and
(4) International Economics, Growth and Development, and Comparative Systems. Each unit contains a number of subunits that cover major economic topics. Each subunit includes a recapitulation of relevant concepts, a statement of the learning objectives, a summary of the article, and a logical sequence of questions carefully crafted to prompt the application of appropriate principles. Some of the articles have been abridged to highlight the principles being studied.

The exercises are intended to supplement an economics textbook. They have been developed so that they can easily be incorporated into lecture material. After assigning a given topic in the text, the instructor may assign a corresponding article in *Economics in the News.* The "Key for Use with Representative Principles of Economics Textbooks" following the Preface illustrates the correspondence between topics in this book and chapters in selected textbooks. The question sheets are perforated so that they can be submitted as homework. Solutions to the exercises are available to instructors on request from the Business and Economics Division at Addison-Wesley.

The second edition of *Economics in the News* also contains ten sets of exercises to accompany videotapes of reports from the "MacNeil/Lehrer Newshour." These videos cover an assortment of micro- and macroeconomic topics and offer an additional dimension to the process of understanding key economic concepts and relating these concepts to issues and events in the news. A guide to using these videos is also available from the Business and Economics Division of Addison-Wesley. It contains some hints on how to integrate the video presentation into the classroom lecture, a detailed description of the video, comprehension questions and answers, the application questions featured in this volume, and suggestions concerning other concepts that can be illustrated with the video.

We hope that this book will help make your economics course satisfying and rewarding.

Acknowledgments

Although the title page only credits the work of the two authors, as with any product this book is the result of the combined inputs of many people. To all of them we would like to offer our sincere thanks.

We are particularly grateful to Joseph Powers, a graduate student at the University of Cincinnati for helping us find topical articles for the second edition. Virginia Farquhar provided invaluable secretarial help with an equanimity under pressure that is enviable. We wish her a long and happy retirement effective January 1993. We hope that we did not cause her to make that decision.

We remain indebted to two people who were responsible for the concept becoming reality in the form of the first edition. Jim Lawler, Territory Manager in the Midwest for Addison-Wesley, believed in our idea, encouraged us, and advocated our proposal to the Business and Economics editors at Addison-Wesley. Critical to the publication of the book was Barbara Rifkind, then Senior Editor, Economics and Finance, (now Executive Editor, Business and Economics). Barbara again deserves recognition for her continued support for the second edition of this book.

Marjorie Williams, Senior Editor, Economics, for this second edition, has ably borne overall responsibility for this book. Christine O'Brien, formerly Associate Editor, Business and Economics, initiated the work for the second edition before becoming Market Research Supervisor. Kari Heen, Assistant Editor, Economics, took over the day-to-day administration of the project. We appreciate her understanding, patience, and especially her good humor.

We would also like to thank Cindy Johnson, who was the project manager. Mary Dyer, Permissions Editor, was invaluable in negotiating the rights to reprint the articles in this book. Her skills meant that very few had to be rewritten using alternative articles. Janice K. Byer did a wonderful job of copyediting our manuscript: we say "wonderful" because she changed very little of it! We are also indebted to Karen Wernholm, Senior Production Supervisor; Kazia Navas, Managing Editor; and Karen Lynch, term-of-project assistant.

More generally, we would like to thank Joseph L. Craycraft, Head of the Department of Economics at the University of Cincinnati, for his encouragement of this project. It is unusual to find such strong support for publications designed to enhance teaching on the part of a head of a Ph.D.-granting, research-oriented, department.

Most of all, we wish to pay special tribute to our families for their forbearance during our preoccupation with the book and frequent seclusion on weekends and evenings. The product proves that the book was not just an excuse.

S.P.
P.K.W.

Key for Use with Representative Principles of Economics Textbooks

Topic and Article # in Economics in the News	Chapters in Selected Textbooks							
	Parkin 2nd ed	Byrns 5th ed	Miller 6th ed	McConnell 11th ed	Gwartney 6th ed	Schiller 5th ed	Baumol 5th ed	Ruffin 4th ed
INTRODUCTION								
Scarcity, Choice, & Opportunity Cost								
1	1	1	1	2	2	1	3	2
2	1	1	1	2	2	1	3	2
3	1	2	4	2/3	2	1	3	2
Production Possibility Frontiers								
4	3	2	1	2	2	1	3	2
5	3	2	1	2	2	1	3	2
Demand and Supply								
6	4	3	2	4	3	2	4	4
7	4	3	2	4	3	2	4	4
8	4	3	2	4	3	2	4	4
9	4	3	2	4	3	2	4	4
10	4	4	2	4	3	2	4	4
11	4	4	2	4	3	2	4	4
12	4	4	2	4	3	2	4	4
MICROECONOMICS								
Elasticity								
13	5	19	19	22	17	19	22	24
14	5	19	19	22	17	19	22	24
15	5	19	19	22	3	19	22	24
Market Interference								
16	6	4	2	22	3	2	4	4
17	6	4	2	22	3	2	4	4
Consumer Equilibrium								
18	7	20	20	23	17	19	21	25
19	8	20	20	23	17	19	21	25
Costs of Production								
20	9	21/22	21	24	18	20	23	27
21	10	22	21	24	18	20	23	27
22	10	22	21	24	18	20	23	27
23	10	22	21	24	App. A	20	23	27

continued

Topic and Article # in Economics in the News	Parkin 2nd ed	Byrns 5th ed	Miller 6th ed	McConnell 11th ed	Gwartney 6th ed	Schiller 5th ed	Baumol 5th ed	Ruffin 4th ed
Perfect Competition								
24	11	23	22	25	19	22	25	28
25	11	23	22	25	19	22	25	28
26	11	23	22	25	19	22	25	28
Monopoly								
27	12	24	24	26	20	23	27	29
28	12	24	24	26	20	23	27	30
29	12	24	24	26	20	23	32	29
Monopolistic Competition and Oligopoly								
30	13	25	25	27	21	24	28	29
31	13	25/26	25	28	21	24	28	31
Labor Markets								
32	14	28	27	29	23	29	36	35
33	14	28	27	30	23	29	36	35
34	14	28	27	30	23	29	36	35
35	14	28	27	30	23	29	36	35
Capital and Natural Resource Markets								
36	16	30	29	30	25	31	35/36	38
37	16	–	–	–	–	34	30	26
38	16	30	29	31	25	31	35	37
39	16	–	–	–	28	–	34	–
Income Distribution								
40	15	28	30	37	24	29	36	38
41	15	29	28	38	26	30	36	36
42	15	29	30	38	24	29	37	38
43	18	36	30	37	27	32	37	38
Government Intervention								
44	19	31	31	6/33	29	27	29/34	39
45	19	31	31	6/33	29	27	29	39
46	21	27	26	34	22	25	31	33
47	21	33	26	34	20	26	27/31	33
MACROECONOMICS								
Introduction to Macroeconomic Variables								
48	22	5/6/7	7	9/10	6	5/6/7	5	5
49	22	6	7	10	7	6	6	5
50	22	5	7	10	7	5	5	5
51	23	7	9	9	6	4	5	6
52	23	6	9	10	6	7	6	5
53	23	7	9	9	6	4	5	6

continued

Topic and Article # in Economics in the News	Parkin 2nd ed	Byrns 5th ed	Miller 6th ed	McConnell 11th ed	Gwartney 6th ed	Schiller 5th ed	Baumol 5th ed	Ruffin 4th ed
Aggregate Demand and Aggregate Supply								
54	24	5	10	11	8/9	5	8/10	10
55	24	5	10	11	8/9	5	8/10	10
Expenditure and Income								
56	25	8	11	12	10	8	7	6
57	26	9	12	12	10	9	9	9
Money and Banking								
58	27	11	14	15	12	12	12	12
59	27	12	14	17	12	13	13	14
60	28	12	16	17	12	13	13	13
61	28	11	15	16	12	12	12	13
Aggregate Demand Fluctuations								
62	29	13/15	13	17	13	14	13	14
63	29	10/15	13	14	11	14	13	11
64	29	–	–	–	11/13	14	–	9
Aggregate Supply Fluctuations								
65	30	15/16	17	19	9	14	16/17	10
66	30	15/16	17	19	8/14	14	16	10
67	30	15/16	17	19	9/14	14	16	10
Inflation								
68	31	16	17	19	14	–	16	15
69	31	16	17	19	7/14	17	11	15
Recession								
70	32	19	–	14	7/15	17	14	10
71	32	19	19	19	14	9	16	10
Stabilization Policy								
72	33	16	18	14	15	14/17	14	18
73	33	16/17	18	14	15	17	14	18
74	33	10	17	19	11	15	14	11
Deficits								
75	34	14	13	20	16	10	15	11
76	34	14	13	20	16	10	15	11

continued

Topic and Article # in Economics in the News	Parkin 2nd ed	Byrns 5th ed	Miller 6th ed	McConnell 11th ed	Gwartney 6th ed	Schiller 5th ed	Baumol 5th ed	Ruffin 4th ed
INTERNATIONAL ECONOMICS, GROWTH AND DEVELOPMENT, AND COMPARATIVE SYSTEMS								
International Economics								
77	35	19	33	39	31	35	18	21
78	35	19	33	39	31	35	18	22
79	36	20	34	40	32	36	19	23
80	36	20	34	40	32	36	19	23
81	36	20	34	40	32	36	20	24
Growth and Development								
82	37	18	36	41	33	37	38	20
83	37	18	36	41	33	37	38	20
Comparative Systems								
84	38	39	37	42	34	38	40	42
85	38	39	37	42	34	38	40	42

CONTENTS

SECTION 2 MICROECONOMICS

SECTION 3 MACROECONOMICS

SECTION 4   INTERNATIONAL ECONOMICS, GROWTH AND DEVELOPMENT, AND COMPARATIVE SYSTEMS   389

SECTION 1

INTRODUCTION

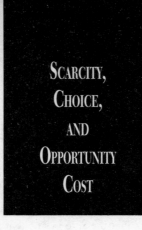

1. Regulations to Reduce Risks Refused

Every choice we make in life involves giving up something else. Economists refer to this as an opportunity cost. It is defined as the value of the best forgone alternative. Sometimes the opportunity costs of a particular course of action are estimated differently by different people, perhaps because they value alternatives differently, or because they perceive costs differently.

In the accompanying article, the Department of Labor and the Office of Management and Budget (OMB) have vastly different notions of the opportunity cost of regulations protecting workers from exposure to hazardous workplace substances.

After studying your text, reading the article, and answering the questions, you should be able to:

◆◆ Define opportunity cost

◆◆ Apply opportunity cost to real world situations

◆◆ Evaluate opportunity cost from different viewpoints

◆◆ Recognize that noneconomic considerations may enter the calculation of opportunity cost

Preview

◆ OMB blocked new workplace health standards proposed by the Department of Labor's Occupational Safety and Health Administration (OSHA).

◆ OSHA argued that the standards would decrease worker exposure to hazardous substances and thereby would save lives.

◆ OMB's position was that the regulations would add to employer costs and cause employers to lower wages or cut employment.

◆ Also, since health is related to income levels, OMB argued that the regulations would actually cost lives.

◆ The Labor Department responded that the inclusion of economic risks was illegal.

◆ This decision was taken as the Bush administration took broad steps to reduce the spread of regulations.

OMB's Logic: Less Protection Saves Lives

The Office of Management and Budget has blocked new health standards for more than 6 million workers in the construction, maritime and agricultural industries on the theory that less protection may save more lives than adding regulatory costs to employers.

The novel theory, outlined in a letter from OMB to the Labor Department last week, argues that added regulatory costs could force an employer to either lower wages or cut employment. If this happens, OMB asserts, it could have a negative impact on workers' health because, it says, higher-paid workers tend to take better care of themselves and if they can no longer afford to do so, more may be killed than saved.

At issue are standards proposed by the Labor Department's Occupational Safety and Health Administration to set permissible exposure limits (PELs) for more than 1,000 substances used in the three industries. The standards, which were approved nearly four years ago for all other industries, are designed to protect workers from excessive exposure to hazardous substances in the workplace.

OMB said it would not consider the proposed regulations until the department completes an analysis showing whether the new rules would have an adverse effect on wages and employment levels in the affected industries. Departmental sources predict such a study could take several years and still would be inconclusive....

The OMB directive comes as the White House has declared a 90-day moratorium on new federal regulations. It also coincides with an announcement by President Bush during a campaign trip to Detroit last week that the auto industry would not have to build cars that would keep gasoline fumes from escaping during refueling.

A senior department official said OMB has put Labor Secretary Lynn Martin in an "incredibly awkward position." Any showdown with OMB is apt to be a major, public test of how much clout Martin has with Bush. Martin, a 10-year veteran of Congress, often has traded on her close ties to the president in dealing with department issues. "This is going to be hot," a department source said.

OMB last Friday refused a formal department request to withdraw the letter. Yesterday, under Martin's direction, the department was drafting a reply to OMB. It questions OMB's legal authority to force OSHA to weigh safety benefits against economic risks for federal health standards. The Supreme Court ruled in 1981 in a case involving cotton dust standards that cost-benefit analysis was illegal in determining health standards.

The draft, being circulated in the department, also suggests that if OMB wants to create a new policy such as the one outlined in the OSHA letter, it should publish a proposal in the Federal Register and let all the regulatory agencies comment on it.

James B. MacRae Jr., acting administrator of OMB's Office of Information and Regulatory Affairs, wrote: "The positive effect on wealth on health has been established both theoretically and empirically. Richer workers on average buy more leisure time, more nutritious food, more preventive health care and smoke and drink less than poorer workers.

"Government regulations often have significant impact on the income and wealth of workers. To the extent that firms cannot pass on regulatory compliance cost increases to consumers, firms will absorb these costs by cutting wages and by reducing employment."

Therefore, MacRae wrote, "OSHA should estimate whether the possible effect of compliance costs on workers' health will outweigh the health improvements that may result from decreased exposure to the regulated substances." He said he was sending the proposed draft regulations back to the Labor Department for further analysis "to compare the health effects of these income changes to the health benefits that OSHA attributes to reduced exposure."

In requesting the analysis, MacRae cited a recent federal appeals court case involving OSHA and the United Auto Workers union. He cited research asserting that every $7.5 million in additional regulatory expenditures may result in an additional death from lowered worker income. Because the proposed OSHA regulations would add an estimated $163 million in annual employer costs, MacRae argued in his letter, the new rules could result in an additional 22 deaths. Because OSHA estimates the new regulations would save 8 to 13 lives a year, MacRae reasoned, there would be a net increase of 8 to 14 deaths a year....

QUESTIONS

1. According to OSHA, what would be the opportunity cost for workers of *not* introducing the proposed OSHA standards for hazardous workplace substances in terms of

   a) safety and health? Explain your answer.

   b) lives saved? Be specific.

2. According to OMB, what would be the opportunity cost for workers of the proposed OSHA standards in terms of

   a) their livelihoods? Why?

   b) general health? Explain why.

   c) the overall number of lives saved? Explain your answer.

3. What would be the opportunity cost for the consumer of goods that would be affected by the proposed OSHA standards? Explain the assumption underlying your answer.

4. What would be the opportunity cost for Secretary of Labor Lynn Martin of fighting OMB over the standards?

5. a) What is the opportunity cost for citizens of not requiring auto producers to prevent the escape of gasoline fumes during refueling?

   b) What would be the opportunity cost for producers and consumers of a regulation requiring auto producers to prevent the emission of fumes during refueling?

6. a) Why might an economist disagree with the blanket moratorium on new federal regulations?

   b) What might have been the reasoning of the White House in deciding to declare a moratorium on new federal regulations?

7. Why might the Supreme Court have ruled that it was illegal to include economic risks in the determination of cotton dust standards?

SCARCITY,
CHOICE,
AND
OPPORTUNITY
COST

2. Ecology and the Economy: The Greens Have the Blues

In our world, resources are scarce and choices have to be made between competing alternatives. The options involve costs in terms of the forgone opportunities which have to be weighed in making a choice. These considerations are relevant whether we are talking about the world as a whole, a country, a city, a family, or an individual. The article reprinted here refers to scarcity, choice, and opportunity cost in the context of the struggle between conservationists and groups advocating the "wise use" of resources.

After studying your text, reading the article, and answering the questions, you should be able to:

◆◆ Recognize the scarcity of resources in the economy

◆◆ Realize that the solution is to make choices

◆◆ Understand the approach of economists in deciding between alternatives

◆◆ Realize that competition in the decision-making process is inevitable

◆◆ Cite examples of opportunity costs for various goods and services

◆◆ Rationalize alternative viewpoints in terms of differing evaluations of opportunity costs

Preview

◆ Ecological concerns are becoming increasingly subordinated to concerns about the economy.

◆ Support for environmental groups is weakening.

◆ Opposition is increasing from "wise-use" groups who argue that resources can be used for economic purposes without destroying nature.

◆ Wise-use groups are using political lobbying to change laws and legal action to compensate those prevented from developing resources.

◆ To ensure its continued viability, the green movement needs to demonstrate that conservation is not incompatible with economic growth.

Gunning for the Greens

Who cares about a few spotted owls when loggers' jobs are at stake? Why worry about caribou when America needs more of Alaska's oil? Who can afford to think about the environment when the economy is the pits?

When times get tough, the questions facing environmentalists get even tougher. And these days, economic anxieties and shifting political winds are threatening to produce a green-out effect that could make tree huggers feel as endangered as the California condor. Epochal events such as the gulf war and the collapse of the Soviet Union have pushed most domestic ecological concerns off the front pages. The recession has prompted many people to question the costs of environmentalism and make it harder for preservation groups to raise money and boost membership. In the presidential campaign, saving the planet has become an orphaned issue. No savvy candidate would dwell on ozone depletion and the need for biodiversity when voters are worrying about whether they'll have a job next year or be able to pay their medical bills.

Environmental groups claim that their members are as committed as ever, but recruits are getting harder to find. For every organization that is still growing—membership in the Nature Conservancy jumped 15% last year, to 620,000—another one seems to have hit a plateau....

... there is no marking time in the opposition camp, which is more organized than ever before. Scores of interest groups—including ranchers, miners, loggers, developers and manufacturers—have become allies in a "wise-use movement" to fight what they see as the extremism of those who put wilderness protection and the rights of endangered animals before the welfare of humans. "There seems to be a coalescing of different economic interests to fight the green devils," observes environmentalist Thomas Lovejoy of the Smithsonian Institution.

This antigreen brigade advocates economic development in wilderness areas, arguing that land can be used wisely for human benefit without destroying Mother Nature. The timing of the campaign is excellent, since two landmark pieces of environmental legislation are up for renewal in Congress this year: the Endangered Species Act, which prohibits development that drives a species to extinction; and the Clean Water Act, which contains a provision protecting wetlands from uncontrolled exploitation. The wise-users are pressuring Congress to weaken those laws as a way to spur economic growth. Another goal is to block proposed reforms of the federal mining law that would make it harder for companies to open mines on public land. "Anytime anyone gets as much power as the environmental movement has achieved, a backlash can be expected," says Oregon logger Tom Hirons....

Hoping to encourage a public and political backlash, the wise-use movement has been adopting many of the tactics long used by environmentalists. Last September timber interests from the Pacific Northwest invited other antigreen groups to join in a five-day lobbying campaign in Washington dubbed the "Fly-In for Freedom." In all, some 370 people from 25 states showed up to stage rallies and urge Congress to roll back environmental regulations. Two months later, many of the same activists met in St. Louis to form the Alliance for America, a potentially powerful umbrella organization that boasts more than 125 member groups. They range from Louisiana shrimpers, who resent federal rules designed to keep them from accidentally snaring sea turtles in their nets, to off-road-vehicle enthusiasts who want to see more trails built in national parks and wilderness areas....

Green activists have long used lawsuits to tie up development projects; now wise-users are turning the tables. "When the environmental movement tells lies that hurt you," Ron Arnold [of the Center for the Defense of Free Enterprise] tells his followers, "sue the bastards." Apple growers have in fact sued the Natural Resources Defense Council, which sounded an alarm three years ago that Alar, a ripening agent sprayed on the fruit, could cause cancer in children. The growers charge that the warning was unjustified and caused them to suffer severe financial losses.

An even more serious challenge to environmentalism comes from lawsuits that seek to compensate landowners who cannot develop their property because of conservation laws. Last year the U.S. Supreme Court let stand a lower-court decision that required the U.S. government to pay $150 million to a coal company in Wyoming that was barred from mining in a protected area. If such payouts became routine, they could undermine environmental laws by making the government more reluctant to control development.

While George Bush is much greener than his predecessor and can point to several accomplishments, such as his tree-planting program and the passage of a strengthened Clean Air Act in 1990, economic woes seem to be threatening his commitment to be the "environment President." White House officials say he is considering a 90-day moratorium on new government regulations and a thorough re-examination of federal rules that put economic burdens on businesses. Since many of the regulations needed to implement the Clean Air Act have yet to be written, environmentalists fear that the Administration will try to weaken the law in the rulemaking process.

That could set off a conflict in Congress, as could efforts by antigreen lobbyists to tamper with the Endangered Species Act and the Clean Water Act.

Though wise-users are on the offensive at the moment, the environmental cause still has strong support in Congress. When the President put forward his energy plan last year, the Senate tabled it because it included a provision to open the Arctic National Wildlife Refuge to oil drilling.

The wise-use movement hopes to gain the upper hand by presenting itself as the voice of moderation in difficult economic times. The only way for environmentalists to counter that strategy is to show more flexibility and demonstrate that conservation is not incompatible with economic growth. Many preservation groups are already moving in that direction, and a consensus is emerging that government regulators should set firm antipollution goals but

give business the latitude to find the most efficient way to meet those goals.

To remain a political force in the 1990s, environmentalists will need to be more adept at touting long-term economic benefits of conservation. They can point out that buying energy-efficient equipment ultimately saves money, that antipollution technologies can create as many jobs as they destroy and that preserving a forest may rescue an overlooked plant that could yield a cure for AIDS or cancer. Greens and wise-users disagree on many issues, but they agree on one inescapable fact: unless society does a better job of reconciling economic growth with the conservation of natural resources, future generations will have neither a healthy environment nor a healthy economy.

—Charles P. Alexander, "Gunning for the Greens," February 3, 1992, *Time*.

QUESTIONS

1. a) Why is it not possible both to protect the spotted owl and to ensure the employment of loggers? Cast your answer in terms of scarcity.

   b) Why has the conflict between loggers and conservationists become more acute? Again, refer to scarcity in formulating your answer.

2. In the face of pressure to save endangered owls and protect jobs, what must the government do? Why?

3. a) What principles would economists use to resolve the problem?

   b) How in practice is the conflict being resolved? Is it a cooperative or competitive process?

   c) Are there any opportunity costs to this process? Does it matter?

4. a) What is the opportunity cost of protecting caribou in Alaska?

b) What is the opportunity cost of drilling for oil in Alaska?

5. If more oil could be found outside Alaska, diminishing the need for Alaskan production, would there be no opportunity cost? Explain your answer.

6. In terms of the economic approach, does it make sense to require economic impact statements to be attached to environmental regulations? Why?

7. One suggestion of conservationists is to have firm antipollution goals but allow businesses the latitude to determine how they will achieve them.

a) How might this reduce the opportunity costs of regulations protecting caribou in Alaska?

b) How might this facilitate economic growth?

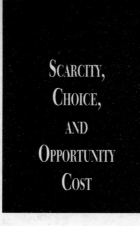

3. Coordinating Choices in the Commonwealth

In every type of economy resources are scarce. Choices have to be made concerning what to produce, how, and for whom. Economists resolve conflicts in the choices preferred by households, firms, and the government through coordination mechanisms. In the USSR a command mechanism was used. Now the Commonwealth of Independent States (CIS) is slowly introducing a market mechanism. The articles reprinted here highlight some of the differences in the two types of mechanisms.

After studying your text, reading the articles, and answering the questions, you should be able to:

◆ ◆ State the chief differences between the coordination mechanisms of the USSR and the CIS

◆ ◆ Explain the distribution of property in command and market economies

◆ ◆ Explain the difference in income inequality in market and planned economies

◆ ◆ Cite the advantages and disadvantages of the market and command mechanisms

Preview

◆ The Soviet economy was run by the state.

◆ Although it had some notable successes, the economy was relatively backward, owing to the characteristics of the command mechanism.

◆ Following the demise of the USSR, Boris Yeltsin introduced the market mechanism in the Russian Republic.

◆ Although the transition was expected to be painful, the market mechanism was seen as the solution of Russian economic problems.

The End

Tyranny is most vulnerable when it tries to reform. For seven decades, the Soviet Union preserved itself entirely by force....

When years of stagnation made change a do-or-die necessity, Mikhail Gorbachev tried to save the Soviet system by making it more humane and more efficient. But the forces of reform soon got out of hand and overwhelmed him, bringing down both the party and the state....

The system invented by Lenin and Stalin was destroyed by its own inner contradictions—as Marxist theorists might say in some other context. The state depended for its existence on total, centralized political and economic control by the Soviet Communist Party. But that leaden hand eventually produced a country that was simply too backward to compete with the rest of the world and too weak politically to hang onto its empire in Eastern Europe. The result was a crisis of self-confidence in Soviet communism. The controls had to be relaxed. Dictatorship turned wimpish, and reform quickly made tyranny untenable.

The Soviet system was an epochal social experiment that captured the imagination of half the world while it appalled and frightened the other half. On the ruins of autocracy, world war and civil strife, it built a new society based on the principle of equality and the abolition of private property. "I have been over into the future, and it works," radical American journalist Lincoln Steffens wrote in 1931, after a visit to the Soviet Union. Marshaling raw resources, both human and material, the Soviet state built a huge industrial base. Despite vast suffering, it summoned up the fighting spirit to defeat the Nazi juggernaut. It produced stunning scientific achievements: a Soviet atomic bomb in 1949, sputnik in 1957, Yuri Gagarin's first manned spaceflight in 1961. "Whether you like it or not, history is on our side," Khrushchev bragged in 1956....

Western socialists began to turn against Soviet communism as early as the 1930s, when Stalin's show trials made gorges rise. By Brezhnev's heyday, genuine belief in communism had all but died out in the Soviet Union itself. It was replaced by bitter cynicism and by a deadly form of egalitarianism that unconsciously prefers shared misery to individual advancement. Rigid central authority was stifling the economy and papering over the ethnic conflicts that would eventually help tear the country apart....

—From Russell Watson with Fred Coleman, "The End," NEWSWEEK, January 6, 1992.

And What Happens Next?

A t the last, the Soviet Union was no more than a shell: an enormous bureaucratic superstructure encompassing bare shelves, empty slogans and hollow men. Can things really get worse under the Commonwealth of Independent States? In the short term, it is all too possible. But that will only start to become clear this week, when Boris Yeltsin's Russian Republic unilaterally imposes sweeping market reforms, including price decontrols that could send consumer goods beyond the reach of most citizens of the former union. "Everyone will find life harder for approximately six months," Yeltsin keeps repeating. "Then prices will fall and goods will begin to fill the market." But not everyone was so confident, perhaps least of all Mikhail Gorbachev. "If we fail to keep the situation under control, it would be awful, for us and for everyone," he said after stepping down last week. A guide to potential flash points:

The Price Crisis Prices for everything but bread, salt, gas, coal and a handful of other staples will soar. Yeltsin's chief economic adviser expects them to double. The former Russian economics minister says they will quadruple. And Soviet newspapers predict that prices for scarce items like lemons could multiply by a factor of 25. At the same time, state stores are to be privatized, but how that will be coordinated is unclear. Most wage ceilings have been removed, raising fears of hyperinflation. Unemployment is also bound to rise. Soup kitchens and special stores will help the neediest to cope. But the possibility of social unrest can't be discounted. Already, war veterans and pensioners have been beaten when they invoked their right to go to the head of food lines.

Food Shortages Parents are panicky about their inability to find dairy products for children. "The prospect is for ongoing food shortages and hunger, if not starvation, in the big cities," said Robert Legvold of Columbia University's Harriman Institute. Yeltsin's strategy assumes that higher prices will shake out food supplies being hoarded in the countryside. But if inflation takes off, food may be withheld by producers waiting for higher prices. And how will workers pay those prices? Many large factories, not yet privatized, could grind to a halt....

Power Failure As a result of the Soviet Union's failure to improve its extraction and distribution systems, coal and oil production have been declining. Now the bills are coming due. Aeroflot, the national airline, has shut down some routes for lack of fuel. There is no gas at all in some provincial capitals, and it's scarce in the big cities. A shortage of diesel fuel compounds the problem of shipping goods over a wrecked road and rail network. The national power grid is overloaded and working at peak capacity. "Should a major breakdown occur, huge regions and even whole sovereign states could find themselves immersed in total darkness," Pravda warned. The most chilling threat of all: widespread shortages of home-heating oil. Says Legvold, "That's the great dread."

—From Tom Masland with Fred Coleman and Anne Underwood, "And What Happens Next?," NEWSWEEK, January 6, 1992.

QUESTIONS

1. In the USSR the command mechanism determined what was produced, how it was produced, and for whom. List the key characteristics of the command mechanism evident in the article.

2. In the CIS the primary economic questions are beginning to be answered through the market mechanism. According to the article, what are the essential features of the market mechanism?

3. a) What distribution of property was needed to make the command mechanism work in the USSR? Why?

   b) Does the market mechanism in the CIS require a different distribution? Why?

4. a) How great was income inequality under the command mechanism? Why?

b) How great will it be under the market mechanism? Why? Substantiate your answer with evidence from the articles.

c) Given the mechanics of each coordination mechanism, how do you explain the difference?

5. a) What were the advantages of the command mechanism of the Soviet Union?

b) What were the disadvantages?

6. a) What are the advantages of the market mechanism of the CIS?

b) What are the disadvantages?

4.
Trade: It Takes Two to Tango

Countries, like people, differ in terms of their abilities to produce various goods and services. It follows that their opportunity costs of producing those items are also different. When one country has lower opportunity costs than another, it has a comparative advantage. It is mutually beneficial for countries to produce more of the goods in which they have a comparative advantage than is necessary for self-sufficiency, because by trading the excess to other countries specializing in the production of other goods, more goods are produced and consumed overall. Without specialization and trade this would be impossible: hence "it takes two to tango."

The editorial considered here relates to the potential benefits of both the United States and Japan freeing trade from protectionist policies.

After studying your text, reading the article, and answering the questions, you should be able to:

◆◆ Explain and represent diagrammatically specialization and self-sufficiency

◆◆ Differentiate between absolute and comparative advantage

◆◆ Understand the basis for, and gains from, trade

Preview

◆ Japan is perceived as a competitor that breaks the rules of free trade.

◆ This has led to calls for the United States to adopt protectionist measures.

◆ Import restraints have saved jobs in some industries.

◆ However, Japanese protectionism is overstated.

◆ Also, U.S. import controls on steel and textiles have caused lower employment in other industries.

◆ President Bush has opened up the Japanese glass, paper, and financial services markets.

◆ The real reason for Japan's export surplus is that their products are better.

America First or America Last?

Are American jobs being lost through a Japanese jujitsu hold on our markets? Does the United States need to keep out imports to save jobs at home? There are now a thousand points of heat between the odd couple of world trade, and not much light. Japan is mythologized every day as a powerful, relentless, dynamic competitor that does not play by the rules. To judge by the noises from New Hampshire, we are developing an inferiority complex that manifests itself in an "America first" call for protectionism. What a folly is in the making!

At the turn of the century we had the same complex about Britain, and the great economist Henry George had the right answer to the clamor then for higher tariffs: "What protection teaches us is to do to ourselves in time of peace what our enemies seek to do to us [with blockades] in time of war." That lesson ought to be burned into our souls from the Great Depression of the 1930s, when Sen. Reed Smoot of Utah and Rep. Willis Hawley of Oregon helped to make it deeper and longer by pushing through an act for higher tariffs. The result: retaliation and lower world trade in 1939 than in 1914.

America-first protectionists never work through to the logical end of their policies; if they did, America would come last. Yes, some jobs may be saved by keeping out a cheaper foreign product. But it does not end there. Take steel. Some 17,000 jobs have been saved through restrictions on imports. But stop cheering. According to the Center for the Study of American Business, the more expensive domestic steel has cost an extra $150,000 for every single job saved. That higher cost has been paid by steel users not simply in cash but also in work lost. In fact, 54,200 jobs were lost in other industries to save the 17,000 in steel. Another example is textiles and apparel. Tariffs are adding about $20 billion annually to consumer bills, leaving less to spend on the output of other workers.

Free trade puts America first. Over the past five years, free trade has contributed much to America's economic growth. Increases in exports, especially high-tech capital goods, have saved this country from an even worse recession. Exports of goods and services, in fact, have contributed about 50 percent of the real growth of the economy over the past five years.

But is Japan cheating? Not if you look at the big picture. Its barriers to trade are lower, on average, than any other country. Its average tariff for industrial products is 2.6 percent, compared with 3 percent for America. Its nontariff barriers, such as quotas and licenses, are similar to those in America, according to the World Bank. No wonder Japan is now one of the world's largest importers. The United States exports more to Japan than it does to Germany, France and Italy combined. Put it this way: Japan imports $394 per capita from America, equal to 1.7 percent of its gross national product, while America imports $360 per capita from Japan, or 1.6 percent of GNP. Our exports to Japan have grown by 115 percent over the past six years. America first.

This is not to say Japan's halo is a perfect circle. Where there is unfairness, where it restricts U.S. goods or companies from its markets, we should respond in a precise way. The day when Admiral Perry could sail into Tokyo Bay and demand everything is gone. President Bush's recent trip was a political disaster because of its ricochet of protectionist and nationalist emotions, but ironically, he and his negotiators made real progress in prying open some tight markets such as glass, paper and financial services. Critically, he raised the concern over trade to the highest political level. So let us be firm abroad—but also frank at home.

The main cause of the Japanese export surplus is that they deliver high-quality goods, designed for consumer taste, accompanied by superior service, at competitive prices. Behind that is a savings and investment level twice as much proportionately as ours and an investment in public infrastructure that is 10 times ours on a per capita basis. Behind our failure is a chronic budget deficit that drains money away from investment and an educational system that fails to produce enough trained personnel. Protectionism is a cop-out because it tries to avoid facing these uncomfortable truths.

America may have a first-class standard of living, but it has a second-class economy and a third-class political system. And protectionism puts America last.

QUESTIONS

In order to keep the analysis simple when answering the following questions, assume that Japan and the United States only produce and consume paper and steel.

1. a) Draw production possibility frontiers for Japan and the United States showing the United States with relatively more resources than Japan and a comparative advantage in machinery manufacture, and Japan with a comparative advantage in steel.

    b) Which country has an absolute advantage in the production of steel and of paper? Explain your reasoning.

    c) Using the concept of opportunity cost, explain how your diagram shows that Japan has a comparative advantage in steel.

    d) Mark points on the frontiers showing where each country might be when protectionism prevents specialization and trade. Label them *J1* and *US1*. Show how much steel and paper is produced and consumed by the two countries. Label it *PC1*.

2. a) On your diagram, draw points (labeled *J2* and *US2*) showing where Japan and the United States might be after agreeing to free trade in steel and paper. Show how much steel and paper is now produced and consumed by the two countries. Label it *PC2*.

b) In terms of your diagram, explain why both countries are better off.

c) Referring to your diagram, explain why the loss of jobs in the U.S. steel industry does not matter in the aggregate.

d) Why, then, does protectionism persist?

3. If the United States heeds the advice of the author of the article, and increases saving, investment, and education such that efficiency is increased in all sectors,

a) how would the production possibility curve of the United States change?

b) should the United States export a different good? Explain your answer.

5.
The Perils and Payoffs of Peace

The scarcity of resources such as labor, capital, and natural resources places limits on the production levels it is possible to achieve. When all resources are fixed and employed, devoting more resources to one use necessarily involves an opportunity cost, that is, less of other goods can be produced.

The maximum combinations of goods it is possible to produce with a given amount of resources can be represented diagrammatically in terms of a production possibility frontier. The slope of the frontier shows the opportunity cost of producing more of one good in terms of another good. The accompanying article concerns the reallocation of government spending between different budget items following the end of the cold war, together with the opportunity costs of alternative choices.

After studying your text, reading the article, and answering the questions, you should be able to:

◆◆ Represent resource allocation decisions in terms of a production possibility frontier

◆◆ Recognize that spending more on one activity involves opportunity costs

◆◆ Demonstrate the principle of opportunity cost using the production possibility frontier

Preview

- The end of the cold war has led to defense budget cuts.

- Analysts argue that productivity and competitiveness may improve as a result.

- Unemployment may increase in states with large defense industries.

- There is disagreement over how to spend the peace dividend.

- President Bush wants to use it in part to reduce taxes.

- Many Democrats would prefer to increase spending on domestic programs.

- Some economists favor reducing the deficit and therefore interest rates.

Cutting Up the Military

James Benson used to earn nearly $20 an hour as a machine parts planner at Lockheed Aeronautics in California. But when the cold war ended and rumors of peace swept the nation last year, Benson was abruptly let go. Now, he faces a bleak future. Nearly 1 million defense-related jobs will be expunged as a result of Washington's previously announced Pentagon budget cuts. And last week, estimates of the body count quickly doubled after President Bush proposed slashing another $50 billion in defense spending over the next five years.

By shrinking America's armed forces and cutting several key weapons systems, such as the B-2 bomber and Seawolf submarine, the president plans to reduce defense outlays from 20 percent to 16 percent of total federal spending by 1997, the lowest level since World War II. Most analysts believe that the shift from guns to butter will have a minimal impact on economic growth in the 1990s but that it could boost America's productivity and global competitiveness. Yet the country will pay a price for peace. Job creation, virtually nonexistent during Bush's White House years, will be further limited, and unemployment, currently more than 7 percent nationally, could jump in a number of states—including California, Connecticut and Virginia—that are heavily reliant on Pentagon spending. "The irony in all this," says John Reed,

a Democratic congressman from Rhode Island, "is that the first message people are getting from the peace dividend is a pink slip. The cuts are all pain and very little gain."

The misery could multiply if the Pentagon's budget is trimmed further, as some in Congress advocate. Senate Majority Leader George Mitchell and other lawmakers, for example, have proposed deeper defense cuts of $100 billion to $150 billion over the next five years. If the higher numbers are adopted, nearly 3 million jobs could be lost.

Savings Squabble In addition to debating the size of the defense reduction, Congress is fighting over the peace dividend. Bush has said that the savings from defense cuts should be available primarily for deficit reduction. But to gain congressional approval, the president is reportedly willing to use a portion of these funds to finance his $24 billion tax cut for families with children. Such a move would violate the 1990 budget agreement, which erected fire walls between different spending categories. Many Democrats, however, want to funnel the peace dividend into domestic spending. Sen. Edward Kennedy of Massachusetts, for example, would like to carve an additional $210 billion from the defense budget and channel the monies into infrastructure, education and health care....

...some economists argue that Washington has no choice but to use the peace dividend for deficit reduction,

since the Reagan administration borrowed heavily and increased the federal budget gap to fund the massive military buildup of the 1980s. "There is no true 'peace dividend' available from lower military spending to finance new personal tax credits or new health and education spending," write Roger Brinner and David Wyss, two DRI/McGraw-Hill economists, in a recent report. "The defense buildup was never paid for in the first place." Chris Probyn, also of DRI/McGraw-Hill, adds that cutting the federal deficit should be the goal of policy makers since it would enable the Federal Reserve to maintain lower interest rates.

Job Losses No matter how the peace dividend is spent, workers in military-related jobs will be hurt....

One way to lessen the pain for laid-off defense workers is through job retraining....

Some companies have attempted to adjust to defense budget cuts by switching to new lines of business....

The cold war is finally over, and America must now radically alter the defense spending that has shaped federal budgets for the past four decades. This change won't come quickly or easily. And in the process, millions of unfortunate workers, loyal soldiers of the defense industry, will become casualties of a new fiscal war that seeks to turn swords into plowshares.

QUESTIONS

1. a) Draw a production possibility frontier showing the maximum combinations of military and other, nonmilitary, goods and services that could be produced given the federal government's budget. Show where the U.S. government was on the frontier during the cold war. Label it point *a*.

    b) Assuming a stable budget, draw a point *b* on your diagram representing the position of the federal government if it was to follow the recommendations of the Democrats cited in the article.

    c) What would be the opportunity cost of such a reallocation of spending? Explain your answer in terms of your diagram.

    d) Would the opportunity cost of each extra $1 million taken from the defense budget increase, decrease, or stay the same? Explain with reference to your diagram.

    e) On your diagram draw the position of the federal government if it were to decide to use the defense cuts to reduce the size of the budget deficit, but maintain the level of spending on nonmilitary programs. Label it point *e*.

2. a) Draw a production possibility frontier showing the maximum combinations of public and private goods and services that could be produced by the U.S. economy given its scarce resources. Mark the position of the United States during the cold war. Label it point *a*.

    b) Show how the position of the United States would change if the defense cuts were to result in unemployment. Label it point *b*.

    c) Mark the position of the United States under the assumption that the peace dividend would be used for income tax cuts (and that there would be no unemployment). Label it point *c*.

    d) Show how your diagram would change if the defense cuts were to be used to reduce the deficit and interest rates such that private investment in productive capital goods would be increased. Label the position of the United States point *d*.

    e) Under what conditions would it be possible to maintain defense spending, raise government spending on civilian programs, increase expenditure on private goods and services, and achieve higher levels of private investment in technologically more advanced machinery? Illustrate the initial and subsequent positions of the United States in a new diagram showing the maximum levels of public and private goods and services that could be produced in the United States.

Demand and Supply

6. Bullish Market for Taurus Cars

Prices and the quantities of goods traded are determined in the economy by the demand for, and supply of, goods and services. Demand reflects the money-backed plans of consumers to buy goods and services in a given period of time. The determinants of demand include the price of the good, the prices of other goods, income, tastes, and population size. The demand for automobiles, as discussed in the following article, illustrates the influence of these factors.

After studying your text, reading the article, and answering the questions, you should be able to:

◆◆ Interpret the demand curve

◆◆ Explain the slope of the demand curve

◆◆ Predict changes in the demand curve given changes in the determinants of demand

◆◆ Distinguish a change in demand from a change in quantity demanded

◆◆ Differentiate between a movement along the demand curve and a shift in the demand curve

◆◆ Recognize substitutes and complements

◆◆ Distinguish between normal and inferior goods

Preview

◆ The Taurus and Ford in general have captured an increased market share in 1992.

◆ A larger market share combined with a recovery in auto sales was expected to produce a profit for Ford.

◆ However, competition from Chrysler and Nissan in the midsize market was imminent.

◆ Taurus sales were helped by competitors' poorer features, old styles, and price increases.

◆ The Taurus' repair record compared well with domestic models, but paled beside the Japanese models.

◆ Minor style changes, advertising and test-drive incentives were also used to attract buyers.

Ford Is Bullish About Its 'New' Taurus

When Ford Motor Co. introduced its "new" 1992 Taurus last year, car critics clucked. Despite Ford's insistence that it had changed virtually every piece of sheet metal, the car looks almost exactly like the original, which ignited Ford's resurgence in the mid-1980s.

But now it's Ford's turn to laugh, so far at least. The Taurus and its twin, the Mercury Sable, have captured 5.5% of the car market since the new-model year began Oct. 1, up from a 4.8% share in the year-earlier period. Largely as a result, Ford has stanched its two-year slide in market share. Ford captured 21.2% of the U.S. car market for the first two months of this year, the same share it received in the year-earlier period and up from 19.9% for all of 1991.

Ford will "get a bigger share" this year, regardless of what happens to the economy, says Ross Roberts, the talkative Texan who took over as general manager of the company's largest marketing division last year.

More than pride is at stake here. Ford has posted $2.8 billion in losses during the past five quarters, and the success of the Taurus and Sable—along with a recovery in overall vehicle sales—are a key to the company's return to the black. During a normal year, these two cars account for about a quarter of Ford's North American automotive profits, says analysis John Casesa of Wertheim Schroder & Co....

This fall, Nissan Motor Co. will make its first serious stab at the midsized-sedan market. More ominously, Chrysler Corp. will introduce a whole new family of midsized cars whose sharp styling may yet make Ford regret its conservative approach with the new Taurus. Even Ford executives concede they're concerned. "There's no question [the Chrysler models] will be targeted directly at Taurus," says Mr. Roberts....

To a large extent, the new Taurus is benefiting from the shortcomings of its competitors. General Motors Corp.'s midsized cars don't have air bags, while the Taurus makes air bags standard for the driver and optional for the passenger.

The latest version of the nation's top-selling car, Honda Motor Co.'s Accord, is now two years old. The Accord outsold the Taurus by 100,000 cars last year, but the gap is narrowing. Since October, Taurus sales are up 6% from the year-earlier period, while Accord sales are flat. Sales of the Mercury Sable have risen 15%, albeit from a much smaller base.

So now Taurus/Sable sales combined handily exceed the Accord's. That isn't quite as good as it sounds because Ford, unlike Honda, sells its cars to rental fleets, although those sales are decreasing.

Meanwhile, the flashy, new Toyota Motor Corp. Camry—also introduced last fall—got a hefty 11.7% price increase to $15,168 (with automatic transmission) and will go up another $430, or 2.8%, on March 13. A similar Honda Accord goes for $14,250, including a recent 2% midyear price rise. The Taurus's base price now stands at $14,980, but company and dealer discounts give the Taurus a price advantage for many buyers....

The March issue of Consumer Reports gives the Taurus good marks in a comparison test that included the Camry, Accord and Chrysler Le Baron. But the magazine notes that while the Taurus has had an average repair record, "among the best of domestic models," it wasn't "in the same league with its Japanese competitors."

Ford will sell 375,000 Tauruses this year, about the same number as in 1988, the top sales year for the model, predicts analyst Susan Jacobs of Jacobs Automotive, a Little Falls, N.J., forecasting firm. She says Taurus will lose market share to Chrysler's new midsized cars late this year, but Taurus sales numbers will keep growing because the overall car market will be expanding by then....

The new Taurus is sleeker and about four inches longer than the original. The only significant change is inside: The new "wraparound" interior makes the dashboard seem to flow into the door.

Ford spent about two years researching the market before committing to the new Taurus. "We researched the car as much as we have anything in our life," says Ford's Mr. Roberts. "And we did what the customer told us to do. It's an example of listening to the customer, instead of doing what we felt like doing."

When it came to marketing, Mr. Roberts adopted a back-to-basics approach that targeted Taurus owners as the best prospects to buy the new cars. "It's five times as hard and five times as expensive to 'conquest' new owners as it is to attract current owners," he notes.

So Ford sent mailers to many of the 1.9 million people who bought the original Taurus. Proclaiming November "test-drive month," Ford offered its Taurus buyers and other existing customers a $50 savings bond to test-drive new Ford cars.

Ford also tailored its mass advertising to attract Taurus owners. A television commercial, entitled "Evolution," showed a picture of the 1991 Taurus fading into a picture of the 1992 Taurus. (A year earlier, Chrysler used a similar commercial to launch its new-version minivan.) "We talked about the changes that were there," Mr. Roberts says. "That we didn't just make changes for changes."

QUESTIONS

1. a) Draw a demand curve for Taurus cars in a diagram of the Taurus car market.

   b) At a given price, what does the demand curve show?

   c) At a given quantity demanded, what does the demand curve show?

   d) What assumption are you making about other influences on demand in drawing the curve?

   e) Why does the demand curve have the slope you have drawn?

2. a) What was expected to happen to the demand curve for Taurus cars as the economy recovered and incomes increased? Illustrate on your diagram above. Does this represent a change in demand or a change in quantity demanded?

   b) Are Taurus cars normal or inferior goods? What evidence is there in the article supporting your position?

3. Which determinant of demand was intended to be influenced by advertising? Draw a diagram showing what was expected to happen to the demand curve for Taurus cars as a result of advertising. State whether a change in demand or quantity demanded would have occurred.

4. a) As the cost of Honda Accords increased, what happened to the demand curve for Taurus cars? Illustrate on a diagram of the market for Taurus cars. Was there a change in demand or a change in quantity demanded?

    b) What kind of goods are Honda Accords and Taurus cars in economic terms? Explain with reference to the relationship between the price of Accords and the demand for Tauruses.

5. a) As the cost of repairing Taurus cars decreased, what happened to the demand curve for Taurus cars? Illustrate on a price-quantity diagram. Was there a change in demand or a change in quantity demanded?

    b) What kind of goods are Tauruses and repairs in economic terms? Explain with reference to the relationship between the price of repairs and the demand for Taurus cars.

DEMAND AND SUPPLY

The quantity of sales of a particular good and its price are determined by the forces of supply and demand. Demand represents the plans of consumers to buy the good in a given period of time. The factors influencing demand include the price of the good, the prices of other goods, income, tastes, and population size. This excerpt relates to the demand for cruise vacations.

After studying your text, reading the article, and answering the questions, you should be able to:

◆ ◆ Interpret the demand curve

◆ ◆ Explain the slope of the demand curve

◆ ◆ Predict changes in the demand curve given changes in the determinants of demand

◆ ◆ Recognize the difference between a change in demand and a change in quantity demanded

◆ ◆ Make a distinction between a movement along the demand curve and a shift in the demand curve

◆ ◆ Define normal and inferior goods

◆ ◆ Characterize the economic properties of substitutes and complements

Preview

◆ During the recession of the early 1990s the demand for cruise vacations increased.

◆ Cruises have gained broader appeal through new onboard attractions and advertising.

◆ Middle-income groups now make up 40 percent of passengers.

◆ Heavy price discounting has helped increase the number of cruise vacations.

◆ Passengers like the inclusive nature of the price.

◆ The extras, such as gambling, shopping, and alcohol, are often priced lower than on land.

◆ In comparison, European tours are seen as pricey and frenzied.

Against the Tide

The Bahamian sun slides into the aquamarine sea as the last passengers of the cruise ship *Nordic Empress* return from a hard day of sunbathing, shell hunting and rum drinking on Coco Cay's white sand beach. "Bring me another Bahama Mama," yells Danny Rivero, 23, from amid 102° hot-tub bubbles high up on the ship's sun deck. Fellow passenger Renato Deoliveira, 19, obediently passes along a lethal concoction of 151 proof Myers's rum, apricot brandy, coconut rum and fruit punch, while Ted and Kay LaTour, a Milwaukee couple in their 60s, laugh indulgently and sink lower in the froth. "Supposedly we're in a recession," says Ted. "But you look around this cruise and wonder."

Everywhere you look around the *Nordic Empress,* people like Ted LaTour are defying the dismal economic news back home....

Whoa, what's going on here? Consumer confidence sank to a 12-year low in January. Airlines are estimating a $2 billion loss for 1991. Hotels are struggling along with occupancy rates barely above 60%. Yet cruise ships are leaving ports from Miami to Los Angeles, New York City to Seattle, with their cabins more than 90% full. Despite the Persian Gulf war and the recession, the cruise industry posted a 10% gain in 1991. A record 4 million Americans took cruises last year, up from a mere half a million in 1970. Carnival Cruise Lines, the world's largest, and No. 2 Royal Caribbean Cruises report record-setting sales this year. In January alone, the two Miami-based companies took bookings from more than 615,000 passengers. "The tide is rising for the cruise industry," exults Carnival's senior vice president of sales and marketing, Bob Dickinson, chairman of the 34-member Cruise Lines International Association. "Cruising is hot."

Until the mid-1980s, the cruise-ship industry was a doddering old lady. TV's long-running *Love Boat* went a long way toward changing perceptions, as did heavy network advertising. Flashy new ships like Carnival's *Fantasy* and Royal Caribbean's *Nordic Empress* now lure passengers with soaring Hyatt-style atriums, neon-lit discos and casinos with low table limits. The elderly can still take a constitutional around the deck, of course, but the trend is toward state-of-the-art fitness spas and sports platforms for water skiers. Princess and Royal Caribbean lines have even bought islands for private beaches....

There's a cruise ship for virtually every taste and pocketbook—122 based in North America alone—from megaliners with more than 2,600 passengers to small exploration-type vessels for fewer than 100. The 250 passengers now taking the full round-the-world cruise on Cunard's *QE2* paid as much as $126,900 for their staterooms and luxurious life-style, but the rich aren't alone on the high seas. About 40% of today's cruise passengers earn $20,000 to $39,000 a year. A three-day cruise in the Bahamas can cost as little as $500 to $800 for two, without airfare. Heavy discounting in the past year has driven prices down even further, especially in the Caribbean, where two-for-one deals were rampant in 1991 and will continue to a lesser extent this year.

What makes cruises particularly popular in these recessionary times is the all-inclusive nature of the ticket. Cruise trips booked through travel agents typically include airfare, room, entertainment and food (six times a day, if not continuously). Book a cruise, and 85% to 90% of the vacation is paid for, vs. 40% to 45% for the typical land-based trip. The only real extras are gambling, shopping and alcohol, which is often priced well below resort levels....

As the cost of cruises has dropped, so has the age of cruise travelers. "They used to say cruises were for the newlywed and nearly dead," laughs Carnival's Dickinson. Now the fastest-growing passenger segment is between the ages of 25 and 40. The median age has dropped from 58 years in 1985 to just under 43 today. Families with children book 28% of all cruise vacations, and there are lines catering to kids, with youth counselors to supervise activities ranging from treasure hunts to computer classes. Premier, the official cruise line of Walt Disney World, sails with Mickey Mouse and other Disney characters on board....

Taking a cruise remains the dream of 58% of all adults, according to the cruise association, yet only 5% to 6% of the U.S. population has ever cruised. By the year 2000, the association predicts, 10 million people will cruise annually. The satisfaction rating for cruises is the highest in the travel business: over 85% are "extremely" or "very satisfied." The ease and safety of cruise traveling has taken on more importance as Americans tire of frenzied, pricey European tours. "I like the days at sea best. There are so many things to do without packing and unpacking, taking taxis and getting places," says Rene Newman, a Chicago resident and veteran cruiser....

There is a definite economy-be-damned attitude among travelers. "People are tightening up, but they haven't stopped taking vacations. Cruises give them value," says Rod McLeod, Royal Caribbean's executive vice president.

QUESTIONS

1. a) What happened to the demand curve for cruises during the recession of 1991, despite lower incomes? Illustrate on a diagram showing the demand for cruises. Was there a change in demand or quantity demanded?

    b) What kind of good is a cruise in economic terms? Explain why with reference to the relationship between income and the demand for cruises.

2. American tastes for cruises have changed radically since the mid-1980s. In a price and quantity diagram, show what has happened to the demand curve for cruises. Has there been a change in demand or quantity demanded?

3. Cruise prices were heavily discounted in 1991 and 1992. How did this affect the demand curve for cruises? Illustrate on a diagram. Was there a change in demand or quantity demanded?

4. a) How have lower gambling prices on cruise ships affected the demand curve for cruises? Illustrate on a diagram of the cruise market. Has there been a change in demand or quantity demanded?

   b) What kind of goods are cruises and gambling in economic terms? Explain why with reference to the relationship between the price of gambling and the demand for cruises.

5. a) As the price of European vacations rose relative to the price of cruises, what happened to the demand curve for cruises? Illustrate on a price-quantity diagram. Was there a change in demand or quantity demanded?

   b) What kind of goods are cruises and European vacations in economic terms? Explain why with reference to the relationships between the prices and quantities of the two goods.

6. In a diagram of the cruise market draw the impact on the demand curve of the aging of babyboomers (who are now middle-aged). Justify your analysis using evidence from the article. Has there been a change in demand or a change in quantity demanded?

DEMAND
AND
SUPPLY

The price and quantity traded of a good or service are the product of supply and demand forces in the economy. Supply relates to the selling plans of producers in a given time period. The amount supplied depends on, among other things, the price of the good, the prices of other goods, the prices of resources used in the production process, technology, and the number of producers. The article reprinted here illustrates the importance of some of these influences in the context of the retail grocery industry.

After studying your text, reading this article, and answering the questions, you should be able to:

◆ ◆ Interpret the supply curve

◆ ◆ Explain the slope of the supply curve

◆ ◆ Predict changes in the supply curve given changes in the determinants of supply

◆ ◆ Distinguish a change in supply from a change in quantity supplied

◆ ◆ Differentiate between a shift in the supply curve and movement along the supply curve

◆ ◆ Define substitutes and complements in production

Preview

◆ Competition and debt are reducing grocery supermarket profits.

◆ High-tech innovations are being adopted to increase advertising and reduce costs.

◆ For example, some companies have introduced shopping cart video screens displaying specials, digital shelf labels, home shopping through computers, and "talking aisles."

◆ Labor costs have been cut by means of check-out scanners.

◆ Some stores have begun frequent-shopper programs.

◆ Consumers do not always like the innovations, especially when they are intrusive.

Grocery-Cart Wars

As Helaine Alpert steers her shopping cart down one aisle and up another at the Food Emporium in Scarsdale, N.Y., an overhead electronic billboard flashes the specials of the day. On the rim of Alpert's cart, a 6-in. by 9-in. video screen automatically displays a list of specials in each aisle she passes. Electronic alert: Cup O'Noodles on sale, two for $1; veal chops, $6.99, a dollar off the regular price. "I used to scour all the flyers for bargains," says Alpert, a lawyer from nearby Edgemont, but now the computer takes care of that. Her basket filled, she takes her place in the check-out line. But rather than browse through the *National Enquirer* or *Redbook,* she passes the time playing a trivia game on the cart's computer. "It's surprising the way they're making shopping more convenient and less boring."

If President George Bush was amazed by the bar-code scanners he saw last month at the National Grocers Association convention in Orlando, he would be truly astounded by some of the technology found in state-of-the-art supermarkets like the Food Emporium. At Vons, a 283-store chain based in Arcadia, Calif., "talking" aisles are equipped with computerized voices that explain products to shoppers. At St. Louis-based Schnuck Markets, electronic "price tags" have replaced paper shelf labels. These new digital labels are linked to a central computer that changes shelf prices for 2,000 to 4,000 items a week and coordinates them with check-out registers. And at Safeway, the nation's third largest chain (after American Stores and Kroger),

customers can shop from home, using a computerized catalog system to order anything from apricot jelly to zucchini. Shoppers can transmit an order, charge it to their credit card, and have delivery arranged—all without a word to anyone at the store.

Not long ago, the most sophisticated piece of technology in most food stores was the produce scale. A grocer's idea of mass marketing was the weekly circular. Growth was taken for granted. But the nation's 31,000 supermarkets today face a different world. After expanding more than 5% a year during the 1980s, they have seen growth slowing since 1989. Last year sales grew only 2%, to $376 billion, largely because of the recession. Now profits are being squeezed more than the Charmin as stores struggle to cope with mounting takeover debt. Six of the top 12 supermarkets, including Safeway, Jewel and Lucky, were snapped up in buyouts during the past decade. The survivors face more competition than ever before. It is not uncommon to find three or four national chains—not to mention a mass merchandiser like K Mart or Wal-Mart—competing in the same territory. With tougher times ahead, grocery chains are turning to computers to gain a competitive edge.

The most vital link in any chain store's system is the check-out scanner. Introduced nearly 20 years ago as labor-saving devices, computerized cash registers are now installed in about 85% of all chain stores. But today's scanners do much more than tally prices. They track what was bought, how often, at what price and quantity and, increasingly, by whom. Stores use these

data to develop promotional programs that target specific groups of customers. About 4,000 store chains have formed frequent-shopper clubs that offer freebies and discounts to customers who sign up, based on how much they spend: Vons, for instance, mailed coupons for free turkeys to its VonsClub members who spent $400 or more at its stores during the eight weeks before Thanksgiving. Richmond-based Ukrop's used its scanner database to pick shoppers living in areas where a competing chain, Kroger, opened new stores and then sent them coupons.

Not every new idea passes muster. Several stores have silenced their "talking" aisles after customers complained of the constant annoyance. Low shopper interest forced New York's D'Agostino chain to pull the plug on an electronic-ordering service that enabled customers to shop from home using their personal computers. The industry is also facing growing public scrutiny over its burgeoning consumer databases, which many see as a threat to individual privacy.

But most of the new supermarket technology is aimed at shoppers inside the store, where buying decisions are made. Last week, in competition with Turner Broadcasting's Checkout Channel, NBC-TV introduced an in-store television system that will carry ads and other programming to shoppers waiting in check-out lines. Such systems will help reduce marketing expenses for companies by pinpointing their promotions more accurately. But they could also mean the end of one of the few remaining refuges from advertising.

QUESTIONS

1. a) There are thousands of grocery stores in the U.S. grocery market, each supplying groceries. Draw a supply curve relating the price of groceries and the quantity of groceries supplied in a diagram of the grocery market.

   b) At a given price, what does the supply curve show?

   c) At a given quantity supplied, what does the supply curve show?

   d) What assumption are you making about other influences on supply in drawing the curve?

   e) Why does the supply curve have the slope you have drawn? Explain in terms of opportunity cost.

2. a) Draw a supply curve for veal chops in a diagram of the veal chop market.

b) When grocery stores offer specials, such as reductions in the price of veal chops, what happens to the supply curve for veal chops? State why. Illustrate your answer on your diagram. Is there a change in supply or quantity supplied?

3. If grocery store owners invest in machinery embodying new technology, such as digital labels, what happens to the supply curve for groceries? Explain why this occurs. Illustrate your response on your diagram in question 1. Is there a change in supply or quantity supplied?

4. a) Draw a supply curve for groceries in a diagram of the grocery market.

b) Given that the prices of goods and services sold by department stores are able to increase faster than grocery prices, what happens to the supply curve for groceries, everything else being equal? Why does this occur? Illustrate your reasoning on your diagram. Is there a change in supply or the quantity supplied?

c) What type of goods are groceries and department store products in economic terms? Explain why in terms of the relationship between the price of department store products and the supply of groceries.

5. a) Draw a supply curve for groceries in a diagram of the market for groceries.

    b) In the grocery market, what was the impact on the supply curve for groceries of the installation of scanners? Explain what happened. Illustrate your answer in terms of your diagram. Was there a change in supply or the quantity supplied?

**DEMAND
AND
SUPPLY**

Supply, together with demand, determine the price of a good or service and the quantity of it that is traded. Supply refers to producers' planned levels of sales of the good or service in a given period of time. The amount supplied depends most significantly on the price of the good, the prices of other goods, the prices of inputs used in the production process, technology, and the number of producers. This article concerning natural gas production highlights the role of these factors in supply decisions.

After studying your text, reading the article, and answering the questions, you should be able to:

◆◆ Interpret the supply curve

◆◆ Explain the slope of the supply curve

◆◆ Predict changes in the supply curve given changes in the determinants of supply

◆◆ Distinguish a change in supply from a change in quantity supplied

Preview

◆ In 1991-1992 the price of natural gas fell to its lowest winter level in more than a decade.

◆ Drilling operations and employment were cut back as a result.

◆ Overseas exploration and development increased as a result of low prices and expanding foreign opportunities.

◆ Prices were low because warm weather reduced demand.

◆ Also, supply was high due to tax incentives, the opening of government-owned blocks in the Gulf of Mexico to drillers, and leaps in drilling technology.

◆ Some companies could afford to continue to supply natural gas at low prices, while others were forced out of the market.

◆ Industry advocates warned that dependence on foreign energy sources would increase.

Collapse in Prices for Natural Gas Shakes Producers

The collapse of natural gas prices in the last three months, to the lowest winter level in more than a decade, is delivering the worst jolt to the nation's weakened oil and gas industry since oil prices fell by more than half in early 1986.

Many giant companies have announced layoffs or reduced spending for new wells, and hundreds of smaller companies, many of them family run, are going out of business. Oil companies are raising their investments overseas, where costs are lower and potential discoveries more promising, increasing the nation's reliance on imported energy....

A Postwar Ebb By some measures, activity in the domestic oil and gas industry is at its lowest ebb since the Administration of Franklin D. Roosevelt. Warm weather and other factors have caused a supply glut that has depressed prices and made costly new drilling unprofitable.

Many industry executives and financial analysts said that the tally of jobs pared from oil and gas production in the United States since the peak month of the last drilling boom, January 1982, could exceed 400,000 by the end of this year, far more than the number lost in the same period in the American auto industry.

Contracts to supply natural gas for March delivery are at $1.25 per 1,000 cubic feet, up about 20 cents from the February contract but down from $2.30 for the October contract and from $1.65 in March 1991. Compared with the highest recorded monthly price, $3.50 in February 1982, natural gas prices have fallen by a yearly average of more than 7 percent in the last 10 years.

Disappointing Winter Gas producers who count on the winter months to generate their biggest sales have watched as prices dropped even below the low point of last summer, an extraordinarily rare development in the winter, when demand for natural gas peaks.

Demand for natural gas has increased in the last few years—to about 25 percent of the nation's total energy supply—as gas became cheaper to burn than fuel oil for thousands of industrial users....

"It would be a disaster for the country for this small producing segment of the industry to be driven out of business by lower prices," said Edwin Rothschild [energy policy director at Consumer Action]. "Natural gas is too important a fuel. It helps reduce our dependence on foreign oil."

And dependence on oil imports is a big burden for the economy. Payments for imported oil amounted to $37.2 billion last year, or more than half of the nation's $66.2 billion trade deficit....

The natural-gas supply glut was caused by many factors. Many big oil companies have kept gas flowing at high rates in the last two years to generate cash from domestic gas fields to invest into more promising fields abroad.

Tax incentives approved by Congress in recent years have also raised output. Companies producing gas from underground coal layers, mainly in northwestern New Mexico and northern Alabama, and from dense rock formations called tight sands in West Texas and other sites, are eligible for big tax credits that make gas sales profitable even if prices fall below $1. The credits amount to as much as 90 cents per 1,000 cubic feet of gas produced through the year 2002 from wells drilled before the end of 1992.

New Drilling Opportunities In addition, a Reagan Administration policy that opened hundreds of Government-owned blocks in the Gulf of Mexico to drillers in 1984 and 1985 has led to rising sales of offshore gas in the last few years. Hundreds of wells developed after those lease sales in the mid-1980's are now in full production.

Leaps in drilling technology have lowered exploration costs and sharpened the eye of oil and gas explorers. High-speed computers are charting three-dimensional maps of drilling prospects by tracking sound waves reflected from rock layers thousands of feet below ground.

While the diversified oil giants and most major independent producers have adjusted to the drop in natural-gas revenues, smaller independents are struggling. Carol Freedenthal [president of a Houston consulting firm] said that small producers were ripe for a shakeout in an industry that he said had become bloated during its last boom, and has since been gradually deregulated.

The Independent Petroleum Association now has about 8,000 members, down from 20,000 in the early 1980's. As natural gas operators are shunned by Wall Street, banks and other sources of financing, the independents must pay for drilling programs mainly from their shrinking revenues. The price collapse has caused many to sharply curtail or halt their drilling efforts....

The purging of small independents has partly come from growing competition that followed the gradual deregulation in natural gas markets during the 1980's.

Bigger companies, with superior exploration technology and lower operating costs, have advantages of larger scale that enables them to operate profitably at lower prices for natural gas and oil prices than the small independents.

QUESTIONS

1. a) Draw a supply curve for natural gas in a diagram of the natural gas market.

    b) At a given price, what does the supply curve show?

    c) At a given quantity supplied, what does the supply curve show?

    d) What assumption are you making about other influences on supply in drawing the curve?

    e) Why does the supply curve have the slope you have drawn? Explain in terms of opportunity costs.

2. The price of natural gas fell.

    a) On the diagram you drew in question 1, show what happened. Explain what occurred. Was there a change in supply or a change in quantity supplied?

    b) Why were some gas rigs closed down?

c) Why was exploration increasingly switched overseas?

3. a) Draw a supply curve for natural gas in a diagram of the natural gas market.

b) Show the effect of tax credits given for gas production on the supply curve of the natural gas industry. (Hint: tax credits for gas production are equivalent to reductions in the cost of inputs.) Explain why this happened. Was there a change in supply or a change in quantity supplied?

4. a) Draw a diagram showing the relationship between the price of natural gas and the quantity of natural gas supplied.

b) Illustrate on your diagram the implications of the opening of Government-owned blocks in the Gulf of Mexico to drillers. Explain why this occurred. Was there a change in supply or a change in quantity supplied?

5. a) In a price-quantity diagram of the market for natural gas, draw a supply curve.

b) Leaps in drilling technology occurred in the natural gas industry. Show what happened to the supply curve for natural gas as a result. Explain why this occurred. Was there a change in supply or a change in quantity supplied?

DEMAND AND SUPPLY

Equilibrium is a state in which opposing forces balance each other and no one can do better given the actions of others and the resource constraints they face. In product markets, equilibrium price and quantity occur where the quantity demanded of a good equals the quantity supplied. Here consumers can make their planned purchases and producers can make their planned sales. There is no incentive for either party to change the price they are willing to accept. The accompanying article compares the one-price strategy of Saturn with the haggling strategy of other auto distributors and illustrates how equilibrium comes about through changes in price.

After studying your text, reading the article, and answering the questions, you should be able to:

◆ ◆ State why there is no tendency to move away from equilibrium in the absence of other changes

◆ ◆ Define shortages and surpluses

◆ ◆ Predict whether shortages or surpluses arise when demand or supply changes

◆ ◆ Explain why prices change to bring about equilibrium

◆ ◆ Explain the benefits of price flexibility

Preview

◆ GM's Saturn division began a no-discount, no-rebate, low-price strategy in 1990.

◆ Sales per dealer have been high owing to the pricing strategy, as well as product quality and service.

◆ Ford emulated Saturn's one-price strategy when introducing the Escort LX.

◆ However, slow sales caused Ford to offer rebates and dealers to haggle over prices.

◆ Most dealers still negotiate between the sticker price and the dealer's cost net of factory rebates and incentives.

The No-Dicker Sticker

When Rosemary Maxam set out to buy a new car last month, the last thing she wanted was fast talk and high pressure. So after taking a quick look at Honda Civic and Plymouth Acclaim sedans in dealer lots—on a Sunday morning, when she knew both dealerships were closed—Maxam went to a Saturn dealership near her home in Plano, Texas. She plunked down the full list price of $12,485 for a blue-green Saturn SL2 sedan with no bargaining and no regrets. "I'd heard that Saturn dealers just don't haggle," Maxam says, "and that sounded good to me."

Saturn, Ford and dozens of independent car dealers around the country seem to have gotten the same simple message: If you make it easy, they will come. Set one price and make it fair, and shoppers will return to the showrooms, grateful to be liberated from inflated sticker prices and stressful haggling.

Just Mats Saturn, a new division of General Motors, announced a no-discount, no-rebate policy in 1990 when it introduced its first models. By setting sticker prices of its compact sedans and coupes below those of the competition, Saturn got dealers to take the corporate line seriously. "We might throw in some floor mats," says Don Lucas, who owns three Saturn dealerships in the San Francisco area and one in Honolulu. "But that's it. Everybody pays list." The Saturn pricing strategy, combined with a growing reputation for quality and service, is paying off. In 1991, its first full year, Saturn sold more cars per dealer than did any other maker, an honor held by Honda the previous two years. This year's pace is faster yet.

Fixed pricing isn't new; over the last 20 years, one hot import after another and a few domestic models like the Corvette have commanded inflexible top dollar. The question is whether bargaining can be taken out of the picture for bread-and-butter cars. Ford will offer its compact Escort LX as a "one-price" car with a below-normal sticker price when the '93 models come out next month. Each of the body styles—three-door and five-door hatchbacks, four-door sedan and station wagon—will be priced at $10,899 ($11,631 with automatic transmission).

The one-price program aims to reduce buyers' stress much as it does to reduce their payments, says David M. Smith, Ford's regional marketing manager. "Our intention is to achieve the same result as Saturn," he says. "What the consumer really needs is less anxiety and confusion." Unlike Saturn, however, Ford probably won't keep its cars at one price for long. In regional tests of the Escort plan last fall, Ford couldn't resist slapping a $500 rebate on the slow-selling five-speed models. What's more, the uniform price represents savings of just $500 on the three-door hatchback against $1,600 on the bigger and more elaborate wagon. To move hatchbacks, dealers are ignoring the pricing policy and getting whatever they can. Smith expects they'll do likewise when the '93s arrive.

Still, a growing number of independent dealers see economic salvation in uniform pricing and are trying to get Saturnized—fast. "Adversity is the mother of invention," says Doris Ehlers of the research firm J.D. Power & Associates. Ehlers counts 38 no-haggle dealers around the country, mostly recession-hit Ford, Chrysler and GM franchises…

Nonetheless, a shopper who knows how to bargain or who happens upon a bona fide sale can usually get a comparable car for less money. Jim Traub, a 26-year-old management consultant, wanted his first new car to be a compact four-door sedan with five-speed transmission, air conditioning, a powerful engine, a sunroof and an AM/FM-cassette. He narrowed his choices to the Honda Civic LX, Mazda Protege LX, and Saturn SL2. "I knew I would be happy with any of those cars," Traub says. "It was a question of where I could get the best deal."

No Deal Traub first visited a Saturn dealer near his home in Chevy Chase, Md., and test drove an SL2 sedan. Priced at $13,445, it was equipped with what he wanted plus alloy wheels, cruise control and power windows and locks. During the test drive, the salesman told him about Saturn's no-haggle policy. "I took it as just another bargaining position for him and assumed that once we got down to business something would happen," says Traub. He offered $11,500, saying he thought he could get a similar Mazda or Honda for much less than the Saturn's sticker price. But instead of making a counteroffer, the Saturn salesman politely suggested that if Traub could find a better deal elsewhere, he should take it.

Traub moved on to a Mazda dealer and drove a Protege LX with the same options as the Saturn. Then he got down to business. The car's list price was about $13,900. Traub knew from a guide that the dealer's cost was $12,100. Two factory incentives—a $1,000 rebate and free air conditioning—lowered the dealer's cost to $10,400. Traub offered $10,000.

"At that point, the salesman clutched his chest and feigned a heart attack," Traub reports. "Then he said, 'I hate selling cars.' I suggested he take my offer to his manager." About 10 minutes later, the salesman returned with a counteroffer of $12,000. Traub offered $10,500. Another 10 minutes, and the salesman came back and said $11,500 was as low as he could go. Traub offered $11,000. The salesman took it.

Anyone with the time and inclination to bargain and the willingness to consider several different makes should do as well.

Q U E S T I O N S

1. Draw a diagram showing an upward-sloping supply curve and a downward-sloping demand curve for the five-speed Ford Escort LX. Suppose that in the regional tests the price was set at the point where the two curves intersected, and the quantity traded was determined in the same way. Mark the equilibrium price and quantity as P_1 and Q_1 respectively.

a) Ford found that it had misjudged the demand for the Escort LX. In the diagram draw the actual demand curve.

b) At P_1, was there a shortage or a surplus? Explain your answer.

c) What happened to the price that consumers were willing to pay for Q_1 and the price at which suppliers were willing to sell Q_1? Explain.

d) As a result of these pressures, what happened to the equilibrium price and quantity traded? Mark the new equilibrium P_2 and Q_2 on your diagram.

e) Did the price settle at the level at which the suppliers were willing to supply Q_1? Explain why or why not.

f) Why was there no tendency for prices and quantities of the Escort LX to change beyond P_2 and Q_2?

2. Draw a diagram illustrating both the supply of and demand for Saturn SL2 sedans. Assume that the price was set at the level where the two curves intersected and the quantity traded was fixed in the same way. Mark these points on the axes as P_1 and Q_1.

a) Why, unlike Ford, were Saturn dealers not willing to reduce the price through haggling? Answer in terms of your diagram.

b) Why did Saturn dealers not have an incentive to increase the price? Answer by referring to your diagram.

c) Suppose that enthusiasm for Saturn SL2 sedans increases due to customers preferring the no-haggle approach to buying a car. In the diagram show what would happen to the demand for and supply of SL2 sedans.

d) At the no-haggle price P_1 would there be a shortage or a surplus? Explain in terms of quantity demanded and quantity supplied.

e) How would Saturn dealers be tempted to change the price and quantity of SL2 sedans? Mark the desired position P_2 and Q_2 on your diagram. Explain your answer in terms of quantity demanded and quantity supplied.

f) Given your answers above, why do most auto producers and dealers prefer a relatively high sticker price, periodic rebates, and haggling?

DEMAND
AND
SUPPLY

Product markets eventually reach an equilibrium state where the quantity demanded equals the quantity supplied. However, there is nothing immutable about the equilibrium price and quantity: They can change due to shifts in supply and demand.

An increase in demand raises both price and quantity, and vice versa. An increase in supply reduces price and raises quantity, and vice versa. An increase in demand and a decrease in supply raises price, and vice versa, but the quantity is indeterminate. A decrease in demand and supply reduces quantity, and vice versa, but the price is indeterminate. This article concerns the market for a college education where significant changes are occurring in supply and demand.

After studying your text, reading the article, and answering the questions, you should be able to:

◆◆ Distinguish the determinants of demand and supply

◆◆ Predict the effects of a change in demand on equilibrium price and quantity

◆◆ Predict the effects of a change in supply on equilibrium price and quantity

◆◆ Predict the consequences for equilibrium price and quantity when both supply and demand change

Preview

◆ Higher education is facing a budget crunch.

◆ The recession has reduced state revenues and forced spending cuts.

◆ Private colleges have been hurt by rising costs and student inability to afford large tuition increases.

◆ Universities are finding it hard to cut administrative expenses further.

◆ They are now cutting programs, departments, library budgets, professors, and capital spending.

◆ Some schools have raised tuition considerably, but financial aid has not kept pace.

Many Colleges Face More Cuts in Basic Services

The University of Maryland at College Park no longer subscribes to the American Journal of Clinical Pathology. Soon, because of a budget crunch, it won't have a Radio, Television and Film Department, either.

In the past 18 months, cutback after cutback in state funding has drained about $40 million from the university's operating budget. As a result, the library has killed subscriptions to 1,534 publications, from Wall Street Transcript to Ukrainian Biochemistry. Most professors haven't had pay raises in two years. Administrators, faculty and staff have been furloughed. And in June the school announced the elimination of an entire college and seven academic departments.

But in this, the University of Maryland isn't alone—not even close to it.

A survey being released today by the American Council on Education finds that 57% of U.S. colleges and universities had to reduce their operating budgets in the 1991–92 academic year, even more than the 45% who did so in the 1990–91 school year. Public institutions suffered the most: 73% of public two-year colleges, 61% of public four-year colleges and 35% of private institutions endured midyear budget cuts, the survey of 411 campuses finds.

In all, nearly half of the public institutions had lower operating budgets in 1991–92 than they did the previous year, the study says. Taking inflation into account, two-thirds of all public institutions lost financial ground during the past academic year.

"Most American colleges and universities are really taking it on the chin financially these days," says Elaine El-Khawas, the report's author and director of the council's research division.

The main culprit has been the recession, which has depleted state revenue coffers and forced broad reductions in state expenditures. Private colleges haven't been immune from budget problems either, hurt by the increasing cost of running an institution of higher learning and growing pressure to rein in tuition increases.

Now, after pinching and scrimping on everything from paper clips to professional travel, many schools fear they have reached the limit of what they can pare, outside of academic programs themselves.

At the University of Vermont, the president's secretary is sick. But he isn't hiring a temporary worker as a replacement. His assistant has left, too. That position hasn't been filled either. Nor have the jobs of assistant director of development or director of the news bureau.

It has come to the point where "the president of the university has said we'll have to make cutbacks in academic areas because up till now most of the cuts have been absorbed in administrative areas," says John Hedin, a spokesman for the school.

But paring academic programs can be traumatic for an institution—and enormously controversial. Already one suggestion helped drive one University of Vermont president from his job. A committee of administration, faculty and staff recommended eliminating the university's entire School of Engineering. The ensuing furor led the president to resign.

But many institutions have no choice but to push ahead with cuts. San Diego State University has decided to just about shut down nine departments, including anthropology, aerospace engineering and German-Russian. At the University of Maryland, the other departments that will be phased out are housing and design; urban studies and planning; industrial, technological and occupational education; recreation; and textiles and consumer economics, as well as the College of Agriculture and extension education.

Though the cuts there were made with relatively little rancor, President William Kirwan worries about the effect on the institution's academic mission. "I think it has had an impact on the quality of education we can offer," he says.

Worse, the pinch has lead to some of the biggest tuition increases in years to cover the shortfall in funds. The University of Connecticut, which has eliminated numerous "low-productivity majors," has pushed up tuition 60% in four years, according to a spokesman. The university put off fixing leaky dorms, labs and other buildings and encouraged more than 250 professors to take early retirement after three years of cuts in state funding.

Prince George's Community College, a two-year community college in suburban Washington, has imposed an extra fee or surcharge on each credit hour. The University of Maryland raised out-of-state tuition 18% last year and in-state tuition 15%.

Moreover, some community colleges are finding it hard to fulfill their mission of admitting everyone who wants to attend. Montgomery College, a two-year school in Montgomery County, Md., considered instituting enrollment caps this year for the first time but was able to avoid it.

"I think access [to higher education] is absolutely threatened," says the Council on Education's Ms. El-Khawas.

In many cases the tuition jump hasn't been met with a corresponding increase in financial aid, from either the federal or the institutional end. Brown University, for example, has ended its long-time "need-blind" admissions policy. And the federal government's Pell grants, with a maximum of $2,400 a year for the poorest students, don't make much of a dent in today's tuition bills, Ms. El-Khawas argues.

So colleges aren't sure how much more they can ask. "We are reaching a point where it's beginning to be, I think, a strain for people," says Maryland's Mr. Kirwan. "I'm not sure there is much more we can do with regard to tuition. We're about at the limit of what we can expect people to pay."

—Hilary Stout, "Many Colleges Face More Cuts in Basic Services," August 3, 1992.
Reprinted by permission of *The Wall Street Journal*, ©1992 Dow Jones & Co., Inc. All Rights Reserved Worldwide.

QUESTIONS

1. In diagrams of the market for public university education, show how supply and/or demand, and the equilibrium price of education and the number of students educated, have been affected by

    a) falling government revenues resulting in program cuts.

    b) decreasing financial aid in real terms (that is, aid relative to tuition levels).

    c) both falling government revenues resulting in program cuts and decreasing financial aid in real terms.

2. In a diagram of the market for private university education, show the implications of both decreasing real student incomes and higher costs of running an institution for the equilibrium price of education and the number of students educated.

3. Universities have responded in various ways. In diagrams of the market for college education in a given state, show the implications of the following approaches on the equilibrium price of education and the number of students educated. Explain why you move the curve(s) you do.

a) reduction in journal subscriptions

b) a restructuring of programs toward popular majors

c) a restructuring of programs toward popular majors and cost savings, such as reductions in faculty, as at the University of Connecticut

d) fewer program offerings at within-state schools, and higher increases in the price of education at out-of-state schools

e) program cutbacks that lower operating costs but reduce the attractiveness of college, as at San Diego State University

12.
Winners and Losers in the Slow-Growth '90s

Product markets are in equilibrium when the market price brings the quantity demanded into balance with the quantity supplied. Although equilibrium is the optimal state for both producers and consumers, it can be disturbed by changes in the conditions of supply or demand, leading to a new price-quantity equilibrium. The accompanying article describes several markets in which there have been, and will be, significant changes in the forces of supply and demand in the 1990s.

After studying your text, reading the article, and answering the questions, you should be able to:

◆◆ Predict the effects of a change in demand on equilibrium price and quantity

◆◆ Predict the effects of a change in supply on equilibrium price and quantity

◆◆ Predict the consequences for equilibrium price and quantity when both supply and demand change

Preview

◆ The recovery from the recession of the early 1990s was expected to be weak.

◆ Certain industries are expected to do better than others in the 1990s.

◆ The winners are expected to include service industries that automate, health care, ceramic tiles, and those that export cereals.

◆ The losers are expected to include construction, credit card companies, consumer electronics, railroads, and basic chemicals.

More Pain Than Gain

Most analysts expect this postrecession recovery to be the weakest since World War II. Joblessness will remain high. Rising real long-term interest rates, which are inhibiting mortgage refinancings, could also retard business investment. Staggering deficits at the state, local and federal levels now equal 7.1 percent of gross domestic product—a record for the Reagan-Bush years. This huge fiscal shortfall will prohibit cash-strapped governments from stimulating the economy. Both consumers and corporations have reduced their crippling debt burden over the past year, but the lingering leverage load is likely to hobble demand for goods and services. The view from abroad is bleak. The German and Japanese economies are slumping badly, a grim harbinger for American exporters, who have prevented the United States from sinking into an even deeper recession.

Most forecasters believe the American economy will experience glacial growth from now until the presidential election. And the fiscal follies of the Reagan-Bush era—combined with weak labor-force growth and sluggish productivity—suggests to many analysts that tough times will persist through the 1990s. In fact, with economic growth expected to remain subdued, the '90s could be the most stagnant period since the '30s. Profits won't come easily in the coming years, and there will be much more pain than gain. A number of the decade's winners and losers are analyzed below.

WINNERS

Service-sector Automation When customers of Plymouth Rock Assurance Corp. in Boston dent a fender on the streets of Beantown, whom do they call? Crashbusters. Plymouth Rock dispatches this aptly named minivan—equipped with computers, video camera and telephone modem—to the scene of the accident so that an adjuster can record the damage, estimate the repairs and issue a check. This speedy approach has given Plymouth Rock Massachusetts's highest customer-satisfaction rating and the industry's lowest overhead.

Unfortunately, most of the $2.5 trillion service sector hasn't caught up with Crashbusters. While productivity in the nation's factories shot up at a 3.9 percent annual rate in the 1980s, output per worker in offices and financial institution sputtered at just 0.9 percent. That presents an opportunity for companies that make service firms more efficient...

Health Care In 1981, Donald Steen hit upon a winning concept: Simple surgery doesn't need to be performed in sophisticated hospitals. Today Steen runs what might be called the Jiffy Lube of outpatient surgery. Medical Care International, his Dallas-based chain of 75 low-cost surgery centers, is the leader in a $3 billion industry that scarcely existed 10 years ago but today performs nearly a quarter of all outpatient surgery.

Steen is working a national calculus of powerful proportions. The nation's health-care costs—$740 billion last year—consume 13 percent of national income and are growing at 9 percent a year. As a result, employers and the federal government, who pay 80 percent of all medical bills, are turning rapidly to low-cost delivery systems.

Medical Care International specializes in simple operations such as knee repair and cataract surgery. Because it maintains no emergency rooms, X-ray labs or trauma centers, it can underprice hospitals by 10 percent to 40 percent...

Cutting-edge Technology In 1922, with Prohibition bottling up its main line of business, the Adolph Coors Co. diversified into medicinal alcohol, confectioner's malt and, curiously enough, ceramic tiles. Today, that quirk of history has made the Colorado brewer a leader in the high-tech ceramics industry, whose revenues reached $11 billion last year and are expected to hit $17 billion by 1995...

Factory Renovation ...If "infrastructure" is the rallying cry of political economy in the 1990s, companies like Honeywell are waiting to respond. Business spending on new plant and equipment plunged 30 percent during the 1981-82 recession, twice the normal recessionary drop: rebounded at only

5.8 percent annually by 1989, half the usual recovery pace, and then drooped 2 percent again in the current recession. Meanwhile, public investment in schools and roads sagged 3 percent annually during the late 1980s. Though businesses, states and cities remain saddled with financial woes, many hope to compensate for their miserable investment record...

Foreign Food Sales Kellogg's annual report last year pictured three executives seated along the banks of the Seine in Paris, boxes of corn flakes before them and Notre Dame towering behind.

Corn flakes in the land of *pain au chocolat?* Yes. Kellogg derived 41 percent of its $5.8 billion in 1991 sales from non-U.S. markets, and is pointing out a profitable path for American business in the 1990s. U.S. exports will suffer as the global recession takes its toll. But Kellogg should move ahead smartly later in the decade, after the world economy picks up. The Battle Creek, Mich., company commands 44 percent of the foreign cereal market, where sales grew twice as fast as in the United States last year. In Latin America, for example, Kellogg has doubled capacity at its Bogotá, Colombia, plant. And in Europe, the firm has capitalized on German reunification...

LOSERS

Construction ...In the overbuilt commercial-industrial market, construction spending plunged 16.6 percent last year—its steepest slide since World War II—and will drop an additional 11.9 percent in 1992 before rebounding sometime later in the decade. In the sluggish residential market, hous-

ing starts slumped to 1 million units in 1991, the lowest level in more than 30 years. And with the adult population growing at its slowest pace since the 1950s, housing starts are expected to creep along at a recessionary pace.

Armstrong, whose profits slipped to $48 million last year from $144 million in 1990, is betting on new high-margin floor coverings for the home-remodeling market, where it derives 38 percent of sales. But with the construction industry still reeling after its explosive growth in the 1980s, hammering out new profits will be difficult in the 1990s.

Credit-card Usage ...Households tripled their credit-card debt to $233 billion during the decade, and banks found credit-card revenues their fastest-growing market.

But today, debt-weary consumers are calling for a divorce. They have cut their debt loads from a postwar peak of 18.6 percent of disposable income in 1989 to 16.9 percent today. Plastic purchases, after expanding at 15 percent annually during the 1980s are expected to grow less than 5 percent a year in the 1990s...

Consumer Electronics ...with a graying batch of baby boomers, their incomes growing at a meager 2.3 percent a year, consumer electronics is in for a low-voltage decade. During the 1980s, domestic sales soared from $10.9 billion to $32.9 billion as boomers approached their peak earning years and bought all the gadgets they'd been hungering for. The 1990s, however, will tell a different story, because household penetration has reached 98 percent for TV sets, 94 percent for stereos and 77 percent for VCRs.

Electronics manufacturers are pinning their hopes on new products designed to wow consumers all over again. Sony, for example, which just announced its first-ever operating loss—$158 million for the current fiscal year—has palm-top televisions and digital-tape products. But in a slow-growth economy, hard-pressed baby boomers will have scant income left for high-tech toys.

Railroads ...Railroads derive almost half their revenues from coal, cars and chemicals, and all three are expected to struggle with single-digit growth because of sluggish consumer and industrial demand.

With volume stagnating and many cost cuts already made, railroad profitability will be squeezed tight over the next few years...

All the cost cutting in the world won't produce a healthy bottom line in the 1990s if the [Chicago-based] Santa Fe's major customers run out of steam.

Basic Chemicals From Korea to Singapore, a forest of smokestacks, silver pipes and tank farms has sprung up since 1980 as the newly industrializing countries of the Far East entered the chemical-refining business. The new refineries have produced a steady flow of basic chemicals for the textile and auto industries of these developing nations, but they are starting to produce a frightening stream of red ink for U.S. chemical makers.

The tremendous growth in the Far East, combined with recession at home, has left U.S. chemical makers operating at 79 percent of capacity, down from 87 percent four years ago.

—David Hage, "More Pain Than Gain," March 30, 1992.

QUESTIONS

The article considers developments in several markets in the U.S. economy. In each of the following cases, draw a supply and demand diagram showing the effects of the reported change(s) on the curves and on the equilibrium price and quantity. Label the initial curves S_0 and D_0 and the new curves S_1 and D_1. Cite which determinant(s) of demand and/or supply changed.

1. In the insurance market, firms are introducing automated innovative approaches, such as "Crashbusters," to reduce costs.

2. In the market for beer, Coors is seeing rising demand in the market for *ceramic tiles*.

3. In the market for cornflakes, Europeans and Latin Americans like cornflakes more and more.

4. In the consumer electronics market, babyboomers are aging.

5. In the credit market, consumers now prefer to borrow less.

6. In the market for basic chemicals, new refineries are appearing, especially in the Far East.

7. In the market for outpatient surgery, outpatient surgery centers are being established without the expensive departments that hospitals have, and employers and the government are changing their health-care benefit plans to encourage or require outpatient surgery.

8. In the market for new homes, the population is growing more slowly than in earlier decades, and builders are finding the prices charged for remodeling old homes increasingly attractive.

9. In the U.S. economy, the recession is over, but the deteriorating infrastructure caused by a paucity of investment could increase costs.

10. In the railroad industry, customers in the coal, car, and chemical industries may suffer a decline, and costs may be reduced more.

SECTION 2

MICROECONOMICS

ELASTICITY

The law of demand states that as the price of a good increases, the quantity demanded falls. The price elasticity of demand summarizes the responsiveness of quantity demanded to a change in the price. In some extreme cases, the price increases but the quantity demanded does not fall. The elasticity of demand is therefore zero. In the accompanying article, which discusses why the health-care market appears not to work, the implicit focus is the elasticity of demand.

After studying your text, reading the article, and answering the questions, you should be able to:

◆◆ Define the price elasticity of demand

◆◆ Understand the implications of the elasticity of demand

◆◆ Calculate the price elasticity of demand

◆◆ State the determinants of the elasticity of demand

◆◆ Define cross-price elasticity of demand

◆◆ Calculate the cross-price elasticity of demand

Preview

◆ Patients pay little attention to the price and quality of health care when deciding which hospital to patronize.

◆ Patients have little information, generally their insurance pays the bills, and they have to go to hospitals where their doctors work.

◆ As a result, hospitals compete to buy the latest technology and pass the cost on, rather than to provide the lowest-cost quality care.

◆ Some employers are assembling networks of lower-cost, higher-quality hospitals that employees have to use.

◆ Certain states, like Pennsylvania, are making more data available.

Laws of Economics Often Don't Apply in Health-Care Field

HARRISBURG, Pa.—James Martz never thought twice about which hospital to go to when doctors told him one of his coronary arteries was so badly clogged he needed a new one.

"There really wasn't any question as to where we would be going," says Mr. Martz, a 54-year-old retired telephone installer. "Our family physician is associated with Harrisburg Hospital."

What Mr. Martz didn't know is that public figures compiled by the government show the death rate for bypass surgery at Harrisburg Hospital is substantially higher than at Lancaster General Hospital, only 38 miles away. Moreover, Harrisburg Hospital charges 50% more than Lancaster, the state estimates.

In a conventional market, a high-cost, low-quality producer would be doomed, or, at the very least, worried. But the laws of economics have been repealed in the health business. Consumers don't comparison-shop and often lack the information to do so. Many hospitals compete to buy the latest technology rather than provide the lowest-cost quality care. And providers resist outsiders' attempts to gauge quality. The result: a seemingly unstoppable increase in the cost of health care.

Rolling the Dice Coronary artery bypass surgery is a good example, though the same holds true for any number of procedures, from gall bladder operations to organ transplants. Bypass surgery is an expensive, complicated procedure that uses a vessel from elsewhere in the body to circumvent clogged arteries near the heart. The odds of surviving it are high, particularly for otherwise healthy, middle-aged people. On average, fewer than 4% die. But the mortality rate varies substantially among the 898 U.S. hospitals where the procedure is done. And few

patients, employers or insurers take that into account.

In fact, most Americans do far more research before buying a car than before allowing a surgeon to cut open their chests....

Ties That Bind If the referring doctor is associated with a particular hospital, then the surgery is done at that facility, explains Dr. Travisano [head of the cardiac surgery team at both Harrisburg and the Polyclinic Medical Center]. Mr. Martz's family doctor is connected to Harrisburg, so Mr. Martz was operated on there. He is doing fine. Since his insurance paid the bill, cost wasn't an issue....

"It's intriguing to me how difficult it is to break established lines of referral," says Lawrence Bonchek, chief bypass surgeon at Lancaster General Hospital. Few of Dr. Bonchek's patients come from Harrisburg. And few patients from Lancaster go to Harrisburg. "Our mortality rate is certainly low. Why aren't we doing more [cases]? Because health care is an inefficient market," he says.

Michael Young, Lancaster General's administrator, finds this downright maddening. The list price for a simple bypass at Lancaster General in 1989 was $17,490, according to Pennsylvania's Health Care Cost Containment Council; at Harrisburg Hospital, it was $28,059. "I am clearly the low-cost provider," Mr. Young says. But employers, who generally pay for most of their employees' health care, "won't give employees incentive to come here." ...

A few patients do shop around, but most rely on their family doctor or cardiologist to pick a surgeon or hospital. And those doctors often aren't familiar with the comparative statistics either. Doctors refer patients to specific hospitals "because that's where they can work. They'll take whatever qual-

ity they can get there. That's the sad truth," says David Blazer, a Lebanon, Pa., cardiologist....

A few employers and insurers are beginning to use objective measures of quality to try to steer patients to better hospitals. Prudential Insurance Co. of America, for instance, designates certain hospitals as "institutes of quality" for organ transplants and is in the process of doing the same for bypass surgery. It negotiates a fixed fee up front and then pays travel expenses for patients who use those institutes.

But Prudential finds some state insurance regulators resistant to its program and very few employers willing to give employees significant financial incentives to take its advice. In Hershey, Pa., Hershey Foods Corp. is using newly available state data to assemble its own network of better-quality doctors and hospitals. Other companies have similar networks, but usually pick doctors and hospitals primarily because they offer discounts, not because of good quality.

If they want it, Pennsylvania residents can get far more information about their hospitals than most Americans. The state Health Care Cost Containment Council publishes comparisons of mortality rates for every hospital in the state, procedure by procedure. Using data gathered from more than 100 hospitals, the council also calculates how many deaths it expects will occur given the age of a hospital's patients and how sick they were when admitted.

The goal is to give prospective patients the sort of information they need to ask educated questions of doctors and hospitals and to make more informed choices. Or, as the council's T-shirts put it, "Check it out before you check in."

QUESTIONS

1. a) Draw a demand curve for the services of hospitals like Harrisburg Hospital.

    b) In numerical terms, approximately what is the price elasticity of demand for the services of the hospitals? How would you characterize the elasticity? (For example, elastic?)

    c) In general, what determines the price elasticity of demand for a product?

    d) Which of these determinants can account for the elasticity of demand for the services of hospitals like Harrisburg identified in question 1b? Cite evidence from the article.

    e) On your diagram, add a supply curve. Show what happens to the price and quantity of, and revenues from, health-care services provided by hospitals like Harrisburg when the costs of surgery, care, and drugs increase. What happens to the revenues of the hospitals? Explain your answer.

2. In the face of rising health-care prices, many employers are changing their benefit plans. Which determinants of the price elasticity of demand for health care are affected by

   a) employees being given a list of participating health-care providers to which they are restricted?

   b) increased copayments by employees for services and higher deductibles (before the employer pays)?

   c) second opinions before surgery is carried out by the first doctor?

3. a) How would the above changes in benefit plans affect the elasticity of demand for the services of hospitals like Harrisburg Hospital?

   b) Draw another supply and demand diagram of the market for the services of hospitals like Harrisburg, depicting the demand curve with its new elasticity.

   c) On your diagram, show what now happens to the price and quantity of health-care services provided by hospitals like Harrisburg when the costs of surgery, care, and drugs increase. What happens to the revenues of the hospitals? How is this different from before the changes in benefit plans?

4. Lancaster General Hospital and Harrisburg Hospital both perform bypass surgery. They are a mere 38 miles apart.

   a) In what range would you expect the cross-price elasticity of demand for bypass surgery between the two hospitals to be? Why?

   b) Harrisburg Hospital charges 50 percent more and has a higher death rate than Lancaster Hospital, yet patients continue to use Harrisburg Hospital. If Harrisburg patients do not switch to Lancaster Hospital when the price of surgery at Harrisburg increases, in what range is the cross-price elasticity? Why?

ELASTICITY

14.
Nintendo
and Sega
Play Price
Games

The demand for a good or service depends on many factors including its price, incomes, and the prices of other goods. When producers are estimating demand in a changing world, they need to consider the impact on demand of changes in each factor. To do this, they need to know the price, income, and cross-price elasticities of demand. The accompanying article illustrates the importance of each.

After studying your text, reading the article, and answering the questions, you should be able to:

◆◆   Understand the usefulness of the concept of the elasticity of demand

◆◆   Calculate elasticities of demand

◆◆   Infer the slope of the demand curve from the value of the elasticity

◆◆   Predict changes in revenue from the value of the elasticity

◆◆   Explain the magnitudes of elasticities of demand

Preview

◆ The prices of advanced video games were being reduced in 1991-1992.

◆ The cause was slow sales growth due to market saturation and a sluggish economy.

◆ Sega's Genesis system was the 16-bit market leader following its price cut in the fall of 1991.

◆ Nintendo's Super NES system was reduced in price in January 1992, and again a few months later.

◆ In response, the price of Genesis systems was decreased by $20.

◆ Nintendo's share of sales rose after the later price cuts from under 40 percent to over 50 percent.

◆ Both companies competed strongly because in 1992-1993 they intended to introduce compact-disc accessories that worked with their 16-bit systems.

Nintendo, Sega Zap Prices as Video-Game War Heats Up

Nintendo Co. and Sega Enterprises Ltd. cut prices on their advanced video-game systems for a second time in recent months, a sign competition is heating up as sales growth slows.

Nintendo cut the suggested retail price of its Super NES system $30 to $149.95, and Sega reduced the price of its Genesis system $20 to $129.95.

The price-cutting reflects sluggish growth, with sales expected to increase just 5% this year from about $4 billion last year, analysts say. In previous years, video-game sales increased by double-digit and even triple-digit figures.

"The video-game market is more mature," says Ted Lannon, president of Fairfield Research, a consumer-polling concern in Nebraska. About 37% of families in the U.S. own a video-game system, and the market is saturated because virtually every family that wants one already has one, he adds.

Nintendo, the industry leader with an estimated 70% of the video-game market last year vs. 20% for Sega and 10% for others, did little or no price-cutting to boost interest in its first-generation system with an 8-bit computer chip. But in January—less than six months after introduction of the second-generation, 16-bit Super NES system—it cut the price on the new product to $179.95 from $199.95.

Bill White, Nintendo's director of marketing and communications, said the company decided to reduce the Super NES price further—to $149.95— "to adjust to softness in the economy." Nintendo, which introduced Super NES last summer, concedes that it fell short of its goal of selling 2.2 million Super NES systems by year end. To boost orders from retailers and win more shelf space, Nintendo also is permitting retailers to delay until Sept. 30 making payments on any Super NES system they order now. The company usually expects payment in 60 days.

At least initially, the price cuts seem to work in Nintendo's favor. At Babbage's Inc., a video game and computer software retailer, Genesis sales were outpacing sales of Super NES by 1.4 to 1 until Friday, when the cuts went into effect, says James McCurry, Babbage's chairman. Over the week-end, however, Super NES sold "slightly" more briskly than Genesis, he adds.

Sega, which beat Nintendo to toy stores with a 16-bit machine and claims a 63% share of the 16-bit market, said it decided to cut its Genesis price because Nintendo recently has gained some momentum. (Nintendo also claims a 60% share of the 16-bit market, although analysts think that Sega's share is higher.) Last fall, Sega had cut the suggested retail price of Genesis to $149.95 from the initial price of $179.95.

The battle for market share is critical because both companies are trying to establish as large a base as possible so they can sell more video-game cartridges and accessories. For example, later this year or early next year both companies plan to introduce compact-disc accessories that work with their 16-bit systems.

"The real brass ring is going to be CD," says John Taylor, an analyst for L.H. Alton & Co. in San Francisco. "What's happening is a fight for control of that market."

QUESTIONS

1. a) Why might it have been useful for Nintendo Co. to calculate the price elasticity of demand for its Super NES system?

    b) The price of Super NES was reduced by $10 relative to the price of Genesis in the spring of 1992. Assume that this was equivalent to a reduction in price of 6 percent, other things being equal. Market share improved from just over 40 percent to slightly more than 50 percent. Assume that quantity demanded also increased by 25 percent. What do you infer about the general slope of the demand curve and the price elasticity of demand at these prices? Explain your reasoning.

    c) What was the effect on Super NES revenues of reducing the price? Explain with reference to the elasticity of demand.

    d) What might have caused the price elasticity of demand to be the magnitude it was? Cite as many reasons as you can.

2. a) Why might it have been useful for Nintendo to calculate the income elasticity of demand for the Super NES System?

b) The recession of the early 1990s led to "softness in the economy" and lower sales. Assuming that the demand for Super NES systems fell by a greater percentage than income, in what range was the income elasticity of demand? Given your response, what type of good in economic terms was the Super NES System?

3. a) Why might it have been useful for Nintendo to calculate the cross-price elasticity of demand for Super NES systems and Sega's Genesis?

   b) In the fall of 1991, the price of Genesis was cut by one-sixth, reducing the demand for Super NES systems. For Nintendo consumers, in what range did the cross-price elasticity lie? In view of this, what kinds of goods in economic terms were Genesis and the Super NES system?

4. In 1992-1993, Nintendo planned to introduce compact-disc (CD) accessories to work with its 16-bit systems.

   a) Why might it have been useful for Nintendo to calculate the cross-price elasticity of demand for its 16-bit systems and CD accessories?

   b) If the price of Nintendo's 16-bit system continued to fall, and the quantity of its CD accessories demanded increased, in what range would the cross-price elasticity be? In view of this, what kind of goods in economic terms would Nintendo's 16-bit system and its CD accessories be?

15. Communist Controls Collapse

The law of supply holds that as price increases, the quantity supplied of a good increases. The amount of additional production seen depends on the elasticity of supply for the product—formally, the responsiveness of the quantity supplied to a change in the price. The focus of the accompanying article is the elasticity of supply in Russia following President Yeltsin's decision to relax controls on prices.

After studying your text, reading the article, and answering the questions, you should be able to:

◆◆ Define elasticity of supply

◆◆ Explain the usefulness of the elasticity of supply

◆◆ Calculate supply elasticities

◆◆ State the determinants of the elasticity of supply

Preview

◆ President Yeltsin liberalized prices in Russia on January 2, 1992.

◆ He hoped that higher prices would entice producers to supply more goods and services.

◆ Prices skyrocketed within a matter of days, much to his surprise.

◆ In response, stores were privatized to induce price competition.

◆ But competition and freedom from state influence were limited by store suppliers being few, imported goods requiring hard currency held by the government, and limits on trade between provinces.

◆ Also, the supply of goods and services was hindered by centralized warehousing and minimum sizes of railroad shipments.

The Battle Against Bottlenecks

The line of rickety trucks heading for Moscow last week chose a strange route through the gathering dusk. Loaded up with 140 Holstein bulls from a collective farm three hours outside the capital, they set off across fields rather than on the asphalt road. Sausage makers in the capital were paying 80 rubles for a kilo of beef. That was more than double their offer just two weeks earlier, before price liberalization, and the collective-farm chairman was finally parting with some of his precious livestock. But the provincial governor recently decreed that no meat could leave his jurisdiction. So the trucks crept over snow-swept meadows and through deep woods. "I'll sell my livestock only when the price is right," the defiant farm chairman said. "No sooner." Now the time had come.

Russian President Boris Yeltsin was hoping that higher prices would lure hoarders to market and bring staples back onto the shelves. But when he liberalized prices on Jan. 2, he evidently didn't expect them to skyrocket as high as they have. In a speech to the Russian Parliament, he charged that criminals were controlling Russia's supply system and suggested that producers' profits should be limited to 50 percent. Meanwhile, leading officials of his own government, from the vice president to the parliamentary chairman, berated him for freeing prices without first privatizing distribution. In an attempt to forestall further attacks, Yeltsin declared that "liquidating trade monopolies and creating competition in this sphere is the most urgent task of the coming weeks."

It will take more than a few weeks. Russian Minister of the Economy Yegor Gaidar says 21,000 stores—out of about 70,000 in Russia—have now been "commercialized." They have taken their first steps toward privatization— such as opening their own bank accounts. But most food stores remain hostage to the same trade-and-distribution monopoly that has been mishandling Soviet supplies for decades. At a rural general store outside Moscow last week, the manager sat idle. She said she couldn't sell anything until she received a new price list from the local trade bosses. Even in the capital, only a few dozen state suppliers serve the entire city of 9 million....

These distributors are a long way from the market economy. "As far as privatization goes, we don't even know where to begin," said Yevgeny Kopeikin, deputy director of the Krasnaya Presnya Fruit and Vegetable Association, Moscow's largest. Some distributors, such as the Proletarsky District Fruit and Vegetable Wholesalers, have broken off into semiprivate "firms" and claim that they're independent of the state. But the trade bureaucrats hold a trump card: imports. Nearly half of the produce in Proletarsky's warehouses comes from overseas—purchased with hard currency that only government officials can provide.

Fortress Mentality Meanwhile, a fortress mentality persists among trade officials. NEWSWEEK found that arranging visits to four food warehouses in Moscow this month was about as difficult as dropping by a nuclear-weapons plant. No wonder: many warehouses stand half empty; at the Krasnaya Presnya Association, 30 percent of contracted supplies never arrived last year. Uzbekistan won't ship its onions to Russia; Ukraine doesn't provide apples anymore. Armed conflict in the Caucasus makes tangerines unthinkable.

In the end, feeding Russia will take a major reallocation of resources from urban to rural areas. In the West, food-storage facilities are located mostly in the countryside, close to the place of production. In Russia, produce generally goes from the field into trucks or railway cars that haul it to city warehouses. The result: shipments of spoiled produce, along with rocks, mud and other refuse. Some of it, such as rotting cabbage leaves, is then shipped back to the countryside to be used for fodder....

Although Yeltsin has issued a decree breaking up state and collective farms, the system is simply not adapted to small producers. The smallest shipment that railway authorities will accept, for example, is usually one full freight car. And for collectives, only the state distribution system can absorb their huge output. "I'm not going to sell my milk liter by liter at the free market," snorted one collective-farm chairman. "It would take forever." Western aid designed to alleviate food shortages is practically irrelevant in the face of these enormous dislocations. Russia needs to overhaul its distribution networks. And Yeltsin will soon find that it can't be done by decree.

—From Carroll Bogert, "The Battle Against Bottlenecks," NEWSWEEK, January 27, 1992.

QUESTIONS

1. a) Draw a price-quantity diagram of the Russian market for cattle, showing the demand and short-run supply curves. Prior to January 1992, there were effective price controls. Mark the controlled price level and the resulting amount of cattle traded.

    b) President Yeltsin set prices free in January 1992. Mark the free market equilibrium price and quantity on your diagram. Given demand and the previous fixed price level, on what did the increase in price depend?

    c) Yeltsin was surprised at the increase in prices. Was he expecting the price elasticity of supply to be more or less elastic than it was? Explain.

2. How was the elasticity of supply in agricultural markets affected by

    a) restrictions on exports from provinces? Explain your answer.

    b) imports having to be paid for with hard currency from the government? Explain your answer.

    c) minimum railroad shipment sizes? Explain your answer.

d) warehouse centralization? Explain your answer.

3. How would Yeltsin's plan to commercialize (that is, privatize) food stores have affected the elasticity of supply of food? Explain your response.

4. Food prices rose rapidly in the first few weeks after being freed. Assuming an unchanging demand curve, why might they eventually decline? Answer in terms of the elasticity of supply. Illustrate your answer on your diagram.

5. The price of beef doubled within a few weeks in January 1992. Calculate the elasticity of supply of beef, assuming the quantity of beef supplied increased by

a) 50 percent?

b) 100 percent?

c) 150 percent?

Show your calculations. For each increase, state whether supply would have been elastic or inelastic.

Market Interference

16. Reds See Red

In unregulated product markets, the prices and quantities traded of goods and services are determined by supply and demand. Where there are effective price ceilings, the forces of supply and demand are overridden. Money prices are lower than in free-market equilibrium, and shortages arise. As a result, there are incentives to spend time queuing or searching for the limited products that are available. Black markets may also develop, where especially those with higher incomes may purchase the products. The accompanying article provides an example of the effects of price controls. It concerns the market for baseball and other entertainment tickets in Cincinnati, Ohio.

After studying your text, reading the article, and answering the questions, you should be able to:

◆◆ State the consequences of effective price ceilings

◆◆ Explain why there are incentives to queue and how long customers are prepared to wait in line

◆◆ Explain why the lower-paid are more likely to queue

◆◆ Explain why a black market is prone to arise

◆◆ Explain who is more likely to buy on the black market

◆◆ Contrast the approaches of economists and noneconomists to the black market

Preview

◆ Tickets for entertainment events, such as Cincinnati Reds baseball games, are often sold by scalpers above the price on the ticket.

◆ The Reds' owner says that the practice is unfair to fans.

◆ Scalpers say that paying a premium is the only way to get good seats.

◆ Scalpers obtain their tickets from season ticket holders and by paying people to queue for tickets.

◆ The Reds' owner wants a countywide ban on scalping.

◆ In opposition, some argue that scalping is a consequence of the free market and that a ban would be unenforceable.

Ticket Scalpers: A Public Service or Consumer Ripoff?

For the price of a ticket, anyone can root for the World Champion Reds, party with the parrotheads at Riverbend or follow a Bengals pass.

But what's the price?

There's a price clearly printed on each ticket, but often that's only the suggested retail price. The real price is often three to four times greater—if a ticket can be found at all.

A middleman has entered the picture—the ticket scalper.

Ticket scalpers, banned in Cincinnati until 1988, have now built a thriving business by being the first to buy tickets at the source for the regular price—or less—and reselling them at higher prices.

Cincinnati Reds owner Marge Schott has had enough, saying the practice is unfair to fans and encourages dishonesty. She wants Cincinnati to reinstate its ordinance banning scalping.

But ticket broker Louise Fisher—who disdains the words "ticket scalper"—said she is serving the fans and condemns Mrs. Schott for attempting to eliminate free enterprise competition....

"You can't go to the ticket window and get a good seat, like behind home plate or where Marge Schott sits," Mrs. Fisher said. It is difficult, if not impossible, for the average fan to get tickets at sporting or entertainment events in premium seating areas....

There are at least three companies in the ticket reselling business in Greater Cincinnati. And national entertainment promoters and professional sports officials say the practice is common in most major U.S. cities.

Several states, primarily in the South, have laws prohibiting the practice. Some states, including California, are considering a ban.

"I don't think it's fair for people to have to pay inflated prices for tickets," Mrs. Schott said. "It's especially not fair for people who travel from out of state to see Reds games. We get support from six states."

She is demanding not only a city ordinance banning ticket resales at inflated prices, but wants the practice banned throughout Hamilton County, which would require a state law.

But fans may be contributing to the problem.

O'Brien and Bengals Business Manager Bill Connelly said season ticket holders are selling some of their tickets to scalpers. A season ticket holder can sell half of his tickets to a scalper—including such favorites as Reds-Dodgers tickets or Bengals-Browns tickets—for inflated prices that cover the entire cost of the season tickets, O'Brien said.

"It makes us look bad," O'Brien said. Scalpers also are posing as representatives of groups to buy large blocks of tickets, he said.

Scalpers and brokers also get tickets by paying people to stand in line to buy them or by buying tickets from people who advertise them for sale in newspapers.

"Bribing ticket sellers (also) is very, very common," said Jerry Pompili of Bill Graham Presidents Inc. in San Francisco. The company promotes rock concerts throughout the United States....

"(But) my personal concern is that anyone who buys a ticket, but later cannot attend the game, be allowed to resell the ticket at face value."

City Council Member Nick Vehr supports the scalpers' argument. "This is a free market system and this is something we ought to let the marketplace decide. There already are enough city restrictions on ticket scalping in the vicinity of the stadium.

"And my concern is that what Mrs. Schott is proposing would be yet another unenforceable law on the city's books."

—Al Andry, "Ticket Scalpers: A Public Service or Consumer Ripoff?," *The Cincinnati Post*, June 6, 1991. Reprinted with permission.

QUESTIONS

1. a) Draw a diagram of the supply of and demand for Cincinnati Reds baseball tickets in a given season. Show the price at which the club sells the tickets, bearing in mind the information given in the article concerning the sales price relative to the free-market price.

    b) Is there a shortage or a surplus? Mark it on your diagram.

    c) Is there a difference between the value consumers place on the tickets and the price at which they are sold by the club? Explain your answer. Illustrate on your diagram.

2. a) Why is there an economic incentive to queue for Reds tickets?

    b) What determines how long people wait in line?

    c) Scalpers pay people to queue. Why would there have been a greater incentive for lower-income people to queue longer than the higher-paid, such as scalpers?

3. a) How do you know that there is a black market in Reds tickets?

    b) Why does a black market in Reds tickets emerge?

    c) How much are fans prepared to pay for baseball tickets on the black market? Answer with reference to your diagram.

    d) What happens to the value of the baseball tickets to fans relative to their price when they are sold on the black market? Explain why your answer is different from that in question 1c.

    e) What would happen in the black market if the Reds had a poor season?

4. a) The owner of the Cincinnati Reds complained that it was not fair for fans to pay inflated prices. How would an economist respond?

    b) Legal solutions to stopping scalping have been proposed. Are these likely to be successful? Why or why not?

    c) How would an economist eliminate the black market?

    d) Compared to the current black market situation, what would happen to the value of the tickets to fans relative to their price under an economist's plan?

17.
Minimizing
the
Minimum
Wage

When markets are free from government interference, equilibrium results in which the prices and quantities of goods and services traded are determined by supply and demand. However, where there is effective interference, disequilibria occur. In the case of effective price floors, there is a surplus at the minimum price. In the same way that these principles can be applied to product markets, they can be applied to labor markets. The accompanying article considers a price floor in the labor market—the minimum wage.

After studying your text, reading the article, and answering the questions, you should be able to:

◆◆ Understand why wage levels may be "unfairly" low

◆◆ Explain who gains and who loses due to changes in the minimum wage

◆◆ Define the circumstances in which the minimum wage creates unemployment

◆◆ Recognize how the minimum wage might add to employment

◆◆ Recognize the conditions when the minimum wage is ineffective

Preview

◆ The D.C. Wage-Hour Board raised the minimum wage from $4.25 to $7.25 an hour on grounds of fairness.

◆ The D.C. Council lowered the increase to $5.25 for fear of loss of businesses and employment.

◆ For example, a day-care center was saved from closure by the council's action.

◆ The mayor recommended linking the minimum wage to the Consumer Price Index and capping any increase at 5 percent.

◆ The Greater Washington Board of Trade recommended matching the federal minimum wage of $4.25.

◆ Labor unions criticized the vote because it kept people well below the poverty wage for Washington.

D.C. Sets Minimum Wage at $5.25

The D.C. Council voted yesterday to set the minimum wage for some workers at $5.25 an hour, repealing an increase from $4.25 to $7.25 that businesses and some politicians said would drive many jobs out of the city.

The council unanimously approved emergency legislation to limit a raise that took effect Sunday for an estimated 17,000 clerical and semi-technical workers in the District. Those affected include secretaries, cashiers, telephone operators and doctors' assistants. Federal and city employees are exempt.

The vote marked a setback for the D.C. Wage-Hour Board, which had raised the minimum wage to $7.25 an hour.

Workers will be paid at that rate until the lower wage takes effect, expected to be sometime today when the mayor signs the emergency legislation.

Council Chairman John A. Wilson offered the $5.25 wage as an alternative to an emergency bill proposed by council member Harold Brazil (D-Ward 6) that would have rescinded the entire increase adopted by the wage board.

Wilson said the $5.25 level would protect businesses and workers, and said the council had to change the board's decision because he did not want to give employers any more "easy excuses" to flee the city.

The new wage—$1 an hour more than the federal minimum wage used in Maryland and Virginia—represented a compromise for a council torn between the needs of constituents in low-paying jobs and the complaints of employers who said they could not afford any increase in a recession.

"The outcry was very loud and very clear" against raising the minimum wage to $7.25, said council member Linda Cropp (D-At Large). "The economic climate cannot at this time withstand such an increase."

Lawrence Landry, chairman of the three-member wage board, disagreed with the council vote.

"I think $7.25 an hour is a fair and reasonable minimum wage," he said. The board approved the $7.25 wage in October, after reviewing a study and holding a public hearing. "We reached that conclusion after a lot of consideration," he said.

Janet King, a 19-year parking lot cashier who had been delighted last week when she heard of the $7.25 minimum wage, was crestfallen yesterday when she heard the council had taken away her increase. She had been making $4.80 an hour.

"I am disappointed," she said. "But I will get a little more, and that is good. Quite frankly, I am very thankful to have a job." ...

Mayor Sharon Pratt Dixon viewed the council's action on the minimum wage as "a responsible one, given the economic situation," said the mayor's spokesman, Vada Manager.

The $5.25 wage is "pretty consistent" with the $5 an hour suggested by the mayor in October, he said. The mayor proposed legislation to curtail the wage board's powers and simply peg annual increases in the minimum wage to the consumer price index, with increases limited to no more than 5 percent a year.

The Wage-Hour Board, formed by Congress in 1918, is appointed by the mayor to represent business, labor and the public. Dixon has not yet made new appointments to the board, which sets wages in nine categories of workers. The board has the power to set wages, but the D.C. Council has authority to overrule the board's decisions.

Some business groups and small businesses lauded the council vote.

McKinley Crudup, administrative director of the Allen AME Church day-care center, had said his center, which serves 100 low-income children, probably would have had to close if forced to pay workers $7.25 an hour.

"I feel that what the council did is in the best interest of everybody. This takes away the strain we all felt about having to close," he said.

Weldon Latham, chairman of regional affairs committee of the Greater Washington Board of Trade, said the $7.25 hourly wage "was out of sync with economic reality."

"The council should next abolish the Wage-Hour Board and adopt a minimum wage in line with Maryland and Virginia, which matches the federal minimum wage standard," he said.

Labor unions criticized the vote.

"For the people whom it affects, it's a tragedy," said Joslyn N. Williams, president of the Metropolitan Washington Council, AFL-CIO. "It's a tragedy because everyone recognizes what it takes to keep body and soul in metropolitan Washington, and $10,000 a year is well below the poverty wage."

—Nell Henderson and Linda Wheeler, "D.C. Sets Minimum Wage at $5.25," *The Washington Post*, December 4, 1991.

QUESTIONS

1. The motivation of the D.C. Wage-Hour Board in raising the minimum wage to $7.25 was to set "fair and reasonable" wages. Labor unions complained that wages were often below poverty wages. Why did employers not set fair and reasonable wages of their own accord? Refer to how wages are set in labor markets.

2. Suppose that in a free market the wage of unskilled workers was $5.25 an hour. On a labor market diagram of wages and unemployment, show how a minimum wage of $7.25 as proposed by the Wage-Hour Board would have led to unemployment and higher wage costs. Separate the unemployed into those who would have been displaced and those who would have been unemployed new entrants to the labor market.

3. Why did the D.C. Council believe that there would be large unemployment effects resulting from a $7.25 minimum wage, while apparently the Wage-Hour Board did not? Focus your answer on the reasons for the size of the two components of the unemployed in your diagram.

4. Using a supply and demand diagram of the day-care industry, demonstrate how a higher minimum wage would have raised the price and reduced the quantity of day care.

5. Draw a new labor market diagram and again show the increase in unemployment caused by a higher minimum wage. Also, show the increase in employment if an increase in the minimum wage had raised consumer incomes.

6. If the free-market wage was $5.25 an hour, as the council chairman appeared to believe,

    a) what was the effect of the Council's legislation on wage costs and unemployment? Illustrate this in a labor market diagram.

    b) what would have been the effect of the Board of Trade's suggestion on wage and employment levels?

7. The mayor proposed legislation linking the minimum wage in D.C. to the consumer price index.

    a) Would this ensure that there would be no unemployment caused by the minimum wage? On what does your answer depend?

    b) Assess the proposal that increases should be limited to 5 percent if inflation in prices and wages were higher.

Households have limited incomes. They decide how to spend their incomes based on their preferences for each good and service. Preferences reflect the satisfaction, or utility, gained from consuming each product. For most products, the marginal utility declines as more units are purchased. Households attempt to maximize their utility by implicitly equalizing the marginal utility of each last dollar spent on each product. When the household pays a price for a good that is below the value or utility placed on it, the household benefits in the form of a consumer surplus. The accompanying article is used to illustrate the marginal utility of regular versus nonalcoholic beer.

After studying your text, reading the article, and answering the questions, you should be able to:

◆◆ Define total utility and marginal utility

◆◆ State how total and marginal utility change as consumption of a good increases

◆◆ Show what happens to utility as tastes change

◆◆ Explain why spending patterns change as utility changes

◆◆ Demonstrate that consumers gain a surplus when they value a product more than its price

Preview

◆ In 1991, the sales of nonalcoholic beers rose while sales of regular premium beers fell.

◆ Social trends and drunk-driving penalties were partly responsible.

◆ Consumers also appreciated the fewer calories and improved taste of nonalcoholic beers.

◆ Increased advertising reinforced such perceptions.

◆ Nevertheless, regular beers still dominate the market.

Big Beer Makers Go After the Sober Set with Assortment of Nonalcoholic Brews

No-alcohol beer has become the fastest growing segment of the beer industry. In 1991, nonalcoholic beers—or brews containing less than 0.5% of alcohol—grew 32%, according to Impact, an alcoholic-beverage industry publication. Meanwhile, light beers rose just 6.7% and regular premium beers fell 6%.

Optimistic Projections While they still account for less than 1% of the beer market, analysts predict that no-alcohol brews could grow to as much as 5% to 10% of total beer sales by the end of the decade. "With societal trends running the way they are, I think the category could reach that," says Rick Burton, brand manager for Sharp's, Miller Brewing Co.'s three-year-old no-alcohol offering.

Those trends include the continuing campaign against drug and alcohol abuse and, more specifically, against drinking and driving. Faced with expensive penalties for driving while drunk, the number of auto deaths in which drivers tested positive for alcohol dropped from 53.1% in 1982 to 46% in 1990. The prospects for no-alcohol beer have also been bolstered by better-tasting products and a marketing push by the nation's biggest beer makers.

Nonalcoholic brews, or near beers, have been around for a long time, but they never made much of a dent until 1989, when Anheuser-Busch Cos. and Phillip Morris Cos.' Miller Brewing decided to add their marketing muscle to the category; Adolph Coors Co. entered the fray last year. The result: 24.1 million cases of near beer were sold last year, up from about 9.6 million in 1989....

There's good reason for the brewers' interest in these brews: profit. Brewers are now locked in a fierce, margin-squeezing discounting battle. Anheuser recently reported that it sold 35% of its beer at discount in 1991. Others estimate that 45.7% of all beer sold was sale-priced in the third quarter of 1991, the latest period for which industry numbers are available.

No-alcohol brews promise some respite from that battle. While introductory advertising expenses—as much as $24 a barrel for Sharp's last year—are eating up some profits, those costs will subside soon. Meanwhile, brewers point out that they don't have to pay federal excise taxes on no-alcohol brews, which boosts their margins by $18 a barrel. No-alcohol brands, Frank Walters [research director for Impact] notes, "generate so much profit, it's easier to pay off the advertising than with other brands."

No wonder, then, that the big brewers have geared up their marketing machines. According to Impact's Mr. Walters, only $1 million was spent on measured media advertising for the brews in 1989. That blossomed to $21 million in 1990. Through the first nine months of 1991, according to estimates by Beer Marketer's Insights, Anheuser spent $8 million on its O'Doul's brand, up 31% from $6.1 million in the same period for 1990.

Those marketing dollars are also backing much improved products, beer experts note. "They're better-tasting products than they used to be," says Benj Steinman of Beer Marketer's Insights.

Each of the Big Three claims its brewing process produces the best taste.

Miller cooks Sharp's at a low temperature, thereby avoiding the production of alcohol. Anheuser makes a regular beer and then removes the alcohol. Coors Cutter is made with a special yeast and a brewing process that produce less alcohol.

No-alcohol brews have another characteristic that bodes well for their long-term prospects in a diet-conscious society: low calories. Domestic no-alcohol brews have 65 to 76 calories, fewer than most light beers, which hover around 95 to 110 calories.

But near beers could get one of their bigger boosts from the continuing battle against drunk driving. Several states are considering lowering their blood-alcohol-content limits for drivers to 0.05% or 0.08% from 0.10%. And the California Highway Patrol recently instructed its officers not to arrest anyone for drinking no-alcohol beers while driving, despite language in the state Vehicle Code that says a beverage with any amount of alcohol is considered alcoholic and therefore isn't compatible with driving motor vehicles.

The growth of near-beer sales isn't all good news for brewers, however. The no-alcohol market is still too tiny to rescue anyone's bottom line, and there isn't any assurance that its popularity will continue. Should brewers get too cocky, they need only remember low-alcohol beers, which enjoyed an initial surge in the mid-1980s and then flopped. Also, brewers are discovering that the new brews aren't attracting as many non-beer drinkers as they had hoped. Impact, the industry newsletter, estimates nearly all drinkers of no-alcohol beer have been recruited from the ranks of regular beer drinkers.

1. a) In a diagram relating marginal utility to the quantity of regular beer consumed in a day, show the marginal utility curve for regular beer consumed by an average beer drinker.

   b) Justify the shape of the marginal utility curve you have drawn. Refer to the article or your general knowledge for possible reasons.

   c) Does total utility increase as consumption increases? Explain your answer.

   d) At what point might total utility decrease as consumption increases?

2. a) Bearing in mind the contents of the article, in your diagram above add a marginal utility curve for nonalcoholic beer for the average beer drinker. Pay careful attention to its position and slope.

   b) Why is the nonalcoholic beer curve in a different position?

   c) Why does it have a different slope?

3. Preferences for regular beer are deteriorating and are increasing for nonalcoholic beer. Supposing that a typical household consumes only regular and nonalcoholic beer and faces stable beer prices and a fixed household beer budget,

a) what is happening to the marginal utility of the last dollar spent on regular beer?

b) to maximize utility, should the household increase or decrease its consumption of regular beer? How should the quantity of nonalcoholic beer bought be changed?

c) what happens as a result of the changes in 3b to the marginal utility of the last dollar spent on nonalcoholic beer and the marginal utility of the last dollar spent on regular beer? Explain your answer.

d) until what point should the amounts of nonalcoholic and regular beer be changed?

4. a) Suppose that dollar values can be placed on utility. Draw a diagram in which the vertical axis is in dollar terms and the horizontal axis represents the number of beers consumed daily by an individual. Show a fixed price for all beer. Now draw curves that show the value of different levels of regular and nonalcoholic beer consumption to the individual, assuming the curves are above the price line at least for low levels of consumption. Shade in the areas that represent the consumer surplus for each drink.

b) Why is the consumer surplus different for each drink?

19. Energy Levels: Oil Runs Out of Gas

A household buys the combination of goods and services that allows it to maximize its utility given its income, the prices of goods and services, and its tastes. In effect, the household equalizes the marginal utilities gained from the last dollars spent on all goods and services. Diagrammatically, the household maximizes its utility at the point where the budget line is tangent to an indifference curve. The accompanying article on alternative types of energy provides an example of a situation in which tastes, incomes, and prices changed to bring about a new consumer equilibrium.

After studying your text, reading the article, and answering the questions, you should be able to:

◆◆ Explain the shapes and slopes of budget lines and indifference curves

◆◆ Define the marginal rate of substitution

◆◆ Select the optimal consumption pattern for a household

◆◆ Predict how changes in income, relative prices, and tastes affect consumer equilibrium

◆◆ Differentiate between an income effect and a substitution effect

Preview

◆ Oil consumption dropped to 41 percent of the national energy pie in 1991.

◆ Domestic oil production reached the lowest levels in decades.

◆ Natural gas sales increased in 1991.

◆ Environmental concerns prompted the substitution of natural gas for oil.

◆ The recession reduced oil consumption and restrained the growth in the demand for natural gas.

◆ Oil and natural gas prices fell.

U.S. Oil Output Drops; Consumption Also Falls

Domestic oil production "has begun a precipitous decline," the American Petroleum Institute said yesterday. In a report summing up last year, it also found that consumption fell, so imports also declined, and that oil's slice of the national energy pie dropped to a 40-year low of 41 percent.

The institute, which is the industry's main trade group, said that producers kept up their output in the early part of 1991 because of the Persian Gulf war, but that fourth-quarter crude production was the lowest for that quarter in 30 years, and outside Alaska it was the lowest since 1950. The number of operational drilling rigs, fewer than 800 in the last five months, is the lowest in nearly 50 years.

Edward H. Murphy, the institute's director of finance, accounting and statistics, said, "It's quite possible that the age of major domestic production is coming to an end."

Dr. Murphy said that while the whole-year figure made production appear flat, it had been inflated early in the year, when the gulf war raised prices and fears, but lagged later. The recession made demand fall substantially for the year as a whole, so imports were down. Imports rose late in the year, however.

Another energy industry group, the American Gas Association, said sales were up last year and would rise further, inasmuch as gas substitutes directly for oil in factories and electricity-generating stations. More and more, the gas association said, natural gas will also be used directly for air-conditioning, displacing electricity made from oil.

With the Clean Air Act of 1990 forcing electric generators to seek cleaner fuels and promoting the use of natural-gas cars and light trucks, among other factors, the gas industry is expecting growth of 5 percent between 1990 and 1994, said Richard D. Farman, chairman of both the association and of the Southern California Gas Company.

But experts say oil consumption is likely to be flat over the same period. Total energy use will increase only about 1 percent in the period, Mr. Farman said. His association is trying to raise natural gas consumption by 14 percent over the next five years.

The contrast between the two fuels last year is instructive; in the face of a national economy that shrank by about 1 percent, delivery of oil products fell by about 2 percent while sales of natural gas rose by about 1.5 percent. Yet the natural gas industry—which overlaps with the oil industry to a large extent—is still weak, because of low prices.

At a luncheon for securities analysts on Wall Street yesterday, Michael Baly 3d, the president of the American Gas Association, said: "Warm weather, the economic recession and some industry financial problems have somewhat masked the strong fundamental outlook for the natural gas industry. But soon, our industry will be taking the mask off." ...

Clash with Environmentalists The American Petroleum Institute blamed the Government for the production decline, both because it changed the tax code to eliminate some breaks for drillers, and because it is keeping drilling rigs out of the Arctic and offshore areas where the goals and hopes of oil drillers and environmentalists collide.

A year ago, when the war in the oilfields of the Persian Gulf was just starting, many oil executives were hopeful of winning access to the Arctic National Wildlife Refuge, as part of a National Energy Strategy. But opponents, most of whom favored new rules on cars instead, requiring better fuel economy, blocked the energy legislation in the Senate in November....

But the statistics released by the institute also point to a continuing shift in the nation's pattern of energy consumption. The amount of energy consumed per dollar of goods and services produced has been roughly flat for the last six years, the group noted, but the amount of oil has declined by more than 7 percent. Part of the difference was made up by natural gas, which substitutes for oil in home heating and in industrial use, and part comes from continuing decline in gasoline demand, as new cars replace old ones.

Drop in Prices Energy demand has also been depressed by mild weather and the recession. And imports have also been encouraged by the drop in prices since the war. Last week, oil dropped below $18 in futures trading on the New York Mercantile Exchange, although it bounced back this week, rising 38 cents yesterday to close at $18.85.

QUESTIONS

1. Draw a diagram showing the quantity of oil on the vertical axis and the quantity of natural gas on the horizontal axis. Add a budget line constraint.

   a) What does the slope of the budget line show?

   b) Now draw a set of indifference curves on the diagram to represent tastes. Should they be relatively steep or flat? Explain why in terms of the marginal rate of substitution.

   c) Show the optimal point of consumption. What makes this point optimal?

2. Concern for the environment and the purchase of more fuel-efficient new cars changed consumers' energy preferences. In a new diagram show the effect of this, if any, on the budget line, indifference curves, and consumer equilibrium. Also, demonstrate what happened to the amounts of each type of energy bought.

3. The recession of the early 1990s reduced incomes. In a new diagram, show the effect of this, if any, on the budget line, indifference curves, and consumer equilibrium. Illustrate what happened to the quantities of each type of energy bought.

4. The prices of both natural gas and oil fell. Assume that the percentage decline in natural gas prices was relatively larger.

   a) In a new diagram show the effect of this, if any, on the budget line, indifference curves, and equilibrium. Show what has happened to the quantities of each type of energy consumed.

   b) What impact did the substitution effect have on the sales of oil and natural gas? Explain your answer.

   c) What impact did the income effect have on the sales of oil and natural gas? Explain your answer.

COSTS OF PRODUCTION

20. Manufacturers Migrate

In any product market, the price and output of a good depend in part on the costs of production. Economists calculate costs with reference to opportunity costs, that is, the value of the best foregone alternative. This reflects the needs of firms to allocate scarce resources optimally among competing uses. Opportunity costs differ from historical costs, which are the customary focus of accountants. In order to be economically efficient and to maximize profits, firms need to minimize their opportunity costs. The accompanying article discusses the costs of production faced by firms in Germany and the gains in economic efficiency that would result from moving abroad.

After studying your text, reading the article, and answering the questions, you should be able to:

◆◆ Define and distinguish between opportunity cost and historical cost

◆◆ Recognize the sources of difference between opportunity and historical cost

◆◆ Explain how to calculate the opportunity costs of inputs that are nondurable, durable, or not directly purchased

◆◆ Explain the requirements of economic efficiency

◆◆ Recognize the different organizational forms of firms

◆◆ Explain the advantages and disadvantages of different forms of organization

Preview

◆ German firms are increasingly producing parts overseas.

◆ New plants are being built abroad rather than in Germany.

◆ The cause is Germany's high costs of labor, corporate taxation, and energy and environmental protection costs.

◆ The need to cut costs is becoming more imperative due to the removing of barriers to trade within the European Community.

German Firms Bemoan Production Costs

Businessmen have always complained loudly about Germany's high production costs and what they call the unrealistic demands of labor. Lately, they have begun to do something about it.

Daimler-Benz AG Chairman Edzard Reuter, the urbane senior statesman of German industry, bluntly sets the tone. "The overwhelming majority of German business leaders are thinking seriously about whether impending investments wouldn't be more sensibly placed abroad" in more cost-effective countries, he told publishers in Dusseldorf this month.

Indeed, Daimler-Benz recently started obtaining diesel engines and auto parts from foreign sources at half the German cost. The company not only isn't likely to build any more major plants in Germany but also wishes it could reverse its decision to locate its newest car plant, due to be completed this year, in Rastatt, Germany. It is even considering producing Mercedes cars in Mexico and Russia.

Jobs Going Abroad Robert Bosch G.m.b.H. last year decided to cut at least 500 jobs by closing a German plant and transferring its production of car stereo speakers to Malaysia. Bosch has also transferred much of its production of cassette-player components to Mexico and gas gauges to Portugal and Turkey, and it recently began producing generators in Wales.

Of the 51 billion marks ($32 billion) that Volkswagen AG plans to invest by 1996, more than half will flow out of Germany for the first time and into low-cost production sites in Portugal, Spain, Mexico, China and Czechoslovakia. Siemens AG is shifting some of its basic production into Eastern Europe and Turkey.

The list keeps growing. German industry groups estimate that jobs are being exported at a rate of more than 100,000 a year, and that doesn't take into account foreign companies that may be bypassing Germany in favor of lower-cost European locations. If production continues to move abroad, Germany's traditional trade surpluses could soon disappear.

German executives maintain that costs are often the driving motive for pulling out of Germany. What it all adds up to is that Germany is becoming less attractive as a manufacturing base at the same time other European countries such as Spain and Portugal are improving their productivity and in-

The Cost of Labor

Average hourly labor costs for 1990 in German marks

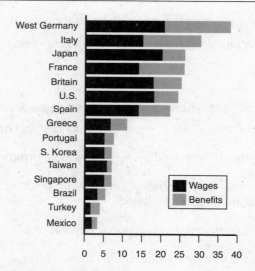

Source: Institute of German Industry, Cologne

dustrial infrastructures. The flight of capital exports German jobs and diminishes Germany's potential future economic growth and tax base. For Eastern Europe and Southern Europe, Germany's loss is their gain.

In 1990 German companies invested a net 29.8 billion marks abroad, nearly three times the 1988 capital outflow, while net foreign capital investments in Germany totaled 2.9 billion marks. The gap continued to widen in 1991.

From 1981 to 1989, Germany drew $14 billion in investments from other Group of Seven industrial nations. By contrast, France and Italy each pulled in $36 billion and Britain a whopping $80 billion.

"What is truly disturbing is that at a time when we need all the foreign capital we can get after unity with the East, we're getting only a tenth of what we are sending abroad," says Ottheinrich von Weitershausen of the Federal Employers' Association, a leading industry group.

Taken together, the disincentives for investing in Germany appear formidable.

German labor costs already are the highest in the world, and labor unions are threatening to try to increase them this year. At the end of 1990, the average German worker cost 37.88 marks ($23.50) an hour in wages and benefits, roughly 50% higher than average labor costs in the U.S., Japan, Britain and France, and five times the wages and benefits of Portuguese workers. By 1995, the average working week in Germany is contractually set to drift down to 35 hours a week from 37.5 hours currently. German workers already spend fewer hours on the job than their counterparts in any of the other Group of Seven countries.

Taxes Remain High Germany has lagged behind reductions in corporate taxes since the late 1980s. At an average 50%, rates at which corporate profits are taxes are half again as high as those in the U.S., Japan and France.

German companies also pay more for energy, for example 20% to 40% more for electricity than competitors in the European Community. Chemical maker BASF would have saved 100 million marks on its power bill last year if it were paying French rates. Costs associated with environmental protection are 60% higher in Germany than the EC average, particularly affecting smokestack industries strapped with some of the tightest environmental legislation anywhere.

Companies that can't easily move abroad are trimming staff in basic production, where profit margins are more sensitive to production costs. Fried. Krupp G.m.b.H plans to cut 10,000 jobs after its proposed merger with Hoesch AG, another steel and engineering group. Thyssen AG, the diversified industry group, is trimming 10,000 jobs, too.

The high cost of doing business has been a recurring grievance for German manufacturers, a few of which started shifting production to cheaper sites in the mid-1980s. But these days the rhetoric has a sharper edge. The European Community's single market looms after this year, and other countries are moving to reduce their production costs even as the German cost problem is growing worse.

The exodus of jobs from Germany worries German policy makers, who are furiously trying to talk militant trade unions out of demanding another round of major pay raises and more time off. German unions are threatening to strike for wage increases of 10% this year after receiving 7% in 1991.

Labor leaders show little inclination to moderate their demands, dismissing predictions of an economic slowdown as "propaganda." But Germany's business leaders argue that the unions' stance could become self-defeating.

QUESTIONS

1. The article lists many costs of production that German producers have to pay.

   a) Which costs would an accountant include in total costs?

   b) Can you think of any costs that an economist would include that an accountant would not?

2. Suppose that automobile producers are storing large inventories of foreign-made parts because their prices have been increasing rapidly due to a changing exchange rate. Would accountants and economists calculate the cost of stored parts used to make automobiles any differently? How? Explain your reasoning.

3. The overhead expenses of automobiles produced by a German manufacturer in a given year include a charge for the cost of the plant. Assuming the facility has an alternative use,

   a) how would an accountant determine the charge?

   b) how would an economist calculate these charges differently?

4. Auto producers have machines specially designed to produce automobile body panels of a unique size and shape.

   a) What would be the cost of such a machine in the eyes of an accountant? Explain your answer.

   b) Would an economist calculate the charge differently? How? Explain your response.

5. The article shows that the cost of producing in Germany is increasing.

   a) In what ways are accounting costs rising?

   b) In what sense is the opportunity cost of producing in Germany increasing?

   c) Why are German companies contemplating moving overseas in response to the changes in the relative costs of production?

6. Many firms are mentioned in the article.

   a) Do they appear to be corporations, partnerships, or proprietorships?

   b) What are the advantages and disadvantages of this type of organization?

21. Railroads Cut Costs to Get Back on Track

Firms are anxious to minimize costs in order to maximize profits and ensure a successful existence free from bankruptcy. Cost minimization requires technological efficiency such that the maximum output is produced from a given set of inputs, and economic efficiency such that the chosen technologically efficient method of producing a given level of output is the least costly. Economists represent these two conditions in terms of production functions and cost curves. In the short run, producers seek to be efficient subject to the constraint that capital is fixed. The accompanying article concerns the efforts of railroads to minimize costs.

After studying your text, reading the article, and answering the questions, you should be able to:

◆◆ Distinguish between the short run and the long run

◆◆ Represent and explain technological efficiency in terms of a production function

◆◆ Represent and explain economic efficiency in terms of cost curves

◆◆ State the difference between fixed and variable costs

◆◆ Predict the effect of exogenous changes on the production function and cost curves

Preview

◆ Railroad freight transportation is becoming more competitive with trucking.

◆ Some companies are expanding rail lines and terminals.

◆ Others are adopting new technology to increase efficiency.

◆ Train crews are now smaller, and management layers have been reduced.

◆ However, freight yards are inefficient and there is overcapacity on some routes.

◆ It remains to convince customers of the timeliness and positive environmental effects of rail transportation.

Railroads Getting in Better Shape for the Long Haul

Long the laggards of freight shipping, railroads are slashing labor costs, revamping management, embracing new technology, exceeding analysts' earnings forecasts during the recession and outperforming the stock market by 100%....

Signs of rejuvenation abound in an industry that not long ago was synonymous with market-share losses to truckers and meager growth prospects. For example, Santa Fe Pacific Corp. is expanding a freight terminal in Chicago and building one in nearby Willow Springs, Ill., to handle a surge of business from companies putting their freight shipments on rail. "We've become a growth industry," says Donald McInnes, a senior vice president of the Santa Fe Railway.

Union Pacific Corp. is spending $267 million to expand a rail line with sidings, double track and new signals to haul low-sulfur Western coal to utilities seeking to meet more stringent air pollution standards. And Consolidated Rail Corp. executives expect to capture more than $1 billion of additional freight business in the next five to seven years.

The chief reason for the industry's turnaround is big cuts in employment. Santa Fe, for instance, has slashed its work force to 14,000 from 23,000 six years ago. Overall, rail industry employment has dropped nearly 50% since 1980 to about 283,000, according to the Association of American Railroads. And railroads expect to save an additional $1 billion a year from new labor pacts that reduce train crews by one or two positions to only an engineer and a conductor. Railroads had been fighting for such contracts for decades.

But some rail industry executives temper predictions of a renaissance. Railroads have problems, including the contraction of some of their largest industrial customers, fierce competition from trucks and strained relations between rail management and labor.

"If they are going to have a renaissance, they better first get the cooperation of their employees," says G. Thomas DuBose, international president of the United Transportation Union. He adds that the militaristic style of management that railroads practiced for decades created a "gap of distrust between the railroads and their employees."

Though main lines have been upgraded and freight train speeds increased, the rail industry has yet to modernize its inefficient freight yards. For example, freight shipments can take as long as 48 hours to maneuver through Santa Fe's sprawling yard in Kansas City, Kan. Santa Fe officials say they need to spend $12 million to streamline the yard to speed shipments.

Shippers complain of delays when freight moves from one railroad to another. Rail executives say railroads still have an anemic return on investment and big excess capacity.

"The rail industry has too much capacity, with too many underutilized rail lines between major markets," says William Greenwood, chief operating officer of Burlington Northern Inc. For example, he says, rail shipments between Chicago and California could be handled on the tracks of just one of the three railroads that now compete for the business.

For railroads, the challenge of the 1990s is to fill this capacity. They plan to use the savings from changes in work rules and the adoption of new technology to boost train frequency while launching aggressive marketing programs to lure back shippers that have defected to trucks. Railroads also are expediting freight shipments by closing or bypassing freight yards that too often caused delays.

Some shippers say they see improvements. "The on-time performance of freight railroads is the best I have ever seen," says Charles Wilkins, director of transportation and traffic at Ford Motor Co., which is switching some freight back to rail.

Railroads are streamlining their management procedures. Rail executives, encouraged by Union Pacific's campaign to slash management layers and shake up the railroad's bureaucracy, are taking similar steps at their railroads. One result, say shippers and competitors, is that railroads are speeding up decision-making, innovating more and entering partnerships with their rivals....

Environmental Response Rail executives expect to capitalize on the nation's environmental problems. They have awakened to the fact that their lines in urban areas could profit from carrying commuter trains to relieve highway congestion. And they see opportunities to move municipal waste, or "suburban ore," as one rail executive calls it. Conrail is moving municipal waste from New Jersey to a disposal site in Texas, while Union Pacific is hauling garbage from Seattle to a landfill in eastern Oregon.

Moreover, environmentalists say railroads use less fuel and create less pollution than trucks moving similar loads without adding to road conges-tion and deterioration....

But the greatest opportunities still lie within the rail industry, say rail executives, to squeeze out inefficiency and move more freight with fewer assets. "We have to avoid spending capital for things we don't need," says Alvin "Pete" Carpenter, president and chief executive officer of CSX Corp.'s rail unit. CSX recently avoided having to buy or rebuild 3,500 coal cars by running more efficient unit trains and storing export coal on the ground at piers rather than in rail cars.

Technological Improvements Rail companies must continue to turn to technology to cut costs and get better control of their far-flung track networks, rail executives say. Some rail lines are weighing plans to centralize their dispatchers, as Union Pacific and CSX have done already. Burlington Northern is experimenting with a car design that could carry 30% more coal and with locomotives fueled by natural gas, which can run longer with less wear and tear. Railroads have begun to place radio tags on containers, locomotives and freight cars as part of an industrywide program to automatically track the entire rail-car fleet by 1995.

—Daniel Machalaba, "Railroads Getting in Better Shape for the Long Haul," February 26, 1992.

QUESTIONS

1. Railroads have a choice of providing their desired levels of service by increasing train frequency with more crews or by expanding and modernizing track and equipment.

   a) Which is the labor-intensive option?

   b) Which is feasible in the short run? Explain your answer.

2. Draw a short-run production function showing the maximum number of ton-miles that can be driven by Burlington Northern as it employs more and more train crews.

   a) What are you assuming about the number of trains in drawing the production function? Why is this realistic?

   b) Given its work force, Burlington Northern under-utilizes its rail lines between major markets. What do you infer about its position in relation to the above production function? Why? How could the number of ton-miles be increased?

c) If Burlington Northern is driving the maximum number of ton-miles it can given its employment level, what is the only way the number of ton-miles can be increased in the short run?

3. a) As more and more train crews are employed, does the last crew added enable more ton-miles to be driven than were added by the previous crew? Explain why or why not using economic reasoning.

b) What happens to the average number of ton-miles as more crews are employed?

c) Draw a diagram depicting the marginal and average product of labor curves you have described in 3a and 3b. Choose an employment level. Explain the slope of the average product curve in relation to the marginal product curve at this point.

4. In a diagram of a production function show what happens to the technologically feasible number of ton-miles, assuming employment is fixed, when

a) the number of employees in a train crew is reduced.

b) track and equipment ages.

5. Railroads are attempting to reduce costs. Identify from the article the costs that can be considered

   a) fixed in the short run.

   b) variable in the short run.

6. Draw a diagram with axes depicting the cost and number of ton-miles driven by Union Pacific. Show the total fixed costs, total variable costs, and total costs, for each level of ton-miles in the short run.

   a) Union Pacific is reducing the number of layers of management. What would you expect to happen to the cost curve in the short run? Why?

   b) When the total cost curve is as low as it can be, how can total costs be reduced in the short run?

7. a) As ton-miles increase, is the cost of the last ton-mile more than that of the previous ton-mile? Explain why using economics.

   b) What happens to the average cost of a ton-mile as the number increases?

   c) Draw a diagram illustrating the short-run marginal and average cost curves you have described in 7a and 7b. Choose a quantity of ton-miles provided. Explain the slope of the average cost curve in relation to the marginal cost curve at this point.

8. In a diagram of Burlington Northern's marginal and average cost in the short run, show the effect of

   a) smaller train crews.

   b) the introduction of new cars and locomotives fueled by natural gas.

22.
The Size of
Sam's
Stores

As in the short run, firms attempt to be technologically and economically efficient in the long run so as to minimize costs and maximize profits. The difference is that in the long run all inputs are variable. Producers are able to select a different plant size as well as alter labor and resource inputs.

The most efficient scale of plant is where long-run average cost is minimized. At lower output levels, there are increasing returns to scale. At higher output levels, there are decreasing returns to scale. However, in certain circumstances it may be more profitable to be in these ranges rather than at the point of lowest long-run average cost.

The accompanying article concerns Wal-Mart's strategy of establishing large stores in order to reap economies of scale.

After studying your text, reading the article, and answering the questions, you should be able to:

◆◆ Define the long run

◆◆ Derive the long-run average cost curve

◆◆ Explain how and why costs change as plant size changes

◆◆ Define increasing, constant, and decreasing returns to scale

◆◆ Explain profit-maximizing deviations from the most efficient scale of plant

◆◆ Discuss the advantages and disadvantages of large economic units

Preview

◆ Wal-Mart stores have spread across the United States.

◆ Their size allows them to price their products below the wholesale cost of smaller competitors.

◆ As a result, local stores have closed, communities have been devastated, and cities have lost tax revenues.

◆ Other stores have been forced to find other niches and to improve store hours and service.

◆ Wal-Mart's size and growth strategy may actually cause its success to falter.

◆ Consumers may stop shopping at Wal-Mart when they realize it is contributing to the decline of their town and to higher taxes.

The Two Sides of the Sam Walton Legacy

When Sam Moore Walton died a week ago after a long battle with cancer, he was eulogized—and rightly so—as a man who had transformed American merchandising and perfected a hands-on management that instilled a sense of team enthusiasm among the 380,000 employees he liked to refer to as "associates."…His passion, his joy, was fine-tuning his vast merchandising network by insisting on such things as brighter smiles and cheerier "Good mornings" to customers from store workers, as well as offering the latest products gathered and stocked through the most sophisticated and efficient inventory technology available.

Wal-Mart merchandising, the brilliantly simple concept of "everyday low price" retailing, has become such a pervasive force (2,000 stories of various kinds, 160 built each year) that it is redesigning the social structure of rural and small-town America more than any other force besides nature. Wal-Mart is beginning to nibble at the edges of large cities and giant shopping malls, many of which are weakened by the general economic malaise.

To millions, the down-home Bentonville, Ark., genius was a hero who brought decent merchandise at low prices to areas scorned by more glitzy entrepreneurs. On Wall Street, Walton was a billionaire god who made countless millionaires of others. Last month President Bush awarded the Medal of Freedom, the country's highest civil tribute, to the ailing Walton….

But even as he was honored, some of Walton's roots were wondering about just what he had wrought….

Steve Bishop, a Church of Christ minister who grew up in Hearne, Texas (pop. 5,400), and served a church there for seven years, fired off an essay a couple of months ago to the Dallas *Morning News,* declaring, "Wal-Mart killed Hearne, Texas—twice … The first death was the end of a downtown that held much more than stores, it held memories, values and people who stayed long enough to make a difference in our lives. Wal-Mart's arrival ended all that. The second killing occurred in December 1990, when Wal-Mart closed its doors in Hearne. It closed because it couldn't turn a profit. Wal-Mart leaves an empty building as testimony to the '80's greed, and it leaves a downtown of vacated shops as testimony to our rush to save a little money—maybe not a very different kind of greed."

Kenneth Stone, professor of economics at Iowa State University, began five years ago to study the Wal-Mart phenomenon in his state after he noted the commercial life of many towns being hollowed out by the huge intruder… "It could be the biggest corporation in the United States," says Stone, and that includes Exxon and General Motors.

Wal-Mart is already the largest retailer, smothering Sears and K Mart. "The impact of a corporation of that size and that involvement in the life of this country is immense," declares Stone, who recently held meetings with the merchants of St. James (pop. 4,300) and Madelia (pop. 2,100), Minn., two small communities gasping in a web of Wal-Marts. He advised them, as he has countless other small-town merchants, on how to deal with the arrival of a Wal-Mart in their region. "I don't fight Wal-Mart," Stone insists. "If you believe in the free-market system as I do, then you cannot keep them out of your community. Much of what I tell you will be to emulate them."

Stone talks about finding special merchandising niches not occupied by Wal-Mart, about improving service, extending store hours….

Yet, for all the delicacy of Stone's presentations and the litany of stores and communities that have survived Wal-Mart, there is a brooding inevitability about the data in Stone's studies. Small communities of static population sooner or later lose business from their downtowns to Wal-Mart, which sinks its roots at their edges. Surrounding communities with no Wal-Mart are devastated. Independent stores in growing areas generally rise with the tide even with Wal-Mart scooping up a big share.

Some of this was surely inevitable in our moiling capitalism; Wal-Mart, perhaps, has done no more than finish off bad shopkeepers and lazy combines. Its bright, clinic-clean stores are the boondocks miracle that Walton wrought.

But few if any American enterprises, no matter how huge and momentarily successful, have enjoyed uninterrupted bliss. The betting in dozens of tiny stores around the country is that Wal-Mart will reach its own plateau. Despite the superb management team Walton left in place, his death will inevitably mean that the soul of his corporation will change. Community irritation at secretive and standoffish ways of Wal-Mart managers, the "us" (Wal-Mart) against "them" (downtown merchants) attitude, and the modest involvement in public affairs and charities by store officers are building resentment.

Then there is the matter of basic economics. James McConkey can't scientifically prove it, but his hunch is that people who drive 20 miles to a Wal-Mart, and so contribute to the decline of their town, end up paying higher taxes, which is a premium for the merchandise they get. Eventually, the pendulum will swing, the market-place will adjust. That is what American capitalism is all about, as Mr. Sam knew as well as any merchant of the modern age.

—Hugh Sidey, "The Two Sides of the Sam Walton Legacy," April 20, 1992, *Time*.

QUESTIONS

1. Companies like Wal-Mart, Sears, and K-Mart have discovered that increased size can bring lower average costs. From the article identify Wal-Mart's

   a) internal economies of scale.

   b) external economies of scale.

2. In a diagram relating costs to output, draw three overlapping sets of short-run average and marginal cost curves for a Wal-Mart store. The middle set should show the current position; the left-hand set should illustrate the situation if the store size was smaller; the right-hand set should be appropriate to a large store size. Draw the long-run average cost curve over these store sizes. Does it show decreasing, constant, or increasing returns to scale? Explain why.

3. When Wal-Mart moved into Hearne, Texas, it caused smaller stores to leave. However, Wal-Mart could not make a profit and so it closed down its store. Assuming the same market demand for the small stores combined as for Wal-Mart, explain how the small stores were able to survive, while Wal-Mart was not. Illustrate your answer with two diagrams showing the long-run average cost curves of a Wal-Mart store and a small store.

4. While Wal-Mart stores have grown in size, in some cases they may have exhibited increasing average costs. What are the sources of these diseconomies? Note down as many as you can find in the article.

5. In a diagram relating costs to output, draw three overlapping sets of short-run average and marginal cost curves for a Wal-Mart store facing increasing costs. As in question 2, the middle set should show the current position, and the outer two should illustrate smaller and larger plant sizes. Draw the long-run average cost curve over this range of output. Does it reveal decreasing, constant, or increasing returns to scale? Justify your answer.

6. Given that diseconomies of scale are evident in some Wal-Mart stores, and therefore that they remain larger than the optimal scale, how do you explain in economically rational terms their reluctance to break up into smaller units?

7. What are the advantages and disadvantages of Wal-Mart's size

    a) for Wal-Mart?

    b) for area consumers?

    c) for neighboring cities?

23.
Reach Out and Touch Something

In the long run, producers choose the least-cost production technique by varying all factors of production. The optimal technique occurs when the marginal rate of substitution between the factors equals the ratio of their prices. Diagrammatically, this is where the isocost line is tangent to an isoquant. At this point, the marginal productivity of the last dollar spent on each factor is equal. The accompanying article focuses on the optimal combination of human and robotic telephone operators at AT&T.

After studying your text, reading the article, and answering the questions, you should be able to:

◆ ◆ Explain what an isocost line and an isoquant represent

◆ ◆ Derive the optimal choice of technique

◆ ◆ Define the marginal rate of substitution between two factors

◆ ◆ Predict the effect of changes in factor prices on the choice of technique both diagrammatically and in terms of the least-cost formula

◆ ◆ Predict the effect of a change in output on the optimum factor combination

Preview

◆ AT&T decided to replace one third of its operators with robotic operators by the end of 1994.

◆ This was facilitated by new technology pioneered by AT&T's Bell Laboratories.

◆ It was part of an ongoing cost-cutting process.

◆ Operator positions were also declining because of decreasing customer usage of operators.

◆ AT&T's largest union, the Communication Workers of America, was angry at the planned cuts in employment.

AT&T to Replace as Many as One-Third of Its Operators with Computer Systems

American Telephone & Telegraph Co. said it will install computerized operator services throughout the country and close 31 offices, or more than 25% of its operator centers nationwide.

AT&T's move could eliminate as many as one-third of its 18,000 operators over the next two years. The company said it will cut 200 to 400 managers and 3,000 to 6,000 operators from its operator services organization by the end of 1994 through dismissals, attrition and transfers.

They'll be replaced by a computerized "voice-recognition" technology pioneered by AT&T Bell Laboratories that responds to a caller's verbal prompts, AT&T said. Instead of talking to a human operator, callers on the AT&T network will tell a robotic operator the type of call they would like to make.

Live Operators Available "The voice prompts the caller to say 'collect; third number; person-to-person; or calling card,'" said an AT&T spokesman about AT&T's newest service breakthrough. When the call is made, he said, "the system will tell the called party, 'I have a collect call from Mr. So and So. Do you accept the call?'" The spokesman added that you can always get a live operator simply by saying "operator."

AT&T's move prompted an angry response from its largest union, the Communications Workers of America. AT&T and the CWA have been at odds over continual massive cutbacks that have trimmed AT&T's ranks by 100,000 workers since its breakup in 1984. But lately their relations have become increasingly strained as the union pegged recent problems with AT&T service, including four major network failures in two years, to overzealous cost-cutting by the telecommunications giant.

"We're outraged by AT&T's move … and by their unbelievable disrespect of our union," said CWA President Morton Bahr. "AT&T's decision to announce layoffs … four weeks before contract talks begin is the worst intimidation tactic we have ever seen." Added J.D. Williams, president of a CWA local representing AT&T operators in Dallas: "It's a sad day in the history of AT&T and the Bell System, which have been offering operator services for more than 100 years." AT&T plans to close the Dallas center, which employs 140 operators.

Two Field Tests But AT&T's spokesman said the company's statistics show that fewer Americans are using live operators these days to help place their calls. "Ninety percent of all long-distance calls are made without an operator and the number of operator-assisted calls has been declining by 8% a year," said AT&T's spokesman. This is a trend, he added, that goes back to 1951 when AT&T introduced direct-dialed long-distance calling. "[Voice recognition] is one more step on that technology path," he said.

AT&T decided to deploy the system after conducting two field tests in the Dallas-Fort Worth area. The company said the trials indicated that customers found the system easy to use and more versatile from a service standpoint. The system uses a method called "word spotting" to filter out automatically any spoken words it doesn't need to act upon, AT&T said.

QUESTIONS

1. AT&T can respond to calls from customers to an operator using various combinations of human and robotic operators. Draw an isoquant showing possible combinations of human and robotic AT&T operators that can respond to a given number of calls. Assume that as more humans are used, more humans are needed for each extra hundred calls because of the use of more inferior labor.

2. Does the marginal rate of substitution of humans for robots rise or fall along the isoquant? Explain your answer.

3. Assuming input prices are constant, add an isocost line to your diagram such that it is tangent to the isoquant. Indicate the optimal mix of human and robotic operators on the axes. Why is this combination the least-cost option?

4. Technical progress has reduced the cost of robotic operators. In a new diagram, show any shifts in the curves and also the former and the new optimum factor combinations assuming the number of calls remained constant. Show the decrease in employment of human operators. Explain how the change(s) in the curve(s) illustrate(s) the price increase.

5. Explain what has happened to the least-cost technique in terms of the marginal rate of factor substitution and the relative factor price ratio.

6. The optimal choice of technique is also where the ratios of the marginal products to the prices of human and robotic operators are equal.

    a) How has the equality been disrupted by the decrease in the price of robotic operators?

    b) What had to happen to the marginal products of human and robotic operators to restore equality?

    c) Draw diagrams of the marginal products of human and robotic operators as the quantity of each factor increases. Show what had to happen to the quantities of each factor employed for the marginal products to change appropriately.

7. Contrary to the assumption in the analyses above, the number of calls to operators has been declining. In a new diagram, illustrate the implications for the curves and the optimum combination of human and robotic operators. Show the decrease in the number of human operators. On what does the change in the number of operator jobs depend?

PERFECT COMPETITION

24.
Farmers
Fight Fish
in Western
Water
Wars

Product markets are characterized by differing degrees of competition between producers. The most fierce competition is to be found in perfectly competitive markets. Their characteristics require producers to accept the market price. Individual producers supply output up to the point where the marginal cost equals the marginal revenue or price in order to maximize profits. Profits or losses may be earned in the short run. Perfectly competitive markets are allocatively efficient when there are no external costs or benefits. The accompanying article about farming provides an illustration of these points.

After studying your text, reading the article, and answering the questions, you should be able to:

◆ ◆ Recognize the characteristics of perfectly competitive markets

◆ ◆ Explain the slope of the firm's demand curve

◆ ◆ Derive the firm's supply curve

◆ ◆ Identify the point at which firms shut down in the short run

◆ ◆ Explain the equilibrium position of firms in the short run

◆ ◆ Recognize whether markets are allocatively efficient

Preview

◆ Irrigation water from federal and state systems was severely limited in 1992.

◆ The causes were the drought and the need to protect salmon.

◆ Environmentalists claimed that farmers used water inefficiently and endangered fish and humans.

◆ Farmers countered that the economic cost of protecting wildlife was too high.

◆ Reductions in agricultural output and in the number of farms were predicted.

U.S. to Tighten Farmers' Water Supply in California in Effort to Save Salmon

California's water wars are about to boil over again.

Today, the federal Bureau of Reclamation is expected to announce severe limitations on how much irrigation water will go to California farmers from federal dam systems this year, according to people familiar with the bureau's plans. The cuts are largely a result of California's withering drought, which is well into its sixth year, despite the heavy storms lashing the state this week.

However, this year's water limits will be far tougher than they've ever been, partly because federal wildlife officials are forcing the bureau to conserve water that would otherwise go to farmers to try to save the fast-disappearing winter run of salmon up the Sacramento River, the key artery of the big federal water system known as the Central Valley Project. The salmon, which are listed as a threatened species under the federal Endangered Species Act, have seen their numbers reduced to 191 from 118,000 over the past 20 years, largely because the water system's dams and pumps kill many fish outright or make it impossible for them to spawn.

The restrictions are certain to trigger predictions of economic doom from farmers, many of whom will receive no federal water for the first time since the drought began. More significantly, the situation also will move toward center stage in the increasingly bitter national debate over the Endangered Species Act's impact on economical growth. The act is up for congressional reauthorization this year, and many business interests are calling for a major overhaul to reduce the economic costs of protecting wildlife.

In California, farmers contend that they are being sacrificed for a fish that even some biologists believe is too far gone to save. Environmentalists counter that farmers' voracious and inefficient water use—farmers sop up 80% of the state's water resources but produce only about 3% of its economic output— threatens not only salmon, but numerous other fish species and ultimately humans, since two-thirds of the state's 30 million people draw their drinking water from the same river systems used by the fish and the farmers....

The Central Valley Project normally provides about a third of the water used by farms in California, the nation's biggest agriculture state. Under the Bureau of Reclamation plan, farmers who received only 25% of their usual federal allotments last year will get no federal water this year.

Moreover, the bureau is contemplating reducing deliveries to so-called "water rights holders"—farmers who owned water rights on the system's rivers before the Central Valley Project was constructed in the 1920s—by about half. That is a potentially explosive move, because water rights holders, many of whom are among the biggest and most politically well-connected agricultural barons in the state, have always maintained that water rights laws and guarantees made by the bureau assure that they can't receive less than 75% of their allotments in a given year, no matter how severe a drought is. The matter likely would end up in court.

Barring months of heavy rain, farmers also face steep cuts in water deliveries from the state's other major water system, the state-owned State Water Project. State water officials have predicted that the state project may ship only about 20% of the water it sends to farmers in a normal year. That's actually an improvement: Last year, farmers got no state water. The overall impact on agriculture is likely to exceed $500 million, by some estimates. That's real money, but California's farm economy typically generates about $17 billion a year.

—Charles McCoy, "U.S. to Tighten Farmers' Water Supply in California in Effort to Save Salmon," February 14, 1992.
Reprinted by permission of *The Wall Street Journal*, ©1992 Dow Jones & Co., Inc. All Rights Reserved Worldwide.

QUESTIONS

1. One of the major agricultural products of central California is tomatoes. Why does the tomato market in central California approximate perfect competition?

2. a) Why is it likely that each farm has to accept the market price for tomatoes, rather than charge a higher price? Refer to the characteristics of the market in question 1.

   b) Why would each farm not charge less than the market price?

   c) What does this imply about the elasticity of the demand curve facing an individual farm?

3. In a diagram relating price and costs to output, draw curves representing a farm's average total cost, average variable cost, and marginal cost of producing tomatoes. Mark the range of output and prices over which the farm is prepared to supply tomatoes.

   a) Why is the farm prepared to sell tomatoes in this range?

b) Why is the farm not prepared to sell any tomatoes below the lower bound of the range you have drawn?

4. Draw a supply and demand diagram of the tomato industry. Show the equilibrium price and quantity. At the side of this diagram draw a second diagram of a tomato farm showing its demand curve and marginal and average cost curves. Identify its output, price, and profits, and explain how each is determined.

5. Irrigation water limitations were made more stringent in 1992.

a) Assuming that the cost of water was unaffected, but that the drought continued and forced some farmers out of business, in two diagrams show the effect of this on the equilibrium price and output of the tomato industry, and the output, price, and profit of a typical tomato farmer who was initially breaking even.

b) Are the prospects for the long-run production of tomatoes as dire as farmers contended in 1992? Why?

6. a) Does society incur any external costs of, or benefits from, tomato production?

b) As a result, are too few or too many resources being allocated to tomato farming?

25. Compact Disks More Compact

In perfect competition in the short run, changes in industry demand and supply cause changes in equilibrium price and quantity. For the individual firm, the change in price affects the quantity supplied as well as profits and losses. The firm's new position is also affected by any changes in its costs curves caused by an initial change in supply. The accompanying article concerns the consequences of different types of exogenous changes in supply and demand on the competitive compact disk retailing industry.

After studying your text, reading the article, and answering the questions, you should be able to:

◆◆ Predict the industry price and quantity traded in the short run following demand and supply shifts

◆◆ Predict changes in the short-run cost curves of a typical firm when fixed and variable costs change

◆◆ Analyze whether the producer or the consumer bears the burden of changes in costs

◆◆ Predict changes in a typical firm's price, output, and profits in the short run following shifts in demand and supply

◆◆ Explain why some firms may choose to shut down in the short run

Preview

◆ Retailers are upset at the ban on large cardboard compact disk packages.

◆ They will have to increase security, use costly plastic security trays, and buy new fixtures for smaller packages.

◆ Retailers warn that consumers will pay higher prices as a result.

◆ The plastic trays may do more harm to the environment than using cardboard.

◆ Record companies are considering compensating retailers for their extra costs.

◆ Also, retailers are being hurt by a tight economy and increased direct sales by record companies to consumers.

Record Makers Giving Retailers the Blues

Record store-owners attending their annual convention here aren't making harmonious noises about the record industry.

The retailers already had complained when the record industry decreed two weeks ago that compact disks will be sold only in jewel box-sized packages starting in a year. It has been planned for several years that the wasteful cardboard boxes that hold the plastic jewel boxes would be banned, but for the past year, the industry has been experimenting with new packages that start out 11 inches long to fit stores' current CD bins, then fold down at home to the jewel-box size.

At the convention of the National Association of Recording Merchandisers, which ends today, it is clear that the ire of the retailers is rising and that this is just one issue increasing tension between retailers and record companies. In a tight economy, the retailers are going to have to spend millions to change fixtures to accommodate the new package, plus increase security to prevent more thefts, a cost they say consumers eventually will bear. And there's more:

this fall, two new technologies will be introduced to consumers, digital compact cassettes and tiny, recordable CDs, Sony Corp.'s Mini Disc, and retailers will have to alter their stores to carry the new disks and cassettes.

At the same time, as Robert Morgado, chairman of Time Warner Inc.'s Warner Music Group, made clear in his keynote address, record companies plan to sell more and more records directly to consumers, not just through record clubs but also catalogs and 800 numbers, thereby competing with the retailers.

"The frustration level is definitely rising," says Russell Solomon, founder and owner of the Tower Records chain. "This CD box thing is the worst decision the record industry ever made, and they did it by royal fiat. Most stores will have to use these plastic security trays called keepers which cost a bundle and are ugly as hell. We can't boycott the record companies, but we'll protest this every way we can."…

Ultimately, the retailers don't expect to get the move reversed: "I'm outraged, but a realist," says Ann Spector Lieff, convention chairman and

head of a 60-store Miami-based chain. But retailers say the change will raise CD retail prices and could hurt the environment, despite the claims of record companies.

Robert Schneider, executive vice president of Western Merchandisers, which supplies records to about 650 Wal-Mart stores and also to "mom and pop" retailers, estimates the industry's total cost for alterations will be $125 million to $150 million. "Bottom line, the consumer will pay 45 cents to 50 cents more for a CD," predicts Mr. Schneider, "and they already think they cost too much." He also says that, according to his calculations, the use of the plastic security devices could add as much as 30 million pounds of plastic to landfills a year, undoing the environmental good of banning the original cardboard box.

After a speech by the association president calling for a reversal of the decision, Jason Berman, head of the Recording Industry Association of America, said, "It won't be reversed." But he said, the record companies have agreed to consider compensating retailers for the added costs.

QUESTIONS

1. a) In a diagram of the retail CD industry, draw the demand and supply curves and mark the equilibrium price and quantity of CDs traded. In a separate diagram at the side, show the marginal and average cost curves and the demand and the marginal revenue curves of a typical store, assuming the market is perfectly competitive and that no profits are being earned. Mark the store's equilibrium price and output.

   b) Show clearly the impact of the recession and the increased proportion of sales of CDs accounted for by direct sales to consumers by record companies. Mark the new retailing industry price and quantity and store price, output, and profits in the short run.

2. a) As in question 1, draw initial equilibria for the CD retailing industry and a store that is breaking even. Illustrate what happens to price, output, and profits when retailers have to incur the cost of a plastic security tray for each CD sold. Pay careful attention to the relative magnitudes of the changes in costs and price.

   b) Are the retailers correct when they say that the consumer pays a higher price as a result of the use of plastic security trays? Does the consumer bear the whole of the increase in cost? Explain your answer and illustrate on your diagram.

c) Why are the retailers upset? Respond in terms of your diagram.

d) Under what economic circumstances will stores decide to shut down in the short run?

3. a) Draw another set of diagrams showing the equilibria of the CD retailing industry and an individual store. Assume that the cost of the plastic security trays are included in the cost curves and that zero profits are earned. If the stores were to receive compensation for the tray costs of each CD sold from the record companies, what would happen to the curves and the equilibrium price, output, and profits in the short run? Illustrate on your diagrams.

b) Do the retail stores benefit from the compensation by the full amount of the subsidy? Explain your answer and illustrate on your diagram.

4. a) In a further set of CD retailing industry and store diagrams, mark the initial equilibria assuming zero profits are made. Show the short-run effect of refitting stores with new fixtures to accommodate new CD packages. What happens to the curves and the industry and firm equilibria?

b) Do consumers bear the cost of refitting the stores? Explain your answer and illustrate on your diagram.

PERFECT COMPETITION

In perfect competition in the long run firms are able to enter and exit the industry in response to short-run profits and losses, respectively. Long-run equilibrium is where profits are zero. As firms enter or exit the industry, factor prices and therefore cost curves may change because of changes in the industry's demand for factors. Where there are increasing costs as the industry grows, the long-run equilibrium price increases with output, implying an upward-rising long-run industry supply curve. Conversely, where there are decreasing costs, the industry supply curve slopes down. The following article illustrates these concepts in relation to the steel industry.

After studying your text, reading the article, and answering the questions, you should be able to:

◆◆ Predict the long-run responses of firms to short-run profits and losses

◆◆ Predict the long-run effect of shifts in demand and supply on price, output, and profits in the industry and the firm

◆◆ Differentiate between the long-run impact of demand and supply shifts when there are increasing, constant, and decreasing factor costs

◆◆ Identify the long-run industry supply curve

Preview

◆ The 1991-1992 recession caused some steel firms to go bankrupt and threatened others.

◆ The major problem was overcapacity and high production, resulting in falling prices.

◆ Also, it was difficult to obtain financing from the stock market or banks to improve capital equipment.

◆ Some firms and plants were kept viable through labor concessions and the deferral of payments.

◆ The improvement in the economy was critical to the survival of many firms, but especially small- and medium-sized firms.

Small, Midsize Steelmakers Are Ripe for a Shakeout

A new shakeout is looming for small and midsize steel companies.

Some steelmakers already are on their last legs after hobbling through last year, when the industry lost an estimated $1 billion and output fell to its lowest level since 1986. Already, companies representing one-fourth of the nation's capacity are operating under Chapter 11 bankruptcy protection, from LTV Corp.'s giant LTV Steel Co. unit in Cleveland, which ships more than seven million tons, to CF&I Steel Corp. of Pueblo, Colo., which makes less than one million. Others are trying to steer clear of bankruptcy by getting rid of unprofitable operations.

"We got to a point in the mid '80s when a lot [of steel companies] were on the ropes," but many of them got another chance, thanks in part to a long strike at U.S. Steel, says U.S. Steel President Thomas J. Usher. "But this year a lot of them will be reeling, and if there's not an upturn, a few will fall by the wayside. A lot don't have the staying power." U.S. Steel, a unit of USX Corp., Pittsburgh, and Bethlehem Steel Corp., of Bethlehem, Pa., earlier this year said they would close one large operation each.

A Few Bright Spots There are a few signs of optimism. Orders have remained relatively strong in January and the nation's steel service centers, which distribute and finish steel, noted that January's average daily shipping rates were up almost 5% from December. Meanwhile, U.S. car makers are vowing to boost U.S. steel purchases.

Still, says Peter Marcus, steel analyst at Paine Webber, "we think that 1992 is shaping up as a more difficult year than 1991 for the steel industry in both the U.S. and abroad."

Just ask Northwestern Steel & Wire Co., of Sterling, Ill. In spite of having the distinction of being one of two U.S. companies certified by Japan to sell steel in that country, the steelmaker has until March 31 to come up with at least $20 million to meet obligations to lenders. In Trenton, Mich., McClouth Steel Corp. asked workers and suppliers for permission to defer payments and is seeking local tax relief as well. American Steel & Wire Corp. said last month it couldn't comply with certain loan agreements. The Cleveland company is now shopping for a partner to supply money and raw materials.

And looking to the next two to three years, American Steel & Wire Chief Executive Thomas Tyrell says, "Unless the economy improves, we can't make the investment necessary to compete."

The biggest problem is capacity. When it comes to adjusting production to meet demand, the industry has shown about as much flexibility as a concrete block. Output remains within 5% of its peak and will likely grow this year as steelmakers restart huge facilities that were shut down last year for repairs.

In turn, prices are being pulled down as steelmakers—trying to maintain high production—battle for a shrinking, or at best static, market. Nucor Corp. of Charlotte, N.C., cut prices earlier this month by $15 a ton on rolled steel because its order rate was sufficient to operate its Crawfordsville, Ind., plant only at 70% capacity. Meanwhile, shortly after U.S. Steel announced a 4% price rise effective in April, Bethlehem Steel announced a smaller price increase. U.S. Steel reluctantly matched that.

"The industry lacks discipline. It has shifted back to the volume-game again," says Christopher Plummer, who follows the steel industry for WEFA Group. "It's a lesson it should have learned in the late '70s and early '80s."

But with 24 U.S. producers of hot rolled band—a standard product used to make everything from car doors to refrigerators—no one wants to be the first to back down. And many in the industry wonder how long or effective any shutdown will be in an industry where old plants have as many comebacks as Muhammad Ali, thanks to labor concessions and the government....

Exports Expected to Shrink Meanwhile, the U.S. overflow has nowhere to go. Mr. Marcus figures there's roughly 45 million metric tons of capacity in the world. Germany, a major importer of steel-intensive capital goods, is in recession and Japan's economy is slowing. That could mean that more foreign steelmakers will try to export to the U.S., which could push up U.S. imports to 18 million tons from 15.7 million tons in 1991, Mr. Marcus says. And after growing in each of the last five years, U.S. exports are expected to recede to four million tons from 7.5 million.

Even if U.S. shipments grow 4% to 5% as expected, it won't be enough to absorb growing capacity. Two thirds of steel goes into capital equipment, and companies won't begin buying new materials until profits improve. Meanwhile, makers of everything from tractors and cars to appliances are trying to trim supplier lists, leaving out marginal producers....

Meanwhile, for sale signs are sprouting up around the country for steel's middle men—about 375 steel distributors. As prices for steel plummeted throughout last year, they were left with high-priced inventory. Banks aren't always willing to finance inventories, while owners of mom and pop shops are nearing retirement and don't want to put any more money in the operations.

"It's a liquidity issue," says Andrew Sharkey, president of the Steel Service Center Institute, which represents the $24 billion steel-service industry. "Small to midsize companies are having a great deal of difficulty getting operating capital and bank lines."

Adds WEFA's Mr. Plummer: "A 4% increase in shipments won't do a heck of a lot for those hanging on the edge."

QUESTIONS

1. a) Draw initial price and output equilibria for the perfectly competitive world steel industry in a supply and demand diagram. In a separate diagram next to it, show the cost, demand, and marginal revenue curves of a typical U.S. steel producer that is breaking even. Identify the equilibrium price and output in each diagram.

   b) Illustrate the short-run effect of the recession of the early 1990s on price and output in the industry and the firm and on producer profits.

   c) Illustrate the reaction of steel producers in the long run. Show what happens to equilibrium price (P_{lr}) and quantity (Q_{lr}) assuming constant costs.

   d) Using a different color, add the long-run industry supply curve to the diagram. Explain what it is and why it has the slope you have drawn.

2. a) During the recession, many steel industry workers agreed to concessions in wages and benefits. Explain why this suggests that steel is an increasing-cost industry.

b) Redraw the short-run equilibria showing the effects of the recession (as in question 1b). Illustrate the long-run equilibria assuming there are increasing costs as scale increases in the industry. State how the firm's cost curves and the price and output of the firm and industry are different from when there are constant costs.

c) Using a different color, draw the long-run industry supply curve on your diagram. Why does it have the slope you have drawn?

3. a) When output grows again, steelmakers will find it easier to obtain finance for investment in more efficient equipment. Explain why this suggests steel may be a decreasing-cost industry.

b) Redraw the short-run equilibria showing the effects of the recession (as in question 1b). Illustrate the long-run equilibria assuming that there are decreasing costs as scale increases in the industry. State how the firm's cost curves and the price and output of the firm and industry are different from when there are constant costs.

c) Using a different color, draw the long-run industry supply curve on your diagram. Why does it have the slope you have drawn?

4. When the economy improves and the demand for steel-using capital equipment increases, what will happen to long-run steel prices, output, and profits? If it is impossible to say, explain what your answer depends upon.

MONOPOLY

At the other end of the spectrum of product markets from perfect competition lies the least competitive type—monopoly. Its chief distinguishing features are a single producer and barriers to new firms entering the market. Since the firm faces the downward-sloping industry demand curve, it is a price setter, rather than a price taker. Profits may be made in both the short run and the long run. Monopoly may have positive benefits in the form of economies of scale and scope and greater innovation, but also may have negative consequences in terms of allocative inefficiency. The article in this section illustrates these points with reference to the monopoly supply of cable television in a local area.

After studying your text, reading the article, and answering the questions, you should be able to:

◆ ◆ Define the characteristics of monopoly

◆ ◆ Recognize the sources of monopoly

◆ ◆ Explain the implications of monopoly for the demand curve and producer equilibrium

◆ ◆ Predict the effects of exogenous changes on equilibrium price, quantity, and profits

◆ ◆ Explain the absence of a supply curve

◆ ◆ State the positive and negative effects of monopoly

Preview

◆ Since deregulation in 1987, cable rates have soared.

◆ As a result, in 1992 the U.S. Senate passed a bill regulating cable television and increasing competition.

◆ The Federal Communications Commission would regulate rates, the number of subscribers, and customer service standards, among other things.

◆ Wireless cable operators and satellite services would have greater access to cable programming.

◆ Cable companies lobbied hard, alleging that the rate increases were necessary for quality programming and because prices had been artificially low.

Senate Clears Bill to Restore Regulation of Cable TV Rates, Foster Competition

The Senate overwhelmingly passed a bill to restore rate regulation for cable television and to encourage competition with cable TV, sending a strong signal that it wants the House to act quickly on similar legislation.

The Senate bill, which passed 73-18, would allow municipalities to regulate rates for basic cable services. To stimulate competition, it would give so-called wireless cable operators and satellite services providers greater access to cable programming. It also would limit both the size and scope of big cable companies, and would let local television stations charge cable systems to use broadcast signals.

In arguing for the bill, Sen. Howard Metzenbaum (D., Ohio), summed up the concern of many senators: "Cable is an industry accountable neither to competition nor regulation." Since 1987, when the industry was largely deregulated, monthly rates have soared nearly 60% nationwide, and rates have more than doubled in many areas....

The vote put the cable industry on the defensive. James Mooney, president of the National Cable Television Association, called the bill "extreme," and said it "would force cable subscribers' dollars to go to support CBS and NBC, at the expense of cable channels like Discovery and CNN."

Sen. Danforth and others dismissed the industry's concerns. "I think it is the nature of the cable industry to exaggerate and try to whip people up," Sen. Danforth said.

The industry lobbied hard for an amendment that would have gutted the bill's main provisions to control rate increases and to spur competition. But the amendment was defeated 54-35.

Cable companies contend that local regulation during the 1970s and early 1980s kept rates artificially low and that customers have been receiving more and better cable programming. Moreover, they argue, the government shouldn't be in the business of setting rates for such cable fare as MTV.

Exemption for Competition The Senate bill would exempt from rate regulation any cable system that competes with another multichannel video service. But for all others, the Federal Communications Commission would be required to set rate guidelines for a basic tier of cable service as well as signal converter boxes and remote-control devices. State or local franchising authorities then could get jurisdiction if they agree to follow the FCC's guidelines.

The measure would thwart any effort by cable systems to skirt rate regulation by stripping popular cable programming from their basic tier. Under the bill, if fewer than 30% of a cable system's subscribers buy the basic service, the FCC could regulate the next tier purchased by at least 30% of the subscribers.

In addition, the FCC could regulate rates for extended basic service, which includes basic broadcast programs and such cable programs as CNN or ESPN, if it receives complaints of excessive rate increases.

An amendment offered by Sen. Patrick Leahy (D., Vt.) would open up a retail market for cable remote-control devices. The provision requires cable systems to allow customers to buy the devices from any retailer. It would also give customers who don't receive scrambled channels the option of connecting their cable directly to their televisions or video cassette recorders. For those who receive scrambled premium channels, only those signals would have to go through converter boxes.

Fair-Price Issue Another major provision would bar cable television programmers, many of whom are owned or controlled by cable operators, from refusing to sell programming to cable industry rivals at fair prices. Beyond that, cable companies couldn't require that they be given a financial interest in a channel as a condition of carrying the channel.

The FCC would set limits on the number of subscribers to any one cable company, and it would limit a cable company's financial interest in programming carried on its local cable systems.

To encourage competition further, the bill also would bar franchising authorities from setting up exclusive arrangements with single cable companies.

To address consumer complaints about shoddy service, the bill would require the FCC to adopt customer service standards and technical standards to ensure signal quality.

QUESTIONS

1. What structural features of the local cable television industry indicate that it is typically a monopoly?

2. What economic factors give local cable companies their monopoly power?

3. a) Draw the cost, demand, and marginal revenue curves in a diagram of a local cable television monopoly. Show the unregulated equilibrium price and number of customers, and profits.

   b) Why is the slope of the demand curve facing a local monopoly cable company as you have drawn it? Explain with reference to the article.

   c) Why does a local cable monopolist not raise prices more and more to increase sales and revenue?

d) Demonstrate what would happen to the equilibrium price, the number of customers, and profits, if the cable television company were to suffer a reduction in demand caused by another cable operator gaining access to cable programming under the proposed legislation.

e) If a curve were drawn between the two equilibria you have identified, would it represent the cable company's supply curve? Explain your answer.

4. Cable companies believe that there are benefits to having a monopoly. Identify from the article any

a) economies of scale or scope.

b) greater potential for innovation.

5. Some politicians criticize monopoly provision of cable service. Why is it believed to be problematic? Again, refer to the article.

6. Both sides devoted a lot of resources to campaigning about local cable monopolies. In how much lobbying is it profitable for cable companies favoring a continued monopoly status to engage?

MONOPOLY

The two polar cases of product market competition are monopoly and perfect competition. Differences in the characteristics of the two product markets lead to contrasts in outcomes. In monopoly, price is higher and the quantity traded is lower than in perfect competition, assuming identical costs. Production is generally at output levels below minimum long-run average total cost. Profits may exist in the long run. Monopoly is less allocatively efficient in that too few resources are put to use in monopolistic industries. As a result, consumer surplus is reduced, producer surplus increases, and a deadweight welfare loss arises. The diminishing hold of the monopoly control of medallion cabs in New York City provides a good illustration of the differences between perfect competition and monopoly.

After studying your text, reading the article, and answering the questions, you should be able to:

◆◆ Contrast the price-quantity equilibria for a perfectly competitive industry and a monopoly

◆◆ Explain the level and distribution of economic welfare in each type of product market

◆◆ Weigh the costs and benefits of monopoly

Preview

◆ In New York City, only yellow taxis may pick up passengers who hail them on the street.

◆ Licenses for yellow cabs—medallions—have not been increased since World War II.

◆ Since medallions exchange for up to $140,000, drivers focus their service on Manhattan where demand is greatest.

◆ It is illegal for door-to-door car services and "gypsy" cabs to pick up passengers on the street although they provide cheap and efficient service.

◆ The mayor has proposed issuing restricted medallions to registered car services which could make pick-ups in ill-served zones.

◆ However, the medallions would be expensive and drivers would have little incentive to take passengers to zones where they could not make pick-ups.

New York Taxi Policy Is a Lemon

In most areas of Manhattan, at most times of the day, hold up your arm and a yellow cab appears—or two or three. But in Harlem and the outer boroughs of New York City, yellow cabs are a rare sight; in the rush hour you can see honest citizens dodging the cops to hire a car of another hue that is prepared to take them where they want to go. How did the Big Apple get into such a rotten state?

The first step was taken decades ago, when the city limited the number of licenses (medallions) issued to yellow taxi-cabs, the only ones allowed to pick up passengers who hail them on the street. There are 11,797 medallions, a number that has not changed since World War II.

The second step was to impose regulations that, when combined with natural market forces, created economic barriers. With no new supply, demand has driven the cost of medallions up to $140,000 in the market that has developed. Eighty-five percent of the drivers rent or lease cabs from the medallion owners. Renting one is so costly that a driver is reluctant to leave high-density Manhattan with no certainty of a return fare.

Non-medallion, non-metered car services offering door-to-door service can be registered without limit. But they are prohibited from picking up people on the street and pay $7,400 per year in licensing and registration fees and taxes. Start-up costs alone can force a newcomer to operate illegally until he's able to go legit.

So the city's third step was to enforce strictly the prohibition of "gypsy" cabs meeting the public demand for cheap, efficient transport and of licensed car services picking up passengers who hail them on the street. One aspect of the plan allows Taxi and Limousine Commission "peace officers" to confiscate the cars of anyone caught providing illegal car service.

Things have gotten so bad that even the limousine liberals have noticed. In late January, New York Mayor David Dinkins proposed, as a solution, still greater regulation of the city's taxi and car-service industries, prompting transport expert Ed Rogoff to comment: "It's hard to see how he could have worked up a plan better designed to honk absolutely everyone off."

The mayor's plan calls for new, restricted medallions that would allow registered car services to pick up passengers who hail them in areas ill-served by yellow cabs. He would drive out the illegal competition with a sixfold increase of enforcement efforts against gypsy cabs. Frank Manzella of the Livery Owners Coalition of New York, the car services' trade organization, believes enforcement will be ineffective. Further, he thinks the cost of the restricted medallions, $15,000, will force legitimate operators to go gypsy, as happened in 1987 when the city began requiring car services to pay registration fees.

Even for New York, the regulations are rich in absurdity. A restricted medallion holder will be able to pick up "hails" only in certain zones. But the zones are ill-served now precisely because they have proved unprofitable for that type of full-time service. And the driver will not want to spend the time to drop off a passenger in midtown Manhattan, where traffic crawls, only to battle back to the outer boroughs empty to take on another fare.

Two groups of customers will be especially inconvenienced by this micromanaged system. First there are residents of the city's poorest and most dangerous neighborhoods who cannot afford cars, and for whom neighborhood taxis are the only recourse for nonstop service. The second are middle-class commuters living outside Manhattan, but within city limits, who rely on hailing a ride from the subways home after work. Their demand is limited to a few hours each day. A guy with a registered car can make a few extra bucks by serving these customers, but not enough to justify paying the city for the right.

—Allen Randolph, "New York Taxi Policy Is a Lemon," March 17, 1992.
Reprinted by permission of *The Wall Street Journal*, ©1992 Dow Jones & Co., Inc. All Rights Reserved Worldwide.

QUESTIONS

1. The medallion-cab owners formerly had a monopoly over cab rides in New York City. Draw the demand, marginal revenue, and marginal cost curves in a price-quantity of the market for cab rides. Show the equilibrium (P_m) and quantity of (Q_m) of rides given by the medallion-cab owners.

2. Competition increased with the growth of gypsy cabs and the entry of door-to-door car services which often illegally picked up passengers who hailed them on the street. The market for cab rides came to approximate perfect competition.

   a) In order to compare the monopoly and perfectly competitive industry equilibria it is necessary to assume, among other things, that the marginal cost curve of the monopoly is equivalent to the short-run industry supply curve in perfect competition. Why is this a reasonable proposition?

   b) Assuming the curves in your diagram are identical to those in the perfectly competitive cab ride industry, show the competitive equilibrium price (P_c) and quantity (Q_c) of cab rides.

3. According to the article, the gypsy cabs and illegal pick-ups by licensed car services met the public demand for cheap, efficient transport. Why was there a difference in fare and service levels between the former monopoly and the perfectly competitive market? Refer to how service levels and fares were set in each type of market.

4. The mayor has proposed new, restricted medallions that would allow registered cars to pick up passengers in areas that are not well served by yellow cabs. Why might the consumer continue to suffer in terms of price and service?

5. Redraw the diagram of the monopoly equilibrium below to the left. Shade in the consumer and producer surpluses and the deadweight loss that arises because of the absence of perfect competition.

a) What does the consumer surplus represent?

b) What does the producer surplus represent?

c) What does the deadweight loss represent?

d) What evidence is there in the article of a deadweight loss due to the monopoly?

6. To the right of the diagram above, depict the perfectly competitive equilibrium. Show the consumer and producer surpluses. With the growth in competition what happened to the

a) level of welfare? Why?

b) distribution of welfare between producers and consumers? Why?

c) deadweight loss? Why?

7. Presumably the city believes that, in spite of the problems identified in earlier questions, monopoly has redeeming features. Are there any in the case of the New York City cab monopoly? Explain your answer.

29.
At the Movies: Slicing and Dicing Prices

Monopolists sometimes charge different groups of consumers different prices. This usually occurs where the groups have different elasticities of demand and there is no possibility of resale. Output may be greater than in a single-price monopoly, depending on the scope for discrimination. The effect is to raise profits. Consumer surplus is reduced to the extent that higher prices charged to consumers offset any gains from increased consumption levels. The focus of the accompanying article is price discrimination by movie theaters that enjoy local monopolies in the showing of first-run movies.

After studying your text, reading the article, and answering the questions, you should be able to:

◆◆ Define price discrimination

◆◆ Explain the sources of price discrimination

◆◆ State the necessary conditions for price discrimination

◆◆ Explain the impact of price discrimination on output, profits, and consumer surplus

Preview

◆ Universal Pictures proposed that exhibitors charge half-price to moviegoers on Tuesdays to encourage midweek attendance.

◆ Movie attendance had declined, possibly due to the recession, home entertainment, and unappealing movies.

◆ Other studios' participation was critical to the success of the plan.

◆ Whether the decrease in price would be offset by the increase in attendance, so that revenue would increase, was hotly debated by theater exhibitors.

◆ "Per-capita" requirements could limit the willingness of theaters to discount tickets.

Coming Soon: Cut-Rate Films on Tuesday

Universal Pictures proposed a half-price ticket plan under which exhibitors would offer movie-goers cut-rate movie admission every Tuesday.

In what it called an "experiment," Universal said it's urging theater owners to adopt a plan that has been widely used in theaters in Canada, where half-price tickets have been offered on Tuesdays for years. The studio said it made the proposal "to encourage midweek theater attendance and demonstrate to the public that the motion picture industry is seriously looking for ways to provide more value for their leisure-time dollars."

The offer comes amid a growing debate in Hollywood over whether declining admissions and box-office receipts are a result of the recession, continued competition from home video and cable television—or just unappealing movies. **Steep Attendance Drop in '91** Total move attendance dropped about 8% last year, yet ticket prices rose a little more than 5%, continuing their climb of the last decade. While the average admission price last year was around $5, a price of $7.50 for a first-run film in major urban areas isn't uncommon.

There wasn't an immediate positive response from other major Hollywood studios, whose across-the-board participation presumably would be critical for the cut-rate-night idea to become a complete success. Movie theater owners said it would be very difficult to explain to customers in multiplex theaters that they have to pay full price for some movies and half price for others.

But Universal, a unit of Matsushita Electric Industrial Co.'s MCA division, said it was pleased by the initial response from major theater chains that said they were embracing the idea, which has been tried locally and at some chains in the past with varying degrees of success. Tom Pollock, chairman of the motion picture group at MCA, said there would be participation by one of North America's largest chains, Cineplex Odeon Corp.—which, not coincidentally, is 49%-owned by MCA—and that he had received expressions of interest from other large chains, such as AMC Entertainment Inc. and Carmike Cinemas Inc.

Mr. Pollock said he was "inviting" all exhibitors and movie studios to go along with the plan for first-run features. "I want to make this very clear, this is an experiment," he said in an interview. "If it turns out that we are not attracting more customers, then none of us are going to want to go along with it." Cineplex Odeon said it would begin the program next Tuesday. The experiment will include Universal's current movie "Fried Green Tomatoes," as well as its coming releases "Stop! Or My Mom Will Shoot," starring Sylvester Stallone, and "American Me," a drama about Hispanic Americans.

Unchanged Exhibitor Contracts While Universal is acting as cheerleader for the half-price movement, it says it won't adjust normal contract terms with exhibitors. Under such terms, studios can get as much as 90% of box-office revenue in the first two weeks of a major blockbuster, with the percentage steadily declining over the run. While Universal and exhibitors that go along with the plan would get less per ticket on Tuesdays, they clearly hope to make up the missing revenue by increased volume. Universal says that in the U.S., the average screen sells less than 40 admissions on a typical mid-week day.

Movie studios don't set ticket prices; theater chains do. One sticky issue, however, is the fact that some studios have contracts with "per-capita" requirements—a minimum amount the studio will accept for each ticket sold—that essentially set a floor on ticket prices. Those requirements would likely hurt theater owners financially if they only charged customers half price, and some executives said studios with such plans would need to re-jigger them to give theater owners a buffer. Universal says it doesn't have such "per-capita" requirements.

Paramount Pictures, Walt Disney Studios and Twentieth Century Fox, among other studios, declined to comment on the Universal proposal.

While some theater exhibitors applauded the idea, others were less enthusiastic. Sony Corp.'s Loews Theaters Management Corp. unit said it doesn't plan to get involved. Alan Friedberg, chairman, said that in his experience, discounting tickets doesn't increase audience size. "What they should do is concentrate on making better films so that 1992 will see a return to the record-breaking [box-office] year of 1989, which wasn't so long ago," Mr. Friedberg said.

Sumner Redstone, president and chief executive officer of theater operator National Amusements Inc., says he hasn't yet decided whether his chain will play along. "I have reservations about whether this is going to solve any major problem, even though they may be on the right track." The issue is sure to be hotly debated at a national convention for theater owners in Las Vegas next week.

Universal also called for theater owners to cut Tuesday prices at their lucrative concession stands. Popcorn and soda sales sometimes make the difference between profit and loss, and theater owners weren't enthusiastic about that request.

But Michael Patrick, president of Carmike Cinemas, is positive about the overall plan. "We welcome this policy. We are eager to do it," he said. His chain had a Tuesday "bargain" night from 1982 to 1986, but had to stop it reluctantly because of some studios' "per-capita" requirements, even though it brought in new movie-goers. "We noticed that the patrons were not our normal patrons by any means. We had the extremely rich bargain-hunters and some lower-income people. You could tell by the cars in the parking lot."

QUESTIONS

1. a) What form of price discrimination was being introduced in the movie theater industry?

   b) What other forms of price discrimination have been, or might be, introduced?

2. a) What economic circumstances allow movie theaters to set and maintain higher prices for most nights while charging less on Tuesdays?

   b) Are these likely to be enduring features that will permit price discrimination to continue? Why or why not?

3. a) Draw a price-quantity diagram for a film shown by a local monopolist movie theater. Include the demand, marginal revenue, and cost curves.

   b) Assume non-Tuesday patrons are the consumers whose valuations of the film account for the upper part of the demand curve, reflecting their relatively inelastic demand. Show the level of ticket sales to non-Tuesday patrons when the price charged exceeds that which would exist in a single-price monopoly.

   c) Assuming that sales in excess of this amount are made to Tuesday patrons at a single lower price than in a one-price monopoly, show the level of sales in total. Shade in the irregular-shaped area representing profit.

4. a)   In what ways do some moviegoers lose and some gain due to price discrimination in this situation?

    b)   Overall, do moviegoers lose or gain? Refer to the change in consumer surplus in your diagram.

5. a)   Some studios have contracts with theater chains stating "per-capita" requirements. In the event that this results in a uniform price of admission, what would happen to the equilibrium price, aggregate sales, and profit of the monopolist theater in question 3? Illustrate in a diagram with the same curves as in question 3.

    b)   Would society as a whole be better or worse off? Explain your answer.

6. Loews Theaters would prefer better films to reduced prices on Tuesdays. Under what conditions does this make economic sense?

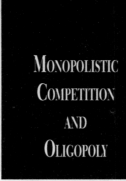

Monopolistic Competition and Oligopoly

30. Frozen Food Fights: Healthy Competition?

Between the polar types of product market competition lies monopolistic competition. Like perfect competition, it is characterized by a large number of firms and consumers and free entry and exit. However, products are heterogeneous, giving firms a downward-sloping demand curve as in monopoly. Profits are possible in the short run. In the long run, free entry erodes any profits and free exit eliminates any losses. Equilibrium output is below that at minimum long-run average cost. While allocative inefficiency exists, society may benefit from product innovation and advertising. The frozen food industry provides a good example of the features and operations of a monopolistically competitive market.

After studying your text, reading the article, and answering the questions, you should be able to:

◆◆ Define monopolistic competition

◆◆ Explain the general slope of the monopolistically competitive firm's demand curve

◆◆ Predict the price charged, quantity produced, and profits earned by a firm in monopolistic competition in the short run and the long run

◆◆ Predict the effects of exogenous changes on the firm's equilibrium position

◆◆ Explain the advantages and disadvantages of monopolistic competition

Preview

◆ In 1989 ConAgra introduced its Healthy Choice frozen dinner brand.

◆ An advertising and price war with other frozen food producers ensued.

◆ Other producers introduced their own brands of healthy frozen dinners.

◆ Industry demand in general was affected by the recession.

◆ Consumers began switching to other types of frozen dinners.

◆ Experts observed that brand loyalty was decreasing.

Once Supermarkets' Leading Stars on Ice, Healthy Choice Frozen Dinners Stumble

Healthy Choice, once the hottest brand in the nation's freezer case, has cooled off.

Its introduction three years ago, taking advantage of a national obsession with eating more healthfully, rejuvenated the frozen-dinners category. Suddenly, less sodium, fat and cholesterol became big selling points. The "healthy" dinners and entrees line also heralded what creator ConAgra Inc. hoped would become a supermarket megabrand.

But Healthy Choice touched off a price war that has proved exceedingly costly to ConAgra. Today, not only are Healthy Choice frozen dinners and entrees losing market share, but they are bleeding their parent. The line's dollar volume is down from a year ago, and first-quarter tonnage sold plummeted....

Millions for Defense Analysts believe ConAgra has been forced to spend millions more than it anticipated defending itself against deep-pocketed competitors such as Nestle S.A. and Phillip Morris Cos.' Kraft General Foods unit, which had ruled the freezer case. "This is an industry that fights with picks and nails," says Goldman Sachs food analyst Nomi Ghez.

Yet even as Nestle's Stouffer Foods unit, Kraft, Campbell Soup Co. and H.J. Heinz Co. battle back, sales statistics show consumers moving on to other microwavable selections such as frozen pasta dishes. For more than a year now, frozen-dinners-and-entrees tonnage sold has been steadily slipping. Information Resources Inc. says volume fell 1.9% in the four weeks ended March 29 alone from a year earlier. But Healthy Choice's decline was more precipitous, down 27.1%.

Partly, that may reflect the recession. With frozen dinners for four costing $12, "you can make it yourself cheaper," says Michael Silverstein of the Boston Consulting Group. He believes that when the economy rebounds, consumers will once again snap up labor-saving prepared foods. But he thinks the category will have to overcome disappointment with predictable fare and bland tastes.

Healthy Choice gained share quickly because it was the right line at the right time. But now "everything is healthy something or choice something," says Ms. Ghez.

Moreover, to recoup lost share ConAgra may be forced back into the test kitchen. The new wave of competitor products puts less emphasis on nutrition and more on taste. Of its recent Le Menu premium-dinner revision, New American Cuisine, Campbell Soup Vice President James Van Stone concedes, "These products are not as 'healthy' as Healthy Choice." But he thinks they are more pleasing to the palate. Campbell grills some meats, roasts others and abandons the traditional heavy starch gravies for packets of sauces that let consumers season to taste. It also is including little extras, such as minimuffins and pieces of Godiva chocolate, with some of its meals.

Some of Healthy Choice's initial success hinged on catching the competition off guard. Stouffer's Lean Cuisine line, for example, was locked in what E. Michael Moone, Stouffer Foods' president, calls a "diet duel" with Heinz's Weight Watchers frozen meals. What's more, "we were too expensive," Mr. Moone admits. Since then the reduced-calorie line has been reformulated, repriced and heavily promoted; Memphis stores recently were selling four boxes for $5.

The results have been dramatic. In the 13 weeks ended March 29, Lean Cuisine's tonnage sold rose nearly 42% from a year earlier, Information Resources reports. Still, Stouffer appears to be sacrificing profits for market share.

Lack of Loyalty Stouffer also recently freshened its traditional "red box" line by adding "HomeStyle" meals, replacing boilable pouches with microwavable trays, reducing cooking time and redesigning the package. "There's been a commodity feel to the category," Mr. Moone admits. The Boston Consulting Group's Mr. Silverstein agrees. "Consumers don't have any loyalty any more. There's not enough uniqueness."

QUESTIONS

1. In what ways do you think the frozen dinner industry approximates monopolistic competition?

2. a) What effect does a firm's claim that its frozen dinners are healthy have on the position and general slope of the demand curve for its frozen dinners?

   b) In what other ways do firms in the frozen dinner industry influence the position and slope of the demand curves for their products?

3. a) In 1989 ConAgra responded to unsatisfied tastes for healthy frozen dinners with Healthy Choice. In a diagram of the market for frozen dinners show the price charged, quantity produced, and profits earned in the short run by a typical frozen dinner producer like ConAgra. Assume all frozen dinners have the same price.

   b) Are sufficient resources being allocated to the production of frozen dinners? Illustrate in your diagram above. Why is this the case?

4. ConAgra's introduction of healthy frozen dinners triggered a costly advertising war between competing brands, increasing costs. Illustrate what happened to the short-run equilibrium price, sales, and profits for a typical firm as a result, assuming a stationary demand curve.

5. a) In the long run, other firms introduced healthy frozen dinners. What happened to the demand for frozen dinners produced by a typical firm like ConAgra? Explain your answer.

    b) Draw the long-run equilibrium of a typical firm. Include the same curves as in question 3 and also the long-run average cost curve. What happened to the price charged, the quantity sold, and the profits from frozen dinners?

    c) In what sense is there excess capacity in a typical firm? Why does it arise in monopolistically competitive firms but not in perfectly competitive firms?

6. An industry expert is quoted in the article as saying, "Consumers don't have any loyalty any more. There's not enough uniqueness." If this is true,

    a) what kind of market structure does the frozen food market have?

    b) how do price, output, and profit of the typical firm in the short run compare with monopolistic competition?

Monopolistic Competition and Oligopoly

Oligopoly is a type of product market that lies between perfect competition and monopoly on the spectrum of competitiveness. It is characterized by a small number of firms whose price and output decisions are interdependent.

One possible outcome is collusion or cooperation where producers are able to maximize their joint profits as a monopoly would. Another outcome is cheating or competition where producers cut price (or change other things such as advertising) in order to gain an advantage over their rivals. The greater the price competition, the more the outcome approximates perfect competition. Sometimes experience restores cooperation. When one producer lowers price, others may follow in the next period to reduce the cheater's profits. This may continue until the cheater realizes that greater profits can be earned through cooperation. The airline fare wars provide an illustration of various oligopolistic strategies.

After studying your text, reading the article, and answering the questions, you should be able to:

◆ ◆ Define oligopoly

◆ ◆ Explain the benefits to producers of cooperation or collusion

◆ ◆ Explain why one firm might cheat and others might follow

◆ ◆ Explain how society benefits from cheating

◆ ◆ Explain why cooperation may be restored by "tit-for-tat" strategies

◆ ◆ Specify different ways in which oligopolists might compete

Preview

◆ American Airlines simplified its fares in April 1992.

◆ Since most fares decreased, more traffic was generated.

◆ The hope was that revenue would eventually increase and that administrative costs would fall, restoring profitability.

◆ The other large airlines emulated American Airlines.

◆ Low-cost rivals TWA and Continental were threatened.

◆ A shakeout was expected to raise fares and airline profits.

Fasten Your Seat Belts for the Fare War

A s American Airlines launched its new streamlined U.S. fare system last week, the traveling public responded with a round of applause and a ring of the reservation phone line. The reforms jettisoned a maddening maze of rates and restrictions and replaced them with just four new fares that provided savings of up to 50% for first-class and nearly 40% for business flyers. Competitors jetted to join the cut-and-simplify frenzy, with United's top executives holding late-night sessions to get their own new fares into ads right on American's heels. "This is good for the traveler and good for the company," says Edmund Greenslet, publisher of *Airline Monitor* trade journal. "This new structure was long overdue."...

But there is a darker side to the fare war: many experts see it as a thinly veiled declaration of war against low-cost rivals like TWA and Continental, which currently fly under the protective wing of the bankruptcy courts and thus pay no interest on part of their debt. Life will get rougher for them once they emerge from Chapter 11 protection and are forced to survive on their own resources—something many analysts fear these weaker carriers may be unable to do for long. Once rid of such pesky competitors and their cutthroat tactics, the major airlines could regain full control of airfares—and might then be free to raise them. "This is the nightmare that the marginal carriers didn't

want to see happen," says John Riener, president of commercial operations for Carlson Travel Network, the largest U.S. travel company. "There's the scent of a final kill in the air."

American insists that it merely wants to bring order to a chaotic fare system that discouraged air travel and encouraged ruinous price wars. Under its old system, American and other carriers offered as many as 200 types of fares and discount plans for any given route, a system that most travelers found confusing and unfair. "Everybody will benefit from this new plan," says Robert Crandall, the company's aggressive chairman, who pioneered innovations like frequent-flyer programs and supersaver fares.

If the new fare structure holds up, it could finally halt the proliferation of discounts in a price-cut-happy industry. "The driving reason for the change is American's desire to get more control over its pricing system than it had when there was a hodge-podge of fares out there," Greenslet says. "American's objective is not to drive TWA out of existence," he asserts. "They can live with TWA operating with a different fare structure, as long as it doesn't declare war."

But Crandall acknowledges that the new fares will draw some traffic away from American's low-cost competitors. "As we close the price gap," he said in an interview with *Time,* "we expect to see business come from the discounters." At the same time, Crandall warned

that he stood ready to lower fares across the board if that proved necessary to match cuts by American's rivals. "We are going to be price competitive. If we have to lower this overall structure, we will do so."

American said it was prepared to take losses for months until the new rate schedule generated enough traffic to make up for the reduction in business fares. "This will hurt earnings in the short run," says Richard Foote, an airline analyst for Argus Research. "But I expect to see a positive impact in the second half of the year." On the brighter side, American expects to save $25 million a year in administrative costs by reducing the number of its fares from a dizzying 500,000 to a relatively stable 70,000.

Whatever its motives, Fort Worth-based American could profit handsomely from an industry shake-out. Staggered by the recession, constant fare fights and a global epidemic of aerophobia growing out of last year's Persian Gulf conflict, U.S. airlines have lost more than $6 billion since 1990. American has been no exception: its parent company, AMR, has lost a combined $279 million in the past two years. All that has led Crandall to predict that the number of major carriers will continue to shrink. Says he: "I think there is probably some consolidation left to happen."

Predictably, Crandall's revolutionary fare changes triggered a dogfight last week with Carl Icahn, the corporate raider turned executive who heads TWA. Icahn challenged the new fares by slashing TWA's rates as much as 40% below American's prices. Icahn also vowed to keep volume discounts for corporate travelers, which American's plan eliminated. "We are here to stay," he told *Time*. "I'm not a passive guy. It's hard to drive a low-cost competitor out of business. And, as far as I'm concerned, it won't work."

Icahn brings some surprising strengths to this skirmish. Bankruptcy-court protection keeps his airline's costs down and permits it to offer some of the industry's lowest prices. TWA has suspended payments on $1 billion of debt and is renegotiating lease payments on some aircraft as it works out a plan to satisfy creditors. While Icahn says he expects to fly TWA out of court late this summer, some analysts argue that he may try to stay in Chapter 11 proceedings while doing battle with American....

Executives of some smaller carriers that generally stuck to their schedules called the new fares dangerous to their health. "This intensifies the battle within the industry between big and small, rich and poor," says Marilyn Hoppe, vice president of revenue management for America West, a Phoenix-based carrier that is in bankruptcy court. "American, United and Delta are not going to take market share from each other," Hoppe declares. "They are going to try to take it from the smaller carriers whose only weapons are lower prices. Bob Crandall would dearly love to get rid of little guys like us."

The air was filled with such suspicions last week. "I'd book and buy my tickets sooner rather than later," quips Carlson Travel's Riener. "If the country ends up with just three carriers, where do you think prices will head—up or down?" Maybe that's an unduly jaundiced view of fare changes that many travelers have happily welcomed. But it squares with the historical winner-take-all nature of the U.S. airline industry, which has dwindled to a handful of major carriers in the 14 years since the country embarked on deregulation in the hope of increasing competition in the skies.

QUESTIONS

1. What features of the airline industry mentioned in the article indicate that it is oligopolistic?

2. American Airlines simplified its fare structure, reducing most fares.

    a) What did it hope to achieve by doing this?

    b) Why did other airlines follow suit? Give two possible reasons.

    c) What was expected to happen to the combined profits of the airlines? Why?

    d) What was expected to happen to the number of passengers transported? Why?

    e) In what other ways did the airlines compete?

    f) Was society better or worse off as a result of the price and traffic changes? Refer to consumer and producer surplus, and any other relevant factors.

3. It was expected that there would be an industry shakeout and that the remaining airlines would raise fares and earn greater profits. One possible implication of the shakeout was that one or two airlines could dominate each hub.

    a) Below and to the left, draw a diagram of the market for air travel at a hub dominated by two airlines. Depict the marginal cost curve and the demand and marginal revenue curves for the hub as a whole. Show the equilibrium fare and number of seats if the two airlines maximized joint profits.

    b) Beside the above diagram draw a diagram of the marginal and average cost curves for one of the two airlines. Show the joint-profit-maximizing price for the hub as a whole. Mark the number of seats sold by the airline and shade the area representing profits.

4. a) Draw a diagram showing the demand for TWA flights assuming that the demand curve has a kink in it at the initial fare level. Add the marginal revenue and marginal cost curves.

    b) Explain and illustrate how bankruptcy helped TWA reduce its fares and increase its traffic levels.

LABOR MARKETS

Wage and employment levels are determined in labor markets by the interaction of labor demand and supply. The demand for labor is a derived demand, labor being used to satisfy the demand for the product. Generally speaking, in competitive labor markets labor demand declines as wages rise. The position of the demand curve reflects the marginal revenue productivity of labor and the cost and productivity of other factors. Western and eastern German labor markets have recently seen significant changes in the demand for labor. The accompanying article explains the many causes.

After studying your text, reading the article, and answering the questions, you should be able to:

◆◆ Derive a demand curve for labor

◆◆ Explain the determinants of labor demand

◆◆ Predict the effect of changes in the determinants of labor demand on wages and employment

◆◆ Explain how the elasticity of demand for labor is affected by changes in its determinants

Preview

◆ In 1992, German wages, benefits, and time off were among the greatest in the world, and the economy was performing well in spite of high interest rates.

◆ But German workers had many complaints.

◆ Eastern Germans were shocked by the effects of the market system on output and employment.

◆ Western Germans were upset that investment in eastern Germany and profits were growing at the expense of western wages.

◆ Also, German firms were reducing employment to remain competitive and in response to technological change.

◆ A massive public sector strike occurred and private sector strikes were threatened.

◆ Privatization was proposed to reduce public sector union power.

151

Germany's Huge Bill for Bailing Out East Is Riling Its Workers

Listening to Germans, you would think Europe's most powerful economy is on the rocks.

Workers complain that despite eight years of steady industrial growth, their wages grew far more slowly than corporate profits, and now they want their share. The giant metalworkers union is threatening work stoppages, and members of a public-employee union that this month mounted Germany's largest strike yesterday rejected a settlement that would have raised their pay 5.4%.

In addition, western Germans are angrily resisting the idea of making further sacrifices to help eastern Germans. And many easterners, accustomed to getting orders from above, are shocked by how much harder and less secure—through perhaps ultimately more lucrative—life can be under capitalism.

Political Implications That national division is leaving both sides of Germany self-absorbed at a time when the former Soviet bloc wants help, when the European Community wants more attention given to politic and monetary union and when President Bush is asking for a "partner in leadership." Amid the turmoil, Chancellor Helmut Kohl's ruling coalition is fighting for survival.

Yet if you look at the German economy, you might wonder what the fuss is all about. German exports surged to a record in March, first-quarter economic growth of 1.2% exceeded expectations, and the stock market is near its highs for the year. And even though the German national debt is soaring and interest rates are so high as to raise fears of a recession, most economists expect nearly 10% annual growth in eastern Germany for at least five years—a surge that would lift national growth to over 3% next year.

And German wages and benefits have climbed so sharply in recent years that in 1991 they were the highest among all major countries. At an average of 40.48 marks ($25.14) an hour, they far exceeded the average $15.88 in the U.S. Even eastern German wages now roughly match those of Americans. Moreover, Germans have some of the shortest working hours and longest vacations in the world....

Psychological Problems "My fear is that we have too many psychological problems between ourselves to play the important role that we need to play now," says Hans Joachim Maaz, an eastern German psychotherapist who recently analyzed Germany in two books. He says the problem is that two sides of the German soul have had trouble getting along—a western side that is efficient, productive and perfectionist and an eastern side that had learned well how to follow commands and respect authorities.

But it is the western side that now is troubled by strikes. "Germans have become self-pitying crybabies," contends Hans Peter Stihl, the president of the German Chambers of Commerce and Industry, whose members account for 70% of the country's output. "They have become the type of people who wrap a much-too-large bandage over a small injury. After the war, when everyone was in bad shape, we pulled together and tackled it. But now, everyone is saturated by his own well-being"—that is, too eager to cling to their affluence....

Meanwhile, many major German companies are working hard, through retooling and downsizing, to be sure they remain competitive in world markets. They are planning layoffs of thousands of workers and shedding thousands more through attrition. General Motors recently joined other car producers in Germany, including Mercedes-Benz, in announcing that it would cut its work force considerably, including a 20% reduction at GM's Opel plant in Reusselsheim, near Frankfurt.

"We are already the dominant economy on the Continent, and we will become even more so," Mr. Stihl says.

However, the road ahead will be rocky. Even many business leaders acknowledge that in normal times, their workers should be getting a bigger slice of the pie.

"The unions' arguments are good ones that can't be easily swept off the table," says Luiz Hoffmann, the president of the German Institute for Economic Research in Berlin. The Institute's own statistics show that the wage share of national income fell to 70% in 1990 from almost 77% in 1982. Yet to pass these profits on to workers now, Mr.

Hoffmann says, would slow investment in eastern Germany, where industrial output fell 35% last year and 15% the year before, and further worsen the national debt. "A correction in profit distribution, which would be a normal event usually, could have grave consequences now," he adds....

Tired of Helping East However, workers and industry disagree about how to divide the cost of unification. Chancellor Kohl asks for more individual sacrifice, but west German workers believe they've done enough....

The mood is especially sour among 3.7 million German metalworkers. Their union, IG Metall, represents workers at automobile, electronics, machine-making and engineering companies—Germany's major exporters. IG Metall seems closer to voting next week for a strike that would begin May 25 as a fifth and final round of wage talks showed no signs of movement.

At one printed-circuit-board plant in Bonn, IG Metall representatives leave strike leaflets on tables in the canteen of Kloeckner-Moeller G.m.b.H., a highly successful family-owned company. The union and the companies are still far apart.

Downstairs from the canteen, most of the women assembling circuit boards say they are ready to strike. But they also sound resigned. They have already been told by management that the machines that were installed last year and have taken some of their jobs are only the beginning of ambitious automation plans that will reduce the work force another 10%. In the past five years, Kloeckner-Moeller has reduced the plant's payroll by more than a third while expanding sales 20% annually....

Yet new economic demands are making these companies rethink their traditionally paternal approach to their workers. When Emil Seidel took over the 1.2 billion-mark electronics and factory-automation company this year, he knew he would have to be tougher than his father-in-law, who still heads the company's supervisory board. "I'm no butcher, but it is striking how much pain he goes through about laying off only 100 people," says Mr. Seidel, 44, an entrepreneur whose can-do manner contrasts sharply with his 70-year-old father-in-law's Old World grace. "I don't like letting people go either, but what other choice do I have?"

The internationalization of the market and rapid technological change are pushing Mr. Seidel to step up automation and narrow the plant's output to more sophisticated core products. He also is buying other companies—something German family businesses never used to do—so he can put his company into the top six in its strongest fields, the production of low-voltage switches and factory-automation systems....

One result of the public employees' strikes has been more pressure on the government to privatize large portions of the public sector, which now accounts for some 20% of the economy. However, Thomas Grueneberg, a postal worker who worked once in the private sector, isn't sure he wants to again.

"If they privatized the post office, perhaps I could earn bonuses for being more productive, but then I would also have to work harder," he says. "Maybe it is better that it stays the way it is—that I earn a little less but also work a little less." Even so, after a raise of more than 5% following the strikes, he will earn 55,000 marks a year (over $33,000) for a 38 1/2-hour week.

—Frederick Kempe, "Germany's Huge Bill for Bailing Out East Is Riling Its Workers," May 15, 1992.
Reprinted by permission of *The Wall Street Journal,* ©1992 Dow Jones & Co., Inc. All Rights Reserved Worldwide.

QUESTIONS

1. a) Draw three sets of axes side-by-side below. In the left-hand diagram draw a marginal product of labor curve for workers in the former East Germany, with employment on the horizontal axis. In the center diagram draw a product demand curve for East Germany prior to reunification when there was little competition. In the right-hand diagram derive the East German labor demand curve from the two diagrams to the left.

    b) Draw corresponding diagrams for eastern Germany after reunification and the introduction of capitalist competition. Assume the marginal product of labor curve has not changed. Make sure your diagrams clearly show the contrasts with the former East Germany.

    c) Explain why the change in product market structure affected the demand for labor in the way it did.

2. a) In the former West Germany, working hours decreased prior to reunification, facilitated by the monopolistic position of many companies. Show the effects of this, everything else being equal, in a further set of three diagrams. What were the ramifications for wage levels at a given level of employment?

b) Before and after reunification, some industries in western Germany saw falling product prices caused by international competition. Illustrate this in another set of three diagrams. What happened to employment at a given wage level?

3. a) In the German electronics industry, automation became feasible. Show the effect on the labor demand curve in a wage-employment diagram of the market for electronics workers. What were the implications for employment at a given wage?

b) At the same time, interest rates were rising, increasing the price of capital. Illustrate the effect of this on the demand for labor in the market for electronics workers. What were the implications for wage rates at a given employment level?

4. Define and explain how the elasticity of demand for labor in Germany would have been affected by

a) the privatization of industry.

b) a falling percentage of labor costs in total costs.

c) the increasing availability of alternative production methods.

33.

Careers in

South

Korea

Wages and employment are determined in the labor market by the forces of labor supply and demand. The supply of labor by a household generally increases with the wage. To begin supplying labor, the wage must be at least equal to the value placed on the last hour of nonmarket activities. This is the reservation wage. Similarly, to supply labor to a particular occupation, the rewards must be at least equal to the value of time in alternative occupations. As the wage rises, labor input is increased until the substitution effect is outweighed by the income effect, causing the labor supply curve to bend back.

The market supply curve for an occupation is the sum of the household curves. The supply curve of labor to a firm is perfectly elastic at the market wage in competitive labor markets. The shortage of workers in South Korea illustrates how household labor supply decisions affect occupational wage rates and employment.

After studying your text, reading the article, and answering the questions, you should be able to:

◆ ◆ Explain the concept of the reservation wage

◆ ◆ Predict whether the reservation wage is likely to be relatively high or low

◆ ◆ Explain the general slope of the labor supply curve of the household with reference to income and substitution effects

◆ ◆ Predict how the labor supply curve changes when a determinant of labor supply changes

◆ ◆ Predict the changes in occupational and firm wage and employment levels when the supply of labor changes

Preview

◆ Many Chinese and other foreign nationals work in South Korea illegally.

◆ South Korea was formerly a net exporter of labor, but now has a growing labor shortage in spite of increasing wage levels.

◆ Causes include rising affluence at home, changing tastes for work and education, smaller families, and a booming economy.

◆ Migrant workers have not been legalized because a supply of older and female workers exists.

Migrants from China Go After Fortunes While Filling Labor Gap in South Korea

Back in the 1930s, when both Korea and the Manchurian provinces of China were occupied by Japan, Kim Chul Shik's grandfather left Korea to build a better life in China.

Now Mr. Kim is back in Korea for the same reason: to build a better life. He and his wife, both Chinese citizens, are working illegally in the land of their ancestors. As soon as they save about $12,000, they are heading back to China.

He says the choice is easy, despite his fascination with the automatic teller machines and electronic ticket vending machines of Seoul. "In Korea, no matter how hard I work, I will always be a poor man," says Mr. Kim, a slight man with wavy black hair. "In China I will be a rich man." There they hope to set up their own business, probably a store.

His dream is to learn how to make a subway ticket vending machine while in Korea and copy it back in China. "Then I could be a millionaire," he says.

Meanwhile, he and his wife do the dirty jobs Koreans avoid. They are but two of an estimated 20,000 Chinese, almost all of Korean descent, who have taken the Golden Bridge ferry across the Yellow Sea to work illegally in South Korea. There are more Chinese in South Korea now than at any time since China invaded during the Korean War 40 years ago. An additional 25,000 workers from the Philippines, Pakistan, Nepal and elsewhere in Asia have flocked to South Korea, entering on 14-day tourist visas, seeking wages that are three to 20 times those paid at home.

Common Problem in Asia The hopeful migrants may or may not hit the jackpot, but they are keeping Korean factories humming. South Korea, which only a few years ago was sending hundreds of thousands of laborers overseas, now faces a growing labor shortage that may threaten its economic growth. Employers here say they need more than 550,000 workers.

The phenomenon is familiar to all the high-growth economies of Asia. Only a few decades ago, experts worried that Asia's teeming masses might overwhelm their nations' available resources. But now these booming economies—in South Korea, Taiwan, Singapore, Hong Kong and Malaysia, as well as Japan—find they don't have enough working people to keep their economies booming. Migrants from the countries that haven't been part of Asia's wave of growth—Pakistan, Bangladesh, India, the Philippines and now China—are pouring in to fill the gap.

The change in South Korea is among the most dramatic. Throughout the 1970s and 1980s, it was a major exporter of labor; its workers carried out many of the Middle East's mammoth construction projects. The outflow hit a peak of 225,159 workers in 1983, when South Koreans sent home more than $1.6 billion in hard currency to a then-poor country bent on industrializing. But with rising affluence at home, the number of overseas Korean workers has been falling by 25% a year.

With rising affluence, more Koreans decline to do the menial, dangerous and difficult jobs. Last year, South Korea became a net importer of labor to fill worker shortages that in some industries are as high as 40%. Employers say they can't fill about 5.5% of office-worker slots. "It isn't a matter of wages," says Park Fun Koo, a labor economist at the Korea Development Institute. "Even with wages going up, employers can't find the people."

And it is getting worse. Thanks to smaller families and more teen-agers going to college, South Korea will have 25% fewer workers entering the job market each year by the end of the decade....

Myth of Misallocation? Korean businessmen, particularly owners of small factories, are pleading with the government to legalize Korean-Chinese migrant workers. But labor officials are reluctant to acknowledge that South Korea's employment problem is severe enough to require imported labor. The Labor Ministry contends that the problem is misallocation of the domestic labor supply. Officials point to a pool of two million women or elderly workers that companies could tap for office and factory jobs but for various reasons don't.

Though manufacturers say they need more workers to survive, some economists say an influx of foreign labor mightn't be good for South Korea's economy. They argue that it's better for industry to move toward higher-value-added products that can match the quality of those produced in Japan or the West and say easy availability of cheap labor might retard that process.

Importing labor, however, does ease upward pressure on South Korean wages, which have risen an average of 18% a year since 1986, bringing the average urban household income to $20,000 a year.

QUESTIONS

1. According to the article, migrant workers like Mr. Kim are prepared to work in menial jobs, whereas South Koreans are not.

   a) Is the reservation wage of South Koreans likely to be relatively low or high for menial jobs? Why?

   b) Draw labor supply curves for migrant workers and South Koreans in a wage-employment diagram for menial jobs. Choose a wage rate such that the workforce is 100 percent migrant workers.

2. Although wages are increasing rapidly, employers still find it difficult to hire South Koreans for menial jobs, like certain office work.

   a) Why might women or elderly people not want to work? Answer in terms of the determinants of the supply of labor.

   b) Draw a labor supply curve illustrating employers' difficulties in attracting South Koreans in a diagram relating office worker wages to employment. Is the income or substitution effect dominant? Explain the reasons for your answer.

   c) Under what circumstances might increasing the wage actually increase the shortage? Explain in terms of income and substitution effects.

3. In the market for South Korean laborers,

    a) what effect does rising college attendance in South Korea have on the supply curve? Illustrate in a diagram. Mark what happens to the number of South Korean laborers offering their services at a given wage. Which determinant of supply is changing?

    b) what effect do higher South Korean wages in general have on the supply curve, everything else being equal? Illustrate in a diagram. Mark what happens to the wage level necessary to employ the same number of laborers as before the wage raises.

4. a) The South Korean economy is booming and is able to employ more workers. In a diagram of the South Korean labor market show the effect of this and the decreasing relative rewards of working outside South Korea on wage and employment levels. Also, illustrate the implications for wages and employment in an individual firm in a second diagram. Explain the magnitude of the change in employment.

    b) Why does the individual firm face a supply curve with the slope you have drawn?

    c) Illustrate in your diagram how more migrant workers would keep wage increases down.

LABOR **MARKETS**	

In competitive labor markets, wages and employment are determined by supply and demand. Changes in real wages and employment occur when the determinants of demand and supply change. For example, when labor productivity or product prices increase, or when wages in alternative occupations or tastes for leisure increase, wages rise. When labor productivity or product prices increase, or alternative wages or tastes for leisure decrease, employment in the occupation increases. The accompanying article describes the changes in supply and demand that caused the glut of graduates in 1992.

After studying your text, reading the article, and answering the questions, you should be able to:

◆◆ Explain how labor supply and demand are affected by changes in their determinants

◆◆ Explain why differences in unemployment levels occur across labor markets

◆◆ Predict changes in equilibrium wages and employment following shifts in the demand for and supply of labor

◆◆ Explain the ways in which equilibrium in the labor market is restored after a disturbance

Preview

◆ Nearly one third of the entry-level positions for new graduates over the 1989-1992 period disappeared in the recession.

◆ In addition, nearly a million managers and professionals were unemployed.

◆ The market was bleakest in New York, California, and Michigan, but was better in the West, Southwest, and South.

◆ Liberal arts students were most affected, while students with engineering and technical degrees had a choice of jobs.

◆ The labor market was expected to improve only slowly.

◆ Students responded by searching for jobs more earnestly, applying to graduate school, living at home, and going abroad.

Graduates Facing Worst Prospects in Last 2 Decades

When bands stop playing at college graduation ceremonies this spring, members of the class of '92, who came of age in a recession, will doff caps and gowns and enter one of the toughest job markets that any class has seen in decades.

Studies by two universities indicate that nearly one-third of the nation's entry-level jobs for new graduates have evaporated during the recession as many large employers have reduced their hiring. At the same time, the market is already glutted with nearly a million unemployed managers and professional workers.

Labor experts say the job market is the worst it has been in a half century in the New York region. And it is not much better in the rest of the Northeast, California and Michigan. Elsewhere, particularly in the West, graduates are not having as hard of a time because either there has been no decline in jobs, or some growth in them. And nationally, the job market is expected to begin growing, though only slightly, over the next year....

Reduced Recruiting Liberal arts students have the toughest scramble ahead, while engineers and students with other technical degrees can expect a choice of jobs. And many graduates will try to skip the recession entirely, as shown by a substantial increase since last year in applications to graduate schools, especially law, business and journalism schools, and to not-for-profit or volunteer organizations....

Campus officials said the overall drop in recruitment combined with the anxiety caused by an eroding job market had noticeable effects.

College placement specialists at several Ivy League schools said that their graduates were adjusting well to the stagnant economy, but that more and more of them were heading for graduate schools. "I am concerned that students are making the graduate school decision by default and may end up in the wrong career," said Mary Giannini, executive director of the Center for Career Services at Columbia University in Manhattan.

At the University of Pennsylvania in Philadelphia, Patricia Rose, director of career planning and placement services, said she had found students to be much more serious about their preparations. "They have been scared into it," she said. "But last year we had fewer than 10 percent looking for work six months after graduation, and I don't expect any change this year."

100 Résumés, No Interview Liberal arts majors are the most fearful. Holly L. Young, an English major at

Job Prospects for the Class of '92

More jobs than graduates

Business and management

Engineering

Health professions

Computer, Information sciences

Engineering technologies

Physical sciences

Graduates and jobs about equal

Education

Mathematics

Architecture

Environmental design

Communications technologies

More graduates than jobs

Social sciences

Communications

Psychology

Life sciences

Visual and performing arts

Liberal arts and general studies

Interdisciplinary studies

Home economics

Public affairs

Agriculture, natural resources

Foreign languages

Philosophy and religion

Theology

Parks and recreation

Ethnic studies

Source: Collegiate Employment Research Institute, Michigan State University

Rice University in Houston, said she knew she was in trouble last summer when she sent out 100 résumés for an internship and did not get an interview. "I've been very nervous all senior year," she said. But she took career workshops at the placement office and narrowed her interests to consulting firms in business technology whose training programs she was interested in. After she had interviewed with more than 15 companies on campus this spring, Ernst & Young, one of the big accounting firms, recently offered her a $31,500-a-year job.

Two university studies suggest that the number of job openings for 1992 graduates has decreased by only 4 percent to 10 percent, but that decline comes on top of two previous annual declines that have, all together, eliminated almost a third of all entry-level positions since the 1989-90 school year. "We have a big pool of talent built up behind this recessionary dam, and it keeps getting bigger and bigger," said Victor R. Lindquist, a dean at Northwestern.

He is also the author of the university's Lindquist-Endicott Report, which has surveyed mid- to large-size businesses about their hiring plans every year since 1945. Nearly half of the 259 businesses surveyed this year said they planned to hire fewer new college graduates. "This is worse than anything I've seen in 20 years," Mr. Lindquist said. One bright spot in the survey: Average salaries are up by a modest 2.7 percent over last year.

A Michigan State University survey of 464 employers in business, industry and government came to the same dismal conclusion as the Northwestern study. "This is the most serious cutback in the job market since we began surveying employers 21 years ago," said L. Patrick Scheetz, author of the survey and director of the Collegiate Employment Research Institute at Michigan State.

The Michigan State study found that about 45 percent of this year's 1.1 million graduates—the largest class ever to graduate from American colleges—are in technical fields, like engineering and the health professions, that have more job openings than candidates. Another 13 percent of the graduates are heading for occupations like education and communication technology that have a balanced supply of jobs and candidates. And 42 percent of the graduates have degrees in areas like the social sciences and communications that are oversupplied with candidates.

Reality Still Shocking Even though this year's graduates are prepared for a tough job search, the reality can still be shocking. "They tell you to start at the bottom, but even the bottom doesn't have much to offer," said Kristan Ginther, a would-be journalist who is graduating from the University of Wisconsin at Madison. Several graduate schools of journalism, havens in the storm, report that applications are up 25 to 75 percent.

What makes the job search more difficult for the class of '92 is that its members are competing with 933,000 unemployed managers and professionals, whose jobless rate has increased by 60 percent in two years, said Samuel M. Ehrenhalt, regional director of the Bureau of Labor Statistics in New York.

"There have been no employment declines in some states in the West, Southwest and South," he said. "But I would say college graduates are facing the toughest job market in a half-century in the New York region. The whole Northeast, Michigan and California are severely affected."

Economists say they expect the job market to improve slowly. Sara L. Johnson, the managing economist for DRI/McGraw-Hill, an economic consulting and forecasting concern in Boston, said the strongest employment growth over the next 12 months will be in the Midwest, the Pacific Northwest and the Southwest, dominated by Texas. "The Northeast will be lagging," she said, "but other parts of the country should see employment gains of 2 percent over the next 12 months."

To some students, the tough market means living at home after college. "I'm going to live at home for at least another two or three years," said Lisa A. Blessing, an economics major at Rutgers University who expects a long search for a job with a modest salary.

For other graduates, the solution is to leave the country.

Marcia L. Recchia, a zoology major at Connecticut College in New London, wants work at La Stazione Zoologica, a marine biology laboratory in Naples, Italy. She is waiting to hear if the Government-subsidized laboratory has a research position for her. "I have no idea about the salary," she said. "I just hope it's enough to live on."

The Peace Corps reports receiving 800 telephone inquiries a day on average, up from 250 a day prior to January. But even the Peace Corps does not have many openings for graduates without technical training. "We can place graduates with degrees in agriculture or forestry within three months, but it takes up to one or two years to place a liberal arts graduate," said Elaine L. Chao, director of the Peace Corps.

Some volunteers sound more pragmatic than idealistic. Sarah Wellinghoff, a major in international relations at the University of Nevada in Reno, is heading off to teach English in the African country of Chad. "If there were more jobs available or teaching assistantships for grad school," she said, "I might not have signed up."

—Michael deCourcy Hinds, "Graduates Facing Worst Prospects in Last 2 Decades," May 12, 1992.

QUESTIONS

1. a) Draw a wage-employment diagram of the labor market for people with college degrees. Show it initially in equilibrium. Mark the equilibrium wage and employment levels.

   b) In the 1989-1992 period the effects of recession were felt. How and why did the demand for college graduates change? Refer to the determinants of the demand for labor.

   c) The class of '92 was the largest ever to graduate from American colleges. How and why did this affect the supply curve? Refer to the determinants of the supply of labor.

   d) Show the effect of the recession and the size of the class on the demand and supply curves in your diagram. At existing wage levels was there a shortage or a surplus? Divide it along the employment axis into new college graduates and unemployed previous graduates.

2. The article discusses ways in which the market began to move back toward equilibrium. Explain which determinant of supply or demand was affected by the following occurrences and what the implications were for the demand or the supply curve:

   a) living with parents longer.

   b) working for the Peace Corps.

   c) going to graduate school.

   d) recovery in the economy.

3. a) Draw two wage-employment diagrams representing the northeastern and the western labor markets for college graduates side-by-side below. Mark their levels of wages and employment. Show the western labor market in equilibrium and a surplus of labor in the northeastern labor market at existing wage rates.

   b) Why was there unemployment of college graduates in the Northeast, but none in the West? Refer to the determinants of labor supply and demand.

4. a) Draw labor market diagrams for graduates in engineering and in liberal arts. Show a surplus of graduates in the liberal arts labor market and a shortage in the engineering market at existing wage rates.

   b) How do you account for the surplus in liberal arts and the shortage in engineering? Couch your response in terms of the determinants of labor supply and demand.

35. Investing in a Career on Wall Street

For an individual to be willing to supply his or her labor to an occupation, the wage must be at least equal to the value of time spent in the best alternative occupation. The wage that is needed to induce the worker to supply his or her labor is termed transfer earnings. The excess of income over transfer earnings is economic rent. The more elastic the supply of labor, the greater the transfer earnings. The accompanying article concerning the career decisions and starting salaries of new MBAs can be interpreted in terms of the concepts of transfer earnings and economic rent.

After studying your text, reading the article, and answering the questions, you should be able to:

◆ ◆   Define economic rent and transfer earnings

◆ ◆   Show diagrammatically the magnitude of economic rent and transfer earnings in an occupational labor market

◆ ◆   Explain the implications of the elasticity of labor supply for the division of wages between economic rent and transfer earnings

◆ ◆   Understand why wages are needed to attract labor

Preview

◆ Wall Street cut back its recruitment of MBAs and cut salaries after the crash of 1987.

◆ Reflecting a buoyant stock market, Wall Street increased its hiring of MBAs considerably in 1992.

◆ MBAs were attracted to Wall Street by relatively high salaries and the lifestyle, pace, and excitement.

◆ However, starting salaries had not changed much for several years, and bonuses for new employees were meager.

◆ Jobs with international duties attracted increasing numbers of MBAs, although some firms had difficulty recruiting in the United States.

They're Back! MBAs Are Rediscovering Wall Street

The Greed Decade may be over, but MBAs are flocking again to Wall Street.

About 750 graduates from the nation's top 25 business schools will be joining Wall Street investment banks this year—double the number of 1991, according to business school recruiters.

That's the biggest torrent of MBAs streaming to the Street since 1987. The October stock-market crash dashed the dreams of many budding investment bankers, as securities firms cut back on recruiting and slashed paychecks amid a painful industry-wide restructuring.

There was much talk that MBAs were turning away from Wall Street's get-rich-quick culture in favor of executive posts in manufacturing firms that made tangible products. But that's not the word from some recent graduates.

"People say the patina had gone out of Wall Street jobs, but the Street still offers a lot of stature," says Jerry Abrahams, a 27-year-old graduate of Columbia Business School recently hired by Smith Barney, Harris Upham & Co. to be an investment banker in its municipal-finance department.

There are few careers that can match Wall Street's challenges and pay, says Mr. Abrahams, who will receive a starting base salary of about $55,000. Besides, he says, Wall Street offers a chance to "eat expensive meals and take radio cars all over town."

Thanks to the buoyant stock market and a boom in new stock and bond issues, Wall Street is enjoying record profits. But the Street's appetite for MBAs is a far cry from the go-go 1980s. This year, 16% of Harvard Business School's new MBAs are expected to go to Wall Street, the school says. That's up from 11.4% in 1988, but still well below the peak of 30.3% in 1987.

And Wall Street's new crop of MBAs no longer scramble to snatch jobs in mergers or real estate, once red-hot fields that have fallen on hard times. Today, MBAs want jobs trading or underwriting stocks and bonds, or selling complex derivatives securities like futures and options.

Sandy Brasher says it's the fast pace of trading that attracted him back to Wall Street. Mr. Brasher had done some corporate-finance work for a Wall Street investment boutique before getting his MBA at Vanderbilt University's Owen School. Now he is close to joining a big Wall Street firm as a trader. "Deals can be done or not done—or take a year and a half," Mr. Brasher says. "I like the quickness and turnaround" of trading.

But MBAs shouldn't expect a windfall right away. Starting pay hasn't risen in several years; typical 1992 base salaries for MBAs range from $50,000 to $70,000, and bonuses typically are thin the first couple of years. "There's tremendous pressure [on Wall Street] to keep salaries flat," says Peter Veruki, placement director at the Owen School. In fact, Mr. Veruki says, some starting salaries "are starting to fall."

Many of today's crop of MBAs are older and more seasoned. Some already are on their second lap on Wall Street. Take Vincent Thompson, a 31-year-old Columbia graduate who was hired as a derivatives salesman by Kidder, Peabody & Co.

After earning his undergraduate degree, Mr. Thompson started as a broker for Dean Witter Reynolds Inc. the week before the market crashed in 1987. It was "frustrating being a broker in a cyclical business," he says. When times are slow, "you're not making any money."

Instead, he wanted to become a portfolio manager, and realized "you've got to have an MBA to walk in the door" on Wall Street. Even after going back to school, however, he found it difficult to hit paydirt: He was "dinged"—business-school parlance for getting rejections—by about three-dozen firms. Though he won't be managing money at Kidder, he is trying to stay flexible by agreeing to sell customized derivatives products to the firm's institutional clients. If nothing else, he says, "it'll be less risky than being a retail broker."

Many MBAs are looking for Wall Street investment-banking jobs outside the U.S., reflecting the globalization of the securities business. Last year, 22% of MBAs from the University of Pennsylvania's Wharton School accepted jobs abroad, up from 17% a year earlier; among the industries with the most jobs with international duties were investment banks, says Chris Hardwick, Wharton's public-affairs director.

The Lehman Brothers division of Shearson Lehman Brothers Inc. is looking to hire "folks with international skills," a Lehman spokesman says. And Lehman recently has begun to scour overseas business schools for candidates. But the biggest crop of MBAs recruited to Wall Street still come from top U.S. business schools such as Harvard, Columbia, Wharton and the University of Chicago.

Perhaps the biggest difference in today's MBAs, university placement directors claim, is their desire for a balanced lifestyle and their professed indifference to pay. Robert Scalise, Harvard's placement director, says students go to Wall Street now "because they really like doing the work—not because it's a ticket to the good life."

Consider S. Rae Yerkey, a Vanderbilt graduate who accepted a $55,000-a-year job at Lehman, hoping to trade derivative products. "Personally, money really didn't have much of an effect" in choosing a Wall Street career, says the 24-year-old Ms. Yerkey. She just wants to be happy in her work. "Hey, I was thrilled with the salary I got," she says.

—Michael Siconolfi, "They're Back! MBAs Are Rediscovering Wall Street," April 23, 1992.

QUESTIONS

1. a) Below and to the left, draw a supply and demand diagram of the Wall Street labor market for new MBAs. The labor supply curve should be drawn bearing in mind that alternative positions in industry were available to MBAs, in some cases at lower, and in other cases at higher, salaries than on Wall Street. Show an equilibrium salary of $55,000 and the associated employment level.

    b) On your diagram, mark the part of total salaries paid that is transfer earnings. Intuitively explain its size relative to total salaries paid.

    c) To the right of your above diagram draw a wage-employment diagram for an individual Wall Street firm, such as Lehman Brothers. Draw the supply curve to the firm assuming the labor market is competitive, and add a demand curve. Mark the equilibrium salary and employment level.

    d) On your second diagram, mark the part of total salaries paid that is transfer earnings. Intuitively explain its size relative to total salaries paid.

2. a) In another set of diagrams of the Wall Street labor market for new MBAs, show how the crash of 1987 decreased salaries and employment in the market in general and in Lehman brothers in particular.

    b) Explain in terms of transfer earnings and economic rent why it was appropriate to reduce salaries in the market in general.

    c) Explain in terms of transfer earnings and economic rent why it was appropriate to reduce salaries at Lehman Brothers.

3. How could Wall Street hire twice as many MBAs in 1992 as in 1991 if starting pay had not increased for several years? Answer in terms of

   a) supply and demand.

   b) transfer earnings and economic rent.

4. The supply of new MBAs with international skills was apparently so invariant with respect to starting salaries that Wall Street firms such as Lehman Brothers recruited overseas.

   a) In a wage-employment diagram for international investment bankers, carefully draw the supply and demand curves.

   b) Shade the area on your diagram that is economic rent. Intuitively, explain its size relative to the total salaries paid.

   c) Why were international investment bankers able to earn these levels of economic rent? Refer to your diagram.

   d) One solution was to raise salaries even higher. In what sense would the money have been wasted? In what way would it have been well spent? Refer to the concepts of economic rent and transfer earnings.

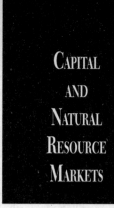

36. School's Out of Professors

Firms generally use capital equipment to complement labor. The demand for capital is the marginal revenue productivity of capital. The supply of capital to the firm in a competitive factor market is perfectly elastic. To maximize profits, the firm increases the capital stock until the additional revenue generated by the last unit of capital equals its price.

Where the benefits and the costs arise in the current period—as when renting equipment or when the lifetime of the equipment is short—the calculation is straightforward. However, capital frequently contributes to production over several periods. In that case, the firm has to calculate the future stream of marginal revenue products (and perhaps costs of capital if payment is delayed) in present value terms, bearing in mind the benefits, the costs, the lifetime of the capital, and the interest rate appropriate for discounting the future.

The same principles can be applied to investment by individuals in human capital. In deciding whether to undertake a particular educational program, people consider the discounted present value of the benefits less the costs over a suitable time horizon. The article reprinted here discusses the reasons for the sharp decline in doctoral recipients.

After studying your text, reading the article, and answering the questions, you should be able to:

◆◆ Explain how firms determine the amount of capital to employ and how individuals decide on the appropriate level of investment in human capital

◆◆ Determine whether it is appropriate to invest in a capital or human capital project given the expected benefits, costs, lifetime of the capital, and interest rate

◆◆ Predict changes in the amount of investment in capital or human capital when circumstances relevant to the investment decision change, such as interest rates and the period over which net benefits arise

Preview

◆ A shortage of college professors in the arts and sciences, especially the humanities, is in prospect.

◆ The cause is a decline in the number of doctoral degrees awarded over the last two decades.

◆ The decline is due to the time and energy required to complete a doctorate, and the claims on time of teaching assistantships.

◆ It is recommended that universities advise students more closely, foster student collegiality, limit teaching assistantships, and increase national fellowships.

◆ Engineering and science doctorates have remained steady because of an influx of foreign students.

Shortage of Professors Is Envisioned

The nation could run short of researchers and college professors in the arts and sciences in the next several years unless graduate programs at American universities are strengthened by new financing and greater attention to students, according to a study on graduate education.

The heart of the problem is that the number of recipients of doctorates in the six areas covered by the study— economics, English, history, mathematics, physics and political science—has sharply declined in the last decade. The doctoral degree is almost always a requirement for appointment as a professor or researcher.

While enough programs exist to produce more doctoral degree recipients, many are so small or so poorly organized that students, hard pressed to find the time or energy to complete a course of work that can last 12 years, often drop out before receiving doctorates, according to the study, which was made public on Monday.

Effects of Inattention "Unless something is done to improve the effectiveness of these programs," said William G. Bowen, co-author of the study, "there will continue to be a waste of human energy, resources that are not used effectively and, quite possibly, an inadequate response by graduate education to the pressures that are going to be felt by the end of the 1990's."

The study, "In Pursuit of the Ph.D.," (Princeton University Press) was conducted by Mr. Bowen, a former president of Princeton who now heads the Andrew J. Mellon Foundation, and Neil L. Rudenstine, who was executive vice president of the foundation before being named president of Harvard University last year.

Despite its importance to the nation, graduate education has received scant attention and comparatively little study, Mr. Bowen said.

American colleges and universities grant approximately one million bachelor's degrees a year, compared with about 300,000 master's degrees and 34,000 doctorates.

Enrollment in graduate schools grew slowly but steadily beginning in the 1920's, then more rapidly in the 1960's until it peaked before graduate student deferments for the Vietnam War were ended in 1968, the report said. More recently, the number of doctoral recipients in the humanities dropped to 3,600 in 1988 from 5,400 in 1973. By contrast, the number of engineering and science degrees has remained steady because of an influx of foreign graduate students who have offset a drop in the number of American students in those areas.

How to End the Decline? The study also found that as many as half of all doctoral students in many programs drop out before finishing.

"The low completion rates and long time-to-degree that often prevail now mean that even modest improvements would increase markedly the number of recipients of doctorates," the authors wrote. "Working to improve the effectiveness of current programs is by far the most sensible way to begin to prepare for the faculty staffing problems that are anticipated by the end of the decade."

A related study co-written by Mr. Bowen in 1989 estimated that the nation would have to increase overall production of doctorates by two-thirds to meet anticipated demands for faculty members and to avert a shortage. The study, "Prospects for Faculty in the Arts and Sciences," projected that by the end of this decade there might be only 30,934 new faculty members to fill 37,091 positions.

The study recommends that universities and graduate departments take several steps to increase the number of doctorates. Among the suggestions are these:

Avoid creating more graduate programs that will be so small and specialized that they cannot meet a minimum standard of excellence.

Advise graduate students more closely and foster a sense of collegiality among them, especially in the trying period when a student is writing a dissertation.

Limit positions as teaching assistants to about two years. Otherwise the positions—which provide financial aid to graduate students in exchange for part-time teaching duties—can interfere with the student's ability to complete a degree program.

The study also recommended that a national fellowship program for the humanities be established, tailoring it after a program being run by the National Science Foundation.

QUESTIONS

1. a) How does an educational program add to a person's marginal revenue product and therefore a person's income? When does the increase occur?

   b) What are the costs of an educational program? When do they arise?

   c) How would an economist evaluate whether it is worthwhile to invest in an educational program? Make clear how future costs and benefits are figured into the calculation.

2. The article cites a number of factors that appear to be related to the decline in doctorates in the humanities. Explain in terms of the investment decision formula you determined in question 1c why the following factors would convince individuals not to invest in a doctoral degree:

   a) the ending of graduate student deferments in 1968.

   b) the long time it takes to obtain a doctorate.

   c) the energy a doctorate requires.

3. Why has there not been a similar decline in doctorates awarded to foreign and U.S. students in engineering and science? Answer in terms of the benefits, costs, time horizon, and the interest rate used to discount future uncertainty.

4. Again referring to the four influences on the educational investment decision, carefully analyze how (and whether) the proposed solutions to the problem of a dearth of doctorates are likely to persuade individuals to complete a doctorate:

   a) better advising by faculty.

   b) greater student collegiality.

   c) higher standards for graduate programs.

   d) fewer years as a teaching assistant.

   e) more national fellowships.

5. What other solutions exist? State whether your recommendations change the benefits, costs, time period, or rate for discounting the future.

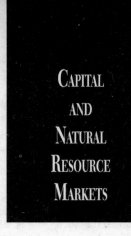

CAPITAL AND NATURAL RESOURCE MARKETS

37.

Auto

Stocks

Accelerate:

Ford—24

to 44 in

Six

Months

In the capital market, households supply their savings and firms demand funds for investment. Households make portfolio choices so as to maximize rates of return, taking account of risk levels. In the context of the stock market, the interest rate is the stock yield. It equals the ratio of the income from a share (dividend and stock market appreciation) to the price of a share.

The price of a share reflects the present value of future profits, based on rational expectations concerning factors such as costs, revenues, and the value of the firm's assets. An increase in expected profits raises the demand of households and others for stock, which in turn inflates the stock price. A primary reason stock changes hands is because investors disagree over future profits. With a higher price, the yield falls unless earnings increase. The price increases until the yield matches the interest rate for assets of similar risk.

A firm's performance is often measured by its price-earnings ratio, that is, its current price relative to the recent profit per share. The ratio increases the greater the expected profit relative to current profit.

The workings of the stock market are illustrated in the accompanying article about auto stocks in 1992.

After studying your text, reading the article, and answering the questions, you should be able to:

◆◆ Define and calculate the stock yield

◆◆ Explain why stock prices rise and fall

◆◆ Explain the limits to stock price fluctuations

◆◆ Define and explain the price-earnings ratio

◆◆ Explain the volume of trading in a stock

Preview

◆ General Motors made a massive stock offering in 1992.

◆ In fact, Ford looked like a better investment in terms of its product, costs, and price-normalized earnings ratio.

◆ GM was less attractive because of its overcapacity, restructuring, model overlap, and falling market share.

◆ Some did not find any auto stocks attractive because of high financial ratios and a bleak long-term outlook.

It's GM's Offering, but Praise Is Going to Ford

Coming soon to a broker near you: the massive stock offering of General Motors.

Around the third week of this month, investors can expect their phones to ring with a friendly broker's suggestion to buy the stock. It's not a bad deal, quite a few money managers say. But have you considered Ford Motor lately? That might be an even better idea.

Ford is acknowledged to be the lowest-cost producer among the big three U.S. car makers. Unlike GM and Chrysler, Ford doesn't have a big, underfunded pension liability. Its reputation for quality is at least equal to that of its U.S. rivals, and it won't have to endure the dislocations GM faces in the next couple of years as it breaks in a new management team, closes 21 assembly plants and shrinks its work force by some 74,000 people.

To the extent GM's shrinkage reduces the industry's excess capacity, it will help profits at all U.S. car producers, not just GM. Yet GM is in some ways the most expensive auto stock. It sells for 12 times GM's average per-share earnings for the past 10 years; the comparable multiple for Ford is only 10 and for Chrysler only six.

"We think Ford is the more interesting," says David Dreman, a managing director with Dreman Value Management, Jersey City, N.J. "Ford in good years ran at 100% plus of capacity, rather than building new plants, which was a wise decision. They trimmed costs more rapidly than GM. Domestically, their strategies are more focused than GM's are." His firm owns a large holding in Ford, and a much smaller one in GM.

GM is making its first common stock offering since 1955, issuing 50 million to 57.5 million shares to the public and expanding the total number of shares outstanding by about 11%. If the stock were priced at yesterday's 40 1/2, off 1/8, proceeds would be at least $2.02 billion....

One East Coast money manager likes the new management at GM, but he is still putting his money in Ford. One problem for GM, he says, is the overlap of its six nameplates, particularly Buick and Oldsmobile. "They've

Auto Stocks in Profile

	GM	FORD	CHRYSLER
Stock Price	40 1/2	44 7/8	18 5/8
Ten-year high	50 1/2	56 5/8	48
Ten-year low	17	3 11/16	1 9/16
Peak earnings[1]	$7.11	$10.96	$6.31
Normalized earnings[2]	$3.26	$4.44	$2.87
Price/peak earnings	6	4	3
Price/normalized earnings	12	10	6
Long-term debt as percent of total capital[3]	54%	65%	60%
Dividend yield	3.9%	3.6%	3.2%
Percentage of analysts recommending stock	57%	66%	47%

[1]Per share, for GM in 1984, Ford in 1988, Chrysler in 1986. [2]Average per-share earnings 1982-1991.
[3]As of Sept. 30, 1991. NOTE: Figures are adjusted for stock splits.

Sources: Value Line Investment Survey, IDD/Tradeline, Zacks Investment Research

done a good job of re-positioning Buick as an American high-end driving car," he says. "But that's really shot Oldsmobile in the heart."

Chevrolet has a far-flung dealer network and a reputation for delivering good value for the money, the manager says. But it has been losing market share to foreign competitors and Ford. "Further difficulty will come from Chrysler's new LH cars," he says.

Many brokerage-house auto analysts won't comment on GM this month because their firms are in—or hope to be in—the offering syndicate. At Argus Research (which provides research to brokerage firms, but doesn't itself buy or sell stocks), analyst John E. Hilton rates Ford "buy," GM "hold," and Chrysler "sell."

Mr. Hilton thinks GM's market-share slide "may very well cease," partly because he has "high hopes for Saturn," GM's import fighter. But he thinks it will take GM awhile to cope with "overcapacity ... a management shakeup [and] plant closings."

GM is "just okay. It's a big company with a huge transition problem," says Greg Smith, investment strategist for Prudential Securities. "I don't think it's going to be one of these sparkling turnaround stories. Closing lots of plants and laying off lots of people almost always takes longer and is more difficult than you anticipate. The one that makes the most sense to me is Chrysler," not at 18 5/8, partly because it is almost purely domestic, and thus could sidestep recessions in Europe this year. "And Chrysler does seem to have a pretty exciting new-product cycle," he says.

Richard Eakle, head of Eakle Associates in Fair Haven, N.J., also likes Chrysler best of the three, though he cautions: "It has more risk in terms of the balance sheet." Among other things, he likes the company's strength in minivans and utility vehicles (Chrysler owns Jeep).

To be sure, GM has strong supporters. "I think there is a major potential for getting market share from the Japanese," says Dan Becker, auto analyst with Wadell & Reed Asset Management in Kansas City. He notes that Japanese car makers were able to get capital very cheaply for years, because of Japan's booming stock market and ankle-high interest rates. Now those advantages have dissipated. "GM's going to get its house in order," he says. "The timing couldn't be better." His firm has been buying both GM and Chrysler shares.

"I think we will have a stronger and longer-lasting recovery than most people anticipate," says Heiko Thieme, manager of the American Heritage Fund. "If that's true, then the auto stocks have not peaked by a long shot." GM "could be 50% higher" in a year or two, he says.

Mr. Thieme likes both GM and Ford. But he prefers GM because it is in the Dow Jones Industrial Average, and therefore is more likely to attract foreign buyers. In the short run, Mr. Thieme says, all the auto stocks are "extended" after a rapid climb. Anticipating a pullback, he suggests buying 25% of one's position immediately, 50% on dips, and the rest when the stocks return to current levels.

Of course, some people wouldn't touch an auto stock, even with gloves on. "I wouldn't buy any of the three," says Stephen Leeb, editor of The Big Picture, a Palisades Park, N.J., market letter. When GM was raking in profits in 1984 and 1988, he says, it sold for five to 5.5 times earnings. Currently it is selling for about six times peak (1984) earnings.

Auto stocks have shot up so much this year that "they've moved out of price ranges where we'd be interested," says one Midwest money manager. "With the recent run, the stocks are higher than normal on price-to-sales and price-to-cash-flow" ratios.

U.S. car makers are "heavily capital-intensive, and mired in huge amounts of debt," says Frederic E. Russell, a money manager in Tulsa, Okla. "They compete with many manufacturers, and cannot distinguish their product in any positive, permanent way."

Frank Curzio, head of FXC Investors Corp. in Queens, N.Y., thinks the auto stocks are still "good for trading" but not for long-term investors. "I could see GM at over 50 this year and Ford at around 55 to 60," he says. But he thinks car sales will fizzle again in 1993 and 1994, as debt-laden consumers find their disposable income crimped by rising federal and local taxes.

QUESTIONS

1. a) Why was GM making a massive stock offering?

   b) What was the expected stock yield given a price of $40 a share and expected income at the normalized earnings level of $3.20 a share?

   c) Why would an economically rational investor have bought GM stock rather than invested in other assets?

2. a) What does the price of a share of stock reflect?

   b) Why do you think the prices of auto stocks rose in 1992 as the economy came out of recession?

   c) If there were only a few days when large volumes of auto stocks were traded, what does this imply about the degree of agreement about expected profits? Explain your answer.

   d) Why were auto stocks expected to increase in price through 1993 and then perhaps decrease?

   e) Why did analysts recommend Ford more than GM or Chrysler? Refer to the information in the article.

f) At what point in the price spiral would investors think that it was not worth investing any more money in auto stocks?

g) What would be the stock yield relative to other stocks and assets at this point?

h) What would be the reaction of investors with money to spend in the stock market at this point?

3. a) What does the price-earnings ratio reflect?

b) What was Ford's price-earnings ratio, given that it was trading at a price of $44 and its normalized earnings for 1982-1991 were $4.40?

c) In contrast, GM's price-earnings ratio was 12. Why would an analyst advise against buying GM stock because of a higher ratio of price to normalized earnings?

d) GM had a ratio of price to peak earnings of 6. Why would an analyst advise against buying GM stock on the ground that the ratio was as high as it was "when GM was raking in profits in 1984 and 1988"?

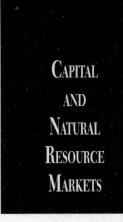

CAPITAL
AND
NATURAL
RESOURCE
MARKETS

Land is a nonexhaustible natural resource in that it can be used again and again in successive time periods without ever being used up. Land rental rates are the prices paid to landowners for the use of their land. They are determined by supply and demand in the market for land in a given area. The supply of land in the area is fixed. The demand for the land reflects its marginal revenue product. The individual firm operating in a competitive land market faces a perfectly elastic supply curve for land at the market price. It rents land so long as the marginal revenue product exceeds or equals the market rental rate. The article reprinted here concerns the rents paid by stores in exclusive shopping districts.

After studying your text, reading the article, and answering the questions, you should be able to:

◆◆ Explain the general slopes of the supply and demand curves for land in the market as a whole and for an individual firm

◆◆ Explain differences in rental rates

◆◆ Predict changes in rental rates following changes in the determinants of the supply of and demand for land

◆◆ Distinguish between economic rent and land rent

Preview

◆ Ron Ross moved his ritzy apparel shop to Studio City, California, after inducements from the landlord.

◆ Many retailers are improving their locations in response to lower rental rates for retailing space and options to cancel.

◆ The cause of the bargain rents is lower demand caused by the slow economy and overbuilding in the 1980s.

◆ Although rental rates are lower, Madison Avenue still typically commands $200 to $300 per square foot, while Rodeo Drive, Beverly Hills costs $100 to $125 per square foot.

Slow Economy Can Open Doors for Small Retailers

Ron Ross moved his ritzy apparel shop to his dream location last week—thanks to the slow economy.

The Tarzana, Calif., retailer decided to anchor a posh but vacancy-ridden shopping center in nearby Studio City after winning sizable inducements from the center's banker. Security Pacific National Bank has run the center since its developer handed over the keys two years ago. Mr. Ross says that the bank footed about 70% of the millions of dollars needed to create a 14,000-square-foot showplace by noted designer Waldo Fernandez.

In better economic times, Mr. Ross probably wouldn't have landed such a generous deal. "Ron's got a great following," says Doane Liu, a Security Pacific vice president. "He's bringing quite a few customers with him to the shopping center." Mr. Ross, whose store carries his name and outfits celebrities such as TV comedian Bob Saget, says the recession simply "has enhanced the scale" of his expansion.

Scores of Opportunities Many small retailers are suddenly discovering scores of opportunities to improve their locations—at a bargain price—during the retail industry's current doldrums. But negotiating the sweetest possible deal can require some fancy footwork by entrepreneurs.

A high number of bankruptcies by failed merchants, coupled with overbuilding during the past decade, have left many shops vacant. Landlords find themselves desperate to improve their cash flow. "A lot of them are feeling the heat from their banks," says Lawrence Holzman, director of retail leasing for Wilrock National Inc., a New York real estate broker.

As a result, numerous small retailers find they can get extra favors from landlords who formerly snubbed them in favor of giant competitors during the 1980s retailing boom. Many big retailers are having trouble expanding because capital is tight. But some small retailers can finance their comparatively modest expansion plans by going to a bank or taking out second mortgages on their homes, says Sid Doolittle, a Chicago retailing consultant.

"Smaller retailers are being opportunistic—and landlords are willing to take them more seriously than a few years ago because demand has fallen off so much," says Bruce Kaplan, president of Northern Realty Group Ltd., a Chicago broker of retail space. "Now, anybody doing deals who is financially stable is a first-class citizen."

Free Rent Small merchants are negotiating lucrative leasing arrangements as new tenants or persuading their landlords to rewrite old leases on

Cheaper Space

Typical annual rental rates per square foot for retail space averaging 1,500 sq. ft.

	4th qtr. 1988	1st qtr. 1992
Beverly Hills, Rodeo Drive	$165–180	$100–125
Boston, Newbury Street	100–115	70–85
Chicago, North Michigan Avenue	100–120	90–120
New York, Madison Avenue	275–350	200–300
Palm Beach, Worth Avenue	100–125	75–85
Philadelphia, Walnut Street	75–100	50–60

Source: Garrick-Aug Associates Inc., N.Y.

terms dictated by current tenants. Thomas Kolp negotiated three months of free rent last year when he opened his Great Harvest Bread Co. franchise in Evanston, Ill....

Options on Lease A few small retailers even have won the right to walk away from a lease if a location proves disappointing. Until now, "[we've] never seen tenants demanding the right to terminate their leases after two or three years if they haven't achieved sales they're comfortable with," says Northern Realty's Mr. Kaplan....

The array of attractive rental options is making expansion-minded smaller retailers think twice about building their own stores. Home Ltd., a New York retailer of ready-to-assemble furniture, opened its first store last fall in a building that it had constructed in Lombard, a Chicago suburb.

But Home Ltd. Chairman John Matthews says the recent retailing turmoil makes space in existing distressed centers more financially appealing. Home Ltd. now is negotiating with landlords to expand into existing buildings at other locations.

Rent Reductions Meanwhile, many small retailers are demanding—and getting—rent reductions from their landlords. "When you're a small-business person, you try everything that comes into your head," says Hugh Porter, a Jenny Craig Inc. weight-loss franchisee in Tucson, Ariz. One of his two outlets is housed near a building that his landlord just completed. When Mr. Porter learned the landlord was offering prospective tenants a cheaper rent in the new building than his own, he sought—and won—a rent cut at his location....

Reducing rent costs also can be a pathway to expansion. Gallery of Gifts and Shoppes Inc. in Hampton, N.H., has renegotiated leases on three of its five stores this year, thereby cutting its entire rental bill 10%, says Robert Coviello, president. He believes that the saving will be "pretty significant" in his effort to return to profitability this year after three years of losses.

A turnaround should help the retail company attract the venture capital needed to add as many as 25 stores in New England over the next five years, Mr. Coviello adds.

QUESTIONS

1. a) What was the general slope of the short-run supply curve in the market for retail space in Studio City, California? How do you know?

   b) Draw a supply and demand diagram of the market for retail space in Studio City. Show why rental rates fell before Mr. Ross moved in.

   c) The opening paragraph of the article attributes the decrease in rental rates to the slow economy, while the fifth paragraph also blames overbuilding. Which is correct? Why?

   d) Explain how the slow economy decreased the demand for retail space in terms of the determinants of the demand for land.

2. a) What was the general slope of the supply curve for retail space for an individual store in Studio City? Justify your answer.

b) Draw a diagram of the supply of and demand for retail space for an individual store in Studio City. Show the implications of the changes in the market as a whole identified in question 1. Assume the store's demand was unchanged.

c) Why did the quantity of land demanded change following the change in rental rates? Answer in terms of the marginal revenue productivity of retail space.

3. Why were rental rates higher on Madison Avenue in Manhattan than on Rodeo Drive in Beverly Hills? Think of as many possible reasons as you can.

4. a) In new diagrams of the demand for and supply of land in Studio City and for an individual store, shade in the areas representing economic rent.

b) In the diagram of the market for land space in Studio City is there a difference between the value of land rent and economic rent? Explain. Are the two types of rent different conceptually?

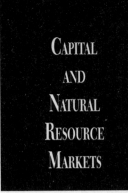

CAPITAL AND NATURAL RESOURCE MARKETS

39. Evaporating Water Supplies in California

Some natural resources are exhaustible in that they cannot be replaced once used. In the market for the stock of an exhaustible natural resource, the supply of the resource is perfectly inelastic. The demand for stocks of the resource depend on the expected yield. In equilibrium, the price of the resource is expected to increase at a rate equal to the interest rate on assets of similar risk.

In the market for the flow of a natural resource, the demand curve reflects the marginal revenue product of the resource as the quantity used increases. Given the stock of the resource, equilibrium occurs where the marginal revenue product equals the marginal cost of the resource.

Over time, the price increases as the stock is depleted. This causes a reduction in the quantity demanded. Eventually, in equilibrium, the stock is exhausted at the same time the choke price is charged, at which point quantity demanded reaches zero. Of course, the process can be disturbed by unexpected changes, for example in interest rates and the stock itself.

The example in the accompanying article concerns water—a resource that can be replaced by rainfall, but, due to the drought, is being depleted faster than it is being replaced in California.

After studying your text, reading the article, and answering the questions, you should be able to:

◆◆ Explain the general slopes of the demand and supply curves for the flow of an exhaustible natural resource

◆◆ Explain the rate at which the equilibrium price of an exhaustible resource increases

◆◆ Explain the rate of use of an exhaustible resource

◆◆ Explain how conservation automatically occurs as resources are depleted

◆◆ Predict the impact of changes in demand and supply on the equilibrium price and quantity used of a natural resource

Preview

◆ California farmers have an abundance of water for which they pay a low price, fixed by long-term contracts.

◆ Meantime, urban areas face a shortage of water in spite of high prices.

◆ Supplies are limited because of the drought and a reluctance of other states to sell their water supplies.

◆ Rising urban demand combined with farmer waste of water, low crop prices, and environmental damage, has prompted a new plan.

◆ Farmers will be allowed to sell water to urban water authorities, letting fields of less valuable crops fall fallow.

◆ Ironically, as the plan was being developed, the drought ended in some parts of California.

Farmers in West May Sell Something More Valuable Than Any Crop: Water

Even as six years of drought turned lawns brown and forced urban Californians to take shorter showers, the farmers in the Palo Verde Valley had plenty of water to go on irrigating such thirsty crops as alfalfa and cotton. And they jealously guarded their rights to cheap Federal water from the Colorado River.

But some profound changes are about to come to this valley between the McCoy and the Dome Rock mountains along the rugged Arizona border. If all goes as planned, nearly a quarter of the valley's acreage will go fallow starting Aug. 1, and, in a two-year experiment, the water saved will be sold to people in urban areas hundreds of miles away.

Slowly, with some reluctance, farmers are beginning to loosen their historic grip on water in the West, transferring some of their supplies to the fast-growing cities and industries—for a price. Such transfers are expected to be an important element of a broad long-range water plan for California to be unveiled April 6 by Gov. Pete Wilson.

The trend has been promoted by an odd twist of Reagan-era deregulation, which has made allies of environmental and urban interests in creating a partial free market in water so that it flows to where it has the most value.

Seeds of Unease   If the trend builds, it could have profound implications, accelerating the already rapid urbanization of agricultural lands that in California produce half the nation's fruits and vegetables. The prospect is stirring unease among farm towns, farm laborers and sellers of seeds, insecticides, tractors and other agricultural needs.

"There's a fairly dramatic change taking place—broad support has developed quickly for agricultural water transfers," said Duane L. Georgeson, assistant general manager of the Metropolitan Water District of Southern California, the powerful agency that plans to buy the water from Blythe. The Met, as it is called, sells water to utilities and communities that are home to 15 million people from Ventura to the Mexican border.

The reasons for the shift are rooted in several factors, including mounting political pressure for more urban water, rising public perception that farmers squander water on low-value surplus crops, concern over damage to chinook salmon fisheries and other environmental harm from years of drought, and low crop prices. Farmers now use more than 80 percent of the available surface water in California that is not set aside for natural resources or does not flow to the ocean....

Drought Loosens Grip   Paradoxically, all this happens as winter and spring storms have swept the West. The once-dun countryside from Sacramento to the deserts has turned green with chapparal and grasses. The drought appears to have ended around Santa Barbara on the once-parched central coast, and Los Angeles and other cities are relaxing water-use restrictions.

But even without drought, pressures persist, both because of a fast-growing population and the demands of environmental laws governing clean water and endangered species. California's population is expected to grow from 30 million today to 41 million within 20 years. If current use patterns remain unchanged, California faces a water shortage of four to six million acre-feet a year for the next 20 years. (An acre-foot is 325,900 gallons, or roughly enough to supply two typical households for a year.)

California will have to meet this demand without additional supplies because there is little money for dams, and neighboring states fiercely resist efforts to take their water.

A result is a breakdown of the historic alliance between urban and agricultural interests in pressing for more dams and reservoirs. On the other side have been the environmentalists, who have long charged that excessive irrigation has caused environmental damage to the Sacramento Delta, San Francisco Bay and other wetlands....

Any change is difficult because it involves revamping half a century of rights rooted in an earlier rural era. A system of 20 dams and 500 miles of aqueducts that harness the Sacramento and San Joaquin Rivers, the 57-year-old Central Valley Project delivers about eight million acre-feet of water, 85 percent of it to nearly 25,000 farms, in normal years. Depending on their contracts, the farms pay as little as $15 an acre-foot under 40-year contracts. Urban users elsewhere in the state pay $200 to $1,900 an acre-foot.

Environmentalists say the Bureau of Reclamation, which manages the project, has caused enormous damage. For example, only 191 chinook salmon returned to spawn in the Sacramento River for the winter run in 1991, compared with 2,422 in 1986 and 118,000 in 1968, contributing to a disastrous collapse of the Pacific salmon industry.

Certain environmentalists, notably Thomas J. Graff and John Krautkraemer of the Environmental Defense Fund, have long championed water marketing to encourage conservation to make more water available for ecological protection. "Why have a low-value crop in a state where there's an increasing premium on water?" Mr. Krautkraemer said. "It doesn't make sense to allot water to irrigated pastures, which don't contribute a lot to the overall economy. If alfalfa is really that valuable, then they should be willing to pay more for water."

Urban interests have joined the chorus. Last September, the Bay Area Economic Forum, representing such companies as the Pacific Gas and Electric Company and water-needy computer and semiconductor makers in Silicon Valley, called for a regulated, market-based water-allocation system, similar to that of utilities which distribute natural gas or electricity. A report by the forum said the area's economic growth was threatened by water policies that have "undermined reliability, availability and quality."

Senator Bradley, chairman of the subcommittee on Water and Power, agrees. "California is a giant sponge," he said in an interview on a recent visit to Los Angeles. "Every year, the equivalent of the City of San Francisco moves to California. The state has a $760 billion economy, of which agriculture contributes only $20 billion. You cannot have 85 percent of the water continue to go to agriculture."...

Farm interests argue that, indirectly, farming represents a much larger proportion of the economy than Mr. Bradley says. Stephen K. Hall, executive director of the California Farm Water Coalition, agreed that all water users will pay more but said that many farmers would be put out of business, with ripple effects on local economies. "There's a misguided notion that if farmers were forced to pay more for water, they'd use it more efficiently and California's water problems would disappear," he said.

—Robert Reinhold, "Farmers in West May Sell Something More Valuable Than Any Crop: Water," April 6, 1992.
Copyright ©1992 by The New York Times Company. Reprinted with permission.

QUESTIONS

1. a) What is the general slope of the short-run supply curve for the stock of water in California? Why? Refer to the article for reasons.

   b) What determines the stock of water in California?

2. a) What determines the demand for water by farmers in California?

   b) Why is the demand for the flow of water by farmers greater than for households? Consider the determinants of the demand for a resource.

3. In the context of the Californian drought, water can be assumed to approximate an exhaustible resource. Farmers hold portfolios of assets consisting of water for farming and other assets. In equilibrium, the rate of return on assets of similar risk are equal. If the market for water were unregulated,

   a) at what rate would the price of water increase each year? Explain your answer.

   b) what would be the rate of use of water each successive year? Explain your answer.

   c) to what extent would there be conservation of the remaining stock of water and a search for alternatives each successive year? Explain your answer.

4. In practice, the supply of water in California is publicly regulated. Farmers typically have contracts that guarantee them water at very low prices for many years. Given this,

   a) what is the rate of use of water each successive year? How is this different from the rate of use in a free market?

b)   to what extent is there conservation of the remaining stock of water and a search for alternatives each successive year? How is this different from the rate of use in a free market?

5.   It is planned to allow farmers to sell water to urban areas. As a result, farmers can hold water for urban use in their portfolios. Given the high price of water in urban areas relative to the price at which some crops are sold, explain why the article says that there will be

a)   more water supplied to urban areas.

b)   less "waste" of water by farmers.

c)   more urbanization of agricultural lands.

6.   If the authorities allow the price of water to urban areas to rise as the stock of water is depleted, why will there be

a)   a reduced rate of use of water in agriculture?

b)   more attempts to conserve the remaining stock of water and to search for alternatives in agriculture?

7.   The drought has ended in some areas of California. If the price of water for urban areas falls as a result, what will happen to the willingness of farmers to sell water to urban areas? Explain your answer.

40.
Cashing In
on College

Education facilitates the development of skills. The resulting greater productivity implies a higher demand for educated workers. The costs of education restrict the supply of educated workers, as a relatively high wage is needed to induce a given number of individuals to supply their labor. As a result, supply and demand cause the wages of educated employees to be greater than those of less educated workers.

The wage differential influences the degree to which individuals invest in their education: economically rational people invest in education if the present discounted value of the future stream of net benefits exceeds zero.

The accompanying article describes the increasing pay differentials earned by those with a college education at a time of stagnating real wages.

After studying your text, reading the article, and answering the questions, you should be able to:

◆◆ Explain why supply and demand differ according to the level of education of workers

◆◆ Explain changes in educational wage differentials

◆◆ Analyze whether a college education is a worthwhile investment

Preview

◆ Real wage reductions, which affected lower- and middle-income groups by the 1980s, began to affect the college-educated in the 1989-1991 period.

◆ For the previous decade, the pay of college-educated people had marginally exceeded inflation.

◆ The recent trend was attributed to the slowdown in the economy, which caused layoffs and lower pay raises.

◆ The real pay of high-school graduates fell about 12 percent over the 1979-1991 period.

◆ Hence the advantage in real pay of a four-year college education increased.

Pay of College Graduates Is Outpaced by Inflation

Two labor economists reported yesterday that the pay of most college-educated people—once thought to be exempt from the wage stagnation that has afflicted most Americans for more than 15 years—had failed since 1989 to keep up with inflation.

The findings, published by the Economic Policy Institute, a Washington research organization that often supports Democratic candidates, suggest that as many high-paying jobs vanish from the workplace, a bachelor of arts degree is becoming less of a ticket to a

rising income—a conclusion that other economists said was probably accurate.

"Unless we create more jobs, the college-educated are going to crowd out the people below them," said Janet L. Norwood, a senior fellow at the Urban Institute and until recently the commissioner of the Labor Department's Bureau of Labor Statistics. "The college-educated can at least go down, but the people below them have nowhere to go."

The study, by Lawrence Mishel, research director at the Economic Policy

Institute, and Jared Bernstein, an economist there, found that among the college-educated, average pay continued to rise at a faster pace than inflation in the last three years only for black women with bachelor of arts degrees and all men and women with at least two years of postgraduate study.

"Black women, educated and uneducated, are becoming the prime wage earners in black America," Mr. Mishel said.

But for most Americans, a marked slowdown in the national economy, starting in early 1989, has pulled down

Education and Earning Power

Change in average hourly wages by education, adjusted for inflation, in percent.

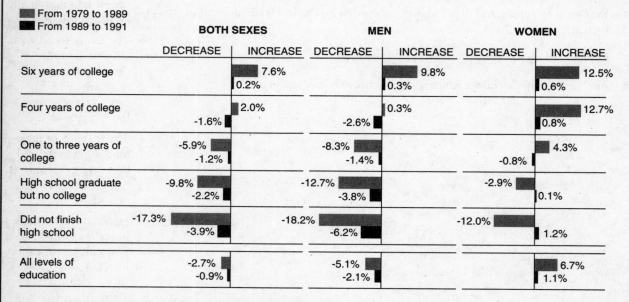

	BOTH SEXES		MEN		WOMEN	
From 1979 to 1989 / From 1989 to 1991	DECREASE	INCREASE	DECREASE	INCREASE	DECREASE	INCREASE
Six years of college		7.6% / 0.2%		9.8% / 0.3%		12.5% / 0.6%
Four years of college	-1.6%	2.0%	-2.6%	0.3%		12.7% / 0.8%
One to three years of college	-5.9% / -1.2%		-8.3% / -1.4%		-0.8%	4.3%
High school graduate but no college	-9.8% / -2.2%		-12.7% / -3.8%		-2.9%	0.1%
Did not finish high school	-17.3% / -3.9%		-18.2% / -6.2%		-12.0%	1.2%
All levels of education	-2.7% / -0.9%		-5.1% / -2.1%			6.7% / 1.1%

Source: Economic Policy Institute, based on Bureau of Labor Statistics figures.

wages. This is true not only for high-school-educated factory and clerical workers, whose pay, adjusted for inflation, continues to shrink, but also for the educated. Indeed, the gap between high school and college graduates, which averaged $5.40 an hour in 1973, is now $5.97 an hour, with the college-educated employee averaging $16.69 an hour, after adjustment for inflation and the high school-trained worker $10.72. That makes a college degree still an advantage, although a diminishing one, since the degree commanded $17.55 an hour in the late 1980's.

Many reasons are offered by economists and sociologists for the newly evident decline in the pay of the college-educated. Prominent among them are the white-collar layoffs in recent years in banking, on Wall Street, in real estate and retailing, and among middle-level managers in many industries as companies adjusted to a weak economy, falling sales and hard-to-get price increases.

The Bush Administration argues that recent wage problems are a result of the recession that is now giving way to a mild recovery. But most economists argue that if the recovery keeps the economy as weak as it was in 1989 before the recession set in, then the wages of the college-educated are likely to continue to suffer.

"You need economic growth far stronger than it has been in recent years to reverse the trend in declining wages," said Richard Freeman, a Harvard University labor economist.

Until 1989, the average hourly earnings of people with a four-year college education had risen over a 10-year period by a total of 2 percent, after adjust-ment for inflation. Over the next three years, 1.6 percent of this gain was lost, the study found—a loss that Mr. Mishel and Mr. Bernstein attributed in part to white-collar layoffs and to raises that were less than the average annual rise of 4.6 percent in the Consumer Price Index since 1989....

All Wages Fell Commenting on the findings, Frank Levy, a labor economist at the University of Maryland, said, "The new trend is striking not so much because the college-educated gained so much ground in the 1980's, but because the bottom fell out of wages for the less educated."

Whatever the reasons, the reversal for the college-educated, combined with a continued fall in inflation-adjusted incomes for people with only a high-school diploma, or less, means that average hourly wages for all the nation's workers fell by nearly a percentage point from 1989 through 1991, on top of a 2.7 percent loss for the 1979-1989 period, the study found....

A Census Bureau study, released earlier this week, reported that the percentage of full-time workers earning less than a low-income $12,195 annually, or $6.10 an hour for a 40-hour week, had risen sharply in the last decade. Other studies show that thousands of entry-level jobs for new college graduates evaporated during the recession that began in July 1990.

From World War II's end until the early 1970's, the incomes of most Americans, whether they were janitors or executives, rose faster than the annual inflation rate. As a result, the constantly rising standard of living for most of the population generated a sense of well-being that began to dissipate by the 1980's—except for the 20 percent of the population at the high end of the income scale, who escaped the stagnation—and in particular the wealthiest 1 percent. College graduates are prominent among the top 20 percent.

An upturn in inflation-adjusted income that appeared to be developing in the mid-1980's failed to materialize, and by early 1989, when the nation's economic growth slowed to 2 percent a year or less, incomes had stagnated again, although college graduates had appeared to be exempt. The upshot is that median hourly wages, adjusted for inflation, for all workers, whatever their education, fell from $11.12 an hour in 1989 to $10.99 an hour last year, the report said.

Coincides with Slowdown The wage problem for the college-educated coincides with the onset, in early 1989, of a slowdown in the growth of the nation's economy, or gross domestic product, to an annual rate of 2 percent or less, from 2.5 percent or more since 1983. That raised the issue of whether a mild recovery now projected by the Bush Administration and most economists—one in which the economy grows at an annual rate of 2 percent to 2.5 percent this year—would be enough to generate new jobs and wage growth as employers compete again for workers.

"It is not clear that people will feel better off if the economy turns up a bit," Mr. Levy said. "People are catching on that beneath the ups and downs in the economy, wages have remained flat."

QUESTIONS

1. a) Draw a diagram with axes showing real wages and employment. Add the supply and demand curves both for college graduates and for people with only four years of high school in 1979. Show the wage differential.

    b) Why would you expect the supply curves to be in different positions?

    c) Why would you expect the demand curves to be in different positions?

2. a) On the same diagram show the 1991 equilibria for the two groups and the new wage differential. Draw them to the right, reflecting the fact that the supply of and demand for both groups increased over the 1979-1991 period. Make sure your diagram shows that the real wages of those with only a high school education were sharply lower than in 1979, while the real wages of college graduates were approximately unchanged.

    b) What might account for the supply curve for high school graduates far outshifting the demand curve? Refer to the determinants of labor supply and demand.

3. What has been the likely effect on college enrollment, other things being equal, of

    a) the increasing wage differential for college graduates? Why?

b) higher real tuition rates? Why?

c) earlier retirements by college-educated male workers? Why?

d) greater uncertainty regarding the path of real wages in the future? Why?

4. a) Draw a real-wage-employment diagram showing the equilibria of people with six years of college and people with four years of college in 1979 and 1991. Show employment of each group increasing over the period. Mark the wage differential in 1979 and 1991.

b) Why might the demand curve for graduates with six years of college have shifted out more than the supply curve, while the demand and supply curves for those with four years of college shifted out approximately equally? Refer to the determinants of labor supply and demand.

41.
Caterpillar
Gives
UAW
Butterflies

Unions tend to negotiate wage levels that are higher than those paid to nonunion workers in similar circumstances. Sometimes this is because unions raise the equilibrium wage by restricting labor supply or by increasing the demand for labor. Alternatively, a union may force the wage above its equilibrium level through its collective bargaining power. Critical to the union's success is an inelastic demand for labor so that wage increases do not significantly reduce employment.

Where one employer dominates the labor market—monopsony—the equilibrium wage is lower than in a competitive labor market, but if a union is present— bilateral monopoly—higher wages are possible, depending on relative bargaining power. The transportation equipment industry provides a good illustration of factors affecting union wage differentials.

After studying your text, reading the article, and answering the questions, you should be able to:

◆ ◆ Explain how unions can raise equilibrium wages

◆ ◆ Explain the constraints on the ability of unions to increase wages

◆ ◆ Define monopsony and bilateral monopoly

◆ ◆ Determine the level of wages and employment in a monopsonistic labor market

◆ ◆ Determine the range within which wages are negotiated in bilateral monopoly

◆ ◆ State typical arguments of unions and employers in collective bargaining

Preview

◆ The UAW was on strike against Caterpillar for several months during 1991-1992.

◆ The UAW and Caterpillar disagreed over pattern bargaining, two-tier wages, layoff protection, and the role of seniority.

◆ While politicians were debating striker replacement, Caterpillar threatened to replace strikers with unemployed workers, in spite of large training costs.

◆ In the interim, Caterpillar used managers and supervisors.

Labor Makes a Stand in Fight for Its Future at Caterpillar Inc.

Last Friday, Caterpillar Inc. Chairman Donald Fites strolled toward a window in the company's seventh-floor executive suite and gazed down at the surrounding factories. For months, they have been rimmed by picketers drawing warmth from wood-burning barrel fires. "I expect our people will return to work," he said. "They've suffered enough."

But yesterday, only a few did return. On the date the company had set for workers to go back to their jobs or risk replacement, Caterpillar says about 300 of the 12,600 striking workers crossed the picket lines at its main production plants.

At the big Cat factories in Aurora and East Peoria that turn out bulldozers, earth movers and other heavy construction equipment, thousands of workers lined the streets, honking car horns, waving picket signs, blaring through bullhorns and training video cameras on plant gates to record the identities of "scabs" who dared cross. By day's end, both sides said they were encouraged by the events, but neither was in a position to claim victory.

The showdown between Caterpillar and the United Auto Workers amounts to more than a frontal assault by a company on one of the few remaining powerful unions in America. With other corporations and unions looking on, it has become a critical battle that could shape labor relations for years to come. Caterpillar not only is trying to put an end to pattern bargaining among companies in a single industry, but has also hauled out management's most potent weapon—the threat of permanently replacing strikers....

Labor unions have made the issue of hiring replacement workers a top priority in this election year. A labor-backed bill to bar permanent replacements has already passed the House. But it faces tougher going in the Senate and a likely veto by President Bush, who believes such legislation would only encourage more strikes. Democratic candidates Bill Clinton and Jerry Brown have said they would take labor's side on the issue. What happens at Caterpillar in the next few days and weeks could have a major impact on the course of the bill.

A Needed Balance Corporate executives and their advisers assert that hiring permanent substitutes is a legitimate counterbalance to unions' right to strike and say that companies would be unfairly handcuffed without that balance. "It would be foolhardy if a company didn't take steps to stay in business and keep customers happy," says Howard Bernstein, a Chicago labor lawyer who represents management in labor disputes....

Seeking Protection Companies are also now prohibited by law from using bankruptcy proceedings to abrogate contracts and hire substitute workers, as Frank Lorenzo did with Continental Airlines in 1983.

Unions want much broader protection, arguing that other industrialized nations prohibit permanent replacements. "It's as basic as our existence," says Joe Uehlein, director of special projects for the AFL-CIO's industrial union department.

Caterpillar can't really afford to keep its plants—now manned mostly by supervisors and other managers—operating at the current, sharply reduced pace. But its workers also are struggling after five months of being out on strike. Many workers say they would like to go back to work, but don't want to cross the picket lines with emotions running as high as they are now. Ultimately, the company should have little trouble finding replacements at a time when unemployment, particularly in Illinois, is high.

Chief among the supporters of Caterpillar's position are the executives of the Big Three auto makers, who employ some 400,000 UAW members. The central issue in the strike—whether Caterpillar should agree to a pact similar to the one that competitor Deere & Co. signed with its UAW workers—will be an issue in next year's labor talks between the Big Three and the UAW. The auto makers, like Caterpillar, want out of the "pattern" bargaining approach that the UAW has forced on companies for decades.

Unlike Deere, Caterpillar wants, among other things, watered-down seniority provisions, the ability to accelerate layoffs and a two-tier wage scale for certain workers that would permit the company to bring on newly hired people at a lower wage than current employees get. (Currently, wages for line workers average about $17 an hour.) The company's refusal to accept a contract similar to Deere's is the main factor that led to the now five-month-old strike.

Recasting the Company Caterpillar believes its stance is crucial to its effort to transform itself from a slow-moving giant to a nimble global competitor. On other fronts, the company is completing a $1.9 billion factory-modernization program. It has also just finished a major reorganization that sliced up the corporate bureaucracy into 17 business units, each with a mandate to make money on its own.

Now comes labor. To Mr. Fites, a 58-year-old former marketing man who looks like a tall Gene Hackman, busting the bargaining pattern means freeing his company to compete with the real enemy: Komatsu Ltd. of Japan, and other competitors in the Far East and Europe. The company, he says, must become "globally competitive, from a U.S. manufacturing base."

Unlike the U.S. auto makers, Caterpillar has hung on to its commanding marketshare lead. World-wide, it is twice the size of Komatsu, and $3.71 billion of its $10.18 billion in 1991 sales came from exports of its big yellow machines. Up through 1991, the company had six years of annual profits; last year, though, it reported a loss of $404 million, caused by the recession and one-time write-offs.

The union says the company can afford its demands. "Global competitiveness is a code for bottom-line greed," says Bill Casstevens, the 63-year old UAW secretary-treasurer leading the battle against Caterpillar.

In the crumbling world of organized labor, the UAW has done better than most unions. Though it lost a third of its membership in the last decade, the UAW stood nearly alone among industrial unions in maintaining its compensation levels. Steelworkers, for example, were able only to muster a 2.5% wage increase for all of the 1980s. Auto workers' wages increased nearly 25% in the period, without adjusting for inflation. And in the last round of negotiations with the Big Three auto makers two years ago, the union insulated its members from expected factory closings by forcing the companies to spend $6 billion to compensate the workers they lay off.

Much of that success results directly from the union's pattern bargaining approach. Its method and goals are simple: Take the best contract possible from the richest of the companies in an industry, and then force similar agreements on the other companies.

The desired effect is to take worker compensation out of competition between companies in the same industry. But increasingly, industrial companies that have UAW work forces are insisting that pattern agreements restrain competition. "The pattern concept is no longer the real world," says one GM official.

If the UAW fails to impose the pattern at Caterpillar, companies such as Deere, Navistar International Corp. and the J1 Case unit of Tenneco Inc. are almost certain to ask for breaks from the union when their UAW contracts expire. The ripple effects could change contracts at smaller suppliers and others.

Caterpillar hopes the threat of replacements will be enough to scare workers back to its factories. It plans to take out help-wanted ads as soon as this week, and advertise as far away as St. Louis and Chicago. The response is likely to be keen: Last week, for example, more than 400 people called Caterpillar's plant outside Aurora seeking jobs.

Local union officials say the decision to hire replacement workers will backfire. "Quality would go to hell, and when quality goes, the customers go," says Jay Roberts, president of a UAW local in York, Pa., where Caterpillar has a parts plant. The company admits it will take time to adequately train replacements, but it says quality won't suffer.

The company insisted on a deal far short of what the UAW achieved at Deere, which makes farm and construction equipment. The union talked about "pattern equity," and drove home its point by submitting one of its demands on Deere stationery. Now, the union says it is willing to talk about any issue. But the company says that its third offer, made Feb. 19, is final. It implemented key parts of the offer yesterday, notably the 13% wage increase over three years that the company had proposed. The union wants much more, but hasn't said exactly how much.

QUESTIONS

1. a) How did the UAW attempt to increase Caterpillar Inc.'s demand for labor?

   b) How did it try to restrict the supply of labor to Caterpillar?

   c) Assuming that the UAW was successful in its use of such tactics throughout the transportation equipment industry, show the impact on the free-market equilibrium wage rate and employment level of transportation equipment workers in the labor market as a whole and in Caterpillar in particular. Assume that the labor market was otherwise perfectly competitive.

2. The UAW also used bargaining to attempt to raise wages.

   a) What arguments did it use to justify its stance in negotiation with Caterpillar in 1992? Refer to the article.

   b) What were the counterarguments of Caterpillar management? Refer to the article.

c) In a diagram of the supply of labor to, and the demand for labor by, Caterpillar, show the effect on wages and employment of a contract yielding above-equilibrium wages.

d) In general, in what way is the elasticity of demand for labor relevant to union negotiating power?

e) Why was the elasticity of demand for labor a constraint on the UAW in its negotiations with Caterpillar? Refer to its determinants in the context of the article.

f) What would be the implications for the elasticity of demand for labor of legislation limiting the replacement of strikers? Why do companies not want the law (and therefore the elasticity of labor demand) changed?

g) Caterpillar wanted to introduce lower wage rates for new hires. Assuming that new hires had the same supply and demand curves as incumbents, would setting the wage below the union contract wage cause an inability to recruit new employees? On what does your answer depend? Draw a diagram to illustrate.

3. In fact, Caterpillar dominated the local labor market.

    a) What was the slope of the labor supply curve it faced?

    b) In the absence of the UAW, what profit-maximizing rule would Caterpillar have followed in determining employment levels? Explain your answer.

    c) Draw a wage-employment diagram of the monopsonistic labor market for Caterpillar workers. Include the demand and supply curves as well as a marginal cost of labor curve. Show the wage and employment level Caterpillar would have chosen if free to do so. Contrast the equilibrium with that in a competitive labor market.

    d) What would have determined the size of the benefit gained by Caterpillar through its control of the labor market? Refer to your diagram.

    e) In fact, Caterpillar had to negotiate with the UAW. On your diagram show the maximum wage Caterpillar would have been prepared to pay at the existing level of employment. Explain your reasoning. What determined the actual wage negotiated?

42. Banging Against Glass Walls

Earnings differences exist between the sexes and between races. Part of the reason is discrimination in employment. Even though people are equally able, women and minorities may be perceived to be less able by employers or customers. Job opportunities become more limited or customers avoid these groups as a result. Either way, the marginal revenue productivity of women and minorities is lowered, reducing employment and wages.

Also contributing to earnings differentials are differences in human capital arising from differences in education, experience, and continuity in the workforce. In the context of sex differentials, the tendency of women to diversify their activities between household and market production further reduces their earning power. The accompanying article shows how occupational segregation causes discrimination and differences in human capital, which, together with work-family conflicts, contribute to sex differences in wages and employment.

After studying your text, reading the article, and answering the questions, you should be able to:

◆◆ Account for differences in earnings between men and women

◆◆ Define discrimination

◆◆ Explain how discrimination affects equilibrium wage and employment levels for women

◆◆ Recognize the factors influencing human capital and explain their impact on female wages and employment

◆◆ Explain how household decisions concerning the allocation of nonmarket activities affect female wages and employment

Preview

◆ A lack of experience in line management positions is hindering the vertical progress of women in organizations.

◆ The causes include unintentional stereotyping of women as support staff, male discomfort with dealing with women, and doubts that women can balance career and family.

◆ Family ties sometimes prevent mobility to gain broader experience.

◆ Some companies are making employees more gender-aware and have introduced cross-functional development plans.

Study Says Women Face Glass Walls as Well as Ceilings

I f the ceiling doesn't stop today's working woman, the walls will, a new study suggests.

For a long time, invisible barriers called "glass ceilings" were viewed as the big obstacle facing women trying to climb the corporate ladder. But the new survey has found that the problem starts before that, with "glass walls" that keep women from moving laterally.

Lack of lateral movement deprives women of the experience, especially in line supervision, that they need to advance vertically, concludes the study conducted by Catalyst, a nonprofit research organization here that focuses on women's issues in the workplace.

The new study is based on interviews with senior managers and focus groups with middle managers from large corporations. It will be released today at a Catalyst conference on strategies for women's advancement.

According to the report, women tend to be placed in staff or support positions in areas such as public relations and human resources and are often steered away from jobs in core areas such as marketing, production and sales.

Catalyst President Felice Schwartz says women get trapped in these kinds of jobs because of unintentional stereotyping that labels them as people who can provide support. Support functions such as human resources, law or finance typically don't offer the critical experience expected of those advancing to senior levels.

"Women are being inadvertently separated," Ms. Schwartz says. "Women go one way, and men go another."

The study says women account for as many as half the professional employees in the largest industrial and service companies, yet they hold fewer than 5% of the senior management positions. And most of the senior jobs they do hold are in areas such as human resources,

finance or public relations.

Among the reasons that few women are assigned to line jobs: Many men still feel uncomfortable dealing with women, and many doubt that the women can balance career and family, says Mary Mattis, Catalyst vice president of research. "Furthermore," she says, "60% of human resources managers who participated in the study reported that putting women in line jobs is perceived as risky."

Several outside experts say that the glass wall has been a longstanding problem but is gaining new importance. As companies pare layers of specialized management, it has become more critical than ever to gain broader management experience, they add.

"The glass wall is just a new name for an old phenomenon called occupational segregation," says Myra H. Strober, a labor economist at Stanford University who is researching issues women face at major corporations. "Jobs get segregated when women begin to move through them," Dr. Strober says. "That's just a way of maintaining old types of discrimination."

Dr. Strober urges women to express their concerns to employers. But she says that corporations bear the ultimate responsibility for breaking down the walls. "If companies are serious about moving women to the top, they have to make sure that women don't get stuck in certain dead-end areas," Dr. Strober says.

Other executives say women need to become more assertive to break through the walls. Eunice Salton, a vice president in a division of Simon and Schuster, recommends that women request transfers and go after important line positions. "The walls are still there," she says, but they're getting weaker....

Encouraging Mentoring The study suggests that women should find out what type of experience companies require of their executives and then seek to get it. At the same time, it says, com-

panies should create programs to encourage mentoring and career development and to discourage gender stereotyping....

While women do face special problems, they're not all the fault of the corporation, Dr. Hauser says. She cites the comparative lack of mobility that many professional women suffer if they're married, because they're more likely than male managers to have professional working spouses. And that can complicate—if not impede—the prospect of moving to a new location. "If you're going to take cross-functional assignments, it often means you have to relocate," Dr. Hauser says....

Taking Steps Some companies are taking steps to move more women into line positions and ultimately into top management. For instance, American Airlines, a unit of AMR Corp., issued a directive that requires all officers to submit detailed, cross-functional development plans for all high-potential women in middle management and above, the report says.

Du Pont Co., Wilmington, Del., has a rotation process that moves men and women through at least two or three functions before they reach top positions in the chemical producer, Catalyst adds.

Arthur Andersen & Co. has started a gender-awareness program, called "Men and Women as Colleagues," the report says. The Chicago-based accounting and consulting firm says the program has helped it attract and retain women. More than 40% of the firm's 4,000 annual hires in the U.S. are women.

Ms. Schwartz, the Catalyst president, says such programs show that women are now entering the second phase of the business revolution. The first phase, she says, brought women into the business world. "The second will bring women into the mainstream of business leadership," she says. "I don't think this is just a dream."

—Julie Amparano Lopez, "Study Says Women Face Glass Walls as Well as Ceilings," March 3, 1992.

QUESTIONS

1. a) Women are largely excluded from positions that provide experience expected of those advancing to senior management levels. What evidence is there in the article for the view that this occurs for discriminatory rather than objective economic reasons?

    b) Draw labor supply and demand diagrams for line managers and staff managers. Show line managers earning more than staff managers. Show what happens to the supply curve in each diagram when qualified women are excluded from line management. Mark the number of male line managers and the combined number of male and female staff managers employed. Illustrate what happens to the salary differential as a result of sex discrimination.

    c) Some companies are discouraging gender stereotyping. Assume that the supply curves return to their initial positions in 1b as a result. Mark the number of male line managers and the number of female line managers on your diagram. Also mark the combined number of male and female staff managers. What are the consequences for the salary differential between line and staff managers? Illustrate clearly on your diagram.

2. a) Why is the human capital of women lower than that of men in general? Refer to the article for evidence.

    b) In a supply and demand diagram of the labor market for senior management, show the impact of women having lower levels of human capital on the employment levels and relative salaries of men and women, assuming that men and women are otherwise alike, including having identical supply curves.

c) Certain companies are giving women cross-functional opportunities. What are the consequences for female employment and salaries? Illustrate in your diagram above.

3. To the extent that balancing a career and a family is a genuine problem for women,

a) how might conflicts affect the demand for their labor compared to that for men? Explain why in terms of the determinants of the demand for labor.

b) how might conflicts affect the supply of their labor compared to that for men? Explain why in terms of the determinants of the supply of labor.

c) In a diagram of the demand for and supply of women in the labor market for senior managers, show the effect of the diversification of roles of women in 3a and 3b above on their employment and salaries.

d) What could an organization do to overcome the consequences of a conflict between career and family? Explain how the supply and/or demand curves would be affected.

43.
The Rich
Got Richer

Income is derived from labor, capital, and natural resources. Its distribution depends on the distribution of resources and the prices of factors. Labor income depends on the amount of human capital possessed, occupational choice, and tastes for leisure, among other things. Assortative mating increases income inequality between households. Interest and rental income depend on wealth, which is determined by bequests and saving.

There are conflicting views on the fairness of the distribution of income and the extent to which the government should seek to reduce inequality through progressive taxation, welfare, and public education and health care.

The accompanying article concerns the debate that raged in the early 1990s about the true changes in the degree of inequality. It also discusses possible causes of the trends and attitudes toward reducing inequality.

After studying your text, reading the article, and answering the questions, you should be able to:

◆ ◆ Draw and interpret Lorenz curves

◆ ◆ State caveats concerning the interpretation of income distribution data

◆ ◆ Explain why incomes differ between households

◆ ◆ Explain why the highest income groups have a disproportionately large share of total income

◆ ◆ Determine the policy implications of different theories of distributive and procedural justice

◆ ◆ Explain the benefits of inequality in a market economy

Preview

◆ Income inequality was a 1992 election campaign issue.

◆ The major share of the gains in average family income in the 1977-1989 period went to the top 1 percent of income recipients.

◆ This held true even after accounting for changes in family size and the effect of taxation.

◆ Conservatives complained that the data included capital gains, underestimated the income of lower-income families, masked the mobility of individual families, and included the Carter presidency.

◆ Liberals responded that the rich still became richer after excluding capital gains and the Carter years.

◆ President Bush's advisor believed the causes were demographic and labor market shifts rather than economic policy.

However You Slice the Data the Richest Did Get Richer

Ironically, when the Congressional Budget Office first released its income data—the numbers on the top 1 percent that are being hurled on the hustings—only a handful of Congressional aides and professional economists paid much attention. And even after the economist Paul R. Krugman of the Massachusetts Institute of Technology crunched the numbers and concluded that the major share of the gains in average family income between 1977 and 1989 had gone to the richest of the rich, he had trouble getting anyone to listen.

But Mr. Krugman's arithmetic ultimately crystallized the issue in much the same way as the misery index—the sum of inflation and unemployment—confirmed what ordinary voters felt had gone wrong during the years of Jimmy Carter's Presidency. And Mr. Krugman's calculation also helped focus the fierce political debate over who won—and who lost—from economic growth in the 1980's.

One reason that the issue remained relatively invisible for so long—in spite of broad agreement among academic economists that income and wealth have grown more unequal—is that statistics on distribution are among the mushiest and murkiest in economics. There are literally dozens of ways to slice and dice the data, not to mention hundreds of different data series.

Alternate Measures Confronted by Republican legislators after Governor Clinton started peppering his speeches with the statistic on the top 1 percent, the budget office was called upon to assess the Krugman calculation. Several weeks later, it issued a report that gave a number of alternate measures of the gains by the top 1 percent. Every measure showed that the top 1 percent of families reaped an outsized share of the gains.

By one calculation 70 percent of the rise in average after-tax family income went to the top 1 percent, rather than the 60 percent figure that Mr. Krugman initially estimated and Governor Clinton has been using. If income gains for the top 1 percent had been the same as for the average family, the budget office economists point out, just 7 percent of the rise would have gone to the very rich.

Adjusting for the fact that families in 1989 were smaller, on average, than families in 1977, 44 percent of the gains went to the top 1 percent. Budget office economists argue that adjusting the average income gain for all families upward to reflect that each family's income was spread over fewer people is a more accurate way of portraying what happened to the well being of families in the middle. Mr. Krugman responds that the adjustment is irrelevant to the question of what happened to the fruits of economic growth.

Other Gains by the Very Rich The Congressional Budget Office also reports other ways of looking at the gains of the very rich. The top 1 percent's share of total after tax income jumped from 7 percent to 12 percent, for example. And 25 percent of the $830 billion rise in the aggregate income of all families—two-thirds of which reflected an increase in the number of families—went to the top 1 percent.

Most conservatives, including Mr. Boskin [President Bush's economic adviser], are not happy with the budget office's figures even after they have been adjusted to accommodate some of their criticisms.

Arguing that the office's data base is flawed, they say that the figures exaggerate the income gains of the rich by including, for example, capital gains; understate the income of everyone else by underestimating incomes in the bottom quintiles; and lump together the Carter and Reagan years by using 1977 or 1979 as a base year.

Conservatives' Arguments "The numbers show that the worst of inequality seems to have built up between 1977 and 1981," said Lawrence A. Kudlow, chief economist at Bear Stearns and a former budget official in the Reagan Administration.

"While there has been some increase in inequality in the last two decades, it is far less than some people allege and its causes—primarily demographic and labor market shifts—have little to do with economic policy," Mr. Boskin said.

"Krugman's 70 percent calculation is not the answer to meaningful questions you'd want to ask," he added. Besides, Republicans say, measuring income shares in a mobile society is as meaningless as measuring which bubbles are at the top of the blender at a given moment in time.

"The whole concept of a static layered society is false except for the underclass," said George Gilder, author of "The Spirit of Enterprise."

Liberals, including Mr. Krugman, see things differently. They argue that capital gains do not distort the overall income data nearly as much as conservatives have claimed, largely because the fastest-growing component of the income at the very top was salaries.

They also respond that measuring the growth of inequality from 1982, the bottom of the worst postwar recession, as Republicans wish to do, swamps any trend in the data. Even so, they point out, the rich even got richer during the expansionary portion of the business cycle—a time when the poor generally increase their share of total income.

And they maintain that mobility was just as great in 1977 as in 1989, so the fact that people can move up and down the economic ladder does nothing to offset the trend toward greater inequality....

The fact is that even before Mr. Krugman rolled his grenade under the tent, the Republicans had recognized inequality as a potential political bombshell and had attempted to diffuse it. Two out of nine chapters in this year's Economic Report of the President, for example, tackled the touchy topic.

Though the report acknowledges

Two Views of Changes in Family Income

How total family income was divided among categories of families in 1977 and 1989, and each group's share of the overall gain in income over the same span of years. The first set of figures is based on the actual income of families. The second set is adjusted for the shrinking size of average families during the period.

Income category	Unadjusted Data			Adjusted for Family Size		
	Share of total income		Share of the average gain in income between '77 and '89*	Share of total income		Share of the average gain in income between '77 and '89*
	1977	1989		1977	1989	
Highest 20 percent:						
Next 4 percent	11	12	25	12	13	19
Top 1 percent	7 %	12 %	70 %	8 %	13 %	44 %
Next 5 percent	10	10	10	10	10	8
Next 10 percent	16	15	11	16	15	11
Second-highest 20 percent	23	22	8	22	21	15
Middle 20 percent	16	15	2	15	15	11
Second-lowest 20 percent	12	10	–7	11	10	3
Lowest 20 percent	6	4	–11	6	4	–7
No income or negative income			–8			–4

* Amount of income gained by families in each category as a percentage of the average gain in income for all families. Negative figures mean that income of families in that category declined an amount equivalent to that percentage of the net gain. All the positive and negative figures total 100 percent of the net gain.

Source: Congressional Budget Office

that the well-off gained more than anyone else, that poverty was higher in 1989 than in 1979 and that the income prospects of families headed by younger and less educated workers were dismal, its main emphasis is on overall growth, rather than on how much more some benefitted than others.

"It's much more important for economic policy to promote growth in family incomes than to redistribute it," Mr. Boskin said.

But some conservatives are fuming because of what they see as the White House's wimpishness on this issue. "The White House is terribly ill suited to take this issue on," said a Republican aide who spoke on the condition that he not be named. "Who's going to fight the fight over fairness? Nicholas Brady? Robert Mossbacher? George Bush? Dan Quayle? There's no one there who comes from the middle class."

Change in Image of the Richest And some Republicans are upset by the notion that some folks at the top got there not by hard work, entrepreneurship or even luck, but by pure thievery, often at the expense of middle-class consumers or taxpayers.

"Voters are less happy with the people at the top," said Kevin P. Phillips, the political commentator and author of "The Politics of Rich and Poor." "By the end of the 1980s, Horatio Alger got replaced by Charles Keating, Michael Milken and Leona Helmsley." ...

"If everybody had done better—even if Donald Trump had gotten three times wealthier—we wouldn't be worrying about inequality," said Richard B. Freeman, an economist at Harvard University.

—Sylvia Nasar, "However You Slice the Data the Richest Did Get Richer," May 11, 1992.
Copyright ©1992 by The New York Times Company. Reprinted with permission.

Q U E S T I O N S

1. In a diagram relating the cumulative percentage of households to the cumulative percentage of total income received, plot the unadjusted family income distribution data points for 1977 and 1989 at each quintile. Add a 45-degree line and draw the Lorenz curves for each year. How do you know from the diagram that inequality increased?

2. Conservatives claimed that the data on the distribution of family income exaggerated the worsening of inequality between families. Explain how misrepresentations could have occurred due to

   a) the exclusion of income taxes.

   b) family mobility within the income distribution.

   c) differential changes in the size of families across the income distribution.

   d) taking 1977 as the base year.

3. Various explanations of the increase in inequality were proposed. Explain why income inequality might have increased due to

   a) labor market shifts.

b) a younger age distribution.

c) increasing benefits of education.

d) the contractionary phase of the business cycle.

e) economic policies.

4. Why did high-income families receive such a large share of total income? Explain in terms of

a) assortative mating.

b) savings.

c) luck.

5. The President's advisor, Mr. Boskin, said that it was more important for economic policy to promote growth in family incomes than to redistribute them.

a) To which theory of justice might he have subscribed? Explain your response.

b) As a practical matter, why was inequality necessary for the functioning of a market economy?

c) Why was it important that family incomes grew?

GOVERNMENT INTERVENTION	44. Licensed to Pollute

When unregulated markets fail to achieve allocative efficiency, there is market failure. A different allocation of resources would increase total production and economic welfare.

One cause of market failure is a public good, where one person's consumption does not reduce the amount available for others and no one can be excluded from consuming the good. In this case, there is an incentive for consumers to be free riders. A private producer would produce less than the allocatively efficient amount.

A second cause of market failure is where private producers impose costs on society which do not figure in the firms' costs. The existence of external costs implies overproduction.

In both cases the government can improve allocative efficiency by intervening in the economy, providing public goods itself, and taxing firms so they internalize external costs. A clean environment is an example of a public good that is suffering from the externalities of many producers. The accompanying article discusses the novel approach to reducing externalities of selling licenses to pollute.

After studying your text, reading the article, and answering the questions, you should be able to:

◆ ◆ Define public goods

◆ ◆ Explain why free ridership might occur

◆ ◆ Explain the circumstances under which the government is able to provide public goods

◆ ◆ Distinguish between internal and external costs and private and social costs

◆ ◆ Explain why too many resources are allocated to firms imposing external costs on society

◆ ◆ Explain how the government can improve allocative efficiency and thereby reduce pollution through taxes on producers in the form of pollution credits

Preview

◆ Conventional regulation of pollution relied on command and control.

◆ Under a new plan, companies will be able to buy or trade pollution credits to the extent they wish.

◆ Companies that find it cheap to reduce pollution will do that and sell the pollution credits to companies facing greater costs of pollution control.

◆ Over time the amount of pollution allowed by the credits in circulation will be reduced, raising the price of credits, and increasing the incentive to cease polluting.

◆ While the overall amount of pollution will be controlled, there will be no control over the emissions of a particular source.

New Rules Harness Power of Free Markets to Curb Air Pollution

TORRANCE, Calif.—In this tidy community of bungalows and palm trees, where even lawn mowers and gas pumps are strictly regulated to fight pollution, Mobil Oil Corp. has just gained the right to spew an additional 900 pounds of noxious gas vapors every day.

So why aren't environmental activists storming the gates of the refinery?

Actually, Mobil is helping usher in a new era in environmental protection. For about $3 million, Mobil's refinery here recently acquired pollution "credits" from the nearby city of South Gate, Calif. South Gate had acquired the credits from General Motors Corp., which closed a plant there in 1985 and sold the city the property. The Torrance refinery will be emitting far less additional pollution than did General Motors.

Mobil bought the pollution rights under a rudimentary version of market-based environmental regulation. The program has been around since the 1970s, but its rules are so cumbersome that pollution "trades" like Mobil's are rare.

That will soon change. A growing number of regulators believe conventional "command and control" regulation—which allows each plant to pollute so much but no more—is failing to stop destruction of the environment. These authorities, encouraged by economists, want to harness the Earth's atmosphere to financial markets and let the markets rid the world of acid rain and global warming.

Using Markets or Else "The 21st century is going to be about using markets to solve social and environmental problems," says Richard L. Sandor, an economist and a director of the Chicago Board of Trade. "Otherwise, the world is going to look like it does in the movie 'Blade Runner.' We're going to be stopping on the road for oxygen tanks."

Commodities exchanges such as the Board of Trade are competing to run legally sanctioned markets that would trade rights to emit sulfur dioxide, nitrogen oxide and reactive vapors like those emitted by Mobil's holding tanks. Utilities, refineries and manufacturers would buy and sell pollution rights, which are supposed to ease the transition to increasingly stringent emission limits. And investors will be able to use the instruments to speculate on the price of eliminating smog.

Not everyone is thrilled about market-based regulation of the environment. Some environmentalists think it is immoral to buy and sell the right to pollute. Others doubt regulators have the tools to enforce market-based programs, which require pinpoint accuracy in monitoring emissions. And some polluters are skeptical that regulators accustomed to commanding and controlling can give a market the freedom it needs to function.

Market Forces Yet in Washington, California and elsewhere, proponents have won over opposition by arguing that traditional regulation gives polluters no incentive to reduce emissions lower than what is allowed. Markets, they say, will create strong competition among companies to find the cheapest and most technologically advanced ways to cut pollution.

A major catalyst for change was the 1990 U.S. Clean Air Act. Starting in 1995, the act will use a market-based program to force power plants across the country to cut emissions of sulfur dioxide, a pollutant that smells like rotten eggs and mixes with clouds to produce acid rain.

Southern California's air-quality regulator, struggling to reduce pollution that regularly violates federal health standards, is now developing markets in each of the three pollutants most responsible for smog. "Previous emission-trading programs, including the sulfur-dioxide program, are like playing checkers," says Joseph Goffman, senior attorney at the Environmental Defense Fund in Washington, who helped write the Clean Air Act. "What they're doing in California is more like elevating it to chess."…

The idea of turning pollutants into a marketable commodity isn't new. Early this century, a British professor named A.C. Pigou argued that a market price for cleaning air and water ought to be established and included among a polluter's expenses, like costs for labor and materials. It wasn't until 1975, however, that the U.S. Environmental Protection Agency created a limited pollution market by authorizing regional air-quality regulators to let companies buy and sell pollution credits.

The rules: To open a plant or add equipment, a company must offset new pollution by buying credits from a polluter reducing its output. The credits are denominated in pounds of pollution allowed per day and typically sell for $1,000 to $4,000 a pound.

A few offset trades have occurred in the Midwest, Maine, Massachusetts and New Jersey, but most—about 100 in the past 18 years—have taken place in California. The pace of such trading has picked up lately, driven by publicity about the Clean Air Act. Among the companies that traded pollution rights last year: Northrop Corp., Allied-Signal Inc., Shell Oil Co. and Mobil.

One argument in favor of emissions trading is that it encourages initiative. That was certainly the case recently at a U.S. Air Force base east of Los Angeles.

Forced to absorb the staff and equipment of a nearby base that is closing, March Air Force Base will soon double the pollution it spews from boilers, vehicle fueling stations and jet-servicing machinery. Base officers were told they would have to offset the increased pollution by buying emission credits.

March recruited pollution-credit brokers that act as middlemen in trades between polluters. Officers also scoured local newspapers and hunted for potential sellers among public documents of previous pollution-credit trades. They made cold calls to refineries and utilities.

A Bargain at $975 a Pound Eventually, March managed to buy the credits it needed from five sellers, for a total of about $1.2 million. They even found a bargain or two, including the right to emit 24 pounds of nitrogen oxide and six pounds of carbon monoxide a day for the rock-bottom price of $975 a pound—from a machinery company that got the credits by closing down a plant. "This company didn't know what it had," says Air Force Lt. Col. Bruce Knapp.

The net effect of the trades: less pollution in the air over California. For every 1.2 pounds of pollution eliminated in a shutdown, the program allows creation of only one pound of new credits....

One shortcoming of market-based regulation is that no one has yet devised a comprehensive way to apply it to the biggest polluter of all: automobiles. Another concern is that while it may result in cleaner air overall, it doesn't force a company to clean any particular plant. In fact, in some cases, it is possible for a plant to buy the right to pollute more than ever.

—Jeffrey Taylor, "New Rules Harness Power of Free Markets to Curb Air Pollution," April 14, 1992.
Reprinted by permission of *The Wall Street Journal,* ©1992 Dow Jones & Co., Inc. All Rights Reserved Worldwide.

1. Why is a clean environment a public good? Give two reasons.

2. The objective of a clean environment receives widespread support, yet many U.S. companies are not willing to pay their share of the cost by reducing their pollution levels. Why do they have an incentive to be free riders?

3. The deterioration in the environment is partly caused by U.S. producers, for whom the costs are external.

   a) How are companies polluting the environment? Pick three examples from the article.

   b) Why are these social costs rather than private costs?

4. Draw a supply and demand diagram for one of the industries identified in question 3a. Label the equilibrium price and output.

   a) Which curve represents marginal private benefit? Explain your answer.

   b) Which curve represents marginal private cost? Explain your answer.

c) On the diagram, draw a marginal social cost curve that includes the external costs of pollution. Show the per-unit value of the externalities at the private equilibrium output level.

d) Mark the equilibrium that is optimal from the point of view of the United States. How does it differ from the private equilibrium? Why?

e) Externalities imply allocative inefficiency. Shade in the deadweight loss. Why is it a misallocation of resources to produce more than the social equilibrium quantity? Refer to the marginal social cost curve and the marginal private benefit curve.

5. Under the new policy, pollution credits allowing certain levels of pollution can be purchased as an alternative to spending money on methods to cease polluting the environment.

a) Assuming that the cost of eliminating pollution is prohibitive, what should the industry's pollution credits cost per unit of output to eliminate the welfare loss? Illustrate in your diagram above.

b) Draw another price-output diagram showing the marginal private benefit and cost curves and the marginal social cost curve including the cost of pollution. Show the initial private equilibrium. Suppose that the cost of the pollution credits exceeds the cost to the industry of eliminating the pollution. Show what would happen to the industry's marginal private cost curve if it decided to eliminate the pollution. Also show the new marginal social cost curve. What has happened to the deadweight loss?

c) What will happen as the price of pollution credits is raised, everything else being equal?

Unregulated markets may be allocatively inefficient where the product is a public good or where there are external benefits. A product is a public good when one person's consumption does not reduce the amount available for others, and when no one can be excluded from consuming the good. In these circumstances, consumers have an incentive to be free riders with the result that there is underproduction from society's view. External benefits arise when society realizes benefits that do not accrue to the consumer. Again, private producers provide less than socially optimal levels of output or service. Public provision and subsidies can remedy these respective problems. Medical research is a good example of a public good and the role of external benefits.

After studying your text, reading the article, and answering the questions, you should be able to:

◆ ◆ Define public goods

◆ ◆ Explain why free ridership might occur

◆ ◆ Explain the circumstances under which the government is able to provide public goods

◆ ◆ Distinguish between internal and external benefits and private and social benefits

◆ ◆ Explain why too few resources are allocated to firms where some benefits of consumption accrue to society at large

◆ ◆ Explain how the government can improve allocative efficiency through unit subsidies

Preview

◆ Sponsors of medical research raise funds from private citizens, but most money comes from the government.

◆ There is debate over whether the government spends too much or too little on AIDS research.

◆ Some say that AIDS spending is too high, but most of the money goes for treatment under entitlement programs.

◆ Although the prospective loss in human potential due to AIDS is greater than that caused by cancer, cancer receives much more government research funding.

◆ The slow increase in AIDS research spending means that scientifically justified research cannot be carried out.

Adequacy of Spending on AIDS Is an Issue Not Easily Resolved

Madonna was there in rhinestone-studded leather. Barry Manilow sang. Luke Perry, heartthrob of TV's "Beverly Hills 90210," spoke. Guests paid as much as $500 to attend and spent thousands more on jewelry auctioned by Christie's. The proceeds went to the American Foundation for AIDS Research, which raised $750,000 on this one December evening at the Regent Beverly Wilshire Hotel in Beverly Hills, Calif.

That money is desperately needed, says foundation board member Peter Staley, because the government "is ob- viously not spending enough" to fight AIDS.

Yet others argue that in view of the many other serious health threats, the U.S. government is in fact spending enough on AIDS—or even too much. "We're spending far more per death on AIDS than we are on these other kill- ers" such as cancer and heart disease, protests Rep. William Dannemeyer, a California Republican.

Such divergent views reflect a grow- ing debate over spending on the dread disease. Yet even as the issue becomes more politicized, there remains wide- spread confusion about how much truly is being spent and in what way.

Budget Proposals There's no ques- tion that federal AIDS spending has gone up tremendously in recent years. President Bush's proposed fiscal 1993 budget calls for authorized spending of $4.9 billion, up from $4.4 billion in the year ending Sept. 30. The budget boasts of a 118% increase in AIDS spending authority since Mr. Bush took office in 1989. In research, the government now spends more on AIDS than on any other disease except cancer.

But the Bush budget exemplifies the AIDS-expenditures confusion. Docu- ments and interviews with federal offi-

Federal Health Efforts

	R&D Funding ($ millions)	Deaths in 1992	Years Lost in 1992
Cancer	$1,984	522,450	1,870,000
HIV/AIDS	1,164	51,000	1,546,000
Heart disease	729	712,254	1,286,000
Alzheimer's disease	282	100,000	N.A.
Diabetes	279	50,468	168,000
Injuries	162	95,085	2,212,000
Stroke	94	142,524	234,000

Notes: R&D funding data represent spending authorized for fiscal year 1992. Deaths and years lost in 1992 are for calendar year; years lost is the estimated years of potential life lost before age 65.

Sources: Public Health Service, Centers for Disease Control, and Alzheimer's Association.

cials show that much of what the administration calls AIDS spending doesn't reflect investment in research, treatment or prevention but rather obligations under entitlement programs; such spending isn't included in government calculations of spending for other diseases, such as cancer....

Apart from treatment, the largest spending category is research. The administration proposes to authorize spending of $1.2 billion, which eclipses that for all other diseases except cancer, at $2 billion. The administration would authorize spending of $772 million on heart disease, $100 million on stroke and $292 million on diabetes next fiscal year, according to the Department of Health and Human Services. More than 712,000 Americans will die of heart disease in calendar 1992, about 522,000 of cancer and 168,000 of diabetes, the government projects. About 51,000 will die of AIDS.

But overall cancer and heart disease rates are level, and declining in some categories, while AIDS is on the rise. For years, the Centers for Disease Control has been estimating that at least a million Americans are infected with HIV. As of January, 209,693 actual AIDS cases had been reported to the disease centers; by the end of 1993, CDC officials estimate, AIDS cases in the U.S. could double, to between 390,000 and 480,000. CDC officials believe that, because of underreporting by doctors, the actual totals are probably 15% to 20% higher. More Americans are expected to die of AIDS this year and in the next two years than in the past 10 combined. And the CDC has proposed expanding the definition of AIDS; if that happens, 160,000 additional HIV-infected people with certain symptoms will be added to the total.

Though the rate of new infections seems to be slowing among homosexual men, it is increasing among heterosexuals, both male and female. Still, in the U.S. the number of AIDS patients who have contracted the disease from a heterosexual partner who doesn't use intravenous drugs is still relatively small— just under 3% of total cases, according to the CDC.

The Public Health Service calculates that by 1993, AIDS will surpass all other diseases in causing a loss of human potential. "It strikes people at a younger age than heart disease and cancer, and the numbers keep growing with AIDS while others remain fairly stable," says a Public Health Service spokesman.

The scientific mobilization to combat AIDS, at least in recent years, has been the subject of praise. Fitzhugh Mullan, the author of "Plagues and Politics: The Story of the U.S. Public Health Service," says, "... the scientific apparatus of the government— particularly NIH [the National Institutes of Health] and the CDC, has been extraordinary."

With federal research assistance, nine drugs have been approved for treatment of AIDS and AIDS-related conditions since the epidemic began about 1981, though no cure has been found. The Food and Drug Administration, under pressure from AIDS activists among others, has put AIDS drugs on a fast-track approval process.

But the rise in AIDS research spending has slowed. For next year, Mr. Bush is asking for a 4% increase in funds for AIDS research, to $1.24 billion—barely above the 3.3% inflation rate projected by his Council of Economic Advisers.

Anthony Fauci, the director at NIH's National Institute of Allergy and Infectious Disease, said under questioning at a recent House hearing that the proposed spending level would lead to a reduction in some NIH research teams and programs and "certainly will slow down" work toward a cure. "I think that we will be able to accomplish a lot," he said, while adding: "We will not be able to do everything that I think would be scientifically justified."

—Hilary Stout, "Adequacy of Spending on AIDS Is an Issue Not Easily Resolved," April 22, 1992.
Reprinted by permission of *The Wall Street Journal*, ©1992 Dow Jones & Co., Inc. All Rights Reserved Worldwide.

QUESTIONS

1. The amount of medical knowledge is determined by the market for medical research.

    a) What private benefits are gained from medical research?

    b) In a price-quantity diagram of the market for medical research, draw a demand curve representing the marginal private benefit of medical research, and a supply curve representing the marginal private cost of medical research.

    c) Why is medical knowledge a public good? Give two reasons.

    d) Why would it be difficult, if not impossible, to have a private market for medical research where members of society pay research establishments to produce medical knowledge?

2. In practice, most medical research is funded by the government.

    a) What are the external benefits of medical research?

b) In your diagram above draw a curve representing the marginal social benefit of medical research. If there are no external costs, which is the marginal social cost curve?

c) Why does the marginal social benefit curve have the slope you have drawn?

d) Why does the marginal social cost curve have the slope you have drawn?

e) Mark society's equilibrium price and quantity of medical research. How does it differ from the private equilibrium? Show the per-unit value of the externalities at the private equilibrium quantity of medical research.

f) Externalities imply allocative inefficiency. Shade in the deadweight loss. Why is it a misallocation of resources to have less medical research than the social equilibrium quantity? Refer to the marginal social benefit curve and the marginal social cost curve.

g) How large a subsidy per unit of medical research would be needed to eliminate the deadweight loss? How would it lead to a social equilibrium?

h) Is enough money being allocated to medical research by the government to create a social equilibrium? Is enough being spent on AIDS research? Justify your answer with information from the article.

| | GOVERNMENT INTERVENTION | **46. Trimming Trucking Trusts** |

Antitrust laws regulate and prohibit certain types of noncompetitive behavior which would otherwise cause markets to fail and allocative inefficiency to arise. The demand for regulation depends on the impact on the consumer's or producer's surplus and the cost of political action. The supply of regulation reflects the size of the added surplus and the associated benefits for politicians and bureaucrats.

According to public interest theory, equilibrium in regulation occurs when allocative efficiency is achieved. Capture theory states that equilibrium occurs when regulations maximize producer surplus. This tends to occur when interest groups are easily identified and have low organization costs, and when the high costs of the decision on regulation are spread thinly over voters.

Allocative inefficiency and sometimes the capture of regulators has led to deregulation in many industries such as interstate trucking. The accompanying article considers the arguments for deregulating *intra*state trucking.

After studying your text, reading the article, and answering the questions, you should be able to:

◆ ◆ Explain the demand for and supply of regulation

◆ ◆ Explain the equilibrium level of regulation in terms of public interest and capture theories

◆ ◆ Predict the impact of regulation on prices, output, and social welfare

◆ ◆ State recent trends in antitrust enforcement

Preview

◆ Some members of Congress attempted to extend the deregulation of interstate trucking to intrastate trucking.

◆ Regulators variously controlled carriers, routes, prices, and the type of freight that could be transported.

◆ Regulation increased the cost of shipping and bloated profits.

◆ Producers wasted resources through shipping goods for in-state customers across state lines to take advantage of lower interstate trucking prices.

◆ Opposition came from the Teamsters union, truckers, state regulators, and certain liberal politicians.

Bust States' Trucking Trusts

Congress voted last year to spend tens of billions of tax dollars to rebuild America's highways. This year, without spending another dime, it can save people who depend on these highways tens of billions of dollars simply by lifting archaic state barriers to competition in the trucking market.

A bill sponsored by Rep. Ron Packard (R., Calif.) would extend the landmark Motor Carrier Act of 1980, which substantially deregulated interstate trucking, to the states themselves. By busting government-sanctioned cartels that drive up the cost of nearly every product shipped in America, the measure could net consumers and businesses savings of as much as $8 billion a year.

Rep. Packard's bill faces fierce opposition from the usual suspects: the Teamsters union and truckers, who stand to lose protected markets; state regulators who resent federal intrusion;

and liberal Democrats who have become born-again advocates of states' rights when it suits the cause of organized labor. Supporting the bill are major shippers, the National Association of Manufacturers, competition-tested truckers, consumer groups and the White House.

High Stakes   The stakes are high. All but eight states currently impose economic regulations on trucking, ranging from controls on which firms can carry what products on which routes to what prices they can charge their customers. In the 20 most tightly regulated states, goods carried within the states cost about $3 billion more to deliver than products travelling a similar distance across state lines under the authority of the Interstate Commerce Commission, according to a 1990 study at the University of Pennsylvania.

Because no state's economy is an island unto itself, those excessive shipping prices exact a regressive tax on the entire nation's commerce and make

American business less competitive internationally. A study by Gellman Research Associates for Federal Express found that trucking regulation in Texas, for example, cost California between $51 million and $64 million in 1990. This broad impact makes state regulation a worthy object of congressional action.

Gellman Associates estimated the total cost of these regulations to the economy at upward of $8 billion, or about $128 on average for a family of four. That bill is much higher than the excess profits reaped by protected carriers, however. The difference is sheer waste. Regulations prompt shippers to choose less efficient modes of transportation, to site warehouses in less advantageous locations, to make longer truck hauls, to run some trucks empty on return trips, and to invest in large, private truck fleets for hauls that specialized truckers could do more cheaply.

The result, notes Transportation Secretary Andrew Card Jr., is "unnec-

Crossing the Line Costs Less

Cargo	Interstate Route	Cost	Intrastate Route	Cost
Filters	Dallas to Kansas City (495 miles)	$495.00	Dallas to Houston (245 miles)	$632.40
Paper Products	Richmond, Va., to Raleigh, N.C. (146 miles)	204.40	Richmond, Va., to Danville, Va. (146 miles)	538.74
Sugar	Sebawaing, Mich., to Toledo, Ohio (174 miles)	283.62	Sebawaing, Mich., to Monroe, Mich. (154 miles)	408.10
Tissue	Palatka, Fla., to Atlanta (354 miles)	265.00	La Grange, Ga., to Atlanta (63 miles)	228.00
Tobacco Products	Shreveport, La., to Sulphur Springs, Texas (125 miles)	450.00	Dallas to Sulphur Springs, Texas (85 miles)	714.00

Source: Americans for Safe and Competitive Trucking

essarily long shipping distances, more diesel fuel consumed, more air pollution, and more wear and tear on the highways."

Consider the case of Overnight Transportation Co., the largest carrier in Virginia. Regulators deny it the right to run trucks between the two most populated areas of the state, Northern Virginia and Tidewater, in order not to subject other carriers to the inconvenience of competition. So Overnight must service Alexandria from its terminal in Landover, Md.—an interstate route that circumvents the authority of Virginia regulators, but also forces trucks needlessly onto the Washington area's notoriously congested Beltway.

In Texas, where a mere four trucking firms control more than 70% of the common carrier market, regulation adds more than a billion dollars a year to the cost of doing business in the state. American Fire Hydrant of Beaumont, for example, says it has paid $603 to ship hydrants to Texarkana, Texas, but only $297 to deliver them to Texarkana, Ark., just over the border. The difference is a few miles by truck and a few thousand miles between regulators.

Frederick Smith, chairman of Federal Express, says his company sends packages going from Denton, Texas to Dallas—a 45-minute drive—by air via Memphis in order to escape state regulations that might put it out of business.

Many major national firms, such as Whirlpool and GE, have moved key warehouses out of state to avoid this transportation tax, even though it means hauling their goods farther to markets deep within Texas. Dallas-based Frito-Lay, for example, saves $95 per truckload by hauling corn chips from its Jackson, Miss., plant to San Antonio, rather than from its Lubbock facility 200 miles closer. Proctor & Gamble supplies Louisiana from its Dallas plant and Texas from its Alexandria, La., plant.

In the heavily regulated state of Washington, foreign steel moves from Seattle to Spokane 31% more cheaply than steel made in Seattle itself, simply because the foreign product falls under more relaxed ICC authority. The high cost of moving goods within the state has cost it business. "We looked at putting warehouses in that state, but did not because trucking rates are higher than elsewhere," says Fred Schaeffer, director of distribution for Clorox.

Defenders of regulation insist that freeing up the markets can only lead to chaos. They claim, on the one hand, that unimpeded trucking leads to destructive competition and, on the other hand, that without regulation a handful of carriers will dominate the market and raise rates at will. Both can hardly be true at the same time. States that never had regulation or have fully deregulated, such as New Jersey and Florida, somehow get along without massive disruption of their markets. And California, which largely deregulated its trucking rates in 1990, enjoyed a 10% fall in inflation-adjusted truckload shipping rates in the first year.

Advocates of regulation also warn that without guarantees of steady profits, truckers will cut corners as they cut costs, deferring maintenance and pushing drivers past their limit. That line of argument may panic the public, but it doesn't sway experts, who note that the fatal accident rate per hundred million miles has fallen 40% since 1979, despite deregulation of interstate trucking. Safety regulation, not rate regulation, is the key to preventing accidents. Paul Jovanis at the University of California-Davis, an international authority on trucking safety, says, "I have found no credible evidence of a connection between economic regulation and safety." Neither did California's Public

Utilities Commission and the California Highway Patrol when they studied the data in 1987.

What is really at stake is the threatened loss of cartel power still enjoyed by some truckers and unionized drivers. The 1980 act saved the country about $15 billion a year, according to a 1990 Brookings Institution study, but it also drove many trucking companies out of business (even as it allowed others to enter the market) and knocked some $3,800 off the wages of the average union driver.

The determined opposition of the Teamsters union to any further reform, in fact, explains much of the politics of this legislation.

Union-Backed Liberals The Reagan administration effectively put further reform of the trucking industry on hold as the price of winning the union's support. Now that the Teamsters have switched loyalties to the Democratic Party, the Bush administration is enthusiastic about completing the reforms spearheaded by Sen. Edward Kennedy and Jimmy Carter in 1980. Union-backed liberals, such as Ted Weiss of New York and Barbara Boxer of California, on the other hand, now warn that further deregulation "could harm consumers and establish an extremely bad precedent of federal interference in the legitimate affairs of the states."

In an increasingly competitive world, the U.S. can't afford to shackle its producers and tax its consumers for the benefit of a few special interests. In a year rife with phony economic nostrums, the proposed deregulation of state trucking stands out as an exceptionally sound way to start meeting the economic challenges of the 1990s.

—Jonathan Marshall, "Bust States' Trucking Trusts," April 28, 1992.
Reprinted by permission of *The Wall Street Journal*, ©1992 Dow Jones & Co., Inc. All Rights Reserved Worldwide.

QUESTIONS

1. The Reagan and Bush administrations shied away from deregulating the intrastate trucking industry.

   a) Does the author explain the persistence of regulation within states in terms of the public interest or capture theories of regulation? Explain the basis for your view.

   b) Why might voters have exhibited a low demand for deregulation?

   c) Why might politicians have decided not to supply voters with deregulation?

   d) Why might unions and trucking companies have exhibited a low demand for deregulation?

   e) Why might unions and intrastate trucking companies have been able to mount considerable opposition to any attempt at deregulation?

   f) Why might politicians have been willing to acquiesce?

2. The government's deregulation of interstate trucking was very aggressive (in contrast to its stance on intrastate trucking).

   a) Why might the demand for deregulation of interstate trucking have been relatively great?

b) Why might the supply of deregulation have been relatively high?

3. As the author suggests, where states regulate intrastate trucking, trucking firms are in effect members of a cartel and act as a monopolist, maximizing joint profits.

a) In a diagram, draw the demand, marginal revenue, and marginal cost curves for a cartel that is fixing prices so as to maximize profits in an otherwise competitive industry.

b) Show how deregulation would alter the equilibrium of the industry.

c) Would allocative efficiency improve? Give the basis for your answer, and illustrate on your diagram.

d) The author states that consumer welfare would improve through breaking up intrastate trucking cartels. Explain why this would follow and illustrate on your diagram.

GOVERNMENT
INTERVENTION

47.
Monoploy
in Utilities:
It's Natural

Natural monopoly is the term used to describe an industry in which one firm can produce for all consumers at a lower price than can two or more firms. Hence the average total cost curve is downward-sloping, reflecting economies of scale. Like any other monopoly, a natural monopoly is capable of earning profits in the short and long runs given a favorable relationship between the demand and average cost curves. Therefore regulation occurs, usually based on target rates of return on capital.

According to public interest theory, regulation achieves allocative efficiency through pricing at marginal cost. However, losses arise. If losses are offset by taxes, allocative inefficiency may be generated in other, labor or product, markets where the tax is levied. Average-cost pricing allows regulated companies to break even and may maximize allocative efficiency subject to the need to cover costs. Capture theory predicts that regulated firms maximize monopoly profits through misleading the regulatory body about cost levels. The focus of the accompanying article is the reaction of regulatory bodies to proposals from utilities to raise rates in response to health-care cost increases.

After studying your text, reading the article, and answering the questions, you should be able to:

◆◆ Define natural monopoly

◆◆ Explain the conditions under which it arises

◆◆ State the benefits of natural monopoly

◆◆ Explain the implications of regulation for prices, service levels, profits, and allocative efficiency

◆◆ State the difficulties of regulating natural monopoly

◆◆ Explain the negative side effects of regulation

Preview

◆ Prompted by a new accounting rule, public utility companies are requesting rate increases to cover the costs of medical benefits to future retirees.

◆ Medical costs for current retirees are already included.

◆ Consumer groups oppose the increases because utility employees receive relatively generous benefits.

◆ This has been facilitated by the ease with which the costs can be passed on to the consumer.

◆ Also, consumer advocates point out that the obligations are unpredictable, and the government may eventually assume more responsibility for health care.

◆ Some states have approved rate increases to cover all or part of the cost increases, while others are studying the issue.

Utilities Want Rates to Cover Health Costs

Public utility companies across the country are applying for substantial rate increases to finance the expensive medical benefits they have promised their current and future retirees. The increases, if granted universally, would add more than $4 billion each year to the nation's electric, gas and telephone bills, according to Government economists.

The requested increases have drawn strong opposition from state officials and consumer groups, in part because utility employees and retirees typically receive far more generous medical benefits than most Americans.

The utilities contend that since active employees are earning their retirement benefits now, part of the cost should be added to current rates. Medical costs for current retirees are already included in the rates.

Southern New England Telephone and Public Service Electric and Gas of New Jersey are among the several major utilities that have requested these increases, and Consolidated Edison of New York plans to.

Consumer advocates are urging state regulators to reject such requests. They accuse the utilities of opportunism, arguing that ratepayers will receive little or no advantage in paying now for largely unpredictable obligations that are decades away.

"Obviously, 20 years from now there will be different ratepayers," said James Pretti, deputy director of the division of ratepayer advocates at the California Public Utility Commission. "It is cheaper for ratepayers to keep the money now, rather than put it up front."

Utilities' health plans have been generous in part because regulators allow the companies to pass along these costs to customers. According to a recent report by the A. Foster Higgins consulting firm, 53 percent of 65 utilities surveyed said they paid 100 percent of the medical costs for retirees and their dependents. But of the 1,189 employers of all types questioned in the same survey only 25 percent said they paid the entire bills....

Higher utility rates to cover retirees' future medical benefits would raise the cost of a broad variety of goods and services, affecting living standards and the international competitiveness of American factories.

Utility companies in at least a dozen states have applied for the increases. A few states, including Connecticut, Florida and North Carolina, have approved some rate increases to cover part of these medical costs. Others, including Georgia and Hawaii, have rejected the companies' requests, with regulators saying they need more time to study the issue.

Regulators are also examining the issue in New York and in California, where seven energy and telephone companies have asked for more than $450 million in higher rates. And in New Jersey, Public Service Electric and Gas, the state's largest utility, recently requested a $50 million increase to cover future health costs of retirees.

A New Accounting Rule The utilities' actions are a response to a new reporting rule, affecting all large companies, that was adopted last year by the semi-official Financial Accounting Standards Board. Before the rule, most companies reported retirees' medical expenses on a pay-as-you-go basis.

Under the rule, each year beginning in 1993, companies must estimate and report a portion of their future medical expenses for retirees. The intention is to alert investors and corporate executives to liabilities that had been largely unnoticed.

The board did not require companies to set aside money for these future costs, but utilities are under special pressures to do so.

The Securities and Exchange Commission staff has questioned whether, in the distant future, state regulators will allow large enough rate increases to cover the potentially enormous obligations of utilities that have not put aside cash for retirees' medical expenses.

The rate requests raise important issues of fairness to current consumers and future generations. Accountants for the utilities say the promises to retirees are a current cost and should be paid now.

"People say, 'let our grandchildren pay for them,' but this is a current cost of service provided today," said Ben McKnight, a partner with Arthur Andersen & Company and chairman of the public utilities committee of the American Institute of Certified Public Accountants....

A Matter of Timing Consumer advocates on the staffs of a number of state regulatory commissions say there should be no urgency about raising rates. They say it is impossible to forecast medical costs accurately, or estimate the interest earnings of money set aside to pay for them.

They also contend that the Government will eventually assume more responsibility for health insurance, shifting the costs for future retirees to taxpayers. The General Accounting Office said recently that the retiree health obligations of all private companies would be reduced by 30 percent if Congress approved a proposal by Representative Dan Rostenkowski, Democrat of Illinois, to expand Medicare, the Federal health insurance program for the elderly.

The struggle over financing retiree costs has intensified pressures to cut back on health benefits and slow the rise in health costs, which have been growing at more than twice the general rate of inflation.

QUESTIONS

1. What causes natural monopoly to arise in

    a) gas and electricity supply?

    b) telephone service?

2. a) Draw a price-output diagram of a utility prior to the Financial Accounting Standards Board (FASB) reporting rule concerning retirees' medical expenses. Include a constant marginal cost curve, a falling average total cost curve (that includes a fair rate of return), and the demand and marginal revenue curves.

    b) Assume that the regulatory body allows the utility to price at average total cost so that it earns a fair rate of return. Show the price and service levels that existed before the new rule.

    c) Show the consumer surplus on your diagram.

    d) Illustrate the impact of the FASB regulations on costs. Also show the new price and service levels that were created when the average-cost pricing rule was applied.

    e) What was the implication for the size of the consumer surplus? Illustrate on your diagram.

    f) If the utility exaggerated the health-care costs beyond the level in 2d so as to maximize its profits, what would have been the price and service levels and the amount of additional profit earned? Illustrate on your diagram.

3. a) What evidence is there in the article of regulators being captured by utilities?

b) What evidence is there of regulation being in the public interest?

4. Compared to most employers elsewhere in the economy, utilities are unusual in the comprehensiveness of their health benefits and in their continued willingness to cover increases in their costs.

a) Draw a pair of diagrams showing the equilibrium price and output of a perfectly competitive industry and the price and output of a representative firm that is breaking even.

b) What would be the effect of an increase in the cost of health benefits on the equilibrium price and output of the industry and the firm, and on the profits of the firm? Illustrate on your diagram.

c) What would happen in the long run if the costs were not reduced?

d) In contrast, why do utilities have little incentive to reduce their health benefits or have their employees contribute toward the cost?

5. Would it be preferable to break up natural monopolies? Why?

SECTION 3

MACROECONOMICS

Introduction to Macroeconomic Variables

The newspapers carry the stories—inflation, recession, recovery, unemployment, budget deficits, trade deficits, federal debt, interest rates, and on and on. When such problems arise, the government is called upon to initiate remedial policies. Proposed policies are often shrouded in political debate as to the most effective and efficient approach to take. The distributional consequences of these policies are also the focus of political debate. These problems and policy issues are the subject matter of macroeconomics, which consists of models of our economic system in aggregate. This article provides an overview of the economic problems facing the American economy in the 1990s.

After studying your text, reading the article, and answering the questions, you should be able to:

◆◆ State the economic problems facing the economy

◆◆ Define the term "business cycle" and explain its consequences for the economy

◆◆ Define inflation and discuss the effects of inflation

◆◆ Define unemployment and discuss the costs and benefits of unemployment

◆◆ Define gross domestic product and debate the advantages and disadvantages of its growth

◆◆ Define the budget deficit and the federal debt

◆◆ Define the trade deficit

Preview

◆ In the 1990s, the American economy is facing a number of challenges.

◆ The most pressing problem in 1992 was to recover from the recession.

◆ Longer-term problems include the need to reduce business and consumer debt, and government and trade deficits.

◆ The low levels of savings and investment will make it difficult to achieve even the meager growth of GDP of the 1980s.

◆ Most economists believe that although consumer confidence in the economy has weakened, the economy will recover.

From Fast Living to Slow Growth

The American economy, still burdened by the excesses of the 1980s, is struggling to regain its footing, a challenge that it will confront through 1992 and perhaps much of the decade.

With a burgeoning array of problems masked by economic growth statistics during the Reagan years, America was surprised when the problems came together at the start of the new decade to throw the country into recession and raise new questions about the nation's future.

Some analysts believe that the unmasking itself is responsible for the sour, uneasy mood of many households and businesses, and therefore also partly responsible for the fact that the economy today is as "flat as a pancake," as one government economist put it last week.

That flatness is widely expected to continue only for a few more months, with growth resuming this spring as consumers and businesses make more progress in digging themselves out from under a mountain of debt. The lowest interest rates in years and a bull market in stocks have paved the way for almost everyone to reduce the cost of their debts.

But no one is looking for a boom. The nation still has a badly battered financial system in which many lenders are unable or unwilling to make many loans they would have made in the past. State and local governments are cutting spending and raising taxes, providing another drag on the economy. And commercial real estate is so badly overbuilt in some parts of the country that there is an estimated 10-year supply of empty space.

By late this year, most forecasters expect the civilian unemployment rate to drop from last month's 7.1 percent rate only to 6.7 percent or so. The good news is that inflation is likely to stay in the 3.5 percent to 4 percent range even if the economic recovery does pick up as predicted.

A simple resumption of growth this year, however, is not going to be enough to get the U.S. economy out of the woods. The legacy of the 1980s is more than a matter of a recession and an incomplete recovery.

The biggest problem in the eyes of many economists is that the long expansion, which led to creation of more than 18 million jobs, came at the expense of a sharp decline in savings and an enormous increase in the total debt of governments, households and businesses.

Instead of consumer spending rising in line with incomes, purchases of new cars, medical care and other goods and services far exceeded growth of after-tax incomes in the '80s. Instead of the federal government keeping its outlays in line with revenue, it ran deficits so large that its debt soared from less than $700 billion to nearly $2.3 trillion. And businesses by the score racked up huge debt increases in connection with takeovers, real estate developments and other expansions, particularly in services such as retailing.

The rise in total debt was paralleled by an unprecedented decline in national saving. Partly as a consequence, business investment other than for replacement of worn out or obsolete plants and equipment was cut nearly in half, relative to the size of the economy.

"The 1980s were a bit of a disaster for the United States and the bill is coming due," economist Rudigar Dornbusch of the Massachusetts Institute of Technology told a large audience at the annual meeting of the American Economics Association in New Orleans a few days ago.

"Like the debts of Latin America, once the growth disappears, debts become a major burden."

On the other hand, there was a singular economic success in the past decade: A rampant inflation was curbed, albeit at the cost of a severe recession, and Federal Reserve actions to keep the flow of money into the economy at moderate levels have kept the lid on since.

But just as the sweeping tax changes of the 1980s failed to provide a magic elixir for the economy, the decline in inflation by itself has not done the trick, either.

Given the low level of savings and investment, some economists now fear that the United States will be lucky during the 1990s to match the record of the '80s when the amount of goods and services produced by each worker rose a scant 0.8 percent a year.

Dornbusch and many other experts regard that as a "poor economic performance" because the slow increase of productivity and a growing concentration of income among more highly paid employees left the real wages of average workers lower than they were 10 or 15 years ago.

Furthermore, with output per worker going up so slowly in the '80s, the major source of economic growth was a rapid increase in the size of the work force as an ever greater share of women sought jobs. U.S. gross domestic product rose an average of 2.2 percent a year only because of all those added workers.

Unfortunately, noted Dornbusch, the work force in the 1990s is projected to expand much more slowly in coming years both because the population is not increasing as rapidly and because it is unlikely that the participation of women will keep rising strongly....

Of course, with the recession and the still incomplete recovery having left the civilian unemployment rate at 7.1 percent, compared to the 5.3 percent rate achieved for most of 1989 and part of 1990, there is a pool of jobless workers. But after the eventual recovery provides work for that pool, economic growth should slow again....

"The economic problems that the United States faced today are not new, they have little to do with a minor [recession], they will not be solved by a tax cut, and they will not go away after the election," said Barry Bosworth, a senior fellow at the Brookings Institution....

The centerpiece of Bosworth's argument was a chart showing that as income gains lagged, consumers kept right on spending. Over the decade, the share of national output going for personal consumption rose from about 63 percent—a level around which it had fluctuated for two decades—to an average of 68 percent in recent years.

Sharp Drop in Savings Meanwhile, for three decades prior to the '80s, total national savings had averaged more than 8 percent of net product—a measure of national income that takes out business allowances for depreciation. In the first half of the 1980s, the figure dropped to 4.9 percent and then to 2.9 percent from 1986 to 1990.

Domestic investment did not fall as sharply as did national saving because a large inflow of money from foreign investors, who bought American stocks, bonds, companies and real estate, supplemented U.S. savings as a source of financing for investment.

Consumers were able to increase their consumption despite the lack of any rise in real average wages for several reasons. First, more consumers went

to work as the share of the population in the labor force rose. Second, the federal government failed to increase total taxes to cover large spending increases for programs such as defense and Social Security. That gave a boost to individuals' after-tax incomes while increasing the federal budget deficit. And third, consumers, like the government and many businesses, went on a borrowing spree.

At the same session in New Orleans at which Dornbusch spoke, Harvard economist Martin S. Feldstein, a former chairman of the Council of Economic Advisers, argued that one byproduct of the ballooning federal deficits of the early 1980s was a large rise in the value of the dollar and a concomitant loss of American competitiveness on world markets. The resulting rise in the U.S. trade deficit was the counterpart of the inflow of foreign capital that kept domestic investment from falling as much as did national saving.

But Feldstein said that research he and other economists have done suggests that in most industrial nations an inflow of foreign money is likely to prop up domestic investment only for a limited time. If a country's level of savings falls and stays down, then its investment will eventually follow, he said. Eventually, continued low investment "would mean a very slow growth in future productivity and in the American standard of living."

An Insecure Look Ahead To an unusual degree, the recession has caused American workers to question what the future will bring. One reason may be that an unusually large share of them suffered through one or more spells of unemployment last year, even though the unemployment rate never passed 7 percent. The number of claims filed for unemployment benefits suggest that 23 million persons lost their jobs last year, compared to 30 million in the previous

recession in 1982 when the unemployment rate hit 10.8 percent.

Since the jobless rate did not go up so much this time, most of those who lost their jobs quickly found other employment. However, the experience with being out of work, some analysts believe, took away the most solid prop under consumer confidence, a feeling of job security.

Once jobs were called into question by the recession, what was left?

"Consumers feel in their bones that they are worse off than 10 years ago," said Dornbusch. "They don't have a lot more income, they have a lot more debt, and they are far more vulnerable. Before, they were willing to believe that everything was going to be all right as long as taxes did not increase....

"They also understand that massive bank failures are not symptoms of prosperity but more nearly the collapse of a house of cards, and above all, an indication that trust in government's wisdom and prudence is altogether misplaced," he continued.

However, the loss of confidence has been overdone, Dornbusch added, though that might not turn out to be a bad thing, depending on how government responds.

"The country is not bankrupt, there will not be another 1930s and the average American will not be paying rent to a Japanese landlord," Dornbusch said. "But a deflation of optimism is not inappropriate if it helps improve policies. Of course, if it is the backdrop for more 'dope'— middle-class tax cuts for instant gratification in an election year or housing-and-health gimmicks—then the country is likely to hop from one crisis to the next, with little prosperity in between."

—John M. Berry, "From Fast Living to Slow Growth," *The Washington Post*, January 12, 1992.

QUESTIONS

1. a) Define the term "business cycle."

   b) What happens to unemployment and aggregate income when the economy is in a recession?

   c) What happens to unemployment and aggregate income when the economy is in the recovery phase of the business cycle?

   d) What happens to stock prices during the economic cycle?

2. The article mentions that the economic success of the 1980s was the curbing of rampant inflation.

   a) Define inflation.

   b) How does inflation tend to change through the economic cycle?

   c) Who gains and who loses from inflation?

   d) Why is it more costly to hold currency when inflation is increasing rapidly?

3. a) Define unemployment.

   b) Define the natural rate of unemployment.

c) Define frictional unemployment.

d) What are the costs and benefits of unemployment?

4. a) Define gross domestic product (GDP).

b) What is real GDP?

c) What are the advantages and disadvantages of a high rate of growth of GDP?

5. a) Define the federal government deficit.

b) Distinguish between the federal debt and the federal deficit.

c) Define the trade deficit.

6. Is the economy in better shape today than it was when the article was written? Refer to inflation, unemployment, the business cycle, GDP growth, the federal deficit, and the trade deficit.

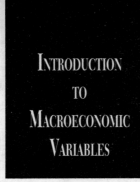

49.
The Job of Counting the Jobless

Once a month, the Bureau of Labor Statistics releases its monthly estimate of unemployment in the United States. This estimate of the unemployment rate is then widely discussed and analyzed. Policymakers may change economic policy as a result. There is often much activity on financial markets in reaction to the unemployment rate.

In spite of all the media coverage that the unemployment rate receives, there is much misconception by the public as to what the unemployment rate shows and what interpretation should be attached to changes in the rate. This article concerns the unemployment rate in 1992.

After studying your text, reading the article, and answering the questions, you should be able to:

◆ ◆ Define and discuss the advantages and disadvantages of the government's statistical definition of the labor force, unemployment, and employment

◆ ◆ Describe changes in the labor force, employment, and unemployment

◆ ◆ Discuss the reasons for changes in the geographical and demographical distribution of unemployment

Preview

◆ The U.S. unemployment rate for January 1992 was 7.1 percent, unchanged from its December value.

◆ The unemployment rate for the Washington, D.C. metropolitan area jumped .3 percentage points to 4.9 percent in December.

◆ Both the national and Washington area unemployment figures were evidence of continued recession.

◆ There was a substantial increase in the number of workers who wanted full-time jobs but could only find part-time work.

◆ The Labor Department survey of businesses found that 91,000 jobs were lost, primarily in manufacturing and retail trade.

U.S. Jobless Rate Stays at 7.1 Pct.

The nation's economic recession apparently continued last month as employers cut payrolls and the unemployment rate remained frozen at a five-year high, government officials reported yesterday.

While the U.S. unemployment rate stayed at 7.1 percent, other figures showed the local jobless rate reaching its highest level in nine years, and analysts predicted the Federal Reserve would come under renewed pressure to cut interest rates once more in hopes of kindling a recovery.

The Washington area unemployment rate jumped 0.3 percentage points to 4.9 percent in December, the highest level of the current economic slump. In 1991, the number of jobs in the region fell 2.1 percent, according to yesterday's figures.

"It looks to me like the recession is deepening," said Richard Groner, chief of labor market information for the D.C. Department of Employment Services, which compiles the area figures....

Nationally, the monthly survey of American households found 389,000 more people at work in January than in December, but many of the new jobs were apparently only part time, the Labor Department reported. The size of the labor force grew more than the number of new jobs, however, so that the total number of jobless rose 38,000 to 8,929,000.

The separate Labor Department survey of businesses found the number of payroll jobs fell 91,000, with manufacturing and retail trade accounting for many of the jobs lost. The Labor Department survey also found that the length of the average workweek fell by two-tenths of an hour, to 34.3 hours....

"The recession is still with us," said Bruce Steinberg, an economist at Merrill Lynch & Co. "A lot of people thought we were bottoming out ... but this data fits with the idea the economy is still shrinking."...

Recession Job Losses

A Look at the Labor Force

Number of People in Millions

	May 1990	Jan. 1992	Change
Civilian labor force	124.96	126.05	+1.09
Employed	118.37	117.12	−1.25
Unemployed	6.59	8.93	+2.34
Working part time for economic reasons	4.88	6.72	+1.84
No longer looking for work*	0.86	1.09	+0.23
Non-farm payroll employment	110.30	108.76	−1.54

* Figures are for 2nd quarter 1990 and 4th quarter 1991 and show individuals who are not looking for work because they believe no job is available. They are not included in unemployment figures.

Source: Labor Department

The decline in both the number of payroll jobs and hours worked surprised many analysts, some of whom had predicted a modest increase. Some analysts said the report put new pressure on the Federal Reserve to cut short-term interest rates soon.

On Capitol Hill, Senate Finance Committee Chairman Lloyd Bentsen (D-Tex.) said the figures "show an economy skating on thin ice" that raised the odds of a renewed recession this year to 50-50....

Asked at a House Budget Committee hearing yesterday whether he thinks the Labor Department report points to a renewed downturn, Michael J. Boskin, chairman of the president's Council of Economic Advisers, replied, "No, I don't."

Predicting the economy would resume growing this spring, Boskin said, "It will take some time as we head further into the year before these indicators start to pick up and to improve."...

The Maryland unemployment rate also rose sharply in December, the state Department of Economic and Employment Development said yesterday. It reached 6.8 percent, up from 6.1 percent in November. State officials blamed the increase on poor Christmas hiring.

Virginia's unemployment rate, reported earlier in the week, fell to 5.5 percent from 5.7 percent in November. The District's unemployment rate, which was reported as part of the local figures yesterday, rose to 8.4 percent from 8.0 percent.

William G. Barron Jr., deputy commissioner of the federal Bureau of Labor Statistics, said the good news of the January increase in unemployment, the first substantial increase since September, was mitigated by a sharp increase in the number of workers who wanted full-time jobs but could only find part-time work.

"At 6.7 million, their number was at its highest level in this recession," Barron told the congressional Joint Economic Committee yesterday.

Barron also noted some other bleak aspects of the Labor Department's report, including a percentage point increase in the jobless rate for blacks to 13.4 percent, the highest rate during this slump.

The unemployment rate for whites last month was 6.2 percent, down from 6.3 percent in December. The rate for persons of Hispanic origin rose from 9.7 percent to 11.3 percent, the Labor Department said.

The 91,000 drop in the number of payroll jobs shown by the survey of businesses last month, Barron said, "brought the total decline since last October to over 300,000. These cutbacks negated all of the increase that had occurred over the prior six months of 1991."

—Anne Swardson and John M. Berry, "U.S. Jobless Rate Stays at 7.1 Pct.," *The Washington Post*, February 8, 1992.

QUESTIONS

1. How is the labor force defined?

2. a) How does the household survey define unemployment?

   b) In what ways does the measured unemployment rate understate "true" unemployment?

   c) Why does the household survey exclude some unemployed people?

   d) In what ways does the unemployment rate exaggerate "true" unemployment?

3. Some people argue that adding jobs is more important than measuring the number of people who might be looking for work. What kind of information does this tell you that the unemployment rate does not?

4. a) According to the household survey data, what happened to the size of the labor force, employment, and unemployment between May 1990 and January 1992? Refer to the article.

b) The monthly Labor Department survey of businesses found the number of jobs decreased by 91,000 in January 1992. This is considerably different from the increase in employment of 389,000 recorded by the household survey. Why do these two surveys provide such different numbers? What do you think really happened to the labor market in January 1992?

5. Several changes occurred in the labor market as a result of the recession. In particular, what happened to

a) the number working part-time but looking for full-time work? Explain this trend.

b) the number no longer looking for work? Explain this trend.

6. Which of the states mentioned in the article had the largest increase in their unemployment rate? Why would you expect these states to have had different unemployment rates?

7. Why might the percentage of the work force that is unemployed be different (and change differently) across demographic groups?

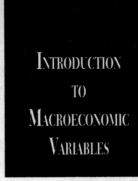

50.
The
Business
Cycle: The
Expansion
Cometh?

Economic activity, such as production or employment, does not proceed in a continuous, smooth manner. Typically, there are upturns invariably followed by downturns. The upswings and downswings in the general level of economic activity are termed business cycles. Over the long term, the increases in economic activity have been greater than decreases, so that the American economy has grown considerably.

Business cycles seem to be an inexorable part of the capitalist system. In the post–World War II period there have been eight business cycles: the average duration of the expansion phases has been a little less than five years and the average period of recession has been slightly less than one year. This article discusses the business cycle and the hope for a recovery from the recession that began in July 1990.

After studying your text, reading the article, and answering the questions, you should be able to:

◆◆ Define a business cycle and its components: contraction, trough, expansion, and peak

◆◆ Describe the postwar movements in economic activity

◆◆ Explain why there is considerable uncertainty in forecasting the start of a recovery or other phases of the cycle

Preview

◆ Good economic news seemed to be frequent in March 1992.

◆ These signs seemed to signal the end of 19 months of recession.

◆ Many economists and politicians had thought that a recovery was underway in the spring of 1991, but it fizzled.

◆ The big difference in 1992 was that the Federal Reserve was more accommodating.

◆ The lower interest rates benefitted both businesses and households, with household net worth up by 6.6 percent in 1991.

◆ Households spent their extra cash, causing employment to increase.

◆ One worry among home builders was that mortgage rates would rise and choke off the recovery.

The Recovery Is Here at Last

John P. O'Leary doesn't need government forecasts to tell him where the economy is going. Since early February, the chief executive of Tuscarora Plastics, a packaging-material maker, has seen shipments and new orders take off. That's all the data he needs. "Our business indicates that the economy is getting better," he says.

Just two weeks ago, O'Leary's assessment might have seemed like just so much wishful thinking. But then, on Mar. 12, the Commerce Dept. announced that retail sales had jumped 1.3% in February, on top of a 2.1% surge in January.

Five days later, in a St. Patrick's Day trio of reports, came more good news: Industrial production picked up by 0.6% in February—its first rise in five months. Housing starts soared by 9.6% during the month, to an annual rate of 1.3 million—the busiest pace for builders since March, 1990. And consumer prices climbed just 0.3% in February, implying a modest inflation rate of 3% annually.

On Mar. 18 came yet another piece of evidence: The Federal Reserve's survey of activity within its 12 regions was also upbeat. In their "Beige Book," the central bankers reported a "slow but widespread advance in the economy since the end of January."

Second Coming So listen up, America: Just as spring arrives, it's looking as if the economy is at last on the mend. The thaw comes after 19 months of recession and stagnation—possibly the longest postwar slump on record. The brutal retreat sent 1.5 million people to the unemployment line, put some 148,000 companies out of business, and made American consumers feel glummer than they had since 1974—on the heels of Watergate, the first oil crisis, and severe recession.

Indeed, convincing consumers that the recession has ended may be the hardest part about keeping this expansion going. After all, the promise of a rebound sounds eerily familiar. Last spring, citing increased industrial production and rising retail shopping, economists and Washington policymakers declared the recession over. But by fall, the U.S. economy was again dead in the water.

This time, economists spot one big difference: a more accommodating Federal Reserve. "The Fed has eased much more dramatically in the past year than in the year before," says Nancy R. Lazar, an economist at the International Strategy & Investment Group. Indeed, the federal funds rate—the rate banks pay to borrow from other banks—now stands at 4%. That's roughly half its level in late 1990.

The result? Consumers and businesses have cleaned up their balance sheets by replacing high-yield borrowings with cheaper debt. DRI/McGraw Hill estimates, for instance, that household net worth grew by 6.6% in 1991, after falling in 1990 for the first time since 1962. "Cash flow has been substantially enhanced by mortgage refinancings, paying down debt, and tapping into home-equity loans," observes Michael R. Paslawskyj, chief economist at CIT Group, lender to midsize companies.

New Hires All that extra cash has sent consumers back into the malls, edging into auto showrooms, and thumbing through real estate listings. Although they're not gobbling up goods and services the way they did in the '80s, there are signs of a new willingness to spend. Take Mark and Laura Greifenkamp. The couple recently bought a Saturn, even though they could have afforded a more expensive car. And they are about to close on a $225,000 house in the Chicago suburb of Western Springs. Mark Greifenkamp, a supervisor at hospital supplier Baxter International Inc., expects that after they move in "we'll spend another $5,000 in the blink of an eye."

Even the unemployment picture seems brighter—another important distinction between last spring's false start and this year's upturn. The economy slipped back into recession last fall partly because American business continued to lay off workers. That hammered personal incomes and slammed consumer spending.

Now, signs of life are sprouting in the labor market: Nonfarm employment rose by 164,000 jobs in February—although economists warn that the bulk of those new hires came in the retail sector, where work is often part-time. But looking ahead, Stuart G. Hoffman, chief economist at Pittsburgh's PNC Financial Corp., thinks that at least 100,000 new jobs will be added, on average, in each of the next few months.

Indeed, businesses, particularly small and midsize outfits, say they're getting ready to hire again. Acme Brick Co. in Fort Worth may be adding 120 workers to its payroll of 1,500. That means the company, a unit of bootmaker Justin Industries Inc., should operate its 16 plants at about 80% of capacity within the next month, up from 72% now. "I feel cautiously optimistic," says President Edward L. Stout Jr.

Times are also busier at Crown Equipment Corp. in New Bremen, Ohio. In February, the maker of electric lifttrucks called back 120 of the 400 workers it had laid off last year. And in Beaver, Pa., the engineering firm of Michael Baker Corp. plans to add 260 to 390 new employees to its work force of 2,600.

House Rule Amid all the evidence of a budding recovery, however, there lurks a spoiler: long-term interest rates. Bond traders, worried about inflation and a massive supply of Treasury debt, have bid long rates up above 8%. After adjusting for inflation, real interest rates are at about 5%—the highest level since 1988. The Fed, which has little sway over long rates, is anxious about Washington's pileup of IOUs. Fed Chairman Alan Greenspan worries that new Treasury borrowings, along with a return of corporations to the credit markets, could cause some crowding out and keep long rates higher and economic growth lower than normal.

One concern is that housing, a key component in a recovery, will take a big hit if mortgage rates climb much higher than 9%. For now, the rebound in housing is spurring a pickup in the production of related items. Appliance output jumped 4.6% in February, for instance, and furniture makers are seeing better demand. The American Furniture Manufacturers Assn. is cautiously projecting a 3.7% increase in shipments for 1992. That would be welcome relief after the industry's four-year downturn.

That's some slump. And it's the very duration of the nation's downturn that has economists convinced the upturn is really here. "There is a replacement cycle. The big-ticket items—the cars, the refrigerators—that people bought in the 1980s are getting old," says PNC Financial's Hoffman. More important, say other economists, the U.S. economy has had time to get its financial house in order. Last year was simply too early for an upturn. This spring, it looks as if the recovery has taken root for good.

QUESTIONS

1. a) Define the term "business cycle."

    b) What are the component phases of a business cycle?

    c) What phase was the economy in when the article was written? Justify your opinion.

    d) What typically happens to the economy in a recovery (or expansion) phase?

    e) Distinguish between the terms recession and depression. Was the downturn of 1990-1992 a recession or a depression? Explain your answer.

2. If the recession that started in July 1990 had ended in February 1992,

    a) how would it have compared with the average recession in terms of duration? Explain the reason for your belief.

    b) how would it have compared with the average recession in terms of intensity? Explain your answer.

    c) how long would the subsequent expansionary phase have lasted, given the average length of previous recoveries?

3. Explain the relationship between the phases of the business cycle and

    a) retail sales.

b) industrial output.

c) employment.

d) inflation.

4. a) Why are leading indicators important in predicting movements of the business cycle?

b) Why do economists literally look at hundreds of economic series to measure and estimate the business cycle?

5. In the spring of 1991, citing increased industrial production and rising retail sales, policymakers and some economists declared the recession to be over. By the fall of 1991, it was obvious that these forecasters were wrong.

a) Why did they err?

b) Why were the authors of the article confident of a recovery in 1992?

6. a) Would recessions be of much concern for you as an individual if you worked for General Motors, or if you worked for the Federal Government? Why?

b) Would recessions be of much concern if they were predictable and regular? Why?

INTRODUCTION
TO
MACROECONOMIC
VARIABLES

51.

Big

Difference?

The gross national product (GNP) measures the total value of goods and services owned by residents of the United States. It is the most widely known measure of the performance of the U.S. economy, but its days are numbered. The Commerce Department has decided to deemphasize GNP in favor of another measure: gross domestic product (GDP). GDP measures the value of goods and services produced *within* the United States. In other words, GNP records the value of production by American residents without regard to their location, while GDP only counts production within U.S. borders.

Although the difference between the two measures is relatively small, the Commerce Department has decided that GDP provides economy-watchers with a better sense of how the U.S. economy is performing. Understanding how the economy and its components are performing is a necessary step to proposing corrective policies. This article discusses the difference between the two measures and why the switch was made.

After studying your text, reading the article, and answering the questions, you should be able to:

◆ ◆ Describe the difference between GNP and GDP

◆ ◆ Discuss the relative strengths and weaknesses of both measures of aggregate economic performance

◆ ◆ Distinguish between changes in real and nominal GNP or GDP

◆ ◆ Describe other modifications to the national income and product accounts of the United States that have been introduced by the Commerce Department

Preview

◆ Commerce Department officials are advising the public to pay closer attention to GDP and less attention to GNP.

◆ The switch to GDP aligns the United States with prevailing measures in most other countries.

◆ Also, by not considering earnings from American-owned investments in other countries, GDP gives a better picture of what is happening to the U.S. economy.

◆ The Commerce Department has made a number of other changes to the national income and product accounts, including a change in the base year.

Painting by a New Set of Numbers

The Commerce Department is likely to announce today that upon closer examination, the American economy grew a little more slowly in the 1980s than it thought.

The conclusion arises from a sweeping revision of what has long been the government's principal economic scorecard, the gross national product. Not only is Commerce recalculating GNP, it is also advising the public to pay attention to a different economic gauge, the gross domestic product, or GDP.

The changes are intended to give the public and policy makers a better sense of how the U.S. economy is performing. As a consequence, Commerce officials said, officials and political leaders will be in a better position to make policy choices.

The officials said they are shifting to GDP from GNP because the former measures production of goods and services in just the United States. GNP, on the other hand, includes the amount by which earnings on American-owned investments in other countries exceed earnings on foreign-owned investments here, sometimes causing the GNP figures to give a misleading reading of the economy's health. Coincidentally,

What's the Difference? GNP vs. GDP

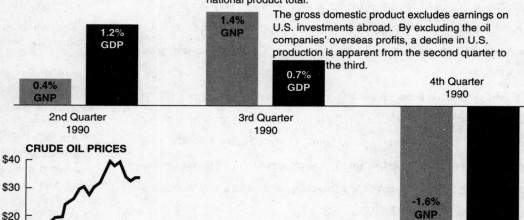

When oil prices shot up last year, oil companies' profits overseas surged and helped inflate the gross national product total.

The gross domestic product excludes earnings on U.S. investments abroad. By excluding the oil companies' overseas profits, a decline in U.S. production is apparent from the second quarter to the third.

1.2% GDP

0.4% GNP

2nd Quarter 1990

1.4% GNP

0.7% GDP

3rd Quarter 1990

4th Quarter 1990

-1.6% GNP

-2.1% GDP

While the fourth-quarter figures for both GNP and GDP declined, the GNP fell less, in part because of continued high profits for U.S. oil companies overseas.

CRUDE OIL PRICES

$40

$30

$20

$10

0

J J A S O
1990

Source: Michael Drew—*The Washington Post*

Japan's Economic Planning Agency said yesterday it will place more emphasis on GDP for the same reason, Bloomberg Business News reported.

Commerce is also changing the base year, or starting point, it uses for calculating the future impact of inflation on the economy.

If the new numbers do show slower growth, they could provide new ammunition for Democratic attacks on President Bush for the economy's lackluster performance in recent years and the lack of a plan to accelerate the nation's recovery from recession.

The change primarily responsible for reducing the country's reported economic growth rate will be a shift to 1987 from 1982 as the base year for Commerce's calculation of changes in the nation's "real," or inflation-adjusted, GNP and GDP.

The department also will provide new "benchmark" estimates for both measures based on a wide range of newly available data from economic censuses, personal and corporate tax returns and other sources.

At the same time, it will change definitions of some types of economic transactions.

All of these changes are meant to account for shifts in prices, consumers' tastes, technological advances and other developments that ultimately are reflected in economic statistics.

Previously published figures incorporating the change in the base year but not the benchmarking or definition changes show that the economy grew an average of 0.2 percentage points less each year from 1981 to 1990 than was the case with the 1982 base year.

On the same basis, the available figures indicate that the recession that began in August 1990 was somewhat deeper than depicted by the current GNP numbers, but that it ended with stronger growth in the second quarter of this year than the current numbers indicate.

In the unrelated switch to emphasizing gross domestic product instead of gross national product, Commerce is seeking to avoid the sort of problem that cropped up a year ago when world oil prices shot up after Iraq invaded Kuwait.

The rise in oil prices and a huge drop in consumer confidence plunged an already weakly growing U. S. economy into recession.

But the extent of the decline in U.S. production of goods and services was masked somewhat in the GNP numbers by a sharp rise in profits that U.S. oil companies earned abroad.

Those profits showed up in GNP as part of what is known as "the rest-of-the-world" sector. This rest-of-the-world sector is not included in gross domestic product.

For that reason, Commerce officials regard gross domestic product not only as a better measure of U.S. production and of the health of the American economy, but as a measure less likely to be distorted by unusual events, such as the volatility of oil company profits or abrupt, large changes in the value of the dollar.

Just as rising oil company profits made the economy's decline look milder late last year than it really was, in terms of U.S. production, the decline in those profits early this year made it appear from the GNP numbers that the economy kept shrinking in the April-June period.

Instead of the 0.5 percent annual rate of decline in real GNP that quarter, real GDP showed a 0.3 percent increase.

—John M. Berry, "Painting by a New Set of Numbers," *The Washington Post*, December 4, 1991.

QUESTIONS

1. a) Define GNP.

    b) Briefly describe how the Department of Commerce calculates GNP by the

        •   expenditure approach.

        •   factor income approach.

        •   output approach.

2. a) Define GDP.

    b) In order to calculate GDP, what changes have to be made to the

        •   expenditure method?

        •   factor income method?

        •   output method?

3. a) Would Honda Corporation's earnings from its U.S. production facilities be counted in U.S. GDP, GNP, or both? Explain your response.

    b) Would Marathon Oil earnings from its Kuwait operations be counted in U.S. GDP, GNP, or both? Explain your answer.

4. a) Define nominal and real GDP.

    b) Why is it useful to distinguish changes in real GDP from changes in nominal GDP?

    c) How is the change in real GDP calculated from the change in nominal GDP?

    d) What is meant by the term "base year"?

    e) Why does the Commerce Department periodically update the base year for the calculation of GDP (or GNP)?

5. a) Commerce Department officials stated that changes in real GDP, rather than GNP, give a more accurate picture of what is happening to the U.S. economy. Do you agree or disagree with the Commerce Department's assessment? Why?

    b) Under what circumstances would there be no difference between the estimate of GDP growth and the estimate of GNP growth?

INTRODUCTION TO MACROECONOMIC VARIABLES

Our economy is quite complex with literally millions of different items changing hands every day. Recording these transactions is difficult enough, but in order to distinguish inflation and economic growth, it is necessary to separate price movements and changes in physical quantities. Two primary methods of measuring inflation are used: the Consumer Price Index (CPI) and the implicit GDP deflator. While both indices have advantages and disadvantages, the CPI receives the most press. This is because many governmental programs, such as Social Security, food stamps, and Federal pensions, have benefits linked to this index. Many unions have negotiated wage increases tied to movements of this index. More than 50 million people have incomes tied to movements in the CPI.

After studying your text, reading the article, and answering the questions, you should be able to:

◆ ◆ Understand the distinction between inflation and changes in relative prices

◆ ◆ Describe the bases of the CPI and the GDP deflator

◆ ◆ Calculate the inflation rates implied by these indices

◆ ◆ Describe and explain changes in the CPI for different product and geographical areas

◆ ◆ Explain the difference between changes in price indexes and changes in the cost of living

Preview

◆ Consumer prices rose .5 percent in March 1992, and at an annual rate of 3.5 percent for the first three months of 1992.

◆ The increase for March 1992 was the largest since October 1990.

◆ Food, clothing, transportation, and energy prices recorded larger increases than other goods and services.

◆ The CPI rose faster in Los Angeles, San Francisco, and New York than elsewhere.

◆ Average weekly earnings failed to keep pace with inflation.

◆ There was disagreement over the prospects for future inflation.

Consumer-Price Increase of 0.5% Is Widespread

The jump in March consumer prices runs counter to recent reassurances that inflation is under control, though many analysts called it a fluke.

The 0.5% increase reported by the Labor Department was the largest since October 1990. The rise was widespread, making it difficult to lay blame on any particular sectors. Nevertheless, economists said the unexpected increase isn't a harbinger of things to come.

"Perhaps this is an example that in any given month and in any given report anything can happen," said Charles Lieberman, economist with Chemical Securities Inc. in New York. "It's inconsistent with the recessionary economy."

"There is no reason to be unduly alarmed," said Victor Zarnowitz, professor emeritus of economics and finance at the University of Chicago. "The problem now is slow growth and not really inflation at this point."

Separately, the Labor Department said Americans' average weekly earnings failed to keep pace with inflation. After adjustment for price increases, earnings fell 0.1% in March, the department said. Before adjustment for inflation, earnings rose to $362.21 a week from $360.13 a week in February. All the figures are adjusted for seasonal changes.

All of the economy's major consumer sectors showed price increases of at least 0.4%. Yet the March rise in prices, which follows increases of 0.1% in January and 0.3% in February, was concentrated particularly in food, clothing, transportation and energy.

Excluding the volatile food and energy prices, March consumer prices still registered a 0.5% increase. So far this year inflation is running at an annual rate of 3.5%. Last year consumer prices rose only 3.1%.

A 6.1% climb in fresh fruit and vegetable prices sparked a 0.5% March increase in food prices, while last month's rise in Japanese auto prices

Consumer prices

Here are the seasonally adjusted changes in the components of the Labor Department's consumer price index for March.

| | % change from | |
	Feb. 1992	March 1991
All items	0.5	3.2
Minus food & energy	0.5	3.9
Food and beverage	0.5	1.8
Housing	0.4	3.0
Apparel	0.6	3.6
Transportation	0.7	1.7
Medical care	0.5	7.8
Entertainment	0.4	3.3
Other	0.5	7.1

March consumer price indexes (1982–1984 equals 100), unadjusted for seasonal variation, together with the percentage increases from March 1991 were:

All urban consumers	139.3	3.2
Urban wage earners & clerical	137.0	3.0
Chicago	139.7	2.6
Los Angeles	145.5	4.2
New York	149.1	4.0
Philadelphia	145.4	3.1
San Francisco	141.9	4.1
Baltimore	138.7	2.7
Boston	147.9	2.8
Cleveland	136.3	2.3
Miami	134.5	1.9
St. Louis	132.6	1.5
Washington D.C.	143.0	2.7

was reflected in the 0.7% jump in transportation prices. Elsewhere, clothing prices climbed 0.6% in March, following a 1.5% jump in February. And energy prices marked their first increase in three months, rising 0.6%, in part due to 0.8% increases in gasoline prices.

Many economists pointed to Labor Department reports showing that wholesale prices inched up a scant 0.2% in March as a sign that retail consumer prices won't accelerate in April.

But while many analysts pegged the March rise as an aberration, not every-

one did. "These data clearly reinforce that inflation will be 4% or higher this year, as opposed to the consensus estimate of 3% to 3.5%," said Marilyn Schaja, economist with Donaldson, Lufkin & Jenrette in New York.

—Jonathan Weil, "Consumer-Price Increase of 0.5% Is Widespread," April 13, 1992.

QUESTIONS

1. a) What does the CPI attempt to measure? Be specific.

   b) Describe the procedure that is used to calculate the CPI.

   c) If the CPI changed from 135 in March 1991 to 139.3 in March 1992, what was the annual percentage change in the CPI?

   d) Look at the changes in the CPI for the various cities listed. Why were they different?

   e) Some analysts saw the monthly increase as an aberration while others viewed the rise as an indication of higher inflation over the next several months. Upon what did the course of inflation depend?

2. Actually, there are two CPIs that are calculated by the Bureau of Labor Statistics. One, CPI-U (all urban consumers) covers 80 percent of the civilian population and the other, CPI-W (urban wage earners and clerical workers), represents about 40 percent of the population.

   a) From the base period (1982-1984) to March 1992, which of the two groups experienced a higher level of inflation?

   b) What was the rate of inflation for each group between March 1991 and March 1992?

   c) Do either of these indexes provide an accurate indication of the inflation you face as a student? Why?

3. a) What is meant by relative prices?

    b) What is meant by the term "inflation"?

    c) Can you have relative prices changing and have no inflation? Explain.

    d) Can you have inflation without relative prices changing? Explain.

4. a) Which prices increased faster in this period? Which increased more slowly?

    b) In general, why did relative prices change?

5. a) Describe the GDP deflator.

    b) Would the GDP deflator produce a different figure for inflation? Why?

53.
A Sexist Approach to GNP?

Microeconomics is the study of the economic behavior of households, individuals, and firms—the "micro" units of the economy. Focusing on a single market, microeconomic analysis looks at output, price, or employment in the market. It is the aggregation of such microeconomic decisions that form the macroeconomic aggregates.

Macroeconomics is the study of the aggregate economy—the collective behavior of the micro units. Macroeconomic analysis uses several models to explain the problems of inflation, unemployment, business cycle fluctuations, and government and international deficits.

Gross national product (GNP) is a macroeconomic concept. It is calculated by aggregating the value of all the final goods and services produced in markets at the microeconomic level. This article examines the microeconomic foundations of GNP, and discusses the appropriate valuation of unpaid housework.

After studying your text, reading the article, and answering the questions, you should be able to:

◆◆ Explain the three ways in which the government measures GNP

◆◆ Understand why GNP focuses on market-priced goods and services as the basis for the calculation

◆◆ Describe three different ways value can be imputed to nonmarket-based services

◆◆ Explain the difference between GNP and other measures of output

◆◆ Describe the utility of the current measure of GNP for economic policymakers

Preview

◆ Housework is omitted from the calculation of GNP.

◆ Advocates for women's rights have claimed that this practice has lowered the status of women.

◆ Economists claim that the omission results from not being able to value housework services.

◆ Economists have devised several measures to impute the value of housework.

◆ The United Nations Decade for Women World Conference adopted a resolution in 1985 to measure and include the unpaid contributions of women in GNP.

If the GNP Counted Housework, Would Women Count for More?

Homemakers often feel their work is taken for granted, and advocates in the women's movement argue that the statistical invisibility of what used to be called women's work has policy implications that undermine a wide range of family issues. And so, there is an international movement to add housework to the gross national product as a way of elevating the work's status and, by extension, that of women.

The idea unsettles some economists and legislators, who say there is no sensible way to attach a price tag to unrenumerated work, and that doing so would compromise the integrity of economic statistics by freighting them with political assumptions.

But proponents of the idea envision it as the magic wand that will force women's issues to the forefront of the American agenda.

"If you raise the status of women," said Representative Barbara-Rose Collins, Democrat of Michigan, "then there wouldn't be such a debate on subjects like the Family Leave Bill, which passed in Congress but the President vetoed. We would be more conscious of the family unit."

Carol A. M. Clark, an economist at Guilford College in Greensboro, N.C., agrees. "If we had been counting women's unwaged work 30 years ago when women began entering the work force," she said, "policy makers would have foreseen and prevented the current child-care and elder-care crises."

Opponents say the idea would only amount to empty symbolism and would create a convenient excuse for the tax collector to reach deeper into the family pocket.

Pricing the Quality of Work Furthermore, economists cannot easily grapple with the question of how to determine the value of particular jobs. The average cook, for example, earns $12,480 annually, according to the Bureau of Labor Statistics, but what is the economic value of the homemaker who can prepare a coulibiac de saumon—or the one who can't even boil eggs?

"There are questions of quality," said Larry Moran, a research economist with the Bureau of Economic Analysis. "I don't know about *your* quality of housework, but the quality of *my* housework would be in trouble."

In October, Ms. Collins introduced a bill to an Education and Labor subcommittee that would require the Bureau of Labor Statistics to determine a dollar value for unpaid services like housework, caring for children or the elderly, agricultural work, volunteer work and work in a family business so that the amount could be added to the G.N.P., the standard measure of all the goods and services produced in a country.

Because the monetary value would apply to the work itself, the legislation would count the efforts of men as well as women if they share or perform household or volunteer work. The legislation, endorsed by the Congressional Women's Caucus, has 31 co-sponsors, including a Republican, Representative Constance A. Morella of Maryland.

At the United Nations Decade for Women World Conference in Nairobi, Kenya, a resolution was adopted calling on all nations to measure and include in their G.N.P.'s the unpaid contributions of women.

"It's important for policy concerns on women," said Dr. Joann Vanek, coordinator for programs on gender statistics in the United Nations statistical office. "The United Nations is particularly concerned about this in developing countries, because so much of what women do in those countries is not reflected in statistics."

The Economists' Ideas Several methods have been devised by economists to value housework.

One is market cost, which measures how much it would cost to take all the services performed inside the home into the market. For women in this county, this value would be about $16,000 per year in 1991 dollars, based on research by the Bureau of Economic Analysis in 1976. This value is comparable to the average salary of a kindergarten teacher, hotel clerk, receptionist, or security guard, according to the Bureau of Labor Statistics.

Another is replacement cost, which measures how much it would cost to get someone to come in to perform all the household jobs. This conjures visions of a home crawling with babysitters, maids and cooks dashing in to perform a task and leaving soon afterward. This value turns out to be the same as the market cost.

And then there is the opportunity cost, which determines how much a person could earn in a job outside the home if he or she weren't doing housework full time. This figure, of course, could vary. If a woman had a law degree, for example, she could potentially earn in the six digits. However, based on a survey of women for a study by the Bureau of Economic Analysis in 1976, this figure was about $17,000 per year in 1991 dollars. This method has been used mostly by lawyers representing women in divorce proceedings.

Despite the United Nations' entreaty to have member nations include unpaid work in their G.N.P.'s—which by some estimates is an additional $4 trillion worldwide—countries have been sluggish, if not unresponsive, about embracing and carrying out the idea.

So far, no country has begun counting women's unpaid work in the G.N.P., but some countries, like France and Norway, have created "satellite" G.N.P. estimates that include it. Others, including Germany, Australia and Canada, have begun studies on the topic, said Dr. Vanek, the U.N. statistician.

QUESTIONS

1. a) Define GNP.

    b) Using a circular flow diagram, illustrate the transactions that would be included in calculating GNP.

    c) How is the value of housework services received by homeowners treated in the calculation of GNP?

    d) Why is housework done by a family member not included in GNP? Explain in terms of your circular flow diagram.

    e) Suppose that the spouses of two different families first clean their own homes, then clean each other's homes for an identical salary. Would GNP include the value of their services before the switch? What would happen to GNP after the switch? Why?

    f) Why might GNP, as measured currently, have increased due to higher female labor force participation rates? Give two reasons, one relating to housework.

    g) Why might the exclusion of housework from GNP cause it to be misleading to compare the levels of GNP across countries?

2. a) What are the arguments cited in the article against the inclusion of unpaid housework in the calculation of GNP?

b) What are the counterarguments mentioned in the article?

3. a) What methods of valuing household services for inclusion in GNP have been suggested? Explain each approach briefly.

   b) Suppose it is determined that housework should be valued at $16,000 per year. What would happen to GNP if a houseworker took a position paying $12,000 a year?

   c) Would it be rational for the person to take a position paying $12,000 per year? Explain your reasoning. Take account of what happens to the housework if the person works.

   d) Which of the three approaches to valuing services do you think would be most appropriate if it were decided to include housework in the calculation of GNP? Why?

4. There have been attempts in the past to include or exclude items from the calculation of GNP. Items that have been suggested for inclusion are pollution and the depletion of the stock of natural resources. Using one of the three approaches described in question 3, explain how you would make this inclusion.

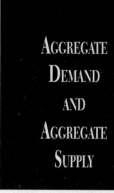

AGGREGATE DEMAND AND AGGREGATE SUPPLY

Macroeconomic equilibrium occurs at the general price level and level of real gross domestic product (GDP) where the forces of aggregate demand and aggregate supply are equated.

The aggregate demand curve represents the inverse relationship between real GNP demanded and the aggregate price level. The curve is drawn holding constant the interest rate, expected inflation, the foreign exchange rate, the quantity of money, and taxes, among other things.

The short-run aggregate supply curve is a direct relationship between the quantity of real GDP supplied and the price level, assuming the prices of factors of production to be constant. The long-run aggregate supply curve shows the full-employment level of real GDP, and is independent of the price level.

These concepts are used to interpret the effects of various strategies to increase U.S. competitiveness described in the accompanying article.

After studying your text, reading this article, and answering the questions, you should be able to:

◆ ◆ Explain the determinants of the aggregate demand curve and the short-run and long-run aggregate supply curves

◆ ◆ Distinguish between a shift in the curves and movements along the curves

◆ ◆ Distinguish between a shift in the short-run aggregate supply curve and a shift in both aggregate supply curves

◆ ◆ Analyze the implications for macroeconomic equilibrium of events that shift the aggregate demand and/or the aggregate supply curves

Preview

◆ The fear is growing that the Japanese economy will soon eclipse the American economy.

◆ Experts from many fields have proposed measures to improve American competitiveness.

◆ The proposals focus on increasing investment, improving productivity, cutting costs, providing better infrastructure, and increasing research and development.

◆ As the economic slump continues, Americans are recognizing that many current economic problems require long-run and not short-run prescriptions.

Attention America! Snap Out of It

Just when Americans should be celebrating their victory in the cold war, they have grown alarmed that they are losing the next big war: the competitiveness war.

After years of watching Japan increase its manufacturing might, Americans have awakened to the dangers of losing the industrial base that long made their nation the envy of the world....

Worried that American workers are ill prepared for the workplace of tomorrow, experts say the country should adopt the German job-training system in which many high school students spend time in factories learning to master modern technologies and solve problems in teams.

Some say Washington should allow banks to own shares in industrial companies, as they do in Germany and Japan, because such a system of large, stable shareholders would enable American companies to think more long-term.

A New Cottage Industry These are just a few of the ideas being churned out by a new cottage industry in which hundreds of economists, think tanks, professors, politicians, columnists and management consultants ruminate full time on how to improve America's competitiveness.

To a surprising degree, these deep thinkers—whether left-of-center or right-of-center, partisan or nonpartisan—have reached a consensus on many prescriptions for America's economic ills. They generally agree that the nation needs to take the following steps.

Increase savings to provide business with more money to invest in buildings and machines that increase productivity and living standards.

Step up efforts to train American workers so they can adapt to the technologies and more flexible factories of tomorrow.

Get companies to think long-term so they will make the strategic investments in equipment, training and research needed to compete with the Japanese and Germans.

Rein in health-care spending, which puts a heavy burden on American industry and now accounts for 13 percent of the nation's gross domestic product, about double Japan's level.

Spend more on research and development so that industry not only maintains its lead in innovation but also improves its ability to turn ideas into hot-selling products.

Invest more in public structures like highways, bridges, railways and airports, which will raise productivity by reducing transportation delays and costs.

"Our greatest problem has been this nation's inability or unwillingness to adequately invest in our future productivity," said Robert B. Reich, a professor at Harvard's Kennedy School of Government, whose book "The Work of Nations" examines competitiveness. "If we have an adequately educated and trained workforce and a state-of-the-art infrastructure linking them together and with the rest of the world, then global capital will come here to create good jobs. If we don't, the only way

global capital will be invested here is if we promise low wages."

As the economic slump extends from months to years, Americans worry increasingly that the nation requires not short-term fixes, but long-term prescriptions. Bruised by recession and foreign competition, G.M., I.B.M. and other stalwarts of Corporate America are laying off thousands of workers, helping to create a palpable eagerness to cure the competitiveness malady before more high-paying jobs vanish.

Evidence of the illness is everywhere. The weekly wages of the average American factory worker have fallen 9 percent since 1973. In recent years, productivity—the key to improved living standards—has grown at one-third the 1960's rate and one-quarter the Japanese rate, although America still leads the world in output per worker....

At the same time, bridges and roads are crumbling, partly because the nation spends a far smaller fraction of gross domestic product on infrastructure than do Japan and Germany. Although Japan has half the population of the United States, its corporations invest more in absolute terms on the plants and equipment that lift a nation's productivity and living standards.

In the Annual Economic Report of the President issued last Wednesday, the President's economic advisers sounded the alarm: "Quite simply, without adequate productivity growth, America's standard of living will neither keep pace with the expectations of our citizens, nor remain the highest in the world."

Ideas from the Gurus The competitiveness gurus have made dozens of other suggestions....Some call for lowering the dollar further to lift exports, while others want to steer more students away from paper-pushing professions like law and toward careers more closely connected to competitiveness, like engineering....

On the education front, experts stress improving primary and secondary education, especially in math and science. Others say far more has to be done to train high-school dropouts so that they can make a bigger contribution to the economy....

Many economists were heartened that in his State of the Union address, President Bush talked at length about strengthening the nation's long-term prospects. Many praised his plan to increase outlays for non-military research and development 7 percent over last year, but most said his competitiveness proposals were just baby steps.

Economists often say one factor is at the heart of all the problems: Americans prefer to consume today rather than save money to be invested for tomorrow.

America seems trapped in a vicious circle because sluggish income growth over the last two decades has made families save less and borrow more in a desperate effort to maintain living standards. The catch is that a low savings rate makes it harder to increase living standards.

Japan's net household savings in 1990 were 14.3 percent of disposable income, and Germany's were 13.9 percent; both dwarfed America's 4.7. This largely explains why in recent years Japan's and Germany's investment as percentage of G.D.P. and productivity growth have far exceeded America's.

Most economists say one crucial way to lift savings and investment would be to slash the Federal budget deficit. But in an election year, President Bush and Congress seem intent on sweeping this gigantic problem under the rug. Many economists expect the deficit to soar to a record $400 billion this year and next year, up from $269 billion in 1991....

According to most economists, the budget deficits and the low savings rate of the 1980's pushed up interest rates, helping to make the cost of capital higher than in Japan. That means American companies need a faster return on their investments, which makes them more short-term oriented....

To make American business more long-term oriented, Mr. Prestowitz [president of the Economic Strategy Institute, a Washington-based think tank] proposed giving shares owned by long-term shareholders more voting power. To increase the time horizons of investors and executives, Professor Reich suggested a much lower capital gains rate for investors holding assets for more than six years. President Bush took a step in that direction by proposing that assets held three years be taxed at a lower rate than those held one year....

While competitiveness experts agree on many measures, there are sizzling disputes over others. President Bush's proposal to cut capital-gains taxes has sparked the hottest debate. He insists it will create an investment boom, but many Democrats in Congress say these cuts will be a windfall for the rich and will barely spur investment.

Who Will Pay? Another huge debate is on how to finance increased spending on education and infrastructure. Many conservatives back a spending cap on discretionary Federal programs. "If they prevented Federal spending from rising by 4 to 5 percent a year, that would free up $50 billion a year," said Martin Anderson, an economist at the Hoover Institution.

But some economists say that once the current downturn ends, the Government should raise taxes to finance needs like improved schools. Advocates of higher taxes often note that in the United States, taxes represent a lower share of G.D.P. than any other major industrial nation. "Higher taxes and more homework—that's my platform," said Charles Schultze, a Brookings Institution economist. "That might not get me elected, but that's what America needs."

Mr. Rohatyn, the investment banker, said cuts in military spending resulting from the end of the cold war should provide plenty of money for programs to increase competitiveness. He also suggests a 50-cent-a-gallon increase in the gasoline tax, still far below the taxes in many European countries. The increase would not only raise $50 billion a year, but would promote conservation, reduce oil imports and cut the trade deficit.

Mr. Rohatyn also proposes that the Government pump $25 billion into the banking system by buying non-voting stock. This would help end the credit crunch that is prolonging the recession and provide money for long-term modernization. President Franklin D. Roosevelt did the same thing to shore up the banking system, and after the banks regained their health, the Government sold its shares at a profit.

—Steven Greenhouse, "Attention America! Snap Out of It," February 9, 1992.

QUESTIONS

1. According to the article, U.S. investment lags investment by two major economic rivals—Japan and Germany.

   a) List at least two types of investment recommended by experts in the article.

   b) Draw a diagram with axes representing the price level and real GDP. Add an aggregate demand curve and a long-run and a short-run aggregate supply curve. Show a macroeconomic equilibrium with unemployment. Label the equilibrium price level and the equilibrium level of real GNP.

   c) Suppose that investment increases, everything else being equal. Show the effect on the aggregate demand curve. Why does it move in the way you have shown?

   d) Also show the effect of increased investment on the aggregate supply curves. Why do they move in this manner?

2. Another approach, cited in the article, is to improve worker productivity.

   a) List two proposals in the article to improve worker productivity.

   b) Illustrate the impact of improved productivity on the aggregate supply curves and on macroeconomic equilibrium in a second diagram.

c) Is there a shift in the aggregate demand curve as a result of the improved productivity? Or is there only a movement along the demand curve? Explain your answer.

d) Would there be a shift in the aggregate demand curve if workers' pay was increased with their productivity? Why or why not? What would be the implications for the price level and real GDP?

3. The article also asserts that American firms need to cut costs in order to improve their competitive position vis-a-vis Japan and Germany.

a) According to the article, where is cost cutting most needed?

b) What would be the impact of cost cutting on the aggregate supply curves and on the price level and real GDP? Illustrate in a third diagram. Explain why you moved the curve(s) you did.

c) Suppose that cost cutting is effective and American prices fall relative to the Japanese; does this further impact the aggregate demand curve and the price level and real GNP? Explain your response.

4. A final area, referred to in the article, is the need for improvements in infrastructure.

    a) Give examples of proposed improvements in public infrastructure.

    b) In a fourth diagram, illustrate what would happen to aggregate prices and real GNP as a result of this change, everything else being equal. Explain why you moved the curves you did.

    c) Improvements to infrastructure are usually very costly and are financed either by raising taxes or by increasing the federal debt. What would be the joint impact on macroeconomic equilibrium of improvements in public infrastructure financed by increased taxes? Illustrate on a further diagram. Explain how and why the outcome is different from the impact in 4b.

AGGREGATE DEMAND AND AGGREGATE SUPPLY

Aggregate demand and aggregate supply are important tools for analyzing the impact of exogenous events or policy proposals on the macroeconomy. If an exogenous event like a supply-side shock occurs, its consequences can be predicted by a comparison of equilibrium values before and after its incidence. Similarly, the likely impact of policy initiatives proposed to either improve macroeconomic performance or compensate those who have been affected by the shock can be analyzed. However, these forecasts are made in an uncertain environment, with the result that outcomes are not always unambiguous. This article considers the impact the 1992 Los Angeles riots and other events had on the Californian economy, and evaluates recommendations that have been made to restore the economic base of the community.

After studying your text, reading the article, and answering the questions, you should be able to:

◆ ◆ Explain the consequences of supply-side shocks and changes in aggregate demand for macroeconomic equilibrium

◆ ◆ Analyze the implications for real GDP and the price level of policies that shift either aggregate demand or aggregate supply

◆ ◆ Discuss the problems of predicting the impact of economic policies

Preview

◆ California's economy has been dealt a number of blows: the recession, defense cutbacks, and the riots in Los Angeles.

◆ Japanese investment and imports were also expected to decline.

◆ The consequences of these events were a dramatic rise in unemployment, a decline in employment growth, a migration of firms, and a fall in real estate prices.

◆ Another important result was a budget deficit for the state that required cutbacks in spending, especially education, and a tax hike.

◆ The northern and central parts of the economy were expected to recover first.

Carnage on the Coast

It was a point of pride with Hoskin Hogan that in the 32 years he had owned the Arco station on the corner of Century Boulevard and Figueroa in south-central Los Angeles he had never laid off one employee. Even last year, as the recession took a 20 to 25 percent bite out of his profits, the businessman found a way to keep all 15 workers on his payroll and off unemployment. But the night the Los Angeles riots began, Hogan's station was torched and destroyed....

California can ill afford another 15 people without jobs. An estimated 20,000 to 40,000 citizens were put out of work as Los Angeles burned, in a state that had already lost a staggering 333,000 jobs last year—2.6 percent of total employment. California's economy, which led the country in job creation in the 1980s, has been savaged by a recession deeper and longer than the national average. The Golden State's unemployment, at 8.0 percent, remains well above the nation's 7.2 percent rate. Defense cuts are decimating California's critical aerospace industry and are expected to vaporize some 250,000 to 375,000 jobs—more than 20 percent of all defense-related employment—in the first half of this decade, according to consultants McKinsey & Co. The California real-estate boom has gone bust, forcing the crippled construction industry to shed more than 40,000 jobs since February 1990, with another 36,000 job losses expected this year. And bad real-estate loans have helped drive bank profits down 80 percent, from $3.4 billion in 1990 to $659 million in 1991.

As a result of this free fall, the state government is approaching the end of its fiscal year in June with a potential $3.7 billion deficit despite a $7.3 billion tax hike, the largest increase ever enacted by any state. Children will be among the deficit's first victims, as the budget squeezes welfare and education....

North vs. South The riots will also exacerbate the troubling division of California into two economies. Most analysts look for Northern and Central California to begin recovering by late this year, led by improvements in agriculture and high technology. But Southern California will continue to be damned by defense cutbacks and overbuilding. Already Los Angeles County groans under a 9.9 percent jobless rate, while San Francisco gets by with 5.7 percent unemployment. With one third of the jobs in the state, Los Angeles County suffered nearly two thirds of the job losses last year. Now it must cope with riot damage estimated at more than $1 billion. And tourism, one of the few bright sectors of the Los Angeles area economy—and its second-largest employer, with 360,000 workers—is shuddering in the long shadow of violence....

The aftershocks of the real-estate bust could shake Southern California for many years to come. With 7.2 million square feet of vacant office space in downtown Los Angeles and 40 million square feet of empty offices in the area outside the central business district, the City of Angels has more unoccupied offices than New York City and Seattle combined....

Southern California is also taking the hardest hit from defense cutbacks. As of 1989, 24 percent of all manufacturing jobs in the Los Angeles area were provided by the aerospace and defense sectors. The region has endured the bulk of the 59,000 California aerospace jobs lost in the last three years. President Bush's State of the Union address sent Southern California reeling as he canceled such local products as Rockwell's Midgetman and MX missiles and limited the planned fleet of Northrop's B-2 bombers to 20 planes. Within a week, Northrop in Los Angeles announced 1,500 job cuts.

These job losses are particularly costly to the state economy because defense contractors pay their workers handsomely. A Southern California Edison study notes that earnings in the aerospace sector averaged $42,600; more-vibrant industries like printing and apparel pay $25,500.

California survived a similar wave of defense cutbacks after the Vietnam War as other manufacturers grew to absorb displaced defense workers in the 1970s. But this time, Californians fear that rather than growing, many nondefense manufacturers are packing their bags, fleeing high costs, regulations and overcrowding. One in 4 medium-to-large companies is considering moving out of state, according to a poll by Mark Baldassare & Associates of Irvine....

With 45 percent of California's budget going to the school system—local governments contribute little because of property-tax limitations—children will inevitably suffer some of the consequences of the state budget crunch. Already California spends less per pupil on education than nearly any other industrial state, and the average class size is the second highest in the nation....

Trade Winds Foreign trade and investment is one bulwark of California's economy that has held strong for the southern half of the state against the waves of recession. More than two thirds of the state's trade passes through Los Angeles, the largest port in the nation. And California exports rose 8 percent last year, to $63.1 billion, helping to create 90,000 desperately needed jobs. One dark spot looms on the horizon, however. As the economy of California's leading trading partner, Japan, turned sluggish, the state's exports to the Pacific power fell 1.2 percent last year. This year's drop is expected to be more dramatic.

Japan's woes are even more perilous to California when it comes to direct investment, where it has pumped a total of more than $14 billion into the state economy....And as California comes to terms with the recent riots in Los Angeles, it is wakening from another fantasy: that the nation's largest state is too diversified to suffer from a deep downturn.

—Don L. Boroughs with Sara Collins, Eva Pomice and Terri Thompson, "Carnage on the Coast," May 18, 1992.
Copyright ©1992 U.S. News & World Report. Reprinted with permission.

QUESTIONS

1. For each subpart of this question, draw a diagram of the California economy with real GDP and the general price level on the axes. Show the aggregate demand curve and the long-run and short-run aggregate supply curves. Assume that in 1990 the economy was at full-employment equilibrium. Mark the equilibrium level of real GDP and the associated price level. Then mark the change in the general price level and in the amount of unemployment caused by the events listed and explain why you shifted the curves you did.

   a) the national recession

   b) Defense Department cuts

   c) the Los Angeles riots

2. As a consequence of the above events, the budget for the state of California was in deficit.

   a) What policies did the state initiate to eliminate its deficit?

   b) What was the impact of at least one of the deficit-reduction policies on macroeconomic equilibrium? Illustrate in a diagram of aggregate supply and demand.

c) Since the state's revenue is closely tied to the income of state residents, did this action improve or worsen the state's economic situation? Explain.

3. The article points to several additional occurrences that will likely impact the California economy. Explain the short-term and long-term impacts on the general price and output level of the economy of Los Angeles of

a) a decline in tourism.

b) the recession in Japan.

c) the emigration of firms from the state.

d) the decline in the quality of education.

4. a) Do the changes described above necessarily mean that the economy of the state will sink further and further as time passes? Explain your answer.

b) What is the value of analyzing the consequences of an event like the Los Angeles riots when it is difficult to predict its occurrence?

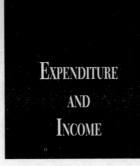

EXPENDITURE
AND
INCOME

Disposable income may be used for consumption expenditure or savings. The saving and spending decisions of millions of households across the United States have a significant bearing on the economy.

First, the relationship between aggregate consumption and GNP is important in understanding fluctuations in the economy because aggregate consumption amounts to 60 percent of gross domestic product (GDP).

Second, personal savings plus business savings represents the pool of funds that is available to be borrowed, either by the government to finance deficits, or by firms to finance investment. The low savings rate in the United States (compared to Japan) is often cited as contributing to low investment and productivity.

This article explores the trend in the relationship between savings and GDP. It also analyzes the causes of the trend and likely future developments.

After studying your text, reading the article, and answering the questions, you should be able to:

◆ ◆ Describe the behavior of the savings rate over time

◆ ◆ Specify the relationship between savings, consumption, and income

◆ ◆ Distinguish between the average propensity to save (APS) and the marginal propensity to save (MPS)

◆ ◆ Explain the savings rate

◆ ◆ Discuss the future course of the savings rate

◆ ◆ Explain the importance of savings to the economy

Preview

◆ In the 1970s, average personal savings reached 9 percent of take-home pay.

◆ Personal savings declined to less than three percent in the late 1980s.

◆ As personal savings go, so goes investment and the economy's long-term ability to increase productivity and raise living standards.

◆ There are potentially many causes of the falling savings rate.

◆ However, the hope that maturing baby boomers will resuscitate personal savings through increased thriftiness has all but disappeared.

Baby Boomers Fail as Born-Again Savers

For years, optimists have been counting on the middle-aging of the baby-boom generation to lift the nation's sagging savings rate. As boomers abandoned late nights at discos for early dinners at home with kids, they were supposed to start saving for retirement or college the way that June and Ward Cleaver did.

If only "Leave It to Beaver" were true today. Personal saving habits peaked in the early 1970's, when the average citizen stashed away more than 9 percent of his or her take-home pay, and declined through the late 80's when personal saving reached a nadir of less than 3 percent.

Maturing Is Not Enough A few years ago it seemed that thrift was getting trendy again, but lately saving has slumped anew. Worse, economists have concluded that there is little reason to believe that younger Americans, merely by maturing, will turn sufficiently thrifty to lift the nation's savings rate much....

That finding is bad news for investment and, hence, for the economy's long-term ability to generate higher productivity growth and living standards. A smaller amount saved by the nation's households, businesses and governments puts a ceiling on new investment—even if some of it can be financed by foreigners. There is already a broad consensus that the nation is investing too little.

The decline of personal thrift is particularly worrisome because Washington is likely to keep racking up huge deficits, and corporate saving, which may well strengthen in the 90's, is not likely to offset the decline in household saving.

But the maturation of the baby boomers will not rescue the nation from its spendthrift ways, many economists believe....

Edward F. McKelvey, an economist at Goldman, Sachs & Company, dismisses as a "cruel hoax" the notion that shifting demographics will cause a savings surge.

In July, the most commonly cited measure of saving, the personal savings rate—after-tax personal income minus consumer expenditures—was 3.7 percent. That was down from 5.2 percent last May.

Economists expect saving to edge up with real income in the recovery, but fewer and fewer expect it to reach its 6.5 percent post-World War II average, much less the double digits that some Wall Street economists have predicted. Forecasters at DRI/McGraw Hill project that the savings rate will hover around 4 percent in the 90's....

More than anything, though, the demographic landscape seemed set for increased saving. Households headed by people 40 to 50 years old historically squirrel away a bigger slice of their income—as much as 16 percent of it, which is more than any other age group does. Now that the leading edge of the baby boom, the generation born between 1946 and 1961, is moving into that age bracket, it would seem to follow that the overall rate would rise.

Actually, it does not follow, several economists say. The boomers are saving more than they did when they were younger—for college education, first homes and retirement—but not as much as their parents did nor enough to affect the overall rate much.

Saving Less

Personal saving as a percentage of disposable income. Figures are monthly beginning in 1988.

Source: Goldman Sachs

"The pace of migration of baby boomers into the high-saving age bracket is much too glacial to deliver the promised increase in saving on its own," Mr. McKelvey of Goldman, Sachs said....

A second problem is that while baby boomers are moving into the high-saving years, the population of Americans 75 and over will also be growing. Like very young Americans, the very old generally spend far more than their current income. "That produces a substantial offset to the small contribution of the aging of the baby-boom generation," Mr. McKelvey said.

Mr. McKelvey also shoots holes in a variant of the aging baby-boomer theme, that of the repentant yuppie. These born-again savers supposedly shopped until they dropped in the 80's and are all shopped out. Besides, they are supposedly tired of materialism and plan to spend the 90's rediscovering traditional values.

But the overwhelming majority of households in the 35-to-44-year-old bracket do not have high incomes to begin with, Mr. McKelvey said. Their average income, $40,000 before taxes in 1989, was "hardly enough to pay for BMW's and trips to the Bahamas on top of basic household expenses."

Besides, contrary to what one might expect if everybody had been splurging on luxuries instead of saving, the fraction of income Americans spent on cars, electronic gizmos and travel did not budge in the 80's. What did take a bigger bite out of budgets, though, was medical care, whose share jumped 4.5 percentage points. That is enough, Mr. McKelvey said, to account for the decline in the savings rate.

There is new historical evidence that casts more doubt on the idea that baby boomers are to blame for the savings slump....

As it turns out, savings rates slipped in all age groups—and in Japan as well as in the United States and Canada—from the early 60's through the mid-80's. Contrary to what most economists have thought, the rates fell furthest among older households. Finally, demographic shifts between high savers and low savers explained virtually none of the slide in saving in the last decade.

One clue to why older households cut back on saving proportionately more than younger households: Saving by homeowners fell much more than that by renters. Prices of houses, which the middle-aged are much more likely to own, were appreciating rapidly in the late 70's and early 80's.

If neither a preponderance of youth nor yuppie excesses caused the decline in saving during the 70's and 80's, middle age and newfound sobriety are not likely to raise it. Mr. McKelvey detects a number of trends that could discourage saving even more, among them the rising birth rate among women in their 30's and the leveling out of the percentage of women in the work force....

"The very generation that is supposed to stop buying too many BMW's may find itself spending money on diapers and day care instead of T-bills," he said.

The true culprit in the savings slump, Mr. Bosworth suggested, may be psychological. People operate with rules of thumb that are formed by critical experiences, like the Great Depression, he said. As the Depression has receded in memory, he added, the rule of frugality has gradually broken down.

Lawrence H. Summers, chief economist at the World Bank, said he believed that people might have less to worry about than they used to. Twenty years ago the rate of poverty among the elderly was twice that of younger Americans. Today it is lower. "My guess," he added, "is that many more people form a view about retirement by looking at whether their parents seem rich or poor than by looking at the report of the Social Security actuaries."

QUESTIONS

1. The article discusses the nation's savings rate.

   a) Define the "savings rate."

   b) How does the definition of "savings rate" compare with the definition of the APS?

   c) What has happened to the nation's savings rate since the 1970s?

   d) What does the behavior of the savings rate tell us about the average propensity to consume since the 1970s?

2. A number of factors that influence savings are discussed in the article. For each of the following, explain how the savings rate would be affected and why.

   a) the maturing of the baby boomers

   b) the recession

   c) a halving of the incidence of poverty among the elderly over the past twenty years

d) an increase in the amount of income spent on nondiscretionary consumption, such as medical care

e) rapid appreciation of the prices of houses

3. a) In order for the APS to increase, what must be true about the MPS and why?

b) Do incomes have to increase for the APS to increase? Why?

4. a) Why is it important for the nation to have an adequate amount of savings?

b) What policy measures could the administration propose to increase savings?

The multiplier is the factor by which an initial change in autonomous expenditure is magnified to produce the final change in income. The basic idea behind the multiplier is that changes in autonomous expenditure induce further changes in spending. When consumption expenditure induced by a change in income changes, there is no multiplier effect.

Although economists typically estimate and apply multipliers at the national level, the multiplier relationship is appropriate for any geographical area. The article provides an example of the working of the multiplier at the local level in the wake of cuts in defense spending.

After studying your text, reading the article, and answering the questions, you should be able to:

◆ ◆ Distinguish between autonomous and induced expenditures

◆ ◆ Describe the multiplier process

◆ ◆ Explain the factors that affect the size of the multiplier

◆ ◆ Calculate changes in employment and income following changes in autonomous expenditure

◆ ◆ Discuss policies that would counteract reductions in income and employment

Preview

◆ Congress is likely to shrink or eliminate the Seawolf submarine program.

◆ Indirectly, the Congress is also considering the end of thousands of jobs in southeastern Connecticut and Rhode Island.

◆ Seventy-two percent of the jobs in the Groton regional economy are defense-dependent.

◆ For Groton, Connecticut, the loss of 15,000 jobs at Electric Boat is causing anxiety among local merchants.

◆ Local officials and business leaders have formed an economic development team to spur job creation.

That Sinking Feeling at Electric Boat

It's the grand opening of Luzzi's Pizza & Deli, but owner Joseph Luzzi is already worrying about going out of business. Located down the block from the Electric Boat Div. of General Dynamics Corp., Luzzi is dependent on the submarine shipyard for customers. He's hoping that reports of possible cuts at the Groton (Conn.) operation aren't true. "People say I've got to be crazy, that there will be no money left around here. I'm going on a prayer," says Luzzi.

He isn't the only one saying novenas. Electric Boat's current backlog is shrinking fast, and the company is banking heavily on the Seawolf nuclear submarine program. But Congress is likely to shrink the program, prompting a drastic downsizing of 91-year-old Electric Boat, which employs 15,000 workers in Groton—11% of total employment in the Groton area. "We need at least one Seawolf a year to remain viable," says an Electric Boat spokesman. "Even with one a year, the division will be half the size it is today by 1996." As they wait for the defense budget to take shape, the folks in Groton are on tenterhooks. Says Mayor Linda B. Krause: "There's a sense of a disaster about to happen."

At Army bases in Kansas, high-tech weapons plants in California, training camps in North Carolina, people feel the same thing: The cold war already is history, and the U.S. is redeploying the resources it once spent to maintain the balance of terror. That's wonderful news for future generations, but right here, right now, the primary support for many towns is being kicked away.

Nowhere is the kick sharper than in Groton. The Electric Boat shipyard there was slated to share construction of 12 Seawolf nuclear submarines. The betting in Washington now is that the Navy will order only three Seawolfs. Says Loren B. Thompson, deputy director of the National Security Studies Program at Georgetown University: "It's basically a dead program."

That news has demoralized Groton and other towns in New London County. Since 1989, Electric Boat has been warning local leaders about possible layoffs. But defense dollars have fueled the local economy for decades, and most businesses and workers didn't know what else to do. "We always had defense and didn't think we'd have to diversify," says Dolores E. Hauber, vice-president at Bank of Mystic and town councillor in Groton.

Aggressive Local officials and business leaders have formed an economic-development team to spur job creation in a region where 72% of the jobs are defense-dependent and defense contracts in 1991 worked out to an amazing $9,085 per capita. "We've gotten a lot more aggressive. If Electric Boat doesn't get the Seawolf contract, we stand to lose close to 28,000 jobs in this area," says Southeastern Connecticut Chamber of Commerce President William D. Moore. The opening of a casino on an Indian reservation in nearby Ledyard next month could mean 2,500 new jobs. But few businesses are expanding.

Most local stores are struggling just to keep the doors open. Richard L. Campo, owner of Campo's Furniture Co., across the Thames River from Electric Boat in New London, is cutting prices to the bone to stimulate trade. Ron K. Wilds, owner of the Fast Attack Convenience Store, next to Luzzi's, fears a cutback at Electric Boat could put him out of business. "I'd love to sell out," he sighs, "if I had a chance."

For now, Electric Boat workers are hoping the clock won't strike midnight. Some say bravely that the cutbacks will never come, that politicians will realize the need to maintain a strong submarine fleet. One chain-smoking 39-year-old designer says he can't imagine working anywhere other than Electric Boat, where he has been for 18 years: "You just keep thinking it can't happen."

Even those who can picture life without Electric Boat are resigned to staying put. Many think job prospects in other parts of the country aren't much better. Says George D. Hodge, a 33-year-old welder: "Where am I going to go? The way the economy is going, jobs are uncertain everywhere."

Joe Luzzi, meanwhile, hopes word-of-mouth will draw more boatyard workers in for a slice of pizza. And he's saying his prayers at night to win Electric Boat the divine intervention it seems now to need.

QUESTIONS

1. Define autonomous and induced expenditure.

2. Identify the following expenditures as autonomous or induced.

   a) the dollars that the federal government pays to Electric Boat for submarine construction

   b) the dollars that local residents pay to merchants in Groton

   c) the taxes that Electric Boat pays to Groton

3. How does a change in an autonomous expenditure induce further changes in expenditure? Describe the process with reference to the cancellation of the Seawolf program by the federal government.

4. According to the article, employment at Electric Boat in Groton is currently about 15,000. Yet if Electric Boat was to suspend operations, the total employment in the area would decrease by 28,000.

   a) What accounts for the difference between the employment loss at Electric Boat and the total employment loss in the area?

   b) Calculate the local multiplier.

c) In general, the size of the multiplier is determined by the proportion of income recirculated in the economy. Describe the leakages in the Groton area that affect the size of the multiplier.

d) Suppose Electric Boat loses 7,000 jobs. What will be the area's total employment loss? Explain your calculations.

5. a) What measures might the Congress or the President take to counteract the employment and income loss in Groton?

b) What can the Groton City Council do to counteract the impact of the loss of Electric Boat jobs?

c) If the federal government spent more money on other programs in the county with the intention of increasing employment by 28,000, would it need to employ all 28,000 itself? If not, how many should it employ? Explain your reasoning.

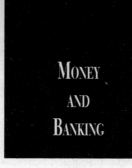

58.
Ruble's Rumble Vigorates Vodka

Money has many important functions in an economy. Indeed, a modern industrial nation cannot function without money, for it facilitates exchange and commerce. By facilitating trade it allows the specialization and mass production that create higher incomes and standard of living. Money also plays a role in determining the price level. This article describes what happens to the functions of money and the behavior of individuals in an economy where inflation is 300 percent annually.

After studying the text, reading the article, and answering the questions, you should be able to:

◆◆ Define money and its functions

◆◆ Describe the different forms of money

◆◆ Explain the determinants of the demand for money

◆◆ Explain the relationship between money and prices

Preview

◆ In January 1992, the inflation rate in Russia was more than 300 percent.

◆ Inflation is a new phenomenon to Russians, and so some people still keep their savings in a savings account that earns 3 percent interest annually.

◆ To maintain their standard of living, some Russians try to raise their wages, while others attempt to be paid in hard currency.

◆ To maintain the value of their savings, Russians are buying shares of newly private companies, apartments, dollars, or vodka.

Getting the Most from Each Ruble

Mindful of Russia's destructively high inflation, the Savings Bank of Russia announced higher interest rates last week for the millions of people who keep their savings in the bank's numerous branches. Rates on passbook accounts went to 3 percent from 2 percent, while the returns on certificates of deposit now range as high as 15 percent for a five-year certificate, up suddenly from 9 percent.

That is not much help when the annual inflation rate is more than 300 percent and a 15,000-ruble account—for many middle-class Russians a once-handsome sum that two years ago could buy a country dacha—is now barely enough to keep a family in food and other necessities for a few months.

Still, Russians are not rushing to withdraw their savings. Wild inflation is still new to them, and they have yet to develop the numerous investment dodges to preserve savings that are so common in the West.

"People got used to government supporting their lives, and now that times are bad, the first reaction is that we have to get the government to take care of us," said Tatyana Zaslavskaya, a sociologist and the director of the Soviet Center for Public Opinion and Market Research. "We still have a great share of such people, but their numbers are declining. Life is teaching them."

The second reaction to the commonwealth's first intense experience with inflation, according to Ms. Zaslavskaya's polls, is a scrambling for ways to increase wages: working more hours, trying to get a raise, holding two jobs, starting a business, trying to get on the payroll of a joint venture involving a foreign partner where wages are sometimes paid in hard currency. That's the good life in a country where a dollar sold on the black market for 100 rubles late last year, is 150 rubles now and might easily be 170 rubles next week.

Only slowly is the Western reaction to inflation and currency devaluation—seeking out clever investments that sustain the value of savings—taking hold. Or, as Ms. Zaslavskaya, 62 years old, puts it: "How can I talk seriously about savings at all when my monthly salary is 2,000 rubles, and I am not a poor woman in this country."

Her own savings totaled 16,000 rubles several years ago, enough to buy a three-room dacha or a small car then, but now she has only 7,000 rubles, equal to $47 in American currency. The cheapest dacha, meanwhile, goes for about 150,000 rubles, and in the last two weeks, the Russian Government has allowed new-car prices to jump to more than 250,000 rubles from 20,000.

"What you have here is a psychological tragedy," said Irina Z. Yarigina, a manager at the Bank for Foreign Economic Affairs. "People did not think of interest income on their savings as valuable. It was a gift from the state, which took care of their needs."

Clearly, such blasé disregard is out of place, and changing attitudes are increasingly evident, particularly in Moscow. Mutual funds and money market accounts with floating interest rates are still unknown here, but stocks aren't. Frequent television commercials and newspaper ads urge Russians to buy shares in newly private companies, promising big returns.

Buying an apartment is now widely permitted, and owning one is viewed as an inflation hedge. So is holding dollars, purchased on the black market in Moscow and a few other major cities. Now officials are saying that ordinary citizens will soon be allowed to buy dollars legally at some banks. That is a step toward making the ruble freely convertible, but one that could make holding dollars a commonplace family investment.

For the moment, owning dollars or stocks or apartments is limited to the most entrepreneurial. For the vast majority, the response to inflation is more primitive. While a New Yorker can easily buy a mutual fund that invests in foreign stocks or bonds—an investment that rises in value when the dollar weakens—a Muscovite buys vodka.

Certain goods have become, in effect, hard currency. Vodka is high on this list, largely because it is so widely consumed, creating a demand that can be counted on to exceed supply. The confidence in vodka's steady value explains why payment in a bottle or two of vodka happens often—to a plumber, for example, to fix a pipe.

Vodka's value as a currency brought Yuri Kislikov to a line that stretched around a corner outside a liquor store recently. "If I go to a worker and ask him to get me a spare part for my car, he'll refuse an offer of money, but he'll do it for vodka," said Mr. Kislikov, a 34-year-old computer dealer who had already made one purchase of second-grade vodka and was in the line for a second time, to buy two more quart-sized bottles at 58 rubles each. "The money is less reliable than the vodka."

—Louis Uchitelle, "Getting the Most from Each Ruble," January 14, 1992.

QUESTIONS

1. a) What is money?

   b) What functions does money perform?

2. a) Which functions of money did the ruble perform in Russia in 1992? Which functions did it not accomplish?

   b) Why did some Russians start buying shares of newly private companies? Explain in terms of the functions of money.

   c) Why did some Russians buy dollars or other hard currencies rather than apartments or shares of stock?

   d) Russians also tried to buy vodka (even those that do not drink!). Why was this rational behavior? Explain in terms of functions of money.

3. What forms can money take?

4. What form of money is

   a) rubles?

   b) dollars?

   c) vodka?

5. Briefly explain the three motives for holding money.

6. As inflation in Russia increased, which motives for holding money

   a) increased in importance? Why?

   b) diminished in importance? Why?

7. a) State the quantity theory of money.

   b) Using the quantity theory of money, explain what was happening to the supply of rubles in Russia in 1992.

8. a) What was happening to the value of money in Russia in 1992? Explain your answer.

   b) If Russian citizens had been able to increase their wages by half of the inflation rate, what would have happened to real wages and the consumption of wage earners? Why?

   c) As a result of the changes in 8b, what would you expect to have happened to industrial production, real investment, and GNP? Explain your response.

59.
The United States' IOUs

The Federal Reserve System is responsible for the nation's monetary policy. Its objectives are to stabilize prices, stimulate economic growth, and moderate business cycle fluctuations. The Fed has a number of policy tools at its disposal. Most important, the Fed can change the rate of growth of the money supply through buying or selling government securities in order to move the economy in the desired direction. However, too much or too little money supply growth may bring about undesirable consequences. This article discusses a policy decision of the Fed to increase its holdings of government securities, and thereby to increase the money supply.

After studying your text, reading the article, and answering the questions, you should be able to:

◆ ◆ Specify the goals and tools of monetary policy

◆ ◆ Explain how open-market operations cause changes in the money supply

◆ ◆ Analyze the beneficial and detrimental consequences of debt monetization

◆ ◆ Explain how changes in the money supply affect aggregate demand

◆ ◆ Define the various monetary aggregates

◆ ◆ Explain the relationship between the money supply and interest rates

Preview

◆ The Fed's purchases of government securities have sharply increased since 1990.

◆ Debt monetization— the Fed's purchases of government securities—creates money.

◆ Some favor debt monetization as a step that will encourage private borrowing and economic recovery through lower interest rates.

◆ Without debt monetization, rising federal deficits would reduce private sector spending.

◆ Others are concerned that inflation will increase as a result.

◆ Historical information suggests that there are long lags between shifts in the Fed's debt share and price changes.

Fed Assumes Bigger Share of U.S. Debt

More of the nation's huge debt burden is being shouldered by a customer with a broad back and very deep pockets: the Federal Reserve System.

The Fed has sharply increased its purchases of Treasury securities since 1990, apparently to allow for more borrowing in the private sector and help spur the economy. Fed Chairman Alan Greenspan and other board governors claim they will keep a lid on inflation. But a growing number of economists view the Fed's new willingness to take on more of the debt as inflationary in the long run.

The Fed's share of the mounting debt pile remains small—less than 3% of a total that's fast approaching $12 trillion. But this share has grown markedly since 1990, in contrast to a previous pattern of persistent shrinkage. Fed holdings of U.S. government securities have risen more than 33% in less than two years; in the same period, total debt rose less than 10% and federal debt about 20%.

"The Fed's recent willingness to hold more of the debt signifies a sea change," says Edward S. Hyman, president of ISI Group Inc. He views the change as "a bad development" since it threatens ultimately to cause steeper price increases. But he also stresses that the lead times between Fed moves to hold more debt and increased inflation tend to be long.

"It's probably not too late for the Fed to change course and avert a new inflationary surge," he says.

For now, "by taking on more of the total debt itself, the Fed is allowing more room in the credit markets for private borrowers," says Robert H. Parks, an economic consultant in New York. Otherwise, interest rates would tend to be higher and less affordable, he says, adding, "The Fed in effect is financing Treasury borrowing with newly created money."

Creating Bank Reserves To increase its debt holdings, the Fed may buy government securities directly from the Treasury, but more typically it does so in the open market. Bank reserves are created in the process, since the Fed can "pay" simply by crediting the amount of its purchases to the account of the bank involved in the transaction. As a result, money is born.

Economists call the process debt monetization. Without it, rising federal deficits tend merely to shuffle spending to the government sector from the private sector, rather than stimulate the economy as a whole.

For all the short-term benefits, a rising money supply, if it goes on long enough and is sharp enough, can eventually outstrip the available supply of goods and services and so fuel inflation. The government's most "potent financing technique" is for the Fed "to monetize the Treasury's debt by purchasing it," says William C. Melton, a former Fed official who now serves as chief economist of IDS Financial Services Inc.

The recent shift in the Fed's overall debt holdings, as opposed to how much of the total is in short-term or long-term securities, has received relatively little notice. Efforts to assess Fed policy have focused mainly on such familiar gauges as the federal funds rate, which banks charge one another on short-term loans, and on aggregates that gauge the money supply.

By and large, these well-publicized indicators suggest an effort by the Fed to loosen the monetary reins. But this endeavor has occasionally seemed halting and marked by caution. The federal funds rate, near 4%, is lower than three months ago, but slightly higher than a few weeks ago. M1, a relatively narrow measure of the money supply, has climbed briskly for many months. But the broader M2, M3 and M4 aggregates have not. Adjusted for inflation, all three are lower now than three years ago.

No Ambivalence There's no such ambivalence in the Fed's recent assumption of more of the debt. In the first quarter of 1990, Fed holdings of U.S. government securities amounted to just over $233.5 billion. The total has been rising sharply ever since, surpassing $312 billion in the final quarter of 1991....

Substantial time often may elapse between shifts in the Fed's willingness to assume debt and developments on the price front. The Fed monetized a rising portion of debt from the early 1960s until nearly the end of the decade, and the trend continued at a slower, more erratic pace until 1976. Yet, inflation remained relatively dormant until the latter half of the 1960s.

A footnote: Unlike the present situation, the Fed's monetizing through the 1960s can hardly be viewed as an effort to relieve credit markets overburdened by federal deficits. Through most of the period, the federal budget was in or close to balance.

The pattern from 1976 to 1990 also shows a long lag between shifts in the Fed's debt share and price developments. The Fed's share of debt fell substantially, a process that economists call demonetization and regard as disinflationary, just as monetization is deemed inflationary. But inflation intensified sharply from 1978 to 1980, well after the Fed's share of debt had begun to fall. As demonetizing continued, inflation finally did abate.

Most economists look for the Fed to adopt a more restrictive policy once the recovery gains strength and the presidential election is over. Some believe that this policy shift may already be at hand. But the hazard is that this could squeeze hard-pressed private borrowers, especially with the federal budget deficit near $400 billion and the economy reviving. The upshot could be appreciably higher interest rates and, once again, a stalled recovery or a new recession.

"The Fed will find it very hard to reverse its recent policy of debt monetization," says Lacy H. Hunt, chief economist in New York for Hong Kong Bank Group. He warns that any return to debt monetization would be "catastrophic" for the recovery, which he believes finally got under way in February.

Some economists disagree with such assessments and caution that the inflationary die is already cast, whatever the Fed decides to do in coming months. "The Fed has already passed the flash point for inflation," claims H. Erich Heinemann, chief economist of Ladenburg, Thalmann & Co.

—Alfred L. Malabre, Jr., "Fed Assumes Bigger Share of U.S. Debt," March 17, 1992.

QUESTIONS

1. a) What goals of monetary policy are referred to in the article?

   b) What policy instruments are available to the Fed to achieve these goals?

2. The Fed has increased its purchases of government securities since 1990. If the purchases have been made in the open market,

   a) how has the composition of the banks' assets changed?

   b) why have banks been able to make more loans?

   c) is it likely that any of the loaned money has reemerged as bank deposits? Explain your answer.

   d) in what ways has the money supply increased?

3. Suppose that the Fed has purchased securities from the Treasury. Would the increase in the money supply have been any different? Why?

4. Supporters of the Fed argue that debt monetization has beneficial effects, especially in a sluggish economy.

   a) Explain how the Fed's increased holdings of government securities could benefit the economy.

b) Why might a recovery be threatened by a reversal of Fed policy?

5. Critics, on the other hand, claim that this process is inflationary. Explain the critics' argument.

6. Indicators of the restrictiveness or looseness of monetary policy include the monetary aggregates.

a) What is the difference between M1, M2, and M3?

b) Do the actions of the Fed to monetize the debt change the supply of M1, M2, and M3? Why?

c) How could M1 "increase briskly" and the broader monetary aggregates, M2 and M3, fall in real terms?

7. Another indicator of the restrictiveness of monetary policy is interest rates. How does an increase in the money supply affect interest rates? Explain the mechanism and the direction of change.

60.
Check the Fed?

The Federal Reserve System, or the Fed, is the central bank of the United States. Central banks are responsible for regulating the monetary and financial institutions and markets, and for monetary policy. Controlling the money supply is arguably the most important function of the Fed because of its implications for the business cycle and the control of inflation.

While the central bank of some countries is part of the elected government, the Fed has a large measure of independence from the President and Congress. This article discusses some strengths and weaknesses of having the present system of autonomy for the Federal Reserve System.

After studying your text, reading the article, and answering the questions, you should be able to:

◆ ◆ Describe the structure of the Federal Reserve System

◆ ◆ Discuss the instruments of monetary policy used by the Fed

◆ ◆ Understand the legal and administrative relationship between the Fed and the U.S. government

◆ ◆ Evaluate the arguments of critics of the present system who advocate increased accountability

Preview

◆ Critics are challenging the present system of an autonomous Fed in order to make the Fed more accountable.

◆ The Fed has considerable influence over the economy, but the government has no direct role in the selection of the presidents of the regional Federal Reserve banks.

◆ The Fed's decisions cannot be vetoed, and its accounts are not subject to outside audit.

◆ Proposed legislation would limit the voting on monetary policy to those governors selected by the President and approved by Congress.

◆ In no other country is monetary policy determined by nongovernment members.

Critics Want Fed's Power Under More Accountability

The Federal Reserve holds an anomalous position in the American system. An enormously powerful Government agency, it is only loosely accountable to the public and to elected officials, and it allows private citizens, basically a banking elite, to help set the Government's economic policy.

When the economy is sour, as it is now, this odd structure tends to become a focus of attention, a sponge that soaks up frustrations over the way the economy is going.

Critics of the central bank had a new twist this morning. At a Senate hearing, several prominent lawmakers, an economist who holds a Nobel Prize and a former vice chairman of the Federal Reserve Board testified in favor of legislation to make the agency more politically accountable. The measure would prevent the presidents of regional Federal Reserve banks, who hold no Government office and answer to no Government official, from voting on Government policy as they do now.

The bill is not likely to be enacted, at least not any time soon, but the legislation has stirred up a new debate on the extent to which the Fed operates outside the bounds of an open society.

"Power without accountability does not fit the American system of democracy," said Representative Lee H. Hamilton, an Indiana Democrat who is a frequent critic of the Federal Reserve and one of the most widely respected members of Congress.

Using its power to raise or lower interest rates, the Federal Reserve has much more influence over the state of the economy than any other Government agency. That is especially true nowadays, when the large budget deficit has caused the White House and Congress to relinquish much of their grip on economic policy.

The Fed sets monetary policy on the basis of votes by the seven governors of the Federal Reserve Board and five of the 12 presidents of the Federal Reserve banks, who vote on a rotating basis.

The governors, like other top Government officials, are nominated by the President and confirmed by the Senate. But the regional Federal Reserve banks are private institutions. Their presidents tend to be career employees of the Federal Reserve, steeped in its culture. They are selected by the banks' directors, who are mostly commercial bankers from the region and who pick officers likely to be sympathetic to their views.

Target of Politicians Many politicians blame the central bank for the current weakness of the economy, saying interest rates should have been driven down more quickly than they were. Frequent reports in the last two years have said that Alan Greenspan, chairman of the board, and most of the other governors have been more inclined toward lower rates than the presidents of the regional banks.

For most of this year, there have been two vacancies on the board, meaning that the bank presidents had as many votes as the Fed governors. The published votes have shown few if any dissents from the policies that have been adopted. But that may be because Mr. Greenspan is careful not to press matters to votes that would show the policy makers to be sharply split.

The legislation under discussion at today's hearing before the Senate Banking Committee would leave all voting on monetary policy to the members of the Federal Reserve Board and would relegate the bank presidents to an advisory capacity. In addition to Mr. Hamilton, the sponsors include Senator Paul S. Sarbanes, Democrat of Maryland, the chairman of the Joint Economic Committee, and Senator Donald W. Riegle Jr., Democrat of Michigan, chairman of the Banking Committee.

"Nowhere else in the Government," Mr. Hamilton said, "are private individuals similarly permitted to participate in decisions which have such an enormous influence over the prosperity and well-being of millions of Americans."

Bank Independence Varies The central banks in the other leading democracies around the world vary in their independence from Government control. But in no other country, according to Prof. John B. Goodman, a student of the subject at the Harvard Business School, are votes on policy cast by people who are not appointed by the Government.

Some legal scholars believe the American system to be unconstitutional, a violation of the appointments clause of the Constitution, which requires policy-making officials to be nominated by the President and confirmed by the Senate. A lawsuit on the matter several years ago was dismissed on a technicality, and the main issue has never been addressed by the courts.

Mr. Hamilton's views about the Fed's lack of accountability apply not only to the legislation at hand but also to other aspects of the central bank's operations.

Meetings of the Federal Open Market Committee, where policy decisions are made, are held behind locked doors. No transcript or official notes are kept that would show who said what. The decisions are not announced for six weeks or more. Even then only a skeletal summary of what transpired is made public, and those who voted do not normally explain their votes the way, say, Supreme Court justices write opinions.

Fed Is Veto-Proof Further, no other branch of government can veto the central Bank's decisions, and the Fed's accounts are not audited by any outside agency.

Over the years, Mr. Hamilton and his allies have offered legislation to change much of this, but the bills have never gotten past the hearings stage. In part, that is because monetary policy is so often unpopular that Presidents and legislators are happy to criticize those policy makers when the economy turns sour.

But another, perhaps more important reason is that the lawmakers and scholars who advocate changing the way the Federal Reserve works are almost always those who want lower interest rates. Preston Martin, who was vice chairman of the Federal Reserve Board from 1982 to 1986, said at today's hearing that the regional bank presidents generally felt much more strongly about keeping interest rates high than did the members of the reserve board.

Many politicians say they favor low interest rates but believe in their hearts that higher rates are necessary to control inflation. These politicians do not want to change a system that they believe would make monetary policy less responsible.

Effect on Markets Mr. Greenspan, like many of his predecessors, has persuaded lawmakers that changes in the Fed's operations would not only give the central bank less flexibility in setting monetary policy but could also cause instability in markets that are familiar with the current system and wary about what changes would mean.

Christopher Whalen, who runs an economic consulting firm here, told his clients in a recent newsletter that the bill to take voting power away from the Federal Reserve bank presidents would "vastly increase the exposure of U.S. monetary policy to overt political pressure."

But supporters of the legislation dismiss those fears. James Tobin, the Nobel Prize-winning economist, was a bit contemptuous of the political pressure argument in his testimony before the Banking Committee today. "Politics?" he said. "In a representative democracy? Think of it. Economic performance necessarily involves political choices."

A Potential Conflict Mr. Tobin said he knew of no instance when private bankers made use of inside information from the Federal Reserve. But he said in an interview during a break in the hearing that he worried about a potential conflict of interest when private citizens held sway over Government policy.

He gave one example. Under the law, the Federal Reserve Board can change the discount rate, the rate the Fed charges commercial banks for loans, only at the request of the directors of at least one regional Federal Reserve bank. Sometimes, when the board wants to change the rate for economic policy reasons, it requests one regional bank or another to make an application. It can be days between the time the request is made and the time the Fed announces that the rate has been lowered.

During that time, Mr. Tobin observed, the commercial bankers who act as directors of the regional bank know something about the direction of monetary policy that they can use for the benefit of their customers that others in the financial markets do not know.

QUESTIONS

1. The three key elements of the Federal Reserve System are the board of governors, the regional Federal Reserve Banks, and the Federal Open Market Committee.

   a) What is the membership of each element?

   b) How are the members of each selected?

   c) To whom are the members of each element responsible?

2. a) Which of the above elements is responsible for determining monetary policy?

   b) Where does the power lie within this element?

   c) What accounts for this locus of power?

   d) What policy tools are available to this part of the Fed to influence the money supply and interest rates?

e) How do these policy tools affect the money supply and interest rates?

f) Why might regional bank presidents wish to keep interest rates relatively high?

g) Why might politically appointed board members wish to keep interest rates relatively low?

3. What arguments cited in the article justify making the Fed more accountable?

4. In response to the argument that more accountability is equivalent to political pressure, James Tobin stated that, "Economic performance necessarily involves political choices." Explain how this statement could justify more accountability.

5. The Fed's ultimate goal is to improve the course of the economy. Do you think that the definition of the goal itself and the way it is pursued should be a political decision? Why?

61.
An Rx for
S&L
Relapse?

Savings and loan associations (S&Ls) are financial institutions whose economic difficulties have cost taxpayers hundreds of billions of dollars. S&Ls were created in the 1930s to provide long-term fixed interest-rate mortgages financed by short-term interest-bearing savings accounts. This was the beginning of the problem. As long as interest rates on savings accounts were lower than mortgage rates, S&Ls could make a profit. When inflation increased, S&Ls had to increase interest rates on savings accounts in order to continue to attract funds. With the value of their principal assets—mortgages—declining, and interest costs paid to passbook holders rising, many S&Ls went broke or came close to it.

In 1980, Congress lightened the regulations governing bank operations in the hope that S&Ls could recover. Although inflation abated in the early 1980s, it was too late for many S&Ls. In an attempt to recoup losses, many S&Ls invested in projects that were risky investments. The Federal Savings and Loan Insurance Corporation, an organization established to safeguard deposits in the event of a bank failure, was also bankrupt, and the government had to either bail out the bankrupt S&Ls or face the possibility of financial disaster. By 1991, the total cost of rescuing these banks was estimated to be $200 billion. This article discusses how the industry got into trouble and how a decline in interest rates is fueling concern of a financial relapse.

After studying your text, reading the article, and answering the questions, you should be able to:

◆◆ Explain the functions of S&Ls

◆◆ Explain the circumstances that led many of the S&Ls to go bankrupt

◆◆ Discuss the pros and cons of bailing out the S&Ls

◆◆ Describe the ways in which S&Ls are regulated

◆◆ Understand the relationship between S&Ls and other financial institutions

◆◆ Debate other means of minimizing the risk of S&L defaults

Preview

◆ The decline in interest rates resulted in a substantial number of homeowners refinancing.

◆ By locking themselves into long-term mortgages at low interest rates, S&Ls expose themselves to the risk of inflation and a return to the S&L failures of the 1980s.

◆ Unlike the situation in the 1980s, commercial banks have increased their real estate holdings, putting them in the same situation as the S&Ls.

◆ The source of the problem may be the public's love of the fixed-rate mortgage.

◆ The possibility of interest-rate risk has led regulators to propose new safeguards such as requiring S&Ls to have more capital.

Lower Interest Rates Revive Fears for Banks and S&Ls

The lower interest rates that are benefiting homeowners and other borrowers are a mixed blessing for banks and savings and loan associations and may even be pushing them into a riskier position.

In the short term, the tidal wave of homeowners seeking to take advantage of the lowest lending rates in nearly 20 years by refinancing their mortgages has provided the banks a much-needed increase in income from fees on the new loans. The lower rates have also widened the spread between the interest rates the banks pay depositors and what they charge borrowers.

But for the long term, the refinancing trend has raised concerns that many large institutions may be risking significant new losses. Federal regulators, academics and some industry executives fear that banks and savings associations, by locking themselves into long-term mortgages at historically low rates, could be devastated if inflation accelerates in the next few years.

The new rates for homeowners, averaging about 8.2 percent for 30-year fixed-rate mortgages, led to more than seven times as many refinancings last year as in 1990, according to the Mortgage Bankers Association. Some fixed-rate mortgages are as low as 7.5 percent.

Agency to Offer Ideas   T. Timothy Ryan Jr., director of the Office of Thrift Supervision, which oversees the nation's savings associations, said that in the next few months his agency would recommend ways to reduce interest-rate risks. "This becomes more important now than before because of the high volume of fixed-rate mortgages that are being held," Mr. Ryan added.

Regulators have proposed requiring savings and loans with high interest-rate risks to have more capital but have encountered industry resistance.

The sort of interest-rate squeeze that regulators now fear is precisely what savings and loans suffered in the 1980's. Revenues from old, fixed-rate mortgages often failed to cover the increasing interest rates they had to pay to attract deposits, which are shorter term. While deregulation, short-sighted investments and corruption all contributed to the crisis, the negative interest-rate spread is now widely acknowledged as the leading cause of the demise of hundreds of savings associations....

Richard H. Diehl, chairman and chief executive of Home Savings of America, the nation's largest savings association, said the potential harm from higher interest rates was worrying the industry more than delinquencies, defaults and the declining values of real estate and other collateral put up to back loans. "It's probably the greatest risk that faces a lender," Mr. Diehl said.

Bankers and regulators have grown more sophisticated in hedging against interest-rate risk but cannot protect themselves completely. "We can hedge to reduce the risk against five-year loans," Mr. Diehl said. "But it's very difficult, if not impossible, to hedge against longer-term loans, such as 30-year fixed loans. It just gets too expensive."

Many analysts believe that the surge of refinancings will grow only stronger in the first few months of this year—particularly if interest rates are cut again—as millions of homeowners realize how much they can save. A new report by Eric I. Hemel, a banking analyst at First Boston, concludes that $1 trillion in fixed-rate mortgages at rates of 10 percent or higher stands to be refinanced.

New Hedging Techniques   Since the savings-industry debacle of the mid-1980's, banks and regulators have developed new techniques to protect against higher interest rates. A large volume of mortgages is being sold to other lenders, including the Federal National Mortgage Association and the Federal Home Loan Mortgage Corporation, which then spread the risk by repackaging the loans as securities that are sold on Wall Street to institutional and individual investors.

Still, experts say interest-rate risks are greater than ever. Commercial banks are more heavily involved in real estate lending than ever before—doubling their exposure in the last decade alone. Analysts say many ailing banks are clearly taking on greater risks in an attempt to bolster their battered financial statements over the short term....

Problem of Fixed Rates   One culprit is the fixed-rate mortgage, which most homeowners, eager to lock in low rates, now prefer to adjustable-rate mortgages. United States banks are the only ones in the industrialized world that promote fixed-rate mortgages widely....

Amount of Capital Needed   Federal regulators are considering whether to require institutions with high interest-rate risk to have more capital. Capital, or net worth, is a critical cushion against losses.

QUESTIONS

1. a) What services do banks, including S&Ls, sell?

   b) How do these institutions make a profit?

   c) Why is the interest rate at which borrowers obtain money generally higher than is paid on savings accounts?

2. In the early 1990s, mortgage interest rates fell from approximately 11 percent to 8 percent, while interest rates on savings fell from approximately 7 percent to 3 percent.

   a) Suppose that S&Ls had agreed to fixed-rate mortgages at an 11 percent interest rate. What happened to the profit made by S&Ls when interest rates fell? What happened to the value of their assets (mortgages)? Explain your answer.

   b) Why did S&Ls refinance existing mortgages when interest rates fell?

3. Assume that mortgages have been refinanced at a rate of 8 percent. Suppose that the S&L industry's fears materialize and an increase in inflation appears likely.

   a) How would the Fed alter the money supply?

   b) What would happen to the interest rate? Why?

   c) What would happen to the interest rate S&Ls pay their depositors? Why?

   d) What would happen to the value of the assets, and the profits, of S&Ls if interest rates paid to savings account holders were to exceed the 8 percent mortgage rate? Explain your answers.

4. a) When a firm goes bankrupt, who generally foots the bill?

   b) Why doesn't the government treat S&Ls as just another firm and refuse to bail them out? Answer in terms of the money supply and also in terms of the implications for output and prices.

5. The article discusses a proposal to require financial institutions with high interest-rate risk to have more capital or net worth as a safeguard against interest-rate risk.

   a) How would this protect the banks and S&Ls?

   b) Why are these financial institutions opposed to this measure?

6. Other solutions exist.

   a) Suppose that the government places a ceiling on the interest rate that S&Ls can pay their depositors (and leaves other financial markets alone). Would this be an effective guard against financial collapse? Explain.

   b) Suppose that S&Ls only offer adjustable-rate mortgages (ARMs). How would an ARM work to solve the problem?

62. Humpty-Dumpty Sunny-Side Down?

Changes in real gross domestic product (GDP) are produced by movements in aggregate demand and aggregate supply. Monetary policy attempts to change real GDP by actions that disturb equilibrium in the money market. The primary mechanism by which monetary policy affects income involves changes in interest rates influencing investment and consumption. Other transmission mechanisms include changes in real balances, wealth, and the exchange rate. The accompanying article illustrates the effects of changing interest rates, real balances, wealth, and exchange rates on real GDP in Japan. Although there are some institutional differences between Japan and the United States, the theory of how policy works is the same.

After studying your text, reading the article, and answering the questions, you should be able to:

◆◆ Explain the impact of changes in the interest rate on investment and consumption and, thereby, on aggregate expenditure and real GDP

◆◆ Explain the effect of changes in real GDP on the demand for real money, investment, and aggregate expenditure

◆◆ Describe alternative mechanisms through which monetary policy actions are transmitted to real GDP

◆◆ Explain the structural conditions of the economy that hinder the speedy operation of monetary policy

Preview

◆ Japan's economy was weakening in 1992.

◆ The Nikkei index was roughly half of its late 1989 level, land values were declining, and bankruptcies were up.

◆ Japan's rapid economic growth since 1985 had been fueled by low interest rates.

◆ Easy credit had stimulated investment and construction, which helped drive real estate and stock market prices higher.

◆ With growth at 5 percent, the fear of inflation led the Bank of Japan to raise interest rates sharply in 1989.

◆ The forces leading to explosive growth reversed, and Japan's economy slowed to a recessionary pace.

Japan's Bubble Bursts

We Americans are so entranced by the Japanese—regarding them either as supermen or demons—that we can't easily see that they make mistakes, too. Well, they do. The current faltering state of Japan's economy is a case in point. The Tokyo stock market is roughly half its peak reached in late 1989 (38,916 on the Nikkei index, which closed Tuesday at 19,918). Land values are declining. In 1991, business bankruptcies rose 66 percent. A dreaded word is being spoken in Tokyo: recession. And Japan's problems are mostly self-inflicted. An orgy of easy credit and speculation drove the economy into a frenzied boom that's now collapsing.

There are fears of a wider financial crisis that would ultimately harm the U.S. and world economies. The grimmest outlook involves a continuing drop of stock and land values, which would undermine Japan's banks and curb the lending needed for recovery. For now, this sort of disaster seems unlikely. Japan's unemployment rate is a mere 2.1 percent. A brief slump will bring no great hardship....

But whatever happens, the punctured boom confounds popular American notions of the Japanese. We see them as a monotonously productive people who disdain all shortcuts to riches. We regard their policies as models of prudence and farsightedness. The imagery is too simple. It won't fit what's now derisively called "the bubble economy": a reference to the hugely inflated stock and land prices of the late 1980s. The period was shaped by private greed and government mistakes.

Government made the biggest blunder. Between 1985 and 1989, the Bank of Japan (Japan's equivalent of our Federal Reserve) kept interest rates too low. The yen was rising on foreign exchange markets, making Japan's exports more expensive abroad. The idea was to stimulate domestic spending to offset a feared loss of exports. The key discount rate dropped to 2.5 percent. Easy credit fueled an explosion of corporate investment in new equipment and factories, residential and office construction.

What ensued was a dizzying cycle of spending and speculation. The construction boom inflated real estate values, because land is so scarce in Japan. Higher real estate prices bloated the stock market, because most major companies have huge land holdings. And a soaring stock market helped companies raise capital to sustain investment spending. Between 1985 and 1990, residential land values in major cities rose 167 percent. The stock market doubled in the two years before its peak. Economic growth in the late 1980s averaged nearly 5 percent annually.

As with all speculative booms, everyone thought success natural and no one imagined the boom would ever end. What finally shut it down was the Bank of Japan's belated recognition that a runaway economy could spawn higher inflation. In late 1989, Yasushi Mieno—the bank's new head—began to raise interest rates sharply. Without easy credit, the speculative machine went into reverse. Land prices, the stock market and corporate investment began to slide. The economy slowed dramatically.

The evidence of excess is everywhere. Many construction projects turned out to be duds. The biggest category of losers were apartments containing "one-room mansions," says analyst Alicia Ogawa of S. G. Warburg Securities in Tokyo.... "There was simply no real demand for this type of project," says Ogawa.

As for stock speculation, it was rampant. Many of Japan's best-known companies committed vast amounts to "*eigyo tokkin*" accounts at brokerage houses. These were funds that could be freely invested in the soaring stock market. It was the disclosure last year that many big companies had been guaranteed against losses on these accounts that prompted the resignation of top executives at Nomura Securities, Japan's biggest brokerage house....

Finally, some of Japan's banks are clearly overextended. Bad real estate loans and low stock prices have hurt them. Banks' capital is heavily concentrated in holdings of corporate stocks. As stock prices drop, so does bank capital. This weakens the banks' ability to make new loans. Ogawa thinks bank profits could be squeezed for three to five years. But she doubts melodramatic predictions of a major financial crisis. The Japanese banking system, she says, is fundamentally sound.

For us, Japan's slowdown is a mixed blessing. Even if it is mild, it will hurt. Demand for our exports will suffer. After Europe and Canada, Japan is our third-largest market....Competition from Japanese firms will intensify, because they try to offset weak domestic sales by exporting more. But beyond these immediate effects, there's a more favorable message in the slowdown.

In the 1980s, Japanese companies acquired an aura of invincibility. They often seemed to have endless amounts of inexpensive capital to finance new plants, research and overseas investment. American and European companies appeared to be at a hopeless disadvantage. What we know now is that the Japanese advantage was largely temporary: the effect of easy credit and high profits from the "bubble economy." Japanese profits are now squeezed. Scarce capital is more expensive. Japanese companies face limits. Less overseas investment may ultimately raise the yen's exchange rate, hurting exports.

Japanese companies won't vanish as fierce competitors. Their strengths lie in quality products and technology. They learn from adversity. But the competition isn't as lopsided as American mythology holds. Japan's economy isn't a miracle machine, and the Japanese aren't supermen. They make mistakes, including—like Americans before them—believing in their own infallibility.

Robert J. Samuelson, "Japan's Bubble Bursts," March 18, 1992. Robert J. Samuelson writes a column on economic affairs for *Newsweek* and *The Washington Post*. Reprinted with permission.

QUESTIONS

1. a) In a diagram of the Japanese money market below to the left, draw the demand and supply curves. Mark the equilibrium interest rate and quantity of real money balances.

   b) In 1985, the Bank of Japan increased the money supply because it was afraid that exports would decline as the yen rose. Show the consequences of this policy on money market equilibrium on your diagram.

   c) Draw a second diagram, positioned in the middle of the page in 1a above, with axes representing the interest rate and the level of investment. Draw an investment demand schedule. Mark the amount of planned investment at the initial interest rate. Show the new investment level that resulted from the change in the money market equilibrium.

   d) On a third diagram, to the right above, draw the aggregate expenditure curve and its components—autonomous expenditure and induced expenditure. Add a 45-degree line and show the initial equilibrium real GDP. Show how real GDP changed following the change in investment.

   e) On your diagram in 1a, illustrate the change in the money demand curve that occurred as a result of the changes in real GDP in 2d. Explain what happened.

2. Following the easing of monetary policy, the Japanese demanded more assets and the stock market index rose, indicating that real GDP was likely to be affected in two other ways. Explain briefly how the increase in the money supply increased real GDP through

   a) the real balances transmission mechanism.

   b) the wealth transmission mechanism.

3. The Bank of Japan raised interest rates in 1989. Assume this was accomplished by a decrease in the money supply. Explain how GDP was affected through

a) the interest rate transmission mechanism.

b) the real balances transmission mechanism.

c) the wealth transmission mechanism.

4. a) The article states that one consequence of a slowdown in the Japanese economy was likely to be a decrease in the demand for U.S. goods. Explain the linkage.

b) It was also expected that the increase in Japanese interest rates would reduce Japanese exports and real GDP. Explain the relationship between the two.

5. What factors determined the length of time between the increase in interest rates and the desired changes in prices and output?

63.
Repercussions
of Fiscal
Policy Tunes

Fiscal policy is the process by which the government uses its purchases, transfers, and taxes to smooth the fluctuations in real GDP and to stimulate economic growth. Government expenditure and taxes produce changes in equilibrium expenditure and real GDP through the multiplier process. Offsetting these changes, resulting changes in the demand for real money affect the interest rate, investment, and real GDP. Thus increased government expenditure may "crowd out" private investment expenditure. This article discusses the repercussions of alternative fiscal policies for the level and composition of real GDP.

After studying your text, reading the article, and answering the questions, you should be able to:

◆ ◆ Describe the impact of government purchases or tax policies on aggregate expenditure and real GDP

◆ ◆ Describe the impact of fiscal policy changes on the money market

◆ ◆ Explain how "crowding out" arises

◆ ◆ Explain the factors that determine the relative effectiveness of monetary and fiscal policy

◆ ◆ Analyze the effects of different fiscal and monetary policy measures on the composition of aggregate demand

Preview

◆ A group of 100 prominent economists proposed that President Bush and Congress should stimulate the economy.

◆ They recommended increasing federal aid to state and local governments and providing business tax credits.

◆ They also urged the Federal Reserve to cut short-term interest rates.

◆ Even though these proposals would increase the federal deficit, the economists argued that the effects would still be beneficial.

◆ When the economy recovered, budget cuts and higher taxes would be needed to reduce the federal deficit.

Economists Urge Investing Stimulus

A group of about 100 prominent economists yesterday called on President Bush and Congress to stimulate the sluggish American economy by increasing federal aid to hard-pressed state and local governments by $50 billion and providing businesses a tax credit if they increase their spending on equipment.

The economists, whose ranks include six Nobel Prize winners, also urged the Federal Reserve to cut short-term interest rates further to make sure any economic recovery this year is strong enough to reduce unemployment significantly.

Acknowledging that adopting their proposal would mean a sizable increase in the federal budget deficit, and probably in long-term interest rates as well, the economists argued that a program focused on stimulating investment would be healthy for the economy even if it increased the deficit in the short term.

The group flatly rejected differing proposals from President Bush, congressional Democrats and Democratic presidential candidate Arkansas Gov. Bill Clinton for personal income tax cuts.

"We believe that cutting income taxes is exactly the wrong approach," said James Tobin, professor emeritus at Yale University, as he read the group's statement at a press conference at the National Press Building. "It would promote consumption, not investment. And although there is a case for a quick, temporary tax cut, history tells us it would be almost impossible to reverse."

Tobin said the goal of economic policy now should be to seek an economic growth rate of 4.5 percent to 5 percent until unemployment falls substantially. Most forecasters believe a recovery is underway, but that the gross domestic product will increase at only a 2.5 percent to 3.5 percent rate in the second half of this year and at a 3 percent to 3.5 percent pace in 1993.

Robert Solow of the Massachusetts Institute of Technology noted that most economists expect the recovery to be "quite weak" compared with those that followed most other recessions since World War II.

"By doing nothing we risk prolonged stagnation, feeble recovery—or worse, no recovery at all," said Marshall Pomer, a professor at the University of California at Berkeley who helped organize the informal economists' group to offer these proposals. "There has been, and still remains, too much complacency."

"For the longer run, the prospect is slow growth of productivity and therefore slow growth of incomes, more and more unequally distributed between the best and the worst off," the group said. "Everyone agrees that the remedy for the long-run problem is more investment: in people, in infrastructure, in technology and in machinery."

To free up resources to finance that investment, the economists argued that the federal deficit will have to come down, a change that ultimately will require higher, not lower, taxes.

"Once the economy has substantially recovered, it will no longer be appropriate to pay for the program by federal borrowing," the statement said. "Instead, we propose that Congress and the president plan now to finance it by a combination of future cuts in defense spending and higher taxes. This program should not be allowed to interfere with continued reduction of the federal budget deficit."

"In the long run, we do have to get some realism into fiscal policy," Tobin said.

Financial analysts expressed skepticism that either the Bush administration or Congress would have much appetite for the second half of the economists' prescription. As a result, any sign the short-term-stimulus portion of the proposal might be adopted likely would cause long-term interest rates to rise, the analysts said.

"Investors would turn around and offer bonds in great quantities," which would drive up long-term interest rates, said Charles Lieberman, managing director of Chemical Banking Securities Corp.

Lieberman was particularly skeptical that Congress would seriously consider a $50 billion increase in aid to state and local governments for education and infrastructure such as roads and pollution-control projects. This year, total federal grants to state and local governments, other than for health and welfare payments to individuals, will be about $64 billion.

—John M. Berry, "Economists Urge Investing Stimulus," *The Washington Post,* March 31, 1992.
©1992 The Washington Post. Reprinted with permission.

QUESTIONS

1. a) Draw a set of three diagrams below. In the left-hand diagram, draw axes representing the interest rate and the quantity of real money. Show the demand for and supply of real money, and mark the equilibrium point. In the middle diagram, the axes should represent the interest rate and the level of investment. Draw an investment curve and show planned investment at the equilibrium interest rate. On the right, draw axes representing aggregate expenditure and real GDP. Draw an aggregate expenditure curve and a 45-degree line showing the economy initially in equilibrium with planned investment as determined in the middle diagram. Show the level of real GDP and aggregate expenditure.

   b) Suppose that the government followed the advice of many politicians and attempted to stimulate the economy through an income tax cut for consumers. In your diagrams illustrate the impact of this increase initially on equilibrium GDP, the money market, the level of investment, and, again, on real GDP.

   c) In the article, James Tobin argues that "cutting income taxes is exactly the wrong approach...it would promote consumption, not investment." Identify and explain what would happen to equilibrium consumption, investment, government expenditure, and net exports.

   d) The magnitude of the change in investment would depend on the slopes of the real money demand curve and the investment demand curve. Under what conditions would there be a large change?

2. The economists are proposing an investment tax credit instead of a tax cut for consumers.

   a) Would the change in GDP following the introduction of an investment tax credit be different from that caused by an income tax cut of the same cost? Why?

   b) How would the change in the composition of GDP be different? Explain your reasoning.

c) Explain why the size of the budget deficit threatens to undermine the impact of the stimulus proposals on investment. Refer to real GDP, the demand for money, interest rates, and investment.

3. The economists also urged the Federal Reserve to cut short-term interest rates to support the economic recovery and their investment tax credit proposal.

a) In a further set of three diagrams (drawn as in Question 1), show how increasing the money supply would decrease interest rates, encourage investment, and increase the economic recovery.

b) Why would monetary policy be used in conjunction with fiscal policy?

The IS-LM model is a convenient diagrammatic device for displaying simultaneous equilibrium in the money and goods markets. The IS curve shows combinations of real GDP and the interest rate at which aggregate planned expenditure equals real GDP. The LM curve shows combinations of the two variables at which the quantity of real money demanded equals that supplied. The intersection of IS and LM shows the equilibrium interest rate and level of real GDP where the goods and money markets are in equilibrium.

The IS-LM model can illustrate the impact on interest rates and real GDP of monetary and fiscal policy, including "crowding out" effects, assuming a fixed price level. In the accompanying article, this model is used to analyze the effects of President Bush's proposals to stimulate the economy.

After studying your text, reading the article, and answering the questions, you should be able to:

◆◆ Describe the characteristics and determinants of the IS and LM curves

◆◆ Predict the impact of changes in monetary and fiscal policy on the equilibrium interest rate and the level of real GDP

◆◆ Evaluate the relative effectiveness of monetary versus fiscal policy

Preview

◆ In his 1992 State of the Union address, President Bush proposed to stimulate the economy using fiscal policy measures in an effort to end the recession.

◆ A $25 billion stimulus to private consumer and business spending was expected to result from lowering individual withholding for income tax purposes.

◆ Other components of the Bush package included an increase in the personal exemption, a tax break for savings, a cut in the capital gains tax, a tax credit for home buyers, and an increase in the depreciation allowance for business.

◆ The budget deficit was expected to increase.

Bush Offers a Plan to End the Recession in This Election Year

For the first time in a decade, the president's State of the Union address has focused on fiscal stimulus rather than spending restraint.

Politically, that may prove astute. But economically, it poses an array of risks, notably increasing the federal deficit to a projected $399 billion in the current fiscal year, a record....

The biggest surprise came when Mr. Bush disclosed that he is unilaterally giving the economy a $25 billion shot in the arm over the next 12 months. In a move that requires no congressional approval, he is ordering employers to withhold less in federal taxes from workers' paychecks almost immediately. The effect will be to give the average family $350 more per worker to spend this year, roughly the equivalent of an extra week's paycheck. But the total tax bite will ultimately be the same; that amount will be made up at tax time next year, when refunds will be smaller or taxes due will increase....

While asking Congress to join with him to save the economy, he also threatened to be combative if it resists. He demanded that Congress act on his plan by March 20. "From the day after that, if it must be: the battle is joined."

If Congress meets Mr. Bush's deadline, the proposals could produce a spurt in business investment and in home sales this year, and could lift consumer spirits a bit. The president's advisers optimistically predict the package could add 500,000 new jobs this year.

The price will be an increase in the budget deficit. The withholding plan, cleverly designed to avoid violating the 1990 budget law, will boost the federal deficit immediately. Some of Mr. Bush's proposals—a new version of Individual Retirement Accounts, for instance—won't increase the deficit now, but will do so eventually....

Not since Ronald Reagan proposed his supply-side tax cuts in 1981 has a president had to ask Congress for help in rescuing a sluggish economy. "It took us just 12 months to go from tax increases are good to tax increases are bad," says economist John Makin of the American Enterprise Institute.

It isn't hard to understand why. The afterglow of the victory over Iraq faded. The economic recovery faltered. The president's popularity plummeted. And consumer confidence still is falling. A year ago, a bare majority—54%—of voters polled by The Wall Street Journal and NBC News said they disapproved of Mr. Bush's handling of the economy. Today, 70% disapprove. In an ominous sign for Mr. Bush's reelection hopes, voters now say Democrats would do a better job handling the economy than Republicans.

In crafting his package, Mr. Bush faced a dilemma. If he proposed big tax cuts or spending increases, they could increase the odds of a strong recovery. But that gain would come at the risk of worsening the long-run problems of inadequate savings and investment. Critics would complain that it was too much, too late.

But if his proposals had aimed exclusively at long-run problems, he would have courted ridicule for ignoring the current sluggish state of the economy. Then the line would be too little, too late.

As he so often does, Mr. Bush decided to walk down the middle, offering a little something for almost everybody....

For the middle class, defined very broadly to include families who make as much as $158,000 a year, Mr. Bush offered a $500-a-child increase in the personal exemption. For those who can afford to save, and who also make less than $120,000 a year, he offered a new tax break for saving. For conservatives, he offered a deeper cut in the capital-gains tax than he has proposed in the past—to a top rate of 15.4%—but only for assets held more than three years.

Spreading the Benefits For would-be home buyers, he offered a new $5,000 tax credit for homes purchased before year-end that administration officials say could turn an additional 250,000 families into homeowners. For homeowners who sell their houses for less than they paid, he offered a new tax break for losses. For the poor, he offered a tax credit of up to $3,750 a year to buy health insurance. For the unemployed, he offered extended jobless benefits. And although he didn't mention it last night, he is also asking to repeal the luxury tax on expensive boats and airplanes.

For business, he offered a temporary increase in first-year depreciation allowances for equipment purchased this year that could increase corporate cash flow by more than $10 billion this year. For the beleaguered real-estate industry, he offered the partial restoration of tax breaks eliminated in 1986 and ways to encourage pension funds to pour money into real estate.

For the Keynesians, he ordered a speed-up of federal spending already in the works to pump an extra $10 billion in the economy in the next six months. But he didn't forget government-spending phobes, either: The budget he is to release today will propose a one-year freeze in domestic spending authority—except for benefit programs like Social Security—at this year's level.

For the regulated, he ordered a 90-day moratorium on "any new federal regulations that could hinder growth."....

Thanks to a sharp cut in interest rates engineered by the Federal Reserve last year, many mainstream economists expect the economy to be growing again, albeit slowly, by spring, which is the soonest any of Mr. Bush's legislative proposals are likely to be enacted. As Sen. Paul Simon, an Illinois Democrat, puts it, "Alan Greenspan has already done more than any tax cut is going to do."

Even some economists inclined toward using fiscal policy to spur a recovery are cowed by the record budget deficit. "Because of the budget pickle we allowed ourselves to get into, we probably shouldn't have any fiscal stimulus," says Alan Blinder, a Princeton University economist. "We don't need tax cuts now."

From the left, Mr. Bush's critics say the president's obsession with tax cuts and spending caps blinds him to the need for added government spending on public causes. "I don't know anybody who believes that a tax cut designed to stimulate the economy of the kind that's being discussed will have any effect on getting us out of the recession," says former Labor Secretary Ray Marshall. He heads a group of liberal Democrats that wants to spend $100 billion on infrastructure and education over the next five years.

From the right, Mr. Bush's critics also accuse the president of timidity, but in the other direction. They want deeper cuts in taxes and spending. The Heritage Foundation, for instance, last week called for a $1,500 tax cut for every child under six and a $1,000 cut for every child between six and 18.

Mr. Bush has crafted his proposal to stay within the bounds of the 1990 budget law. But the risk is that Congress will see the president, and raise him. Or, as Salomon Brothers economist Susan Hering puts it, "In an election year, the president's package will be only the starting point for a possibly dangerous competition with the political opposition to woo voters with fiscal favors."....

Economic Boost Elements of the program are undeniably potent stimuli for the economy. Take the withholding tax maneuver, a way to give American consumers about $25 billion a year in cash that they otherwise wouldn't have received until they got tax refund checks next year.

Nearly 85% of all taxpayers have too much money taken out of their checks, essentially giving the government an interest-free loan. Mr. Bush is ordering the Internal Revenue Service to change tax-withholding formulas so that employers take less in taxes each week from checks of workers who earn less than $90,000.

The investment incentive is also likely to give the economy a kick. The president's Investment Tax Allowance—additional depreciation in the first year of 15% of the purchase price—would give businesses an incentive to buy equipment or other assets besides real estate before the end of the year.

"That's the one temporary tax cut where the temporariness makes it work better," says Brookings Institution economist Charles Schultze, who was among Jimmy Carter's advisers. "If you are going to goose spending, dear God, we ought to boost investment spending."

Of course, as auto makers have demonstrated with their rebates, temporary incentives tend to increase demand for equipment today, then reduce demand for equipment after the tax break expires. "You're just borrowing from the future," says Allan Meltzer of Pittsburgh's Carnegie-Mellon University. "It's silly."

Echoes of Keynes True, concedes Princeton's Prof. Blinder. But, he adds, it's also precisely what John Maynard Keynes prescribed for countering recessions: "Counter-cyclical policy is about filling in holes and shaving-off peaks."

Similarly, the $5,000 tax credit for first-time home buyers who act by year-end should lure off the fence Americans who have been thinking about buying in the next few years. And it comes at a time when the National Association of Realtors figures that lower mortgage rates already have made houses more affordable to middle-income Americans than at any time in the past 18 years. About 840,000 homes sold last year, or about one-fifth of the total, went to first-time buyers, the Mortgage Bankers Association says. The administration is counting on a "ripple-up" effect, figuring that it can boost consumer confidence by making it easier for existing home buyers to sell their residences.

Other parts of the Bush package probably won't do very much to help the economy right now. The increase in the personal tax exemption won't mean a nickel to families without children. And for those who do, it doesn't kick in until Oct. 1.

For a working family with three children, $40,000 in wage income and no extraordinary deductions, the Treasury estimates the proposal would mean a tax cut of only $56.25, about 1.5%, in 1992 and $225 in 1993. That's $4.32 a week.

QUESTIONS

1. a) What is the IS curve?

    b) Why is it drawn with a negative slope?

    c) What factors are held constant in moving along the curve?

2. a) What is the LM curve?

    b) Why is it drawn with a positive slope?

    c) What factors are held constant in moving along the curve?

3. Consider President Bush's proposal to reduce personal income taxes.

    a) Draw a diagram with axes showing the interest rate and real GDP. Add the IS and LM curves. Mark the initial equilibrium.

    b) Show the impact of the tax cuts on the curve(s) and on the equilibrium interest rate and level of GDP. Why did you move the curve(s) you did?

    c) Explain why the new equilibrium depended on the slope of the LM curve.

    d) Under what circumstances would the tax cuts have had no effect on real GDP?

4. The article refers to the sharp cuts in interest rates engineered by the Federal Reserve in 1991.

   a) Draw a further IS-LM diagram. Show the economy initially in equilibrium.

   b) Show the impact of the expansion of the money supply on the equilibrium interest rate and level of GDP.

   c) Explain why the new equilibrium depends on the slope of the IS curve.

5. The impact of the substantial cuts in interest rates had not materialized by January 1992.

   a) Explain why an expansion of the money supply might not increase real GDP.

   b) Explain the probable economic reasoning underlying the statement by Senator Paul Simon that "Alan Greenspan has already done more than any tax cut is going to do."

   c) Suppose that fiscal policy measures were initiated at the same time that the Fed expanded the money supply. Explain what would have happened to the economy.

AGGREGATE SUPPLY FLUCTUATIONS

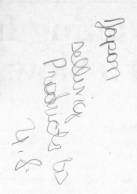

Japan declining Productivity 4-8

**65.
Sluggish
Economy
Growing at
Snail's
Pace**

Wages and employment are determined in the U.S. labor market by the interaction of aggregate labor demand and aggregate labor supply. The aggregate demand for labor is inversely related to the real wage. It reflects labor's marginal revenue productivity as well as the cost and productivity of other inputs. The aggregate supply of labor is positively related to the real wage. As the real wage increases, the higher wage induces current workers to offer more hours and new workers are attracted into the labor market. Changes in real wages and the level of employment occur when the determinants of labor demand and/or supply change. This article discusses the labor market undercurrents of the slow recovery from the recession of the early 1990s.

After studying your text, reading the article, and answering the questions, you should be able to:

◆◆ Explain the determinants of the aggregate demand for labor curve and the aggregate supply of labor curve

◆◆ Predict how employment and the real wage change as the aggregate labor demand and/or supply curves shift

◆◆ Explain the determinants of the aggregate production function

◆◆ Predict changes in real gross domestic product (GDP) following changes in employment and productivity

Preview

◆ Although in March 1992 most Americans were awaiting the end of the recession, it had already ended, according to many economists.

◆ In fact, the economy was in a period of slow growth in which unemployment and consumer uncertainty remained problems.

◆ Signs of recovery included increases in housing construction, and in furniture and appliance sales.

◆ Recovery was hampered by debt problems, corporate restructuring, a lack of a government stimulus, and the slowdown in the Japanese economy.

◆ The fast growth of the labor force of the 1980s had slowed, and poor productivity growth continued.

Daunting Implications of a Slow Recovery

Most Americans are longing for the recession to end. The problem is, it did so nearly a year ago.

That's what most economists say. They believe the downturn, which began in the second half of 1990, gave way to recovery sometime in the first half of 1991. What the country has been witnessing since then is not continued recession, but what Georgia State University's Donald Ratajczak calls "a very, very slow liftoff."

To many, the distinction between an actual recession and an anemic recovery is irrelevant. When you use the "common sense duck test," notes Michael Boskin, President Bush's chief economist, most would agree that "it's been a lousy period."

But a slow-growth economy has significant implications—especially during an election year. On the one hand, it means that the unemployed still have a rough time finding jobs, consumer confidence remains bleak and the possibility of tipping back into recession is all the more likely. On the other hand, the economy holds just enough promise for the Federal Reserve to keep from easing interest rates further. It is, in short, the economic equivalent of purgatory.

Perhaps even more important is what the current state of the economy may reveal about the future. Although it's a mistake to confuse a regular business cycle with the forces shaping the long-term economic landscape, slow growth has become a theme that's common to both. In this sense, some fear that the snail's-pace recovery is providing a taste of things to come.

Exactly when the recession ended and the recovery began will be decided by the Business Cycle Dating Committee of the National Bureau of Economic Research, a private group in Cambridge, Mass. When making its official determination, this panel of economists examines a range of data, from retail sales to industrial production to gross domestic product.

Since the second quarter of last year, real GDP has been expanding steadily, but barely. In the past few weeks, clear signs have emerged that the pace of growth is picking up. Home sales and home construction are increasing, and that has spawned scattered sales of furniture and appliances. The hope is those early spring buds will flower into better growth later this year. And some economists say they wouldn't rule out a strong bounce back. Don't take slow-growth predictions "as gospel," says American Enterprise Institute's Herbert Stein, given how poorly economists have forecast other aspects of this cycle.

Nevertheless, most analysts argue the recovery will continue to be well below par. Among the reasons: continued debt problems, corporate restructurings and a lack of the kind of fiscal and monetary stimuli that have tweaked the economy in the past.

Moreover, the Japanese economy is putting on the brakes just as the U.S. economy is starting to accelerate. Despite all the talk about their "closed markets," the Japanese buy more goods from the U.S. than any other country except Canada—nearly $50 billion a year. As their economy slows, ours is sure to suffer. And in past slowdowns, Japanese industry has responded by trying to ship even more goods abroad— a strategy that would cause a double blow to U.S. industry.

At the Federal Reserve Board, top officials also say they're worried about another spillover effect from Japan's current problems. The sharp drop in the Tokyo stock market may force Japanese investors to sell off U.S. securities and pull their money home to cover losses. That, in turn, could cause long-term interest rates here to rise.

In the White House, the implications of slow growth are well understood. In the past, an economic recovery that began by the spring would have been sufficient to re-elect a president in November. But this time, the president's advisers privately warn that growth likely won't be sufficient to eliminate the economy as the top campaign issue.

For the rest of the nation, continued slow growth this year will underscore already serious questions about the longer-term. Real GDP grew at an annual average of 3.8% from 1961 to 1971, but it fell to 2.3% from 1981 to 1991. For a year and a half before the recession, real GDP grew at an annual rate of just about 1.25%. And the future is daunting. Growth in the labor force, which helped fuel the expansion of the 1980s, will be down sharply in coming years because of demographic changes, according to the Labor Department. And gains in productivity— the measure of output per hour of work—have been disappointing for two decades. "We may just have to lower our aspirations as far as growth is concerned," says Stanford economist Robert Hall, who chairs the Business Cycle Dating Committee.

The consensus is that near-term growth will be slow. But even once the shackles are off, we may find we don't run as fast as we used to.

—Rick Wartzman, "Daunting Implications of a Slow Recovery," March 23, 1992.

QUESTIONS

1. a) Draw a short-run aggregate production function showing the relationship between aggregate output and the quantity of labor in the United States in 1980.

    b) During the 1980s, the growth of the labor force fueled an expansion of real GDP (aggregate output). Illustrate this on your diagram above. Assume everything else was constant.

    c) What might have been responsible for the growth in the labor force? Explain in terms of the determinants of the supply of labor.

    d) As the labor force grew, what happened to the size of sequential increases in real GDP, ceteris paribus? Why?

2. Also, output per hour of work increased slowly in the 1980s.

    a) Illustrate the impact of the growth in labor productivity on real GDP on a further diagram of the aggregate production function of the United States. Assume everything else was unchanged.

    b) What factors might have positively affected productivity?

    c) What factors might have held productivity growth back?

3. The article argues that the growth of real GDP is, and will continue to be, slow in the 1990s. A number of causes are cited. For each of the causes below, show the implications for the real wage and the level of employment in a diagram of the aggregate demand for and supply of labor, and also for the level of employment and real GDP in a diagram of the aggregate production function.

    a) decreased exports to Japan

    b) consumer uncertainty and unemployment

    c) rising interest rates

    d) corporate restructuring that raises efficiency but increases unemployment

    e) slow growth in the labor force and labor productivity

    f) small increases in furniture and appliance sales

66.

Is Unemployment Natural and Sticky?

Wages and employment are determined in the U.S. labor market by the interactions of the aggregate demand for and supply of labor. According to the flexible wage theory, the real wage continually adjusts to restore equality between aggregate demand and supply. The equilibrium amount of employment is where the quantity of labor demanded is equal to the quantity of labor supplied. Any resulting unemployment is "natural," that is, the result of labor market flows into and out of the labor force.

The sticky wage theory states that labor markets may not adjust because labor contracts fix nominal wages for a given period. Therefore, unemployment, over and above the natural rate, can result where wages are sticky.

There is a difference, however, between unemployment defined for statistical purposes and unemployment that is natural or due to sticky wages. The accompanying article describes the unemployment problem of the United States in 1992 and provides evidence that can be used to assess whether unemployment is natural or the result of sticky wages.

After studying your text, reading the article, and answering the questions, you should be able to:

◆◆ Define and recognize natural and sticky wage unemployment

◆◆ Distinguish between the natural and sticky wage unemployment rate and the official definition of unemployment

◆◆ Explain how wage contracts cause unemployment when aggregate demand in the economy, and aggregate labor demand in the labor market, decrease

◆◆ Explain how flexible wages prevent additional unemployment when aggregate demand in the economy, and aggregate labor demand in the labor market, decrease

◆◆ Explain the causes of natural and sticky wage unemployment

◆◆ Discuss policy measures that are appropriate to reducing natural and sticky wage unemployment

Preview

◆ The April 1992 unemployment rate decreased from 7.3 to 7.2 percent.

◆ Payroll employment and payrolls increased.

◆ Business services, which lead broader job growth, grew.

◆ There was an improvement in the unemployment rate for teenagers, whites, and Hispanics, and the number of longer-term unemployed decreased.

◆ Average weekly hours eased a little, while income remained virtually unchanged.

◆ The overall gains in the labor market indicate a slow sustainable expansion.

Jobless Rate Dropped to 7.2% in April; Nation's Payroll Increased by 126,000

The employment picture showed several signs of continued improvement in April, suggesting that the pickup in economic activity is having a slow but perceptible impact on the labor market.

The unemployment rate fell in April for the first time in nine months, the Labor Department said, dropping to 7.2% of the work force from 7.3% in February and March. In addition, employers added 126,000 people to their payrolls last month—the largest increase since last May—mostly in the services and retail trade. All the figures are adjusted for normal seasonal variations.

Although the report didn't point to particularly robust growth in the labor market, analysts said it was probably strong enough to keep the Federal Reserve from easing interest rates further. "If we had only gotten 30,000 growth in payrolls and no drop in the unemployment rate, the Fed would have probably eased," said Donald Ratajczak, director of the Economic Forecasting Center at Georgia State University.

The drop in the unemployment rate, while statistically insignificant, comes at a time when the labor force—those people who have jobs or are looking for work—is growing briskly by 290,000 a month. Analysts said it was an encouraging sign that the unemployment rate hasn't actually crept upward with that swift growth.

"These numbers suggest a slow, but sustainable, economic expansion," said Mellon Bank chief economist Norman Robertson. "It suggests the economy is on the right track."

Particularly encouraging was the marked job growth in the business service industry, led mainly by temporary-help companies. Increases in business services are often considered a bellwether of job growth as employers are hesitant to begin hiring permanent employees until they are certain economic growth will continue.

Mitchell Fromstein, president and chief executive officer of Manpower Temporary Services, said that company has seen a 20% increase from last year in the number of temporary workers companies are seeking....

Other positive labor market news: The unemployment rates for teen-agers, whites and Hispanics declined in April. Also, the number of people without work for 15 or more weeks fell by 165,000 last month, and the number of part-time workers who would rather have full-time jobs declined by 227,000.

The gradual improvement taking place in the labor market isn't likely to translate immediately into more consumer spending, because while the number of people on U.S. payrolls increased in April, average hours worked per week declined and income has been virtually stagnant.

However, the overall gains in the labor market are "indicative of a substantial improvement down the road for an inverse in permanent hires," Mr. Fromstein said. "I don't know if we are ready to break out the champagne bottles, but maybe we could go out and buy some glasses."

—Lucinda Harper, "Jobless Rate Dropped to 7.2% in April; Nation's Payroll Increased by 126,000," May 11, 1992.
Reprinted by permission of *The Wall Street Journal,* ©1992 Dow Jones & Co., Inc. All Rights Reserved Worldwide.

QUESTIONS

1. a) What evidence is there in the article that at least some of the unemployment was caused by sticky wages?

   b) Did the official unemployment rate capture all the unemployment caused by sticky wages? Explain your answer.

   c) Draw a diagram below to the left with axes representing real wages and employment. Add the aggregate labor demand curve and the aggregate labor supply curve. Show wage contracts set at the equilibrium wage level. Illustrate the impact of the recession, ceteris paribus.

   d) Draw a diagram to the right above with axes showing the aggregate price level and the level of real gross domestic product (GDP). Add the aggregate demand curve and both the short-run and the long-run aggregate supply curves. Show the U.S. economy initially in equilibrium at the full-employment level of real GDP. Illustrate the impact of the recession, ceteris paribus.

   e) Did the recession cause any unemployment above the natural rate? Mark the extent on your diagrams.

   f) If so, why did the recession result in unemployment? Refer to your diagrams.

   g) Given the recession and your answers to 1e and 1f, what could have helped to reduce unemployment?

   h) Explain whether higher aggregate demand would have helped.

2. a) What evidence is there in the article that wages were at least somewhat flexible?

b) Draw a diagram below to the left with axes representing real wages and employment. Add the aggregate labor demand curve and the aggregate labor supply curve. Show the equilibrium wage and employment level. Illustrate the impact of the recession, assuming completely flexible wages.

c) Draw a diagram above to the right with axes showing the aggregate price level and the level of real GDP. Add the aggregate demand curve and both the short-run and the long-run aggregate supply curves. Show the U.S. economy initially in equilibrium at the full-employment level of real GDP. Illustrate the impact of the recession, assuming flexible wages.

d) Had wages been completely flexible, would the recession have caused any unemployment above the natural rate? Mark the extent on your diagrams.

e) If not, why not? Refer to your diagrams.

f) What evidence is there in the article that the natural rate of unemployment was greater than zero?

g) Does the official unemployment rate capture all "natural" unemployment? Explain your response.

h) Given the recession and your answers to 2d and 2e, what would have helped reduce unemployment?

i) Was there a role for increasing aggregate demand? Explain your answer.

AGGREGATE SUPPLY FLUCTUATIONS

67. Union Raises Raise Scare of Supply-Side Shock

The aggregate supply curves are constantly changing. The long-run curve shifts position as the productive capacity of the economy changes due to changes in the amounts or productivities of factors of production.

The short-run aggregate supply curve shifts for the same reasons, as well as when factor prices change, such as when new wage contracts are negotiated. Movements along the short-run aggregate supply curve happen only when the aggregate price level changes, such as following aggregate demand changes. Such movements reflect a change in the real price of factors of production.

Supply-side shocks are unanticipated events—such as a sudden rise in the price of an important input, or a drought—that cause either or both aggregate supply curves to shift. This article explores the implications of German unions' wage demands for macroeconomic equilibrium.

After studying the text, reading the article, and answering the questions, you should be able to:

◆◆ Define the term "supply-side shocks"

◆◆ Explain the factors that shift the aggregate supply curves

◆◆ Analyze the consequences of a supply-side shock for short-run and long-run macroeconomic equilibria

◆◆ Explain how full employment can be restored following a supply-side shock

◆◆ Determine the distribution of the gains and losses from a supply-side shock

Preview

◆ After a costly 11-day strike in the German public sector, labor unrest was threatening to spill over to the private sector.

◆ Public sector unions had negotiated a 5.4 percent wage increase.

◆ Private sector unions were seeking even higher settlements.

◆ Negotiations between employers and the unions were unusually bitter.

◆ There was concern in business and government that high wage increases would reduce the country's competitiveness and cause unemployment.

Myopic

Already battered by public-sector strikes, Germany now faces the prospect of a far more damaging one in the private sector. IG Metall, a German engineering union, threatens to call out its 3.7m members on May 25th if employers do not raise their 3.3% pay offer. So far, Gesamtmetall, the engineering employers' association, refuses to budge. But even if peace does break out before the deadline, the once-cosy relationship between capital and labour in Germany will still be in doubt.

IG Metall and other private-sector unions such as IG Medien, which represents print workers, want a higher settlement than the 5.4% rise offered to public-sector workers after their recent 11-day strike. IG Metall has even asked for a 9.5% rise, though it has hinted it would accept a lower figure.…Franz Steinkühler, IG Metall's boss, blames "the Rambos" in the employers' ranks for refusing to compromise.…

Hans-Joachim Gottschol, the association's president, has given warning that a big wage rise could cost the industry hundreds of thousands of jobs.

Such mud-slinging is not uncommon in wage negotiations. Yet there are signs of a general worsening in German labour relations. Unification is partly to blame. Higher income taxes in western Germany have stiffened the unions' resolve. They are also betting that a show of strength in western Germany will help recruitment in the east. Employers' attitudes have hardened too. "We have the feeling that something has changed on the employers' side," says Karl Feldengut of the Deutsche Gewerkschaftsbund, Germany's trade-union confederation. "They have been so hard, so unwilling to compromise," he adds. This new toughness has raised fears that the employers want to modify the social contract that has long governed German labour relations.

These fears may be justified. Though German managers still sing the praises of *Mitbestimmung,* the system which allows workers' representatives to sit on companies' supervisory boards and share in decision-making, they say that, when it comes to pay and conditions, German unions have lost touch with reality. "There is a lot of day-dreaming going on," complains Klaus Steilmann, boss of the Steilmann group, Europe's biggest clothing manufacturer.

Mr. Steilmann and other German chief executives worry that *Standort Deutschland,* or Germany as a manufacturing centre, is becoming increasingly expensive because of German workers' high wages and long holidays. There have been similar warnings in the past, but this time companies are doing something about it. On May 8th Werner Niefer, the head of Mercedes Benz, said the car company would axe 20,000 jobs or 11% of its workforce.

Germany's car-component suppliers are also in a fix. They agreed to pay rises of 6% in 1990 and 6.7% in 1991, but could not raise prices because car makers were driving hard bargains to keep their own costs down. Those component firms that dared to raise their prices lost business to cheaper foreign suppliers. Several other branches of the engineering industry suffered the same fate.

No wonder, then, that German employers are presenting such a solid front to the unions. They want to keep pay rises down, at least until they have reduced other costs. The unions are equally determined to keep pay rises up. So if the bill for German unity continues to rise, expect even more disunity at the negotiating table.

—"Myopic," May 16, 1992. ©1992 The Economist Newspaper Ltd. Reprinted with permission.

QUESTIONS

1. a) Draw a diagram with axes representing the aggregate price level and real GDP. Add the aggregate demand curve and the short-run and the long-run aggregate supply curves. Show the German economy at full-employment equilibrium at the beginning of 1992.

    b) Assuming that prior to the public sector strike and subsequent settlement, wages were increasing in 1992 at 3.5 percent and productive capacity was also growing at 3.5 percent per year. Show the effect of these developments on the aggregate demand and supply curves. Also mark on your diagram the forecasted macroeconomic full-employment equilibrium at the beginning of 1993.

    c) The wage settlement with the German public sector unions was much larger than expected. What happened to the short-run aggregate supply curve as a result of the settlement? Explain your answer.

    d) What happened to the long-run aggregate supply curve? Explain your answer.

    e) Many politicians and business people were predicting higher inflation and greater unemployment as a result of the settlement. On the diagram above, illustrate why the wage increases were expected to have this effect.

    f) Suppose that, later in 1992, private sector unions received their proposed wage increases. On your diagram show the effects on the curve(s), labeling the shift(s) *f*. Also, show what would have happened to real GDP and the general price level.

    g) The public union settlement was expected to add $10 billion to the German budget deficit. One fear of a rising budget deficit was that taxes might be increased and government investment in eastern Germany might be reduced. Show clearly on your diagram the potential effects of these occurrences on the curves, labeling the shift(s) *g*. Also, show what would have happened to real GDP and the general price level.

2. Germany was faced with reestablishing macroeconomic equilibrium. If workers had moderated their pay demands, what would have happened to the general price level and real GDP? Illustrate in a new diagram of aggregate supply and aggregate demand where the initial equilibrium was below full-employment GDP.

3. Many business people were worried that wage settlements would make German products less competitive. What were the implications for real GDP and the general price level of a decline in German competitiveness? Illustrate your answers in a new diagram of aggregate supply and aggregate demand where the initial equilibrium is at full employment.

4. The title of the article is "Myopic." Who do you think is myopic and why?

INFLATION

Economic agents act on their expectations concerning real magnitudes of variables such as wages and interest rates. Since most contracts are stated in nominal rather than real terms it is necessary that economic agents forecast inflation. Signals of future price movements are given by various markets and economic indexes.

When individuals' expectations of inflation are correct, there is no reason for their behavior to change. When individuals' expectations of inflation are not correct, important consequences follow for real gross domestic product (GDP) and the price level. This article describes the impact of inflation and inflationary expectations in Switzerland.

After studying your text, reading the article, and answering the questions, you should be able to:

◆ ◆ Explain the effect of wage inflation and indexation on the short-run aggregate supply curve and macroeconomic equilibrium

◆ ◆ Explain how indexation of wages and prices can prolong attempts to reduce inflation

◆ ◆ Describe the role of expectations in formulating decisions

◆ ◆ Explain how expectations of future prices are formed

◆ ◆ Explain the difference between, and implications of, anticipated and unanticipated inflation

Preview

◆ The Swiss economy, traditionally one of the most stable in Europe, has been experiencing inflation and unemployment.

◆ The inflation rate in 1991 was 5.9 percent and the jobless rate reached 2.2 percent, triple its 1989 level.

◆ The initial cause of the inflationary surge was an expansion of the money supply in 1988, in response to the world stock market crash of October 1987.

◆ Although monetary policy has since contracted, government spending, indexation, and cartelization have continued to push prices up.

◆ Wages are indexed to the previous year's inflation and housing rents are indexed to mortgage interest rates.

Switzerland's Slippery Slope

For years Switzerland was as famous for price stability as for cuckoo clocks and yodelling. Europe's richest economy used to boast one of the lowest inflation rates in the world and one of the strongest currencies, thanks to sound monetary policies and prudent public finances. Switzerland also enjoyed stable growth and the lowest unemployment rate in the industrialized world. No longer. Over the past couple of years it has picked up some nasty foreign habits: high inflation and rising unemployment.

Last year Switzerland's inflation rate averaged 5.9%, up from 0.7% in 1986 and higher than the average of the countries in the European Community for the first time in two decades. Over the past year the once cast-iron Swiss franc has been the weakest of the big currencies, with a 12% slide against the dollar. Meanwhile, Switzerland's attraction as a financial centre also seems to have faded. Tight monetary policies to mop up this mess have pushed the economy into recession. GDP fell by an estimated 0.5% last year and is forecast to grow by only 1-1.5% in 1992. The jobless rate has more than tripled since 1989, to 2.2%, which is low by the standards of most other countries but is viewed with horror in Switzerland.

Many Swiss blame the Swiss National Bank (SNB), which allowed the money supply to explode in 1988, for their country's economic problems. Like Germany's Bundesbank, the SNB is independent of politicians and has price stability as its main objective. This should have helped preserve its credibility as an inflation fighter. Yet Switzerland and Germany, the countries with the world's most independent central banks, are both suffering uncomfortably high inflation. What has gone wrong? In the long term independent central banks do help to keep inflation lower, but in the short term their task may, as in Switzerland's case, be complicated by structural factors.

The blame for the initial surge in inflation does, however, lie with the SNB. For years its monetary policy depended on controlling the monetary base, a policy which was clearly successful. But monetary compasses are not as reliable as Swiss watches. The relationship between the monetary base and nominal GDP broke down in 1988. A change in bank-reserve requirements and the introduction of a new electronic bank-clearing system made it harder to interpret the different monetary measures. Unfortunately, these institutional changes occurred soon after the world stockmarket crash in October 1987, when the SNB, like many other central banks, eased its monetary policies to avoid a sudden contraction in demand. Instead, interest rates fell too far and the economy overheated.

Although the SNB may be guilty on this first charge, it is not to blame for the fact that several years later inflation remains too high, at 4.9% in the 12 months to January. The SNB tightened its policy in late 1988, but inflation has been slow to respond. One reason for this is that the government went on a spending spree, undermining the SNB's tight monetary policy. The total budget (central and local government and social-security funds) swung into deficit in 1991 for the first time since 1984. Some of this reflects the effect of the recession, but the structural budget balance has deteriorated sharply.

Another problem has been the indexation and cartelization common throughout the Swiss economy. Housing rents, for example, are, in effect, indexed to mortgage interest rates. When the government raises interest rates in order to squeeze inflation, rents—and hence the consumer-price index—automatically increase. With two-thirds of the population living in rented accommodation, and rents accounting for almost a fifth of the consumer-price index, this simply ratchets inflation up another notch.

A second factor is that another two-fifths of all prices are determined either by the hundreds of private cartels that operate in Switzerland, particularly in the professions and in distribution, or by state firms, such as the telecommunications monopoly. Both have used their excessive power to push up prices.

Combine these upward pressures on consumer prices with Switzerland's traditional practice of indexing wages to the previous year's inflation and it is easy to see why inflation has been so slow to respond to tighter monetary policy. To bring its inflation rate down to acceptable levels, Switzerland will now have to endure a more prolonged slowdown than might otherwise have been necessary.

Switzerland needs to dismantle cartels and scrap indexation agreements not only to bolster the SNB's fight against inflation, but also to give a much-needed boost to economic efficiency. In December the Swiss will vote in a referendum on whether to join the European Economic Area (a free-trade zone which will link the EC with EFTA, of which Switzerland is a member). Membership would oblige Switzerland to dismantle cartels and encourage competition.

The government is also now in favour of eventual full membership of the EC. But sufficient public support for the interim stage of joining the European Economic Area, let alone full membership of the EC, is far from guaranteed. For example, joining the EC would require Switzerland to introduce a value-added tax. But such a tax has already been turned down by Swiss voters in three different referendums.

Switzerland's current mess is partly due to its previous economic success, which meant that the government faced less pressure to liberalize the economy than governments in other countries. How many years of sluggish growth and high inflation must the Swiss suffer before they, too, decide to act?

QUESTIONS

1. a) Draw a diagram of the Swiss economy with axes showing real GDP and the general price level. Add the aggregate short-run and long-run supply curves and the aggregate demand curve. Assume that the Swiss economy was in full-employment macroeconomic equilibrium in 1987. Identify the equilibrium output and price level.

    b) Fearful of a sudden drop in aggregate demand as a result of the world stock market crash in October 1987, the Swiss National Bank (SNB) expanded the money supply in 1988. On the above diagram, illustrate the consequences for the equilibrium levels of real GDP and prices in 1988. Assume, as indicated in the article, that the money supply was increased by an amount greater than needed to maintain full-employment equilibrium. Also assume that everything else was unchanged.

2. A substantial number of Swiss workers have their wages indexed to the previous year's inflation. Assume that as a result of the SNB's actions, actual inflation was 2 percent in 1988 and that wages rose accordingly in 1989.

    a) What happened to the aggregate supply curve(s) as a result of wage indexation? What happened to the equilibrium price level and real GDP? Illustrate clearly on your diagram.

    b) What happened to wage increases in 1990, ceteris paribus? What happened to real GDP and the price level as a result?

3. The Swiss responded to growing inflation with monetary restraint.

    a) The article states that in spite of recent contractions in monetary policy, the inflation rate has been decreasing only slowly. Explain why this might be, given your answers to question 2.

b) The Swiss also index rents to interest rates. Why might rising interest rates frustrate the purpose of the restrictive monetary policy?

4. The author of the article suggests that the Swiss scrap indexation agreements.

a) If indexation is abolished, why will the Swiss wish to form expectations of price level movements?

b) How might rational expectations of inflation be formed?

c) How else might individuals form expectations about inflation? Explain the methods.

d) Would it be problematic if inflation were unanticipated? Why or why not?

69. Abolish Capital Punishment: Index Capital Gains

Indexation is a policy that ties the increase in a variable to the inflation rate. For example, social security benefits increase as the rate of inflation, measured by the Consumer Price Index (CPI), increases. Unions have negotiated escalator clauses that adjust wages in accordance with changes in inflation. In recent years, income tax brackets have been indexed to inflation. Some economists have called for complete indexing of the tax system, as well as government payments, such as unemployment compensation. This article discusses the indexation of the capital gains for tax purposes.

After studying your text, reading this article, and answering the questions, you should be able to:

◆ ◆ Define a capital gain

◆ ◆ Explain how capital gains arise

◆ ◆ Explain how indexing operates

◆ ◆ Analyze the economic and political benefits and costs of indexing capital gains

◆ ◆ Compare the relative economic and political merits of indexing income tax brackets and capital gains

Preview

◆ President Bush announced in 1992 that he wanted to reduce the capital gains tax.

◆ Congress opposed the reduction because it meant a windfall for the rich.

◆ There were a number of complex provisions that treated gains on specific assets in different ways and subjected them to different rates.

◆ Consequently, investors would have made decisions based on the tax conse-quences rather than on the merits of the investment opportu-nity.

◆ Indexation would have been more equitable and less distorting.

◆ Income tax brackets have been indexed since the early 1980s.

Why Not Index Capital Gains?

When President Bush called for a cut in the capital-gains tax in his State of the Union speech, he should have added: "Read my lip service." Democrats, as expected, are attacking the proposal as a boon for the wealthy. Less predictably, champions of a capital-gains reduction are concluding that the plan benefits entrepreneurs and risk takers far less than the president's rhetoric would suggest.

Bush would like to cut the capital-gains tax from the current 28 percent to 15.4 percent on assets sold after being held for at least three years. But the catch is that individuals who realize sizable investment profits in a single year could have a big chunk of it taxed at close to 24 percent, courtesy of the complex alternative minimum tax. After a barrage of complaints, the administration late last week adjusted its plan so that profits from the sale of all real estate and small businesses—yet to be defined—would not be exposed to the alternative minimum tax. But stock and bond gains still would be....

The complexity of the package is daunting. To encourage long-term investing, the antiregulation Bush administration has come up with a true Rube Goldberg of a holding schedule. Profits taken on investments after one year would be subject to a 23.8 percent rate, those owned two years or more to a 19.6 percent rate and those held three years or longer to a 15.4 percent rate. Beyond the record-keeping burden, planning would be impossible. Year after year, investors would have to decide whether to sell profitable assets or wait for a lower capital-gains rate to kick in, worrying that their gains could meanwhile dwindle or disappear.

A Not-So-New Idea "The whole plan is bogus; there are few real incentives and it won't do much to unlock frozen capital," complains Bear Stearns & Co. Chief Economist Lawrence Kudlow, a top official at the Office of Management and Budget in the first Reagan administration and a staunch supporter of capital-gains reduction. "The president would have been better off leaving rates where they are, avoiding the political controversy and simply asking for investments to be indexed against inflation."

Index against inflation? Why not? Texas Republican Rep. William Archer has pushed bills for more than a decade to index capital gains. Such a plan almost passed Congress twice: In 1978, the House approved indexing but the Senate wouldn't; in 1980, the Senate wanted it but the House balked. Supporters range from conservative economist Milton Friedman to Sen. Bob Kerrey, the presidential hopeful from Nebraska. Friedman likes indexing because, as he declares, "No one can claim that indexing is inequitable." He favors eliminating capital-gains taxes entirely, as Germany has done. Short of that, taxing only real gains would be "a more effective long-term reform" than merely lowering the capital-gains rate.

Indexing's biggest advantage, says Friedman, is that it would eliminate a distortion in the investment process. Investors could buy assets on their merits. They would not have to worry about the impact inflation will have on future returns or time their selling to artificial holding periods. And Friedman observes that, once in place, indexing would be politically harder to undo than a preferential capital-gains rate, which has been yo-yoed up and down over the years by Washington and would inevitably be the focus of endless future tinkering.

Indexing would work straightforwardly. The government would publish an annual inflation adjustment, as it has done for income-tax brackets since the early 1980s. If an investment was bought for $1,000, say, and five years later inflation was up by 25 percent, the purchase price would be adjusted to $1,250 to make up for lost buying power. If the investment was then sold for $2,000, only the $750 difference would be taxed. As for interest, Friedman would index not only interest income but also interest paid out. For tax purposes, business borrowers would be able to deduct only the portion of what they paid on loans that was in excess of the rate of inflation. Indexing stalwart William Archer says business opposition to such interest treatment would make congressional approval almost impossible.

A capital-gains reduction this year is a slim possibility, with the Democrats in control of Congress. A Democratic version of a cut probably would be tied to a boost in the top rate for wealthy taxpayers, which Bush has said he will oppose. Of course, the administration and Congress could halt the partisan shell game and accept indexing. But in an election year, that might be too much to expect.

QUESTIONS

1. President Bush argued in his State of the Union address in 1992 that cuts in the capital gains tax paid were necessary.

   a) Define a capital gain.

   b) Why do capital gains arise?

   c) Are all capital gains real capital gains? Why or why not?

   d) Explain why indexing capital gains would reduce capital gains tax payments.

   e) Milton Friedman believes that indexing capital gains would be equitable. Explain why this might be true.

   f) What economic problems result from the capital gains tax structure failing to anticipate inflation in capital gains?

   g) What impact would indexing capital gains, and thereby reducing capital gains taxes, have on aggregate demand, ceteris paribus? Explain your response.

   h) What effect would it have on short-run and long-run aggregate supply? Explain why.

i) Draw a diagram with the axes representing the price level and real gross domestic product (GDP). Add the aggregate demand and aggregate supply curves. Show the U.S. economy in equilibrium below the full employment level of GDP. Illustrate the impact of the change in aggregate demand on real GDP and the price level.

j) How would you expect the following parties to react to indexation of capital gains? Why?

  • businesses

  • private investors

  • the government

  • congressional democrats

2. The article points out that income tax brackets are indexed.

a) Why is this less justifiable from an economic standpoint than indexing capital gains? Refer to the implications of income tax indexation for aggregate supply and aggregate demand, and for macroeconomic equilibrium.

b) Why is it more justifiable in political terms?

RECESSION

Recessions arise because of sharp and significant movements in aggregate supply and/or aggregate demand. The resulting declines in real output, employment, sales, and personal incomes take time to occur, and may happen at different times. As a result, dating recessions is not easy.

The body responsible for dating the start and end of a recession is the Business Cycle Dating Committee of the National Bureau of Economic Research, a group comprising seven prominent economists. The committee examines many different economic series, concentrating on employment, output, income, and sales, in reaching their decision. When contractions in these areas last six months or more, the committee declares the start of a recession. The variability of these series adds to the delay in the committee officially declaring a recession. This article discusses the causes of the 1990 recession and the process of dating it.

After studying your text, reading the article, and answering the questions, you should be able to:

◆◆ Explain how decreases in aggregate demand and supply-side shocks cause recessions

◆◆ Explain the interrelationship between the goods market and the labor market in the course of a contraction

◆◆ Describe the role of economic indicators in dating and forecasting recessions

◆◆ Understand the sources of uncertainty in dating and forecasting

◆◆ Compare the frequency and duration of previous recessions

◆◆ Predict the effect of corrective monetary policies on the macroeconomy

Preview

◆ The ninth recession of the post-World War II era started in July 1990 and ended 92 months of expansion.

◆ The date of the recession was determined by the Business Cycle Dating Committee of the National Bureau of Economic Research.

◆ The recession was caused by the oil price increase and collapse in consumer confidence that followed the invasion of Kuwait.

◆ The Dating Committee made its decision based on trends in jobs, personal income, sales, and industrial production.

◆ Recessions tend to be of short duration; the average recession lasts 12 months.

It's Official: July Saw the Recession's Start

The committee of seven prominent economists that is the arbiter of when recessions officially begin and end, ruled today that the current one started nine months ago, in July. The panel made no attempt to guess when it might end.

The decision of the Business Cycle Dating Committee of the National Bureau of Economic Research, a private organization whose rulings go into numerous record books, means the American economy began to contract before Iraq's invasion of Kuwait on Aug. 2. But, committee members said, the initial contraction might never have evolved into a full-blown recession without the damage to the economy that resulted from the Persian Gulf crisis.

"The war plainly did not create the overall economic slowdown that was very evident even in June," said Robert Hall, a Stanford University economist and chairman of the committee. "However, the increase in oil prices that followed the invasion probably did play a role in the sharp contraction that occurred in the fall."

Characteristic Contraction That sharp contraction in the four areas that the committee watches most closely—jobs, personal income, sales and industrial production—is a phenomenon that is characteristic of nearly every recession, with or without a political crisis. Without that sharp contraction, concentrated this time in October and November, the slowdown might never have turned into a genuine recession, in the committee's view.

"It is what the business press would call a free fall," Mr. Hall said. Although the committee concerned itself today only with dating the recession's starting point, Mr. Hall and other members said the economy was still contracting.

"It will be a long time, I predict, before we meet again to date the trough—the end of the recession," Mr. Hall said. The Bush Administration, the Federal Reserve and many private economic forecasters say that the Persian Gulf crisis, with its impact on oil prices and consumer confidence, caused the recession, and they say it is now coming to an end. The committee, in effect, steered clear of both contentions.

Today, the Labor Department said the number of people filing new claims for state unemployment insurance climbed by 47,000 to 498,000, in the week ended April 13. That reversed

How This Recession Stacks Up

Percentage changes of assorted indicators during recent recessions. Figures for 1990 recession are estimated.

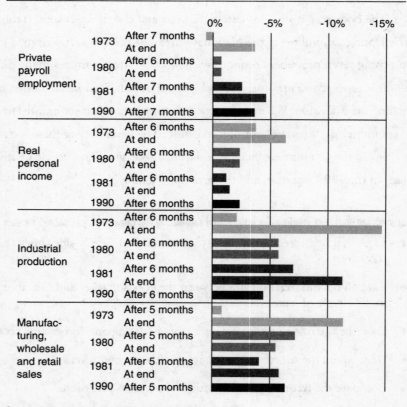

		0%	-5%	-10%	-15%
Private payroll employment	1973 After 7 months / At end				
	1980 After 6 months / At end				
	1981 After 7 months / At end				
	1990 After 7 months				
Real personal income	1973 After 6 months / At end				
	1980 After 6 months / At end				
	1981 After 6 months / At end				
	1990 After 6 months				
Industrial production	1973 After 6 months / At end				
	1980 After 6 months / At end				
	1981 After 6 months / At end				
	1990 After 6 months				
Manufacturing, wholesale and retail sales	1973 After 5 months / At end				
	1980 After 5 months / At end				
	1981 After 5 months / At end				
	1990 After 5 months				

Source: Robert J. Gordon, Northwestern University

two weeks of decline. President Bush promptly chided the Federal Reserve for not doing more to push down interest rates.

The committee members, by a unanimous vote, provided a starting date for the recession that will appear in thousands of Government documents and business publications. The record now lists eight other recessions since World War II with an average length of 12 months. If this one is average it would end in June.

Geoffry Moore, a committee member from Columbia University, said, "So far this one does look to me very much like an average recession, although it is hard to find evidence that it is ending."

The Popular Definition The National Bureau, a private organization that finances research, has pinpointed not only recession dates but also the beginnings and ends of booms. In that role, the ruling today served the additional function of defining the economic expansion that started in November 1982, at the end of the last recession, and lasted for 92 months, until last July.

Only one other expansion since 1854 was longer: The booming 1960's produced 105 months of constant growth, from early 1961 until the final months of the decade.

The popular definition of a recession is two quarters of contraction by the gross national product, which is the value of all goods and services produced in a given period. By that definition, the current recession started in last year's fourth quarter, when the G.N.P. declined by 1.6 percent at an annual rate, and this year's first quarter, when the G.N.P. decline was more than 2 percent and perhaps much more, according to most estimates. The Commerce Department will announce the first-quarter figure tomorrow.

The Dating Committee also prefers that a downturn last at least six months to qualify as a recession. But it frequently dates recessions as starting in the midst of a quarter—in this case in the early weeks of last year's third quarter.

This time July became a sort of average for four key developments. The committee decided that job growth peaked in June, then jobs began to disappear as layoffs accelerated. Personal income, adjusted for inflation, grew to its highest level in July and has fallen ever since. Sales by manufacturers, wholesalers and retailers peaked in August and then declined, and industrial production went into decline in September.

The other committee members are Martin Feldstein of Harvard, president of the National Bureau; Robert J. Gordon of Northwestern University; Benjamin Friedman of Harvard; Victor Zarnowitz of the University of Chicago; and William Branson of Princeton.

QUESTIONS

1. a) In a diagram of the U.S. economy in June 1990, with axes representing real GDP and the general price level, draw an aggregate demand curve and a short- and a long-run aggregate supply curve. Show the United States at full-employment equilibrium. Identify the equilibrium price level and level of real GDP.

   b) As a result of Iraq's invasion of Kuwait, there was an unexpected large increase in the price of oil. What was the effect on the aggregate demand and supply curves? Explain your answer.

   c) Illustrate on your diagram the resulting impact on real GDP and the price level.

   d) Draw a diagram of the U.S. labor market showing the aggregate labor demand and aggregate labor supply curves. Illustrate what happened to the curve(s) and equilibrium real wages and employment as a result of the above events.

   e) What happened to the total amount of personal income as a result, ceteris paribus?

2. In addition, consumers become uncertain about the future course of the economy.

   a) Draw another diagram of the U.S. economy in June 1990 as in question 1a.

   b) What was the result of declining consumer confidence for aggregate demand and/or supply? Explain your reasoning.

c) On your diagram, show the effect of lower consumer confidence on real GDP and the price level.

d) What were the consequences of these changes for the labor market? Illustrate in another diagram of the U.S. labor market.

3. Your analyses in questions 1 and 2 show that higher oil prices and lower consumer confidence caused changes in output (and therefore sales), prices, employment, and wages (and personal income). According to the article, which of these economic indicators revealed

a) the first signs of recession? Why do you think it was the first to show significant change?

b) most change over past recessions? Hypothesize why this might be.

4. The article states that as a consequence of an increase in new claims for unemployment insurance, President Bush "chided the Federal Reserve for not doing more to push down interest rates."

a) Given the state of the U.S. economy in questions 1 and 2, what would have been the impact of a decline in interest rates? Explain your answer.

b) Why was the Fed reluctant to agree to the President's wishes?

71.
It's Not Over Until It's Over

The precise link between unemployment and recession has puzzled economists for many years. Classical theories assume that as the demand for labor decreases, so would real wages, thereby maintaining equilibrium in the labor market. Many modern monetarists adopt the classical view, but also believe that the labor supply is quite responsive to changes in the real wage. Keynesian economists believe that sticky wages cause the labor market to adjust slowly and result in unemployment. The accompanying article discusses the trends in the goods and labor market in the recession of 1990-1991 and the ensuing recovery.

After studying your text, reading the article, and answering the questions, you should be able to:

◆◆ Explain how changes in the components of aggregate demand impact the labor market

◆◆ Explain the adjustments in the labor market during the economic cycle when wages are flexible and when wages are sticky

◆◆ Understand the difficulty in discriminating between the two theories using empirical evidence

◆◆ Make policy prescriptions to reduce unemployment when wages are sticky and when wages are flexible

Preview

◆ Economic data in early 1992 indicated that a recovery might be in progress.

◆ Consumer spending was up, largely due to increased government transfer payments, overtime pay, and low interest rates.

◆ However, unemployment was still high and job growth outside retailing and automobile manufacturing had not begun.

◆ Robert Solow, a Nobel laureate economist, estimated that a 3 percent growth in GDP was needed to keep unemployment from increasing.

◆ The outlook for the economy rested on lower interest rates, higher investment, and the recovery of exports.

Recovery Held Too Weak to Generate Jobs

For all the robust gains showing up in recent economic reports, most economists say that the evidence available so far is not sufficient to demonstrate that a strong enough recovery is under way to generate new job growth.

Unless job growth resumes soon, they say, there will not be enough additional family income to sustain the jump in consumer spending that began 60 days ago. That could mean a renewal of the recession or, at the very least, a continuation of the stagnation that has plagued the American economy for three years. A similar upturn last spring, also hailed as the first stage of a recovery, came to a halt in August after failing to increase jobs.

"I don't think you can go past May without significant job growth and keep a recovery going," said David Wyss, senior economist at DRI/McGraw-Hill, a data-gathering and consulting service. One million fewer Americans hold jobs since the recession began in July 1990.

Healthy increases in retail sales, new home construction and auto and truck production since December have prompted many economists to predict that by midsummer, the economy will be growing at an annual rate of more than 3 percent. The Federal Reserve's periodic survey of regional economic conditions released yesterday confirmed the upturn in consumer buying, but noted that manufacturing layoffs persisted.

A 3 percent growth rate by midsummer would mark the first time since the winter of 1989 that the growth rate has exceeded even 2 percent—a slowdown that has blurred the distinction between stagnation and recession.

Strictly speaking, a recession means that the gross domestic product, measuring all the new wealth created in the United States in a given period, is shrinking, as it did from the summer of 1990 until last spring. Since then, growth has been so anemic that economists and the public alike have often called it a recession.

The reason for this blurring of definitions is the loss of jobs. By almost every estimate, if jobs are to be created again, rather than lost through layoffs and attrition, then the gross domestic product must grow at an annual rate of more than 2 percent for several quarters, and perhaps by as much as 3 percent. Only then, said Nancy Lazar, senior economist at ISI Group, a consulting firm, would there be "a tone change in the economy."

Three percent growth, adds Robert M. Solow, a Nobel laureate in economic sciences, "is just about enough to keep the unemployment rate constant or slightly diminishing."

Whatever the long-term outlook, President Bush can point to the incipient upturn as evidence that an election-year recovery is under way. And his Democratic opponents, with equal authority, can hammer away at the missing jobs and the rising unemployment rate: 7.3 percent today, compared with 5.3 percent when the recession started. "They'll each be able to put their spin on the data," Mr. Solow said.

Ms. Lazar and some other forecasters say that 3 percent growth is likely by Election Day, and could endure into 1993. They base their optimism on two conditions lacking last spring, when consumer buying also surged. One is the decline in interest rates for mortgages and auto loans since last year, although some rates have recently turned up a bit. The other is healthier banks, specifically those that have written off many of their uncollectible loans and now seem more willing to finance new activity.

But in a dozen interviews with economists, their doubts about job growth, the most important factor of all, repeatedly came to the surface....

New Cut in Rates? Reflecting this caution, David W. Mullins, vice chairman of the Federal Reserve, suggests that the Fed might bring short-term interest rates even lower than their present 4 percent level if the upturn shows signs of fading. "In the current, complex, sluggish environment, we are watching the situation very carefully because last summer, the economy started to take off and the environment snuffed out that recovery," he said, noting that rising rates a year ago had discouraged consumers and businesses.

Perhaps the main reason for the current upturn is a sudden rise in personal disposable income, the money Americans can spend or save after paying their taxes. After declining for most of last year, total disposable income jumped 1.5 percent in January from December's level, even after adjusting for inflation. And February brought an additional 2.2 percent increase.

These were far and away the largest increases since the summer of 1990, when the recession began—but they did not come from job growth or from noticeably higher wages, economists say. The bulk of the gains came from more fragile sources: a rise in overtime pay, the extended unemployment benefits recently granted by Congress, higher Social Security checks and the Government's early mailing of veterans' benefits and income tax refunds.

"We do have some stimulus out there and our surveys show a recent strengthening in consumer confidence, suggesting a turnaround," said Richard T. Curtin, director of the University of Michigan's monthly consumer sentiment surveys. Mild inflation—the Consumer Price Index is rising at an annual rate of less than 3 percent—also helps to stretch family budgets, and lower interest rates have reduced millions of mortgage payments, Mr. Curtin noted.

Doubts on Employment "But more fundamentally," he said, "when consumers look to the year ahead or to the next five years, they are not seeing the employment problem solved and that will inhibit any recovery."

Thomas Plewes, associate commissioner of the Labor Department's Bureau of Labor Statistics, also doubts that the employment problem has been solved, although 164,000 jobs were added to the labor force in February, the first rise since last November. "The figures that we put out were not incompatible with a recovery, but they did not demonstrate one either," he said.

Most of the reported job gains were at retailers and auto factories. But the rise in retail jobs was partly artificial: a formula used to adjust for seasonal variations increased retail employment by 133,000 instead of the 50,000 or so jobs actually created. And the more than 10,000 new jobs at auto makers mostly represented call-backs of hourly workers temporarily laid off, industry executives said....

The current upturn has to weather three other hazards, economists say. One is a possible decline in exports. What growth there has been in recent months has come partly from strong exports, now threatened by declining economies in Europe and Japan.

Another hazard is rising imports. When the economy revived last spring, a portion of the new purchases was imported goods, creating jobs abroad but not at home.

Finally, many economists argue that a consumer-led recovery cannot, by itself, sustain sufficient growth, unless rising production also stimulates investment in new machinery and factories. That would require a reversal of a trend that saw net new investment in plant and equipment drop to 5 percent of the gross domestic product in the late 1980's from 7.8 percent in the late 1960's.

"One thing that saved us in the 1980's was investment by foreigners in the United States," Mr. Wyss of DRI/McGraw-Hill, said. "Lately, there has not been enough consumption to make investment rise."

—Louis Uchitelle, "Recovery Held Too Weak to Generate Jobs," March 19, 1992.

QUESTIONS

1. a) Draw a diagram of the U.S. labor market with the real wage and the level of employment in hours on the axes. Add a labor supply curve and a labor demand curve. Illustrate the position of the economy in June 1990 when it could be considered to have been at full employment. Identify the equilibrium real wage and level of employment.

   b) In 1990-1991, there was a decrease in aggregate demand that produced a recession. What happened to the demand for labor as a result of this decrease? Shift the appropriate curve in the above diagram. Illustrate what happened to the equilibrium real wage and volume of employment, assuming flexible wages.

   c) Did unemployment result from the change in the demand for labor? Explain your answer.

2. According to the article, there were a number of signs in 1992 that economic activity had increased.

   a) What was the impact of lowered interest rates on aggregate demand? Explain your response.

   b) What was the impact of increased personal disposable income on aggregate demand? Explain your answer.

   c) What were some of the sources of increased personal disposable income cited in the article?

3. a) What happened to the demand for labor as a result of the increase in aggregate demand? Illustrate on your diagram in question 1. What happened to the equilibrium real wage and the level of employment?

   b) The article points to an increase in overtime pay yet no decrease in the unemployment rate. Is this consistent with your answer to 3a? Explain your answer.

c) What determined the magnitude of the employment adjustment to the increase in aggregate demand?

4. Now assume that wages were sticky in the face of changes in aggregate demand.

    a) What factors might have been responsible for wages being sticky?

    b) In a second diagram of the U.S. labor market, show what happened to real wages and employment as a result of the decrease in aggregate demand. Illustrate any resulting unemployment.

    c) How did real wages, employment, and unemployment change in the recovery? Illustrate on your diagram.

5. If you were to look at the change in the real wage and level of employment that result from the supply and demand shifts would you be able to tell whether the sticky or flexible wage theory of the labor market was more appropriate? Why or why not?

6. Why does it matter from a policymaking viewpoint whether the labor market is flexible or sticky?

Desirable macroeconomic outcomes include real variables—low unemployment, steady growth, and balanced international trade—and nominal variables—low inflation and appropriate exchange rates. These macroeconomic objectives are not automatically attained all the time. Stabilization policies are needed. The chief instruments used are monetary and fiscal policy. The key players involved in formulating and implementing policy are the Congress, the President, and the Federal Reserve. The accompanying article concerns the policy proposals of these key players to stimulate a recovery.

After studying your text, reading the article, and answering the questions, you should be able to:

◆ ◆ State the targets of macroeconomic policy and explain their importance

◆ ◆ Explain the roles of the key players in formulating and executing macroeconomic policy

◆ ◆ Analyze the impact of alternative proposed policies on macroeconomic performance

◆ ◆ Predict the effects on the macroeconomy of policies that are too weak or too strong

Preview

◆ Congressional members were unhappy about the state of the economy.

◆ They criticized the Federal Reserve for interest rate cuts that they said were "too little too late."

◆ Alan Greenspan, chairman of the Federal Reserve, defended the slow steady decline in interest rates as the best policy that could have been formulated.

◆ Greenspan thought that interest rate cuts would be sufficient to effect a recovery.

◆ Greenspan feared that tax cuts and other fiscal stimuli would increase the budget deficit and reduce investment.

Greenspan Faces Barrage of Senators' Complaints

Republican Sen. Alfonse M. D'Amato of New York recalled yesterday that a year ago he asked Federal Reserve Chairman Alan Greenspan, "What world do you live in? You were worried about inflation. Businesses are closing. We're in a recession. Cut the interest rates."

After more months of recession and a stalled recovery, D'Amato complained that rather than following his advice, the Fed "did too little too late" and the country suffered as a result. "I think a great deal of the pain that we have endured could have been minimized" with faster action by the Fed to cut interest rates, the senator said.

Greenspan, seeking confirmation to a second four-year term as chairman of the Federal Reserve Board, listened yesterday to a barrage of such complaints from D'Amato and other members of the Senate Banking Committee who were unhappy about the state of the American economy.

Several of those most critical of the Fed nevertheless stressed their respect for Greenspan, and no senator indicated that he planned to vote against another term for Greenspan as chairman or against a new 14-year term as a board member.

The complaints were bipartisan. Sen. Jim Sasser (D–Tenn.) wanted to know why the Fed did not act more quickly to cut interest rates in the fall of 1990 "when we were sitting there on the cusp of a recession."

Saying he was hearing talk of suicides among Florida developers, Republican Sen. Connie Mack wanted to know how real estate values could be stabilized and a "downward spiral" be avoided.

Through it all, Greenspan agreed that the American economy has turned out to have more problems than he had thought when he and the other central bank policy makers were making their decisions at the time.

But he defended the slow, steady decline in interest rates beginning in the spring of 1989 as the best that could have been done, given the fear of future inflation by investors—a fear that has until recently kept long-term interest rates high despite repeated cuts in short-term rates by the Fed.

And Greenspan pointedly rejected an argument from Sen. John F. Kerry (D–Mass.) that economic growth has been strongest when inflation has been running at a 5 percent to 6 percent rate. Under current circumstances, Kerry suggested, some added inflation could help stabilize real estate values.

"Would you rather have inflation or deflation?" Kerry asked.

"I prefer neither. I think they are both destructive," replied Greenspan.

The Fed chairman agreed that fast growth and inflation have historically sometimes gone hand in hand, but he cautioned, "I'm not sure which is cause and which is effect…"

The inflation issue went to the heart of the disagreements between most of the committee members and Greenspan. To Greenspan, it is also a key to the Fed's role in the U.S. economy.

"I see the fundamental task of monetary policy as fostering the financial conditions most conductive to the…economy performing at its fullest potential," he told the committee in a brief opening statement. "As I have often noted, there is every reason to believe that the main contribution the central bank can make to the achievement of this national economic objective over long periods is to promote reasonable price stability….

"But a central bank must also recognize that the long run is made up of a series of short runs. Our policies do affect output and employment in the short and intermediate terms, and we must be mindful of these effects…We have been taking actions designed to assist in returning the economy to a solid growth path.

"However, the Federal Reserve… must also be conscious of the limits of its capabilities. We can try to provide a backdrop for stable, sustainable growth, but we cannot iron out every fluctuation, and attempts to do so could be counterproductive," Greenspan said.

The Fed chairman also sparked disagreement from several committee members by saying it was his current judgment that the economy will pick up this spring without any further reduction in interest rates or any package of tax cuts or spending increases. Greenspan said he feared that a bidding war could develop as details of a stimulus program are negotiated, with the budget's "structural" deficit increased as a result.

If that happened, he warned, investors' inflationary expectations would rise and, as a consequence, so would long-term interest rates. But Banking Committee Chairman Donald W. Riegle, Jr. (D–Mich.) asserted, "Well, I think we need a stronger answer. I mean, I think we've got to come up with a strategy to respond to the country's economic situation. I think it's got to be bigger and stronger, and it's got to kick in now….I don't think we can continue to gamble that what we've done may or may not work."

—John M. Berry, "Greenspan Faces Barrage of Senators' Complaints," *The Washington Post,* January 30, 1992.
©1992 The Washington Post. Reprinted with permission.

QUESTIONS

1. A number of policy targets are mentioned in the article. Briefly explain why economic policymakers would choose to

   a) have the "economy performing at its fullest potential."

   b) have "stable, sustainable growth."

   c) "promote reasonable price stability."

2. The article reveals a tussle over who should be responsible for economic policy. Explain the role of the following key players in formulating and administering stabilization policy:

   a) the Congress

   b) the President

   c) the Federal Reserve

3. a) Draw a diagram with real GDP and the price level on the axes. Add the aggregate demand and supply curves. Show the economy in 1992 in macroeconomic equilibrium below the full-employment level of real GDP.

b) Mr. Greenspan was concerned at the prospect of a stimulus program. Describe how tax cuts and spending increases were supposed to stimulate the economy. Illustrate their impact on macroeconomic equilibrium in your diagram.

4. Mr. Greenspan argued that "the economy will pick up ... without ... any package of tax cuts or spending increases."

a) Describe how monetary policy was supposed to stimulate the economy.

b) In a second diagram, show the impact of the Fed's monetary policy on macroeconomic equilibrium.

c) According to the article, some members of Congress were not enthusiastic about Mr. Greenspan's policy efforts. What reservations did the Congress have about the Fed's policy measures?

5. Mr. Greenspan feared that the competing policy measures might be added together and push up the federal budget deficit and long-term interest rates. Suppose that interest rates were reduced, and tax cuts to consumers and investment tax credits to businesses were enacted.

a) Why might the federal budget deficit increase?

b) Why might long-term interest rates have increased?

c) What would have been the effects on the policy targets in question 1? Explain your predictions.

73.

The Faux Pas of Fine-Tuning?

Stabilization policies are designed to influence macroeconomic activity in order to avoid inflation and high unemployment, and to achieve steady growth in real GDP. To achieve these goals, decision makers employ a variety of tools, including monetary and fiscal policy. Not only must these tools be used with the appropriate intensity, but also they must be used with the right timing. Many economists believe that in the absence of shocks to the economy, prudent use of these policies would achieve stabilization. Other economists believe that the policies disrupt stability. This article discusses whether appropriate policies can be adopted to allow the economy to avoid inflation and recession.

After studying the text, reading the article, and answering the questions, you should be able to:

◆ ◆ Explain how corrective monetary and fiscal policy is supposed to produce a full employment macroeconomic equilibrium

◆ ◆ Discuss the problems involved in "fine-tuning" the economy

◆ ◆ Explain and evaluate how fixed-rule and feedback-rule policies operate

◆ ◆ Analyze the impact of fiscal policy measures on real GNP, growth, and the budget deficit

Preview

◆ The economics establishment has lost confidence in the government's ability to implement an anti-recession policy.

◆ While economists in the 1970s thought they knew how to fight recessions and implement stabilization policies, there is a great deal more skepticism today.

◆ Part of the skepticism stems from recent experience with fixed- and feedback-rule policies, and from supply-side economics.

◆ Another group of economists dismisses fiscal policy measures entirely, arguing that rational behavior on the part of individuals will offset the direct policy effects.

◆ Others argue that the slow growth in productivity is our principal economic problem and any proposal that lowers savings should be avoided.

367

Spurning Fine-Tuning

Republicans and Democrats alike are hard at work seeking ways to pump up the American economy and let the good times roll again.

That is what prominent economists used to think Government was all about. But now the economics establishment has generally lost confidence in the ability of the Government to fine-tune the economy, afraid that anything that Washington might do would be as likely to harm as help....

In part, the misgivings are based on the conviction that allowing Washington to renegotiate last year's deficit reduction deal is akin to inviting Imelda Marcos to window shop at Gucci. But it also reflects fundamental intellectual doubts about the value of fiscal measures in fighting economic downturns, as well as the more specific worry that any pre-election fix would undermine long-term efforts to increase savings and growth.

As recently as the early 1970's most economists thought they knew how to take the sting out of recessions. A decline in the inclination of businesses and consumers to spend, they said, could leave a gap between the total demand for goods and the economy's capacity to provide them. And while the gap would eventually close without government intervention, eventually could be a very long time indeed. What was needed to offset swings in private demand, they argued, was some combination of tax cuts and government spending, plus an increase in funds available for bank loans.

The size, timing and the proper mix of fiscal and monetary stimulus have always been a matter of fierce debate. The intellectual heirs to the great British economist John Maynard Keynes emphasized the merits of reducing taxes and increasing government spending; the resulting budget deficits, they argued, would pose no burden to society as long as the extra demand for goods and services could be met from farms and factories that would otherwise be idled.

Followers of Milton Friedman of the University of Chicago much preferred to rely on monetary measures. They were convinced that business cycles could be smoothed away simply by requiring that the Federal Reserve keep the growth in the supply of money on an even keel. But the two camps grudgingly shared an intellectual framework of how the economy worked, as well as an implicit belief that stabilization policies could be perfected.

Faith Is Shaken The last two decades on a roller coaster of recession and growth, however, have shaken public faith in economists' capacities as scientists of stability, and speeded a parallel drift within the profession. Virtually all economists would still use fiscal and monetary tools to offset Depression-magnitude swings in demand. But there is no longer anything approaching a consensus on the virtues of intervention in a crisis of current dimensions, where unemployment remains low by historic benchmarks.

The ranks of orthodox monetarists have declined. But as the non-monetarist Robert Gordon of Northwestern University notes, their core idea—that steady-at-the-helm works best (if not always very well)—has been filched, not abandoned. Pragmatists like Robert Hall of the Hoover Institution in California have convinced the Federal Reserve Board to change course infrequently, and to aim at a simple and easily measured target: the rate of growth of total spending in the economy. It is really the Keynesians, with their enormous investment in the concept of fine-tuning with fiscal policy, who have suffered most.

One striking challenge came from "supply-side" economists, most notably Arthur Laffer, who contended that the sheer waste and perverse incentives associated with high tax rates created opportunities to cut tax rates without cutting tax revenues. There was thus no need to think of fiscal policy as a mechanism for fine-tuning: The fiscal spigot could and should be left wide open to spur economic growth.

Supply-side economics did not work as Mr. Laffer and his disciples expected. After the big income tax cut of 1981, the budget deficit ballooned to levels unprecedented in peacetime. But neither did it confirm the Keynesian view that wide-open deficit spending would lead to uncontrolled inflation.

Substantially increased government borrowing to finance the deficit did not "crowd out" private borrowers because foreign lenders proved ready and willing to make up the difference. Moreover, collapsing energy prices and sharply increased world competition in manufactures kept inflation to a pleasing minimum. And while few research economists were converted to the supply-siders' cause, stable (if relatively slow) growth of the Reagan years certainly undermined public confidence in the logic of fiscal fine-tuning.

Cut Taxes Now The boldest critique of Keynesian theory from within the economics establishment has come from Robert Barro of Harvard. When the Government cuts taxes or increases spending it borrows to cover the extra deficit. Thus in the process of cutting taxes today, Mr. Barro said, the Government is creating a future liability—the added debt—that will have to be financed by raising taxes tomorrow. And taxpayers are likely to respond by curtailing current spending, offsetting the direct fiscal stimulus.

Mr. Gordon of Northwestern probably speaks for most policy-oriented economists in dismissing the Barro critique as "aerie fairie" theory, hardly related to how people actually behave. But its sheer ingenuousness has made it the grist of a hundred academic journal articles and a thousand graduate school classes. Mr. Hall of the Hoover Institution argues that the Barro punchline—that the consequences of fiscal stimulus might be both complicated and unintuitive—"has shifted the ground" under the Keynesian monolith and made it fair game for more practical-minded critics of fine-tuning.

Gregory Mankiw of Harvard lays out a smorgasbord of these qualms.

Once the need for fiscal stimulus is recognized, he notes, it may take months to pass the necessary legislation. Hence the full impact may only hit the economy after the recovery is under way and the stimulus is no longer welcome. Even if the stimulus does hit in timely fashion, public fears that it will ignite inflation may push up interest rates and slow business investments.

That should not be a significant problem if the public is convinced that the spending or tax stimulus is indeed temporary and will evaporate by the time offices and factories are running full tilt. But such convictions do not come easily to a public grown cynical about Washington: "Whenever I hear a politician say 'never again' I don't believe it," Mr. Mankiw, the Harvard economist, said.

John Taylor, who just returned to Stanford University from President Bush's Council of Economic Advisors, points out that a credible temporary cut in payroll or income taxes would have its own drawbacks. If the increase in take-home pay is scheduled to last just a year or so, research suggests that just 20 or 30 cents out of every extra dollar will actually be spent; the rest would end up as private savings. And while there is nothing wrong with people saving more, it is no virtue in this context: most of the intended stimulus would be lost, even as the budget deficit rose.

The bang from a buck of direct government spending—say, highway construction—is far greater than the punch from a tax cut. But Mr. Mankiw noted that the time it took to put a workable spending plan in place in-creased the likelihood that the stimulus would come too late.

Specific Objections Some economists who might otherwise take a chance with fine-tuning offer specific objections to a fiscal fix in the current climate. Mr. Taylor, for example, believes that the nation's core economic problem remains slow growth in productivity—a condition that is worsened, if not caused, by Americans' historically low rate of savings. And he fears that any tampering with the deal to cut the deficit in half by the mid-1990's will dim the prospects for a collective turn toward thrift. "We ought to be thinking about the long term," Mr. Taylor said.

Would it be possible to devise a fiscal package that mollifies the skeptics' most pressing concerns? Two unrepentant Keynesians, the Nobel Prize winner Robert Solow of the Massachusetts Institute of Technology and Francis Bator of the Kennedy School of Government at Harvard, think part of the answer is a one-time increase in Federal aid to states and localities. Much of the money, they believe, would be used to restore spending on public investment projects in progress that have been delayed by the budget pinch.

That need not conflict with long-term growth objectives, Mr. Bator argues, since "we need the increase in public investment." And pressure to extend the program beyond a year should be containable because state and local government revenues will rise with the economic recovery.

Neal Soss, chief economist at the First Boston Corporation, seconds the motion for increased public spending because he doubts there is any easier way to light a fire under private spending. In this third year of the economic slowdown—output, he notes, has barely budged since 1988—"businesses and consumers have become allergic to risk."

Mr. Hall of the Hoover Institution points out that the temporary nature of a tax break can cut either way. While people would probably spend little of a one-time income tax reduction because it would have little effect on their lifetime purchasing power, businesses would likely jump at a one-time chance of a tax credit on new investment they had planned to make next year or the next.

Stimulus Plan …Could even the most carefully crafted stimulus misfire? Might public confidence—and public spending—fall in response to a pre-election fix? Might the last best hope for convincing Washington to keep government outlays within sight of revenues be lost? Almost anything is possible, Mr. Bator of the Kennedy School concedes. But "it would be an odd reaction," he said, one out of tune with the "empirical regularities of the past."

He argues, moreover, that there is a parallel risk in sitting tight. If the economy slips deeper into decline, the demand for relief could overwhelm an orderly effort to stabilize the economy without sacrificing long-term productivity goals. A deeper slide might not be likely, Mr. Bator says, "but do you want to take a chance?"

Official Washington plainly does not. And economists who would rather stay the course are rapidly losing their influence.

QUESTIONS

1. a) What types of policy instruments are the focus of this article?

   b) Which agencies are responsible for implementing them?

2. a) Draw a diagram with axes representing real wages and real GDP. Add the aggregate demand and aggregate supply curves. Show the economy in macroeconomic equilibrium at the natural rate of unemployment.

   b) Following the example in the article, suppose that there is a decline in the inclination of businesses and consumers to spend. Demonstrate the consequences for macroeconomic equilibrium.

   c) Suppose that corrective fiscal and monetary policies are viable. Illustrate clearly the impact of a tax cut and an increase in the funds available for bank loans on equilibrium.

   d) Explain how problems might develop in correcting economic fluctuations due to

   • the size of the fiscal and monetary stimulus.

   • the timing of the stimulus.

   • the proper mix of stimuli.

3. a) The article refers to "steady-at-the-helm" or fixed-rule policies. Explain what fixed-rule policies for stabilizing the economy are.

b) Explain how a fixed-rule policy (such as a zero rate of growth of the money supply) would correct the economic downturn described in question 2.

c) Another approach to stabilizing the economy is to use feedback-rule policies. What is a feedback-rule policy?

d) How would a feedback-rule policy counter the decline in spending described in question 2?

e) Why do some economists argue that a fixed-rule works best?

4. Some economists argue that the effects of fiscal policy are neutralized by offsetting adjustments in spending.

a) Explain how public spending may "crowd out" other types of spending.

b) Why would some fiscal policy measures hurt long-term growth?

c) Supply-siders, such as Arthur Laffer, do not believe tax cuts increase the federal deficit. What is their argument? Does the evidence from the 1980s support their case?

74.
A Sprinkle
of
Skepticism
for Supply-
Side
Success

STABILIZATION POLICY

Supply-siders argue that the U.S. tax structure induces the prospect of stagflation. Marginal tax rates are said to be so high that productive effort is actually discouraged. The lack of investment is held to cause production bottlenecks and capacity constraints, resulting in goods being produced at ever-increasing costs. Monetary policy is deemed ineffective because any attempt to stimulate the economy raises inflationary expectations. Fiscal policy is seen to be similarly impotent because any attempt to increase aggregate demand increases inflationary pressures on the economy.

The "supply-side" remedy consists of changes in the tax laws to encourage work effort, investment, and saving. With an increase in investment and productive capacity, employment can be increased without increasing inflationary pressures on the economy. This article examines the supply-side effects of Jerry Brown's flat-tax proposal to stimulate the economy.

After studying your text, reading the article, and answering the questions, you should be able to:

◆ ◆ Analyze the positive and negative impacts of fiscal and monetary policy on macroeconomic equilibrium

◆ ◆ Explain the supply-side approach to stabilization

◆ ◆ Explain the mechanisms through which changes in the tax laws would influence output, employment, and prices

◆ ◆ Explain the implications of the Laffer curve

◆ ◆ Discuss the potential disadvantages of the supply-side approach

Preview

◆ When campaigning for the Democratic presidential nomination, Jerry Brown proposed a tax plan to stimulate the economy.

◆ The proposal consisted of replacing a multitude of personal and corporate income taxes with a flat tax on income and a value-added tax (VAT).

◆ Supply-siders argued that the proposed income tax plan would reduce the disincentives to work, save, and invest, increase tax revenues by increasing economic activity, while shareholders would bear the VAT.

◆ Tax experts doubt the program would work.

Brown's Flat Tax Plan Draws Support of Supply Siders from Reagan Camp

Jerry Brown's flat tax proposal, under heavy attack in New York, is nevertheless finding support among supply-side refugees from the Reagan administration.

Two former officials from Mr. Reagan's Treasury Department—Gary Robbins and Aldona Robbins—released a report this week praising the Brown tax plan. They said that over the next four years, the proposal would create two million jobs. That compares with their estimates of less than a half million jobs created under President Bush's economic plan, and 250,000 jobs lost under Arkansas Gov. Bill Clinton's economic plan.

Economist Arthur Laffer and his partner Victor Canto also have been talking up the flat tax proposal. At a conference they sponsored here last month, "there was a lot of support—surprisingly so"—for the Brown tax plan, according to Mr. Canto.

The former California governor's plan would eliminate all existing federal taxes and replace it with two new taxes—a 13% flat tax on all income, and a 13% "value-added tax" on goods and services. Mortgage interest, rent and charitable contributions would all be allowed as deductions under the flat tax.

Many conservatives have long favored the notion of a flat tax, as well as a value-added tax, arguing that it would reduce the disincentives to work, save and invest. But the Brown proposal has come under heavy fire from tax experts of all persuasions who argue it would shift much of the tax burden from well-to-do people to poor people, and because it wouldn't raise as much money as the current tax system.

Criticism of the plan has been so harsh that even Mr. Brown has begun to back away from it, indicating he would be willing to add measures to reduce the burden the plan places on the poor and increase its burden on the well-to-do.

But the supply siders dismiss such criticisms of the Brown plan. While most economists argue the burden of the value-added tax would fall on consumers, Mr. Canto contends it would fall on "the owners of capital"—or corporate shareholders. Since such shareholders tend to be relatively well-to-do, his analysis suggests the plan wouldn't put an undue burden on the poor, or be a boon to the rich.

And Mr. and Mrs. Robbins, using a "dynamic" economic model to estimate the revenue effects, argue the Brown plan would "raise $250 billion per year more revenue than the current tax system." That estimate is based on the assumption that Mr. Brown's tax plan would lead to a surge in economic growth. Similar assumptions were used to make supply-side calculations that the 1981 tax bill wouldn't lead to a budget deficit.

The supply siders aren't likely to find other economists and tax experts rushing to embrace their analysis. James Poterba, an economist at the Massachusetts Institute of Technology, says the notion that the burden of a value-added tax falls largely on consumers "is one of the least controversial areas of tax policy." The value-added tax, he says, is roughly "the equivalent of a sales tax."

Nobel-prize-winning economist Paul Samuelson says Mr. Brown's tax system would "emasculate the distributional equity of a progressive tax system." He adds however, "If I were a supply sider I'd be for it, because I don't give a rip about distributional equity."

And even some of the supply siders' allies have doubts about joining up with a liberal Democrat like Mr. Brown. "There is an awful lot of merit to a flat-tax rate proposal," says Lawrence Kudlow, chief economist at Bear, Stearns & Co., and a speaker at the Laffer-Canto conference. "But I'm not a Jerry Brown supporter....He is not regarded as a free-market supporter, and he is not regarded as someone who wants to limit government."

QUESTIONS

1. a) Draw a diagram with real GDP and the price level on the axes. Using aggregate demand and supply curves, show the U.S. economy in 1992 in equilibrium below full employment.

   b) If government spending had been increased, what would have happened to macroeconomic equilibrium? Explain your answer. Illustrate the changes in your diagram.

   c) Suppose that the government had cut taxes to stimulate the economy. Would your answer change? Explain your response.

   d) Why might the consequences for the federal budget deficit have been problematic?

2. In fact, the Federal Reserve attempted to stimulate the economy by lowering interest rates.

   a) What were the likely consequences of an increase in the supply of money for macroeconomic equilibrium? In your answer, include reference to inflationary expectations.

   b) Although short-term interest rates decreased significantly as a result of Fed policies, long-term interest rates did not decrease very much. What were the implications of stagnant long-term interest rates for capital spending and investment? Why?

3. As an alternative to the fiscal and monetary policies analyzed above, the Brown proposal sought to lower tax rates. One effect would have been to reduce taxes on capital income. What would have happened to

    a) investment? Why?

    b) macroeconomic equilibrium? Illustrate in a further diagram showing the United States initially in equilibrium below full employment.

4. The flat tax plan would also have lowered the tax rate on wages and salaries for most middle- and upper-income taxpayers. According to supply-siders, what would have happened to

    a) macroeconomic equilibrium? Explain your answer. Draw a further diagram to illustrate, assuming that the United States was initially at less than full employment equilibrium.

    b) tax collections and the federal budget deficit? Explain the reasoning behind this belief. Draw a Laffer curve to illustrate.

5. One of the arguments against a supply-side approach to stabilizing the economy is the lag from implementation to realization.

   a) What does this imply about the shape of the investment demand schedule?

   b) Why are lags a problem for stabilization?

6. Another argument against the supply-side approach is that the tax burden for the poor would increase while the tax burden of the rich would decrease.

   a) Explain how the poor would be hurt and the rich would benefit from

   • a flat income tax (compared to the current progressive tax).

   • a value-added tax (that is higher than current sales taxes).

   b) Is this a political or economic argument against the flat-tax proposal? Explain.

7. a) Why is it unusual for a politician who believes in a prominent role for government to be also a supply-sider?

   b) How can the two policies be pursued without causing a huge federal deficit?

75.
Will the
Real
Deficit
Please
Step
Forward?

Are the recent budget deficits evidence of fiscal irresponsibility, and therefore additional controls on government spending are needed? Or is the deficit under control? Both the Gramm-Rudman-Hollings Act of 1985 and proposed constitutional amendments contain the implicit assumption that the optimal size of the deficit is zero. Economists tend to be more concerned with the underlying, structural deficit, or the ratio of public debt to GDP. The optimal amount of debt using these guidelines need not be zero. In fact, some think that deficits per se don't matter.

So how large should the deficit be? The accompanying article argues that the concern with the official size of the deficit is misplaced, and that the deficit should only include those elements that affect the working of the economy.

After studying your text, reading the article, and answering the questions, you should be able to:

◆ ◆ Distinguish the official budget deficit from the primary budget deficit

◆ ◆ State the sizes of the official budget deficit and the primary budget deficit

◆ ◆ Explain the importance of changes in, and comparisons over time and space of, the ratio of public debt to GDP

◆ ◆ Justify adjusting the deficit for the business cycle

◆ ◆ Explain how to calculate a cyclically adjusted deficit

Preview

◆ Economists do not agree on either the importance of the deficit to the workings of the economy nor the process by which the deficit impacts important economic variables.

◆ There is agreement among economists that the primary budget deficit and the ratio of publicly held debt to GDP are the two most important measures.

◆ The primary budget was in surplus rather than deficit from 1988 to 1990.

◆ The ratio of federal debt to GDP is forecast to stabilize at 55 percent, a rate about the same as that of Germany and France.

◆ The uses to which government spending is put is more important than the deficit.

Worry About Under-Investment, Not Deficits

"**C**BO projects that the deficit will exceed $350 billion in 1992, setting a new record for the second year in a row....[T]he 1992 deficit will amount to 6.0% of GDP, just shy of the postwar high reached in 1983."

This is the way the Congressional Budget Office began its January discussion of the budget outlook, but its handwringing is unwarranted. Because CBO's budget numbers include too much and too little, they misrepresent the country's fiscal position and direct attention away from real economic issues—such as how resources are used or how tax laws favor consumption over investment. After a decade of self-flagellation about the deficit and forecasts of disasters that did not occur, it is useful to pause long enough to ask what the published numbers mean.

Economists do not agree whether or how budget deficits affect the economy. They do agree, however, that if deficits matter, the two deficit measures that matter most are (1) the primary budget deficit and (2) the ratio of publicly held debt to some broad measure of spending such as GDP or GNP.

Primary Budget Deficit The primary budget deficit excludes interest payments and the massive outlays for the thrift bailout, two expenditures that have no impact on economic activity, aggregate spending or prices. Interest payments are a pure transfer. The government collects revenue from some people that it then pays as interest to others. This may have modest distributive consequences, but it does not affect the workings of the economy.

The huge expenditures on the thrift bailout pay for losses incurred in the past, when resources were wasted in unproductive projects or in some cases were stolen. Had the government kept its accounts more accurately, the losses would have been recorded when the net worth of many S&Ls became negative. Instead, they are recorded now as part of the deficit. That makes both the reported current deficit larger and reported earlier deficits smaller. When the assets of the failed S&Ls are sold, future deficits will be reduced. Again, all this bookkeeping has no economic significance.

The ratio of public debt to GDP signals that the national debt may be rising faster than the economy's capacity to pay. From the repeated experience of countries in Latin America and elsewhere, we know that an ever-increasing ratio of debt to GDP may be followed by inflation or even hyperinflation. This may be a problem for Russia or Brazil, but hyperinflation is a remote danger for the U.S., where inflation has fallen during the years of handwringing about the deficit.

In fact, neither the primary deficit nor the debt ratio suggests that the U.S. budget deficit should be high on the list of current concerns. The primary budget was in surplus from 1988 to 1990. Last year the government reported a cyclical primary deficit of about $50 billion resulting from the recession. Before the president's tax and spending initiatives the CBO projected relatively small primary deficits for 1992 and 1993, reflecting its forecasts of sluggish growth in output, employment and tax revenues, with continued growth in non-defense spending. The CBO estimated that if the economy were at full employment, the primary budget would show a surplus of 0.5% to 1% of GDP for the fiscal years 1993 to 1997.

During the 1980s the ratio of federal debt to GDP jumped from the mid-20% range to the low-40% range. Financing the S&L bailout and rising government spending (including interest payments) will move the debt ratio to about 55% of GDP in the 1990s. Thereafter the debt ratio should remain stable, according to government and responsible private projections. If the projections are correct, the debt ratio will be returning to its mid-1950s level, before the inflation of the 1970s reduced the real value of the debt. At 55% the U.S. debt to GDP ratio is not much larger than the ratios in Germany and France.

If the primary deficit and the debt ratio were all that mattered, we could be confident that the budget posed no long-term threat to economic stability. Unfortunately, the government accounts are not as inclusive as they could be. Government liabilities for civilian and military employee pensions are as much an obligation as a formal bond contract.

These claims are not included as part of the government's debt, but they should be. Estimates by Henning Bohn of the Wharton School show that pension obligations for government employees increased the federal government's liabilities at the end of 1989 by $1.2 trillion—and government pensions are only one of many liabilities excluded from the debt-to-GDP ratio. Among some of the notable others: federal deposit insurance, guarantees of private pensions and of shareholders' brokerage accounts. The thrift crisis is an example of a contingent liability that came due.

Accounting for the federal government's hidden liabilities is not a mere matter of detail. While official documents show that the federal government added $1 trillion to its net debt between 1982 and 1990, Mr. Bohn estimates that a more accurate measure of the increase in net government liabilities for these years is $1.5 trillion—and even that is without including future obligations for Social Security and Medicare.

The government reported total net financial liabilities of $1.6 trillion at the end of 1989. But Prof. Bohn estimates that the government's total negative net worth is in fact twice that amount, again excluding Medicare and Social Security liabilities. If Mr. Bohn is correct, the federal government's indebtedness is equal to about 27% of Americans' total private wealth.

Mistaken assumptions about deficits and the public debt matter because they lead presidential and congressional candidates, journalists and citizens to draw incorrect conclusions and become concerned about the wrong set of issues.

The major question is not the deficit itself, but how the federal budget affects the way Americans use resources. Looking at the deficit alone makes it seem that federal investment in infrastructure has the same effect as hiring more regulators. The effects on the economy of these two ways of spending money are, however, quite different. If the government's investment is effective, private sector productivity is enhanced. Consequently, the government adds assets that offset its liability for debt. The private sector too may add additional assets, so wealth increases.

On the other side, regulators often reduce private sector productivity by diverting resources to unproductive tasks. And here there is no asset to offset the liability. Computation of government net worth shows that the government has accumulated debt without generating assets to pay for it, either directly or by increasing productivity in the private sector.

Of course governments everywhere are concerned with issues other than productivity, such as the protection of persons and property, protection of the environment and redistribution of incomes and wealth. These concerns are not advanced by fevered worry about an imprecise or mismeasured number.

None of this should suggest that federal deficits are irrelevant. But when many express concern about what this generation will leave to its progeny, we need to be clear about what government has done and can do and what we as a nation want it to do. Instead of concentrating on the deficit, we should ask three questions about administration and congressional spending and tax proposals:

1) Does the program benefit the present at the expense of the future?

2) Does it further the practice of encouraging consumption at the expense of saving and investment?

3) Does it encourage growth or redistribution?

Present and Future With a few exceptions, most of what has been proposed this year by the president or Congress favors the present over the future, consumption over saving and redistribution over growth. These choices do not address public concern about slow growth of income and productivity. They add to future liabilities without providing government assets or encouraging acquisition of private wealth to pay for debts when they fall due.

It is a mistake to allow concerns about the budget position to prevent actions that raise standards of living and add as much or more to assets than to debt. Budget decisions that encourage investment, raise productivity and reverse the bias toward current consumption should be welcome, even if the people with green eyeshades turn blue.

—Alan H. Meltzer, "Worry About Under-Investment, Not Deficits," March 17, 1992.
Reprinted by permission of *The Wall Street Journal*, ©1992 Dow Jones & Co., Inc. All Rights Reserved Worldwide.

QUESTIONS

1. The main issue raised in the article is how the deficit is calculated.

   a) How is the federal deficit conventionally defined?

   b) What was it projected to be in 1992?

   c) How is the primary budget deficit defined?

   d) Should the current primary budget deficit include

   • interest payments on federal debt? Why or why not?

   • current losses from S&L failures? Why or why not?

   • future pension obligations for current government employees? Why or why not?

   • current salaries for the military? Why or why not?

   • welfare payments? Why or why not?

   e) What was the primary budget deficit expected to be in 1992?

2. Another measure that economists prefer is the ratio of government debt to GDP.

   a) Why is it useful to calculate the change in the debt-GDP ratio?

   b) How has the ratio changed since the early 1980s?

c) What might be worrisome from an economic standpoint about a rising ratio? Explain your answer.

d) Why is it useful to compare the ratio now with the ratio in the 1950s?

e) Why is it useful to compare the ratio in the United States with the ratios in other major economies, such as France and Germany?

3. A further adjustment discussed in the article is to correct for the effects of the business cycle, producing a cyclically adjusted deficit.

   a) How do government revenues and expenditures behave in a recession? Why?

   b) How do government revenues and expenditures behave in a recovery? Why?

   c) What is the advantage of looking at a cyclically adjusted budget deficit?

   d) How would a cyclically adjusted deficit be calculated?

   e) What are the implications for the size of the deficit of adjusting the forecasted 1993 deficit for the cycle? Refer to the article.

DEFICITS

In 1985, Congress passed the Balanced Budget Reduction Act—more commonly known as the Gramm-Rudman-Hollings Act. This act legislated mandatory budget deficit reductions to meet predetermined targets. The deficit was supposed to decrease to zero within a number of years. Since 1985, both the targets and the budget deficits have increased. In 1990, congressional and administration officials hammered out a budget agreement that required revenue increases for spending beyond targeted levels.

At various times, Congress has considered constitutional amendments requiring a balanced budget. The amendments have been defeated. The accompanying article concerns another proposal to balance the budget through a constitutional amendment.

After studying your text, reading the article, and answering the questions, you will be able to:

◆ ◆ Distinguish the federal deficit from the federal debt

◆ ◆ Discuss the real burden of the debt on future generations and on investment

◆ ◆ Explain the rationales for various legislative measures to control the government deficit

◆ ◆ Explain the consequences of relatively large public sector claims on resources

Preview

◆ Another balanced-budget amendment to the constitution has been proposed.

◆ The Simon-Stenholm approach would necessitate tax increases or spending reductions if the federal government's budget goes into deficit.

◆ Tax increases are more likely since spending cuts have never been popular with Congress.

◆ The Kasten amendment would require two-thirds majorities to raise taxes more than economic growth or to deficit-spend.

◆ Contributing to the boom in budget deficits was a 1974 law that stripped the administration of impoundment powers.

◆ Therefore, the article suggests a presidential line-item veto to control government spending.

Simon's Tax Increase

Faster than you can say "House Bank scandal," Congress is suddenly enamored of a constitutional amendment to balance the federal budget. We know what you're thinking, and yes, it's too good to be true.

The House Budget Committee, heretofore uninterested in the amendment, plans to hold hearings. House Speaker Tom Foley predicts the amendment will pass this year, despite his personal opposition. Texas Democrat Charles Stenholm's amendment bill has 268 co-sponsors, including 110 Democrats. In the Senate, Democrat Paul Simon of Illinois declares, "I think we have a real chance of passing it." The last time the Senate even allowed a vote on the amendment was 1986, the year before George Mitchell's liberal Democratic faction took over.

We suppose it's healthy that the Members are feeling enough political pressure to do something, anything, about a runaway federal budget. Yet this Beltway groundswell has all the sincerity of a trial lawyers' convention. Mr. Simon, who ran for President as the only true New Deal heir in 1988, wants us to believe he's worried about federal spending.

Mr. Simon's political camouflage would allow Members to tell angry voters that they're really champions of fiscal probity because they support a "balanced budget." Yet it contains no restraint on the real problem, which is spending and taxes.

The Simon propaganda on the bill stresses "the deficit," never *spending.*

He frets about "staggering deficits year after year," and "sending the bill to our grandchildren," but he can't find anything but defense spending to actually cut. Mr. Stenholm has a much better personal record on spending, but his amendment also lacks a tax-and-spend limitation.

The Simon-Stenholm approach would in effect create an automatic tax-increase mechanism. Every time the budget would go into deficit, Congress and the President would have to close the gap. The choices would be lower spending or higher taxes. But spending cuts never pass because the Members are in political hock to active, vociferous lobbies (such as public-employee unions).

Higher taxes may be unpopular, but a balanced-budget amendment would create a political "necessity" that makes it easier for politicians to justify more new taxes. This has more or less been the experience in states that have balanced-budget laws. Just ask California's Republican Governor Pete Wilson, who had "no choice" but to sign a record tax hike in 1991.

By contrast, Republican Senator Robert Kasten of Wisconsin is offering a balanced-budget amendment that has real teeth. It'd require a three-fifths supermajority in Congress to deficit-spend. But it also requires a three-fifths vote to increase taxes above the rate of economic growth. In short, if voters had to tighten their belts in a recession, so would the federal government.

The Kasten amendment is supported by the various groups that care about the size of government, such as the American Farm Bureau Federation. President Bush has said that any balanced-budget amendment "should include safeguards against a resort to higher taxes," presumably of the Kasten sort. Because it's for real, Mr. Kasten's bill has only 16 Senate co-sponsors. Mr. Foley may not let a similar bill even get a vote in the House.

As we've argued here for nearly two decades, the deficit boom began with the Budget Act "reform" of 1974. Passed over a Watergate-weakened President, that bill stripped the executive of the impoundment power and made Congress's 535 logrollers the dominant budget force.

This is obvious from the cynical way Congress is now lobotomizing the $7.9 billion in spending "rescissions" (cuts) that President Bush has proposed. Speaker Foley's Democrats have stripped them back to $5.7 billion, and replaced many of Mr. Bush's proposals with their own cuts, which punish Members who have had the temerity to support rescissions. Republican Harris Fawell of Illinois has seen funding for the renowned Fermi National Laboratory in his district gutted. The status quo Congress punishes its heretics.

The solution is to make someone besides the logrollers accountable again. Our belief has been that the best way to do this is to put the President back into the process with a line-item veto. Maybe President Bush should propose a deal: He'll sign a phony balanced-budget amendment if Congress will pass a real item veto.

QUESTIONS

1. Distinguish between the federal deficit and the federal debt.

2. One of the major concerns that is raised in the article is that the federal deficit might be a burden to future generations.

   a) If the government taxes the American people in the future in order to pay the interest on the debt to fellow Americans, is the tax a burden on future generations of Americans? Explain your response.

   b) Does your answer to 2a change if the interest is paid to foreigners who are holding the debt? Explain why or why not.

   c) Does your answer change if the government sells treasury bonds to the Fed? Explain your answer.

3. A further problem is the impact of the deficit on the level of private investment.

   a) Draw a diagram with the real interest rate and the dollar value of loans on the axes. Add curves representing the supply of and demand for loans. Show what happens to the equilibrium interest rate and the value of loans when the federal deficit rises and is financed by borrowing.

b) Draw a diagram with axes showing the real interest rate and the level of investment in dollar terms. Draw an investment schedule. Show what happens to the level of investment as a result of the events in 3a.

c) Some people argue that the real problem is not the debt per se, but the low level of saving in the United States. How would a higher savings rate decrease the burden of the debt? Explain in terms of the market for loans and the investment function.

4. A number of measures designed to reduce the federal deficit have been proposed or implemented. Explain how each of the following is expected to reduce the deficit.

a) the Gramm-Rudman-Hollings Act

b) the balanced-budget constitutional amendment

c) a presidential line-item veto

5. The author of the article is clearly not only concerned with the deficit, but also with the level of government spending and taxation. What is problematic from an economic viewpoint, if anything, about increasing the size of the public sector's claims on resources at the expense of the private sector?

SECTION 4

INTERNATIONAL ECONOMICS, GROWTH AND
DEVELOPMENT, AND COMPARATIVE SYSTEMS

77.
Games in Trade: Chinese Checkers

Economists have long argued for free trade as a policy that can increase the wealth of a nation and increase the efficiency with which resources are used. In order for there to be gains from trade, countries should specialize in the production of goods in which they are relatively efficient, that is, goods for which they have a comparative advantage. Specialization necessitates a change in the production mix of the country, and exchange allows a change in the consumption mix. Both changes improve resource utilization and the wealth or well-being of each country.

The restriction of international trade is called "protectionism." Tariffs and quotas are the principal tools of protectionism. Protectionist policies by one country often lead to retaliation by other countries and a consequent loss of the benefits of trade. This article examines the consequences of the imposition of tariffs for the trade and welfare of the United States and China.

After studying your text, reading the articles, and answering the questions, you should be able to:

◆◆ Explain the relationship between opportunity cost and comparative advantage

◆◆ Discuss the relationship between efficiency, specialization, and exchange

◆◆ Understand the basis for, and gains from, trade between countries

◆◆ Describe the consequences of the imposition of trade barriers

Preview

◆ China imports goods from the United States that have copyrights, trademarks, or patents.

◆ China has been lax in enforcing international laws protecting these property rights.

◆ Therefore, the United States has threatened to impose tariffs on approximately $1.5 billion of imports from China unless intellectual property rights are better protected.

◆ China has threatened to retaliate and impose tariffs on over $1.2 billion of imports of American goods.

China Threatens to Boost Duties on American Products if U.S. Imposes Tariffs

China today threatened to raise import duties on U.S. airplanes, corn, steel and other items if the United States imposes punitive tariffs on Chinese products.

The announcement could worsen the two nations' dispute over China's copyright, trademark and patent laws. The United States has given China until Jan. 16 to improve its protection of intellectual property rights or face tariffs of up to 100 percent on a wide range of goods.

The U.S. Trade Representative's Office says the Chinese products that could be targeted represent $1.5 billion in annual imports, and include beer, textiles, pharmaceuticals, footwear and jewelry.

China, in turn, has warned that it could retaliate, but its threat today was the most specific yet on what form the response might take.

The two sides are to meet in Washington this week for a final round of talks.

China is considering "retaliatory duties on some of the U.S. commodities," said China's state-run New China News Agency. Imports of U.S. aircraft, cotton, corn, steel and chemicals worth about $1.2 billion would be affected, the report said, citing information from the Ministry of Foreign Economic Relations and Trade.

Aircraft account for the biggest share of U.S. exports to China, with aircraft and parts worth $575 million sold in the first half of 1991 alone.

Like the United States, the Chinese targeted items that can be bought elsewhere. Airbus and other European airplane manufacturers, for example, would welcome a chance to replace the Americans as suppliers.

China also buys more than 4 million tons of U.S. grain annually, but can also get it from countries such as Canada and Argentina.

The U.S. Trade Representative's Office began a six-month investigation in April into China's protection of intellectual property rights.

U.S. companies say Chinese factories pirate hundreds of millions of dollars of computer software, pharmaceuticals, clothing designs, musical recordings and books—more than any other country. China introduced its first copyright law last summer, but the United States says it is inadequate and poorly enforced.

Negotiations on improving protection broke down in November, but the United States extended the deadline for the penalties to take effect and held more talks in December, which U.S. officials said made no progress.

China, however, maintains that it has improved protection for intellectual property rights and should be given more time to bring protection up to U.S. standards. Officials stress that it will not bow to U.S. pressure.

QUESTIONS

1. The United States has a comparative advantage in corn production. Define comparative advantage. Be sure to include the concept of opportunity cost in your definition.

2. Assume that the United States and China each produce grain and textiles. Suppose that the United States has a comparative advantage in the production of grain and China has a comparative advantage in the production of textiles.

   a) Draw production possibility curves for each country. Mark the amounts of grain and textiles that the United States and China would have produced and consumed in the absence of trade.

   b) In practice, when the article was written, free trade existed. On each diagram draw a line representing the rate at which goods could be exchanged internationally.

   c) Mark the amounts of grain and textiles that the United States and China produced. How did the amount of each good produced in the two countries differ from in a no-trade situation?

   d) Mark the amounts of grain and textiles that the U.S. and China consumed. How did the amount of each good produced in the two countries differ from in a no-trade situation?

   e) Identify the gains from trade for each country. Upon what did the gains from trade depend?

   f) Explain why trade brought gains to each country.

3. Focus on the market for textiles.

   a) In a price-quantity diagram draw the export supply and import demand curve for Chinese textiles in the United States.

   b) What was the free trade price of textiles in the United States? What was the level of textile imports by the United States? Illustrate on your diagram.

4. Suppose that the United States had imposed a tariff on the importation of textiles from China.

   a) Illustrate on the above diagram the change in Chinese export supply as a result of the tariff.

   b) Show what would have happened to the price and quantity of textiles traded.

   c) What would have happened to the gains from trade described in question 2? Explain your answer.

   d) Assuming that China had imposed a tariff on grain imports in retaliation for U.S. tariffs on textiles, who would have gained and who would have lost from these policies?

5. Given your answers to the above questions, do you think the United States should impose tariffs on Chinese goods because of China's lax enforcement of intellectual property rights? Assume that China would retaliate. Explain your position.

International Economics

Free trade is international trade that is unrestricted by tariffs, quotas, or other administrative regulations. Although the vast majority of economists agree that trade restrictions lower real income, these arguments have not dissuaded legislators from initiating a variety of protectionist policies. These policies protect jobs in certain industries. Advocates of protection claim that this is only a short-run necessity because the protected industries soon become highly competitive. The arguments for and against protectionism are discussed in this article.

After studying your text, reading the article, and answering the questions, you should be able to:

◆ ◆ State the arguments offered by the proponents of free trade

◆ ◆ Define and distinguish different types of protection

◆ ◆ Outline the arguments offered by the proponents of protectionism

◆ ◆ Analyze and compare the impact of various protectionist measures on prices, output, and welfare

◆ ◆ Determine who benefits from, and who is harmed by, free trade and protectionism

Preview

◆ A call for protection was raised in the presidential election campaign of 1992.

◆ Economists noted that previous and existing import restrictions had only limited benefits.

◆ While some industries benefitted, other industries were worse off.

◆ Others attributed the poor performance of protectionist measures to an inappropriate selection of the type of protection.

◆ Protected firms benefitted where they invested in equipment and improved product quality, as the steel industry did.

◆ Price increases and restricted choice are the short-run costs of protection.

◆ Long-run benefits may be lower prices and increased choice.

Trade Curbs: Do They Do the Job?

In the midst of the recession and election campaign, protectionist pressures have boiled to the surface, but economists say that import restrictions have had glaringly mixed results for the industries they were supposed to help.

For a few industries like motorcycle manufacturers, protection has provided the breathing room they wanted to begin to regain their strength. But several other industries, most notably autos, are worse off. For some industries, like steel and machine tools, the results of protection have been less than desired. And in most cases, economists generally agree, one clear loser is the American consumer.

"Except for motorcycles, I can't think of a case where the benefits that protection gives to producers outweigh the injury suffered by consumers," said Gary Hufbauer, a fellow at the Institute for International Economics in Washington. He figures that in the mid-1980's quotas on Japanese car imports cost American car buyers an average of $500 a car, whether the car was imported or domestically made....

Weighing Costs and Benefits
Several Presidential candidates, including Patrick J. Buchanan, a Republican, and Edmund G. Brown Jr., a Democrat, have backed protection, viewing it as much-needed medicine for the nation's ailing industries. President Bush and Gov. Bill Clinton of Arkansas say they support free but fair trade and have shunned strong protectionist rhetoric.

Many economists say they are unenthusiastic about protection because, in their view, Washington's trade negotiators have often failed to choose its most effective forms. This has sometimes produced painful results, as when import quotas prompted Japanese car makers to build factories in Detroit's backyard.

Tariffs are generally more helpful than quotas, because they have a direct effect in making foreign products less competitive. In contrast, quotas, which limit a product's supply, can strengthen foreign competitors by enabling them to raise prices and profits, giving them more money to expand or develop new products.

Companies can grow stronger under protection if they use it as an opportunity to invest in equipment, improve product quality and otherwise shape up, economists say, although lazy companies can use protection as a cushion.

"Quotas give you a window of opportunity," said Eli Lustgarten, an industrial analyst at Paine Webber. "If you don't take advantage of that window to solve your problems, then you're going to disappear."

Labor unions are often the biggest fans of quotas and voluntary restraint agreements. "They are designed to provide an industry with time to adjust to specific foreign competition," said Rudy Oswald, chief economist for the A.F.L.-C.I.O. "It's desirable to allow industries to do that because, otherwise, we will put whole industries out of business."

While most economists say protection means higher prices and fewer choices for consumers, Mr. Oswald argues that protection can mean more competition and lower prices in the long run by preventing Japanese cartels from dominating the American market and jacking up prices.

But in the view of many economists, the political debate about protection too often focuses on the needs of industry, while ignoring consumers, many economists say.

"Protection has cost American consumers big bucks," Mr. Hufbauer said. "If people knew how much it was going to cost them, wouldn't they insist that the nation, that the industries involved, get a better payoff from protection?"

QUESTIONS

1. The article discusses the impact of Voluntary Restraint Agreements (VRAs) and quotas.

   a) What is a Voluntary Restraint Agreement?

   b) What is a quota?

   c) What is the distinction between a VRA and a quota?

   d) Describe two other measures that can be applied to protect domestic industry from foreign competition.

2. The United States had relatively higher steel production costs than overseas producers in 1984.

   a) Draw a price-quantity diagram showing the import demand of the United States for steel and the export supply of steel by other countries. Mark the price and the level of U.S. steel imports under free trade.

   b) Who benefitted and who lost due to the free trade of steel (compared to a no-trade situation)?

3. a) In the above diagram draw a curve representing the steel VRA of 1984-1992. Identify the resulting domestic (U.S.) price and the quantity of steel imports.

b) For each of the following economic agents, state whether and explain why they gained or lost when VRAs replaced free trade.

- U.S. consumers

- U.S. steel producers

- U.S. automobile manufacturers

- U.S. Treasury

- foreign exporters of steel to the United States

- other foreign (nonsteel) exporters

4. Protectionism has been suggested as a way of maintaining employment.

a) What arguments do industries make when soliciting protectionist measures?

b) In the steel industry example above, did the imposition of a VRA "save" jobs in the steel industry? Explain your response.

c) What happened to the sales and prices of products that used steel as an input?

d) What happened to wage rates and employment in steel-using industries?

e) Evaluate the argument that protection maintains employment.

5. The article argues that tariffs might be preferable to VRAs.

   a) Suppose that instead of a VRA the government were to impose a tariff on imports of steel. Draw a diagram as in question 2a. Show the effect on the price of steel of a tariff that reduces imports to the level seen under the VRA. How is the impact of a tariff on price different from that of a VRA?

   b) For each of the following economic agents state whether and explain why they would prefer a tariff (T) to a VRA, a VRA (V) to a tariff, or be indifferent (I). Why?

   - U.S. consumers

   - U.S. steel producers

   - U.S. steel importers

   - U.S. automobile manufacturers

   - U.S. Treasury

   - foreign exporters to the United States

   - other foreign (nonsteel) exporters

6. Suppose that you were campaigning for elected office in an area where there is a potential for large job losses because of foreign competition. What policy position might you advocate without compromising your concern for the welfare of the nation? Explain your stance.

**79.
The
Unbalanced
(?) Balance
of
Payments**

Over the past few years, one of the more closely followed economic indicators has been the monthly balance of trade report issued by the Department of Commerce. The primary reason for this attention is that the United States, which had had a balance of trade surplus for most of the post-World War II era, began having merchandise trade deficits in the 1970s. In the 1970s, the deficits were offset by trade surpluses in services, leading to a current account surplus. In the 1980s, however, the merchandise trade deficits increased dramatically, exceeding trade surpluses in services. Although the merchandise trade deficit declined in the late 1980s and early 1990s, it was still high. Forecasts of a resultant reduction in the standard of living in the United States and foreign takeovers of U.S. assets have been commonplace. The article that follows discusses the trends in, and the components, causes, and ramifications of, the trade deficit.

After studying your text, reading the article, and answering the questions, you should be able to:

◆◆ Describe the components of the balance of payments accounts

◆◆ Calculate the current account deficit or surplus

◆◆ Explain the relationship between entries in one of the component accounts and deficits or surpluses in the others

◆◆ Explain the causes of deficits and surpluses

◆◆ Evaluate the measures that have been proposed to reduce the balance of trade deficit

◆◆ Understand the implications of a balance of payments deficit

Preview

◆ 1991 saw the smallest U.S. merchandise trade deficit in eight years.

◆ However, December's trade gap widened by $1.77 billion.

◆ The 1991 results were attributed by some economists to the weakened U.S. economy and a declining dollar.

◆ By December 1991, however, the recession in Europe was dampening demand for U.S. exports.

◆ The U.S. trade surplus with Western Europe quadrupled in 1991, while the trade deficit with Japan and China widened.

U.S. Exports Fell 2.2% in December, Reflecting Global Economic Slowdown

After reaching record levels in 1991, U.S. exports appear to be weakening, reflecting a global economic slowdown that analysts say could last through 1992.

The Commerce Department announced that exports fell 2.2% in December to $36.13 billion. That was the second consecutive monthly decline. Meanwhile, imports jumped 2.3% in December to $42.07 billion. As a result, the monthly trade deficit swelled by $1.77 billion to $5.93 billion.

Exports were one of the few sources of strength for the U.S. economy for most of 1991, and the softening at year end isn't good news. "I guess the bottom line here is that for 1992 we're going to have to have a domestically based recovery, because we're not going to have any support from the foreign-trade sector," said Bruce Steinberg, economist with Merrill Lynch & Co.

"Most European countries are either in or close to recession," he added.

"Canada remains in recession, and Japan is slowing down."

Auto Exports Fall The decline in exports was concentrated in capital goods, consumer goods and automobiles. Exports of autos nosedived 10.3%. The import figures reflected increases in capital goods, industrial supplies and consumer goods.

Despite the deterioration in the trade balance in December, Acting Commerce Secretary Rockwell Schnabel pointed enthusiastically to figures indicating the trade deficit for the full year narrowed to $66.20 billion, the smallest trade gap since 1983, from $101.72 billion in 1990. Exports in 1991 totaled a record $421.85 billion, while imports, at $488.06 billion, posted their first annual decline since 1982.

Analysts have warned for months that the trade gap would widen once consumer demand picks up in the U.S. Trade deficits typically shrink during recessions because of lower domestic demand.

According to the trade report, the U.S. trade surplus with Western Europe more than quadrupled in 1991 to $16.13 billion from $4.03 billion in 1990. That shift partly reflected strong demand in Europe, combined with a decline in the value of the dollar, which made U.S. exports less expensive. The U.S. trade deficit with Germany narrowed to $4.91 billion from $9.40 billion, as the absorption of East Germany led to an increase in demand for goods from the U.S. and elsewhere.

"Generally, Europeans had money to spend and people in the U.S. didn't," said Allen Sinai, chief economist for Boston Co.

Deficit with Japan Widens The U.S. trade deficit with Japan last year widened to $43.44 billion from $41.10 billion in 1990, and the trade gap with China swelled to $12.69 billion from $10.43 billion. The deficit with Taiwan narrowed to $9.84 billion from $11.18 billion.

QUESTIONS

1. The article describes the behavior of the merchandise trade account.

   a) What is the merchandise trade account?

   b) How are U.S. exports of automobiles treated in the current account of the United States?

   c) How are U.S. exports of automobiles treated in the current account of the importing country?

2. a) What are the other components of the U.S. balance of payments current account?

   b) Describe in general terms the nonmerchandise items that would be included in each of the components in 2a.

   c) Why is foreign tourism to the United States treated as an export?

3. a) How is the U.S. deficit on current account paid for in an accounting sense?

   b) How is this represented in the balance of payments accounts?

4. The article points to a disagreement concerning the cause of the reduction in the deficit. Explain how each of the following would have improved the balance of trade.

   a) a strong European economy

b) German reunification

c) the slide in the value of the U.S. dollar

d) the U.S. recession

5. The decline in the value of the U.S. dollar does not only affect the balance of payments. What are the implications for

a) Japanese investment in the United States? Why?

b) the standard of living of U.S. residents? Why?

80.
Made in
the USA—
by Foreign
Enterprise

For most of the 1980s and 1990s, the United States has run a current account deficit. This, coupled with a weak dollar and high interest rates, has resulted in significant capital inflows. When foreigners purchase U.S. assets, many people are upset. Not only is it regarded as a sign of U.S. weakness, but also fears are raised that other countries might gain some political control over the United States or compromise national security. Others are concerned that financial instability could result from foreigners withdrawing their money. These concerns raise demands for protection. This article discusses the recent experiences of Japanese purchases of U.S. assets and the advantages and disadvantages of foreign ownership.

After studying your text, reading the article, and answering the questions, you should be able to:

◆◆ Describe the changes in the economic position of the United States vis-à-vis other countries that have encouraged foreign ownership of U.S. assets

◆◆ Explain the relationship between the trade deficit, the federal budget deficit, and the private sector deficit

◆◆ Explain the causes of fluctuations in the level of Japanese purchases of U.S. assets

◆◆ Discuss the arguments for and against foreign ownership

◆◆ Discuss policies that could be applied to reduce foreign ownership

Preview

◆ During the 1980s, Japanese investors, supported by a surging yen, low interest rates, and soaring asset values, started buying U.S. properties.

◆ These acquisitions have not paid off so far because the U.S. recession has reduced their value.

◆ These losses, coupled with Japan's recession, have discouraged new Japanese investment in the United States.

◆ One investment strategy that has paid off is the decision to build automobile factories in the United States.

◆ Because of Japan's huge trade surpluses, many analysts believe that Japanese purchases of U.S. assets have only been temporarily slowed.

Reversal of Fortune

Japan continued to bad-mouth America last week with Prime Minister Kiichi Miyazawa's claim that U.S. workers have forgotten how "to live by the sweat of their brow." This insult, the latest in a series of trans-Pacific slurs, echoes recent assertions by some Japanese politicians that Americans are lazy and illiterate. Despite their public antipathy toward the United States, however, many in Japan still crave America's lifestyle and covet some of this country's prized possessions. In the midst of the current name-calling, for example, a Japanese-led group is trying to purchase Seattle's baseball team....

The Japanese are used to dealing with American hostility. During the 1980s, they were vilified when they shelled out billions for prestigious U.S. properties like Rockefeller Center, Columbia Pictures and Firestone Tire. But America's mudslinging did nothing to bog down Japan's relentless money machine. Propelled by low interest rates, soaring stock prices, skyrocketing property values and a surging yen, Japanese investors roared into America faster than a bullet train from Tokyo to Osaka.

Losing Luster Today, with the American economy tarnished by recession, many of Japan's high-profile U.S. acquisitions look less than lustrous. In real estate, for example, the $75 billion the Japanese spent in 35 states and 67 metropolitan areas is now worth $60 billion or less, according to Jack Rodman of Kenneth Leventhal & Co., an accounting firm....Burdened by underperforming real-estate loans in America, Japanese banks have taken large losses....Meanwhile, on the corporate front, Bridgestone Corp., Japan's biggest tire maker, has struggled with its $2.6 billion takeover of Firestone. After purchasing the American company, Bridgestone was forced to sink $1.5 billion into aging factories and to

inject $1.4 billion in new capital just as the U.S. tire market skidded.

America's economic downturn and Tokyo's growing financial distress have discouraged new Japanese investment in the United States. Japan is now faced with tighter credit, sagging real-estate values and a plunging stock market. Over the last two years, the Nikkei Index has dropped from 38.916 to 22.000. This sell-off, combined with the property bust, has dramatically eroded capital and reduced Japanese banks' ability to lend. As a result, Tokyo's holdings of U.S. stocks and bonds have been sliced by $27 billion since 1988. Japanese purchases of U.S. corporations dropped from $11.9 billion in 1990 to just $3.8 billion last year. And between April and September of 1991, Japanese direct investment in America fell almost 40 percent from a year earlier.

The most noticeable pullback has been in the property market. Since 1988, Japanese investments in U.S. real estate have plummeted from $16.5 billion a year to less than $5 billion annually....

Like its real-estate ventures, Japan's forays into corporate America haven't always met with quick—or easy—success. The Bridgestone-Firestone deal is a case in point. In its fury to outbid Italy's Pirelli, Bridgestone may have moved too quickly in acquiring Firestone, according to Daniel Schwartz of Ulmer Brothers, a New York-based investment bank. Then, lacking a cohesive strategy for running the American tire maker, the Japanese company moved too slowly in consolidating operations. Rather than streamlining, as analysts had recommended, Bridgestone hired 500 quality-control experts. Quality has improved at Firestone but productivity is still only 60 percent of Japanese levels.

In addition to outright acquisitions, Japanese firms have purchased equity

stakes in at least 180 technology-oriented companies since 1986. Peter Peterson, chairman of the Blackstone Group, a New York investment bank, says these strategic alliances are a cheaper and less risky proposition than buying a company outright. Taking a minority equity position "gives Japanese companies a chance to adjust to American companies' cultures and operations," adds Schwartz....

Made in America One investment strategy that has benefited both Japan and the United States is Tokyo's decision to build automobile factories in America's heartland. This transplanted car production accounts for 17.6 percent of the U.S. auto market and has helped dampen protectionist fever. So far, Japanese car makers have poured roughly $9 billion into transplant factories, which now employ 30,080 workers. Japan Inc. has invested two or three times more in plants and equipment than have its U.S. counterparts, according to Blackstone's Peterson. This investment philosophy, he adds, explains why "some Japanese have decided to take the green-field approach and build their American plants and their work force culture from the ground up rather than make large and higher-profile investments in acquiring existing companies."

Although Japanese investment in the United States has slowed, most analysts don't expect Tokyo to remain on the sidelines for long, because Japan's huge and growing trade surpluses will eventually need to be recycled. In fact, Japan has announced that its current-account surplus doubled in 1991, to $72.6 billion. As a result, says Deutsche Bank economist Kenneth Courtis, Tokyo will direct at least $700 billion into foreign markets over the next decade. Only this time, chastened Japanese firms are likely to be more careful where they throw their yen.

QUESTIONS

1. Japanese investment in the United States has its roots partly in the U.S. trade deficits of the 1980s, which caused the United States to become a net borrower.

   a) Explain the general relationship between the trade deficit, the federal budget deficit, and the private sector deficit.

   b) Was the federal budget deficit or the private sector deficit primarily responsible for the U.S. trade deficits experienced in the 1980s? Explain.

   c) Explain the process by which increases in government purchases of goods and services resulted in trade deficits.

   d) Why did foreign investment in the United States exceed U.S. investment abroad when the United States ran a trade deficit?

   e) Why did the rising value of the yen against the dollar give the Japanese an incentive to invest in U.S. assets?

   f) Why are foreign lenders buying firms and corporate assets rather than simply holding bonds?

   g) The United States is a net borrower. Distinguish the United States from countries that are both net borrowers and debtor nations.

   h) Does it matter whether foreign lenders are financing U.S. consumption or U.S. investment? Explain your answer.

2. Explain why the Japanese reduced their level of new investment in the United States due to

    a) the recession in the United States.

    b) the recession in Japan.

3. In 1991, Japan had a current-account surplus of $72.6 billion.

    a) How does a current-account surplus materialize?

    b) Is there any relationship between Japan's current-account surplus and the fact that Japan has one of the highest savings rates? Explain.

    c) The article states that this current-account surplus needs to be recycled. Why? Explain your answer.

4. The article discusses some of the investments in U.S. firms by Japanese firms.

    a) How might American tire buyers benefit from Bridgestone's purchase of the Firestone tire company? Explain your response.

    b) How might American car buyers benefit from Japan's decision to build automobile factories in the United States? Why?

c) What is the likely impact of the Japanese investments in U.S. companies on U.S. employment? Explain your answer.

d) What is the likely impact of the Japanese investments in U.S. companies on their U.S. competitors? Justify your answer.

e) What are the economic disadvantages of foreign ownership of U.S. firms?

5. During the 1980s, as foreign ownership was growing, there were increased demands for policies to prohibit foreign takeover of American assets. Suppose that foreign ownership reached a critical point in a certain industry that was vital to the national security of the United States. What options would be available to our government?

International Economics

Money facilitates the exchange of goods and services. When a purchase is made, the seller expects to be paid in the national currency of his or her country. A gas station in Detroit wants dollars for any gas that is sold and a Parisian bakery expects francs for its bread. When a good or service is imported into a country the seller generally asks to be paid in his or her own currency. The nation's currency that is needed to pay for the import is termed foreign exchange, and the price at which one currency can be converted into another currency is called the foreign exchange rate. The foreign exchange rate for each currency is determined by the demand for and supply of foreign exchange.

These transactions are not costless. Markets have to be established and resources devoted to accomplishing these exchanges, thereby reducing the amount exchanged. This article discusses the determination of exchange rates and the implications of establishing a common European currency.

After studying your text, reading the article, and answering the questions, you should be able to:

◆ ◆ Explain the determinants of the exchange rate

◆ ◆ Understand how the exchange rate is determined under three different foreign exchange regimes

◆ ◆ Explain the mechanics of currency appreciation and depreciation

◆ ◆ Discuss the impact of a common currency on European firms, European consumers, foreign firms, foreign consumers, and governments

◆ ◆ Discuss the impact of a common currency on a member country's monetary and fiscal policies

Preview

◆ The European Community has created a monetary union that will establish a common central bank and a single currency.

◆ The European Currency Unit, or ECU, will replace the current currency of the individual European nations.

◆ Each nation that joins the monetary union will relinquish control over its money supply and interest rates in exchange for forecasted growth in trade and investment.

◆ Member countries will also give up the power to devalue their currency and manage their budget deficits.

◆ Besides lowering the cost of doing business in Europe, a common currency will raise investor confidence by reducing the risk of devaluation and exchange rate fluctuations.

European Monetary Union: Now Much More Than Talk

After years of talk, European Community governments seem set to relinquish control over their monetary policies and form a landmark monetary union that will include a common central bank and a single currency.

Despite Britain's objections, the plan calls for setting up a common currency in several European countries, perhaps as soon as 1997 and no later than 1999.

If all goes according to plan, the European Currency Unit, or ECU, will become the currency of hundreds of millions of Europeans—and could someday rival the dollar in importance. European officials say the plan will bolster growth and investment, push down inflation and interest rates, and improve Europe's competitiveness versus the United States and Japan.

Over time, there will be trade-offs for countries that join the monetary union. For example, they will relinquish sovereign power over their money supply. Each nation will stop issuing its own money and forfeit control over the setting of interest rates, since those powers would go to a common central bank.

These countries will still influence overall monetary policy because they will have representatives on the board of the common central bank. Member countries will also give up the power to devalue their currencies. Many European countries with competitiveness problems and trade deficits have devalued their currencies, because it raises their exports by making them cheaper abroad.

Also, countries will no longer have full freedom over their budget policies.

Concerned that large deficits can push up inflation and interest rates, the community plans warnings and even fines against countries with deficits that exceed 3 percent of their gross domestic product.

Still, every community member except Britain insists that the benefits of monetary union will outweigh any of the losses.

Although the decisions taken next week in Maastricht, the Netherlands, will not have overnight repercussions, monetary union will ultimately have far-reaching effects on people and businesses both here and in the United States.

Germans who travel to France and the Netherlands will no longer have to worry about changing their marks to French francs and Dutch guilders; all three countries will have the same currency. Similarly, vacationing Americans who travel from Nice to Florence will not have to fret about their leftover francs.

And businesses will be able to end the bothersome and costly practice of preparing invoices in separate currencies for different countries. Companies will also save money by eliminating the European currency-hedging operations they use to protect the value of shipments against currency fluctuations.

American banks and manufacturers doing business in Europe strongly support monetary union, saying it will lower costs and, they hope, stimulate the Continent's economy.

"Imagine what it would be like operating our business in the United States with 12 different currencies," said Ursus Jaeggi, director of government affairs for Du Pont in Europe. "It would have a hell of a negative impact on our bottom line, because our costs would go up significantly.

"As soon as these European currencies can be replaced by a single currency, we can simplify internal administration. It would help our costs, our bottom line, and our ability to compete."

Builds on Existing System The plan for monetary union will build on the existing 10-nation European Monetary System, which pegs exchange rates among the community nations. Monetary union will improve on this by creating a large currency zone that raises investors' confidence by eliminating the threat of devaluations and exchange-rate fluctuations.

It is unclear now how many nations will join a common central bank and use a common currency. After bitterly fighting monetary union to preserve its own currency and sovereignty, Britain is likely to opt out. Several other nations may also be excluded if they do not rein in their inflation rates and budget deficits. Many European officials predict that seven nations, including France and Germany, will make up the first group to use a common currency and form a joint central bank.

Since July 1, 1990, when the first stage of the monetary union plan took effect, community nations have sought to make their economic policies and performance converge by lowering inflation rates and budget deficits. Europe's currencies can only be fused together if community members bring down their inflation rates so that they are in a narrow range, European officials say. These officials add that community members need to slash their budget deficits to ease pressures on inflation and interest rates.

In 1994, a Second Stage The second stage of monetary union—which begins on Jan. 1, 1994—calls for an embryonic European central bank, known as the European Monetary Institute, to guide and put pressure on the 12 nations to bring their inflation rates, interest rates and budget deficits into line.

"Monetary union will not only create certainty, but it will create a better consensus on economic policies over all that are strongly influenced by the idea of lowering inflation," said Jean-Louis Beffa, chairman of Saint-Gobain, the French glass and packaging company.

By the end of 1996, the community's members plan to vote on a third and final stage of monetary union—to create a common central bank and set permanent exchange rates. These moves require unanimous approval. Officials from several nations hope a decision to form a single currency will also be taken then.

Worried that a lack of unanimity would cause a single currency to fall by the wayside, France won a compromise from other nations this week that aims to insure the creation of a single currency. A new vote is to be taken by late 1998, and according to the compromise a simple majority of nations will suffice to form a common central bank and currency.

Similar to Fed System Once a common central bank is formed, the central banks of France, Germany and other nations will take on functions not unlike the role of the regional Federal Reserve Banks in the United States.

France, Spain and Italy want a communitywide central bank because they are frustrated that Germany's Bundesbank so dominates the European Monetary System. These countries contend that the German central bank, with its high interest rates, too often favors fighting inflation over promoting economic growth.

"You won't have a policy that is totally influenced by the specifics of one country," said Mr. Beffa of Saint-Gobain. "It could be a little more growth-oriented. It could take into account a little more the situation of other countries."

Germans Are Wary …Many Germans are wary of embracing the ECU, which they fear will be weaker than the mark. The ECU's value will be based on a weighted "basket" of community currencies.

"Some people feel this is a very unique opportunity, and we shouldn't let it slip by," said Ulrich Schroeder, an economist with Deutsche Bank. "But others say we should proceed a little more cautiously, that we shouldn't commit ourselves right now."

The Germans insist that the new central bank be independent of government pressure, which would allow it to concentrate on keeping prices stable rather than on easing credit, as many politicians want. They also fear that if community members fail to bring down inflation, the common currency will prove far flimsier than the mark.

Conditions for Joining The plan sets several conditions that a nation must satisfy to join the monetary union:

Its inflation rate must not exceed by more than 1.5 percentage points the average rate of the three community nations with the lowest rates.

Its budget deficit must not exceed 3 percent of its gross domestic product and its overall Government debt must not exceed 60 percent of G.D.P.

Long-term interest rates must not exceed by more than 2 points the average interest rate of the three countries with the lowest inflation rates.

Its exchange rate must not fall, for two years, more than 2.25 percent below the average of the European Monetary System.

Currently, only France and Luxembourg meet all of these criteria. Even Germany does not meet all of them, because the costs of reunification have pushed its budget deficits to 5 percent of G.D.P.

Italy does not meet any of the conditions. Its deficit is about 10 percent of G.D.P., and its overall debt is more than 100 percent of G.D.P.

QUESTIONS

1. The German mark could be exchanged for 3.39 French francs in mid-April 1992. Assume that the market for foreign exchange between the mark and the French franc was unregulated by central authorities.

   a) What determined the demand for francs by Germans?

   b) What were the determinants of the shape and slope of the demand curve?

   c) What determined the supply of francs?

   d) What were the determinants of the shape and slope of the supply curve?

   e) How was the exchange rate determined?

   f) Draw a diagram of the supply of and demand for French francs in terms of German marks. Mark the exchange rate and the equilibrium number of French francs exchanged. (Make sure you label the axes correctly!)

   g) Illustrate on your diagram what would have happened to the value of the French franc relative to the mark if the demand for francs had increased.

2. Suppose that there is a floating exchange rate between France and Germany. Describe what happens to the demand for and supply of marks if

   a) there is much higher inflation in France than in Germany, assuming that incomes in the two countries increase in proportion to the rate of inflation.

   b) the rate of interest rises in Germany and falls in France.

c) the French budget deficit doubles while that of Germany decreases, assuming that the French budget deficit is partly financed by borrowing from German citizens.

3. In fact, in 1992 the 10-nation European Monetary System was an example of a managed foreign exchange market.

a) Draw a diagram of the supply of and demand for French francs in terms of German marks. You may assume any upper and lower limits to the exchange rate.

b) Explain the shape of the supply curve you have drawn.

c) Illustrate what would have happened to the exchange rate and the quantity of francs traded had the demand for French francs increased significantly.

d) How would the foreign exchange market operate to achieve this exchange rate?

4. If a monetary union among the European nations is formed in the late 1990s, what type of exchange rate will exist between

a) France and Germany?

b) the United States and France?

c) the United States and the ECU?

5. Assume there is a fixed exchange rate between French francs and German marks in the latter part of the decade.

a) Draw a diagram illustrating the equilibrium of the regulated foreign exchange market for French francs in terms of German marks.

b) Explain the shape of the supply curve you have drawn.

c) Illustrate what will happen to the exchange rate in this regulated market if the demand for francs increases significantly.

d) How will the foreign exchange market operate to achieve this exchange rate?

e) Given your answers to question 2, explain why a country that joins the European Monetary Union will have to relinquish control over its money supply, interest rates, and (to some extent) its budget deficit.

6. a) What are the benefits to a monetary union? Refer to the article.

b) Who benefits, and why do they benefit?

GROWTH AND DEVELOPMENT

82. Gaps, Gains, and Growth

There is a large gap between rich and poor nations. The gap is growing: per-capita income for the rich nations is increasing faster. The poorest countries seem to be mired in poverty. Attempts to improve their lot have failed. In some countries formerly designated as "developing," economic development strategies have been so successful that the economies are now designated as "newly industrialized." Economic growth rates for some of the newly industrialized countries have far surpassed the growth rates for countries that are termed "industrialized."

This article examines the characteristics of developing, newly industralized, and industrialized countries. It also describes the strategies that developing nations have pursued to escape their poverty.

After studying your text, reading the article, and answering the questions, you should be able to:

◆◆ Describe the characteristics of developing, newly industrialized, and industrialized nations

◆◆ Discuss the sources and process of economic growth

◆◆ Understand the obstacles to economic growth

◆◆ Evaluate various strategies for improving economic growth and development

Preview

- Following the General Agreement on Tariffs and Trade talks in 1948, the industrialized nations generally opted for free trade.

- However, most of the developing countries retained their protectionist postures.

- Nations that selected free trade prospered, while the countries eschewing free trade did not.

- Around 1980, developing countries began to lower their tariffs and quotas.

- The delay can be attributed to the gains from trade being widely dispersed, while the benefits of protection were more apparent.

- Also, the International Monetary Fund (IMF) and the World Bank requested that debtor nations introduce free trade in return for debt relief.

Why the Third World Is Embracing Free Trade

When the General Agreement on Tariffs and Trade was established in 1948, the founders assumed there would have to be special rules for "developing" countries. These countries, the reasoning went, couldn't compete on even terms with industrial nations like the U.S. While they were building themselves up, they would be allowed various forms of trade protection, such as import quotas and tariffs, the sort of things that the sturdy industrial countries were vowing to get rid of.

The industrial countries did indeed opt for free trade. There was an explosive expansion of world trade, and that helped to spur international prosperity that, in turn, softened any hardship caused by the steady removal of protection. As expected, the developing countries dragged their feet on reducing protection. In fact, their remedy for any trade troubles still was more, not less, protection, just as it had been in the past. For the Third World, the road to free trade seemed to keep stretching farther and farther into the future.

There were exceptions. The Asian tigers—South Korea, Taiwan, Singapore and Hong Kong—opted increasingly to open their markets. It worked, too, but the four examples seemed to do little or nothing to convince other developing countries that this was the real road to development.

Then, about 1980, things began to change. Developing countries, which had fought off free trade like the plague, suddenly seemed to decide that it was their economic salvation.

Why the rush to free trade? Why did it take so long to develop? And, perhaps most important of all, will it last? Dani Rodrik, who somehow manages to divide his time among the Hoover Institution, Stanford University, Harvard and the National Bureau of Economic Research, deals with those questions in a new paper (NBER Working Paper No. 3947).

The author offers a variety of examples of the rush to freedom, including countries in Latin America, the Caribbean, Africa, Asia and the Mideast. As he remarks, putting all these countries together with the newly opening-up nations of Eastern Europe adds up to a genuine revolution in policy making.

The transition was a long time coming in part because many politically well-connected people had an interest in the status quo. Tariffs and quotas limit the low-cost, high-quality imports that otherwise would compete with the products of domestic manufacturers, an arrangement the manufacturers would like to see continue.

It is possible to demonstrate that the average citizen and the entire economy would benefit from the elimination of such special privileges, and Mr. Rodrik does so, quite persuasively. "At this point," Mr. Rodrik writes, "the economics professor usually stops and rests his case, feeling smug after this unassailable demonstration of the superiority of free trade."

But the gains from free trade are widely dispersed and difficult to see. They may materialize only over a period of considerable time. A domestic manufacturer, on the other hand, can claim, accurately or not, that a new higher tariff "saved" the jobs of 1,000 workers, and in the U.S. he can even bring some of those workers up to Congress to argue for tariffs. Only an occasional economist ever shows up in Washington to lobby for free trade.

It's awfully hard for a politician to take income away from one group to give it to another group—when he can't quite understand how and why that other group is benefiting.

So how did the developing countries ever get started toward free trade? To some extent, the answer is that they got pushed. All of the oil money the Organization of Petroleum Exporting Countries was getting was going into the banks, and the banks were "recycling" it to the developing countries. But the Third World couldn't use the money productively and soon was deeply in debt.

The World Bank and the International Monetary Fund bailed out many of the debtors, but in return insisted on broad and often painful economic reforms—including free trade. Some of the debtors had friends in the industrial world and managed to soften the World Bank-IMF prescriptions. In most cases, too, reform had a home-grown elements. The debt situation had become so desperate that many countries were ready to experiment with something as new as free trade. Mexico, for instance, has moved more aggressively to trade freedom than the World Bank intended.

With year after year of negative growth and with inflation running into triple digits, it's hardly surprising that countries became willing to experiment. One of the more interesting experiments came in Chile. In 1973 Chile had the same problems as its neighbors, high inflation and very low growth. The country also had a Marxist government, which was pushed out by Gen. Augusto Pinochet, a dictator.

Gen. Pinochet was in no rush to get the country back to democracy, but he had thoughts about the economy—mostly opening it up and slowing inflation. The reforms worked, leading some skeptics to say that an essential element in such reform was dictatorship. But the country had a free election, democracy was restored, and free trade was hardly an issue in the voting. Free trade was a success, and it's hard to argue with success.

Will it last—in Chile and elsewhere? The growing number of successes are one thing that it has going for it. In addition, nations have become increasingly aware that free trade sells better when it's linked with anti-inflationary reform. Free trade may be hard to see, but everyone can appreciate stable prices. As Mr. Rodrik concludes, "Nothing will help sustain open trade policies more than a stable macro-economic environment."

QUESTIONS

1. The article refers to developing countries, industrial countries, and countries like South Korea and Hong Kong, which can be termed "newly industrialized" countries. Define

    a) developing nation.

    b) newly industrialized country.

    c) industrialized nation.

2. What are the typical characteristics of developing nations in terms of

    a) income?

    b) distribution of income?

    c) proportion impoverished?

    d) demographics?

    e) balance of payments?

3. Trade increases the prosperity of participants. Prosperity is usually defined in terms of income per capita.

    a) Explain why income per capita is a better indicator of economic development than simply using the level of income or GDP.

    b) What causes a country's per-capita income to change? Draw a per capita production function to illustrate.

4. Developing countries face many obstacles to economic growth. Explain how each of the following is a barrier to economic growth.

   a) a high population growth rate

   b) a low savings rate

   c) international debt

5. The article mentions various policies historically adopted by developing countries to promote economic development. What have been the rationales for

   a) protection to develop export industries (rather than free trade)?

   b) import substitution (rather than export promotion)?

   c) the encouragement of foreign investment (rather than constraining foreign capital)?

6. The article points to a number of cases in which free trade has increased economic growth.

   a) Suppose that a ban is placed on the import of steel into Hong Kong. Below and to the left, draw a diagram of the demand for and the supply of steel in Hong Kong. Mark the equilibrium price and quantity.

b) Now assume that a steel manufacturing plant is constructed in South Korea. Above, and in the center of the page, draw a diagram of the South Korean steel industry, with price and quantity on the axes. Draw a supply curve.

c) Suppose that Hong Kong drops its protectionist policies so that South Korean steel is imported into Hong Kong. Above and to the right, in a third diagram, draw the new supply curve facing Hong Kong consumers. Mark the new equilibrium price and quantity, and the level of imports.

d) Why is Hong Kong better off?

e) What happens to income, employment, and output in South Korea? Explain your response.

83. Population Pill Difficult to Swallow

There is a great deal of inequality in the distribution of income and wealth among the countries of the world. Only about 20 percent of the people of the world live in "industrialized" countries that have relatively high living standards and per-capita income. Very few countries in the twentieth century have made the transition from "underdeveloped" or "less-developed" countries to industrialized nations. For the others, poverty and its attendant maladies are endemic. The rate of population growth is one significant obstacle to economic development. This article discusses the relationship between population growth and economic development.

After studying your text, reading this article, and answering the questions, you should be able to:

◆◆ Explain the relationship between population growth, resource allocation and development, and output per capita

◆◆ Describe the relationship between population growth, savings, and economic development

◆◆ Explain the impact of trade deficits and foreign debt on economic development

◆◆ Discuss the problems associated with implementing birth control in third world countries

Preview

◆ Nearly half the population of Central America is under the age of 15.

◆ In 1950, there were 4 million children under the age of 15; in 1970, 8 million; in 1990, 13 million.

◆ Both the amount and speed of growth is of great concern.

◆ Population growth is overwhelming the region's cultures, economies, social systems, and natural resource base.

◆ Population gains have swamped economic development, producing lower standards of living.

◆ A major problem is emerging for which there is no short-term solution.

◆ It is difficult to gain acceptance for population control.

The Population Explosion: Threatening the Third World's Future

I was walking through the streets of Cartago, Costa Rica, some 20 years ago when the bells rang and the elementary schools let out. A thousand scrubbed and uniformed children flooded the streets. That Lilliputian world was a dramatic reminder that Costa Rica, like the rest of Central America, is a nation of children. Nearly half the population is under the age of 15.

Central America's population explosion—and the population explosion taking place throughout the Third World—was captured for me in that incident. Today, ever-larger numbers of children are pressing hard on small and, in some cases, shrinking economies. The 8 million Central American children under the age of 15 in 1970 represented a large increase from the 4 million children in 1950. There are 13 million Central American children under the age of 15 now. If projections hold true, there will be 19 million by 2025.

In one lifetime, Central America's population is not just doubling or tripling. It is rising by a factor of seven—if the ecology can support it. And growth will not stop in 2025.

The population explosion that began in the 1950s and continues today is arguably Central America's most significant historical event, overriding the importance of the Spanish conquest and the independence movement 270 years later. Never has the region experienced anything of this magnitude and force. Not only is the amount of growth of serious concern, but also the speed with which it is occurring.

Overwhelming population growth is wreaking havoc on the region's cultures, economies, social systems, and natural-resource base. Forget the failure of political systems and civil wars as the leading issue. Forget economic depression and unemployment, affecting as much as half the labor force. Forget old debates over land-holding systems where power is concentrated in the hands of a few export-crop producers. Forget low standards of living and miserable urban slums that appear occasionally to be clusters of smoking cardboard and tin boxes strung along the arroyos. Forget the exodus of tens and hundreds of thousands headed north to cross the porous Mexican—U.S. border in search of jobs.

Focus instead on the rise in population as the single basic issue. It has put an incredible burden on attempts to resolve old problems and has, meanwhile, created new ones. In Central America today, you truly must run faster and faster just to stay in place.

The concept of "economic development" has dominated, for the most part, the Third World's view of its future since the 1960s. A fast pace of economic growth was expected to more than offset rapid population gains. Population growth was still considered a given. The idea of slowing it down offended many—for religious and political reasons—and grated deeply on personal convictions. But it was always recognized that economic growth had to keep pace with population growth. If the economies faltered, the continuing population gains would slip right by, producing lower and lower standards of living. This is precisely what has happened.

Central America offers a typical case of the demographic forces working in the Third World. Demographers—not only in Central America, but in many developing nations around the world with rapidly growing populations—have informed politicians that they see a very major problem emerging for which there is no short-term solution. Further, the problem is guaranteed to continue to intensify for the next half century and longer.

Slowly but surely, the soundness of these alarming population projections is being recognized. These projections, accompanied by common-sense observations in the increasingly crowded streets outside, are convincing politicians that a serious and intractable problem has emerged.

The Third World's demographic future contains hard messages that are difficult to swallow. But, with rapid population growth still accelerating, neither Central America nor other developing nations are likely to stabilize and take the pressures off their social, ecological, and economic systems—or those in the First World.

—"The Population Explosion: Threatening the Third World's Future," THE FUTURIST, January/February 1992. Published by the World Future Society, Bethesda, MD. Reprinted with permission.

QUESTIONS

1. Costa Rica's population growth was 2.5 percent in 1989. Its total population was estimated to be 3 million.

   a) Assuming that the growth rate remains constant over the 1989-1999 period, estimate Costa Rica's population in 1999. By what percentage does the population increase?

   b) If the United States' population growth rate is 1 percent and this rate is also assumed to be constant over the next ten years, by how much will the population grow? Compare this with your estimate of Costa Rica's population growth.

2. Actual population growth is the difference between the birth and death rates. The death rate in Costa Rica is 4 per 100,000, while the birth rate is 29 per 100,000. The figures for the United States are 8.5 and 16.4 respectively.

   a) What is happening to the percentage of people under 15 in Costa Rica? Explain your answer.

   b) Why is the death rate higher in the United States than in Costa Rica?

3. The article argues that the rapid population growth rate in Central America is wreaking havoc with the economy and society.

   a) Draw a per-capita production function with capital per capita measured on the horizontal axis and output per capita on the vertical axis. Select a point on the production function to represent the Costa Rican economy in 1970.

b) The population has grown rapidly since 1970. The amount of labor has therefore increased. If Costa Rica is typical of Central America, what has happened to total output in this period? What do you think has happened to output per capita? Illustrate on your diagram above.

c) What has happened to the standard of living and the level of poverty as a result of your answer in 3b? Explain why this has occurred.

d) Suppose that education per worker has increased during the period. How would your answer to 3b change? Illustrate the outcome on your diagram.

e) What are the economic obstacles to increasing educational attainment in a country like Costa Rica?

f) What are the implications for other productive resources of a fast-growing population?

g) Had there been a greater amount of capital investment since 1970 incorporating the latest technological advances, how would your answers to 3b be different? Explain your answer and illustrate in a new diagram.

4. A further, related, obstacle to economic development associated with a high rate of population growth is the low savings rate.

   a) Why are savings important to economic development?

b) Why might savings be low in countries like Costa Rica?

c) How does the fact that the Central American countries have large current account deficits and foreign debt affect economic development in these countries?

5. One remedy for the problems resulting from high rates of population growth is birth control. What are the obstacles to more widespread adoption of birth control? Refer to the article.

84.
For Richer
or Poorer?
Russia
Weds
Capitalism

In the post–World War II period, the world's two principal economic and political systems have been capitalism and socialism, epitomized by the United States and the Soviet Union. In 1991, the Soviet Union as a political entity collapsed, the member republics becoming separate countries. The collapse of the political system resulted from the failure of the Soviet economic system. Capitalism and market reforms are now replacing socialism and central planning. The transition from socialism to capitalism, however, has not been without hardship. The accompanying article discusses the reforms being made in Russia to change from a socialist economy to a capitalist economy, and points out the difficulties that Russia is experiencing.

After studying your text, reading the article, and answering the questions, you should be able to:

◆◆ Describe the characteristics of capitalism and socialism as economic systems

◆◆ Explain how resources are allocated in a free market system

◆◆ Understand how resources were allocated in the centrally planned economy of the Soviet Union

◆◆ Understand some of the problems that led to a marked decline in the growth of the Soviet economy

◆◆ Describe the objectives of the economic reforms

◆◆ Discuss some of the consequences of the reforms that have been implemented

Preview

◆ In 1992, industrial production was down and unemployment was up all across the former Soviet Union.

◆ The hardship generated by the reforms led to pleas for relief and a retreat from their implementation.

◆ The release of previously controlled prices had dramatically increased production costs.

◆ Tight credit and the collapse of the banking system had made it difficult to raise capital.

◆ Central planning had been reduced, but industry was not yet privatized.

◆ Consumers and firms had difficulty paying higher prices.

◆ There was considerable disagreement whether the Russian economy's ills called for shock therapy or a more gradual approach.

Reform Has Russia's Factories on the Mat

In the cavernous Red Proletariat machine-tool factory in central Moscow, half-finished lathes gather dust, and some workers on a break play dominoes.

The assembly line has been cut back to one eight-hour shift a day. At the end of last year, 500 of the plant's 5,000 workers were fired, and another 500 may go soon. Demand has shriveled for such high-cost products as industrial robots and equipment for making computer disks, so the plant is producing more low-cost lathes.

What's happening at this factory, once an industrial showcase for the Soviet Union, is happening all over Russia. Production is collapsing at an alarming rate, and the collapse threatens to derail the radical reforms designed to get the fledgling capitalist economy rolling. So far this year, industrial production is falling an average of about 15% a month. In the worst-hit sectors, such as farm machinery, output is in a free fall, plunging as much as 50% a month.

Unprecedented Unemployment Government officials gloomily predict that the declines will continue at least through the third quarter, and they now openly say they fear widespread bankruptcies. Unemployment, in a country with practically no social insurance system, may reach an unheard-of 6%, or five million people, by year's end, according to even the more conservative government estimates.

The International Labor Organization expects Russian unemployment to soar to 15%, or 11 million of Russia's 75 million work force. The ILO, an agency of the United Nations, said this week that Russian jobless rolls could even swell to as high as 30 million people if Moscow goes ahead with plans to let domestic oil prices rise to world levels and allows bankrupt state enterprises to go under.

As the economy sinks, a rising tide of discontent is leading to increasingly forceful calls for a step back from the radical reform plan. Some go so far as to call for the ouster of President Boris Yeltsin. But the main target is Yegor Gaidar, the Russian economic chief who has drawn international praise for his ruthless but consistent austerity policy aimed at curbing the deficit and forestalling hyperinflation.

To hear some businessmen, economists and factory managers tell it, everything has gone wrong with reform. The government's program of price liberalization has sent costs of raw materials and utilities up as much as tenfold and caused labor costs to skyrocket. Tight credit and the collapse of the banking system have made it impossible to raise operating capital. Meanwhile, high taxes are bleeding businesses dry, and the ending of old supplier relationships has made procurement a nightmare.

Many critics argue that industry, which is almost entirely state-owned, should be made private before prices are freed, so that producers can respond to market signals. But the government argues that privatization takes too long and says a stable currency and realistic price structure must come first.

Elusive Priorities "Maybe Gaidar is a little doctrinaire, but liberalization of prices was the first and only thing to do," says a Western economist who monitors Russia's economy. "People won't begin to be businessmen and have an economic perspective if you don't have . . . stability."

But, faced with the prospect of industrial collapse, some in the government argue for a softening of the austerity program. "I generally agree with Gaidar, but I think the danger of industrial failure is no less than the danger of hyperinflation," says Economics Minister Andrei Nechayev, Mr. Gaidar's deputy, who advocates new subsidies for some industries.

In the past, Soviet enterprises operated on centrally dictated orders. A factory knew exactly how many widgets it had to make, to whom to deliver them and where to get parts. Unprofitable factories were propped up by the government.

Last year, the former Soviet government started edging away from all that, though hesitantly as new freedoms led to rising chaos. Then, after the attempted putsch last August, the whole system collapsed, and the Russian government introduced shock therapy Jan. 1, with price liberalization, an austerity budget and a new tax system.

The Vladimir Tractor Factory, 100 miles east of Moscow, illustrates the ripple effects of price liberalization. Anatoli Grishin, the jovial 14-year-veteran director, has had to raise salaries as much as 70% in the past month so his workers can afford higher prices. He also brings in food to sell his workers at subsidized prices.

To cover such higher costs, tractor prices had to jump tenfold. Sales plummeted. The factory once turned out 30,000 tractors a year under the central plan. This year it expects to sell only 16,000.

Russia's cooperative and state farms are being broken up, and the land is being turned over to individuals, but "no private farmer has the funds to buy expensive equipment," says Boris Nefyodov, a top adviser in the Russian Union of Industrialists and Entrepreneurs. "Actually, now we're at a pre-World War II level of tractor production—and all this just before the spring planting campaign."

Even when factories are delivering products, customers often can't pay. So far this year, buyers haven't paid for goods valued at a total of 200 billion rubles ($2.22 billion), estimates Mr. Nechayev, the economics minister.

—Elisabeth Rubinfien, "Reform Has Russia's Factories on the Mat," April 1, 1992.

Q U E S·T·I O N S

1. As the article states, in the former Soviet Union, central planners allocated resources to industries such as the farm machinery industry.

   a) Draw a diagram with axes representing the price and quantity of farm machinery. Add the demand curve for farm machinery.

   b) Draw the supply curve for farm machinery and explain its slope and position.

   c) Add a vertical curve showing the target level of output set by central planners. Mark the price of farm machinery and the quantity traded.

   d) Was the farm machinery industry allocatively efficient? Explain and illustrate on your diagram.

   e) At the price you have marked, show the excess supply or demand. Was the price too low or too high? How did producers and consumers react?

   f) What could producers do to restore equilibrium? What did planners do to bring supply and demand into equilibrium? Illustrate your answer.

2. In 1992, Russia was in transition from a socialist economy to a capitalist economy. Prices and quantities were freed from central control.

   a) Draw a set of demand and supply curves for farm machinery identical to those in question 1. Show the socialist equilibrium.

   b) What determined the price and quantity of farm machinery traded when the market was freed from controls? Mark the capitalist equilibrium on your diagram, assuming that the curves were unchanged.

c) In fact, the demand and supply curves shifted. The breaking up of state farms meant that farmers were unable to afford as much farm equipment as before. Also, price liberalization led to increased raw material costs. Bearing in mind the magnitudes of these changes described in the article, illustrate the consequences on your diagram. Show the impact on the output of farm equipment.

d) At the price you have marked, was there excess supply or demand? Why or why not?

e) Why was the Russian economy more allocatively efficient when production and prices were liberalized than under centralized planning? Refer to your diagram.

f) Show total social welfare after the shifts in the curves. Was a free market economy a "better" system than socialism? Explain your response.

g) Would it have been better to gradually lift price controls on raw materials and other goods—say by 10 percent a year? Explain why or why not.

COMPARATIVE SYSTEMS

The inefficiencies of centrally planned economies have led to the wholesale abandonment of socialism and a rush to capitalism. Capitalism is a system in which there is private ownership of the means of production, and markets allocate resources. There is, however, no unique model of capitalism.

Some productive resources can be owned by the state. Resources can be allocated by planners as well as by markets. Which decisions are left to the market and which are appropriate for government varies across countries. National defense, law and order, and income distribution questions are typically left to government. There are a number of other goods, such as education and pollution control, where many call for more government provision, while others feel that the private sector can best handle allocation questions. The market mechanism generally allocates other types of goods and services. This article argues that there is a role for social policy in capitalism, and it should not be equated with socialism.

After studying your text, reading the article, and answering the questions, you should be able to:

◆◆ Define different types of economic system

◆◆ Describe the provision of goods and services when resources are allocated by the market and when they are allocated by the government

◆◆ Understand the advantages and disadvantages of capitalism

◆◆ Outline the determinants of income inequality in capitalism

◆◆ Discuss the need for, and fairness of, inequality in capitalism

Preview

◆ The fall of communism in Eastern Europe does not mean that capitalism is without faults, such as social problems.

◆ The stigma of socialism has restricted public debate on social policy.

◆ Conservatives have equated a large and active government with socialism.

◆ Low taxes and a dearth of social programs have created incentives for engaging in illegal activity that are greater than the rewards for working honestly.

◆ Given that antisocial behavior is inappropriate, there are strong positive economic reasons for more social programs.

◆ The "proper" level of taxes and social programs is an empirical question and not an ideological issue.

Improve Capitalism.
Use Some Socialism.

By arguing that Communism's spectacular failure after 70 years proves capitalism's success, American ideology has fallen into a trap of faulty logic.

When Communism failed in Eastern Europe, the number of people living in poverty in the U.S. did not change. Our rivers did not become cleaner, nor did the drug problem become less threatening.

The collapse of Communism (or socialism, as its leaders called it) can benefit our economy if we consider it an opportunity to examine our system critically without fear that the process and outcome of such scrutiny will be stigmatized as socialist.

The fear of socialist taint (even from Western socialisms) and the effect of that fear on social policy debate have long distracted us from our main task of making capitalism, the most productive economic system known to man, more humane.

That fear has been evident in the conservatives' equating a large and active U.S. Government with socialism. During the Reagan Administration, this equation paved the way for the Government's abdication of its responsibilities in education, housing, poverty, health care and care for the homeless. New York's ills that Vice President Dan Quayle attacked on Thursday are as much a result of the Reagan "small-Government" years as of the big-Government years preceding them.

In a capitalist system, people are in effect paid according to how much society would lose if it were to do without their services. The fees a famous brain surgeon earns can be rationalized by considering what would happen if the surgeon stopped operating: we would lose the services of all of those he would have saved.

But our society has produced a group of people whose productive contribution is minimal—for example, an illiterate 17-year-old who depends on drugs and lacks the discipline to hold a job. If such a person were deducted from our economy, our gross national product would stay the same or might go up, since this person may have been engaged in activities that harmed others and hence the economy.

Like everyone, such people rationally respond to incentives and strive to increase earnings. In their case, they will weigh the benefits of working honestly, at an almost zero wage, or criminal activities that will bring a better return, even after adjustment for the risk of being jailed.

Critics of high tax rates maintain that they smack of welfare state practices and erode the incentives of our most productive citizens. What they don't acknowledge is that our country has a dual-incentive system: one for the rich, one for the poor. When tax rates on the wealthy are low and social programs are small, this creates incentive for antisocial behavior by the poor that decreases everyone's quality of life. When tax rates for the rich are higher and social programs are large, the poor have incentives to behave less destructively to themselves and others. Thus, the question of which combination of taxes and social programs maximizes the nation's quality of life should be empirical, not ideological.

The price capitalism pays for its failure to provide proper incentives to the underclass so that its members can seek honest rather than criminal employment is readily visible. You can't rely on the incentive system to bring you the Apple computer without understanding that it will also bring you your local crack dealer. You can't rely on the incentive system to bring you 50 cable TV channels without also having your windshield washed by an army of homeless men when you drive across town.

In the past, the response would be, "Well, this is bad, but would you rather live in Russia?" Obviously nobody wants to live in Russia, but that does not make it any easier to live in America. It could be easier if we re-examined the defects of capitalism without contaminating the analytic process by importing into it our hostility toward socialism. Inevitably, we would conclude that if the underclass has improper incentives, they must be changed.

But changing them may involve measures that to some smack of socialism. Take a family with a poor woman who heads a household with four children and has no high school degree. Whose incentives are we worried about? Clearly not hers; unfortunately, the economic battle for her is probably lost. What we must care about is offering the right incentives to her children by creating an environment where honest work is preferable to dishonest work. This means educating and otherwise preparing them to respond effectively to new incentives.

This may also entail a dole to the mother—welfare not workfare—but so what? Despite the national hostility toward welfare, especially in this election year when welfare is becoming an issue, enlightened selfishness suggests that, despite the weak economy, in the long term it would be wise to subsidize her in order to allow her to provide for her children.

When all government actions in the U.S. were judged by their distance from socialist doctrine, such interventions as national health care, the dole and regulation of industry were considered dangerous. With Communism dead, rational policies may be considered on their merits, not their ideological implications.

QUESTIONS

1. It is often argued that communism (or socialism) has failed, and that capitalism has been successful.

   a) Define capitalism.

   b) Define communism. How is communism different from socialism?

   c) Define socialism.

2. a) The article says that critics of high tax rates state that they smack of welfare state capitalism. What is welfare state capitalism? Give an example of a good produced in the United States that fits the description of welfare state capitalism.

   b) How is market socialism different from welfare state capitalism? Give an example of a good produced in the United States that fits the description of market socialism.

3. The U.S. government has reduced its provision of goods and services, and has left the private sector to fill the gap. For each of the following items mentioned in the article, state how the provision (for example, the price, quantity, and quality) of the good or service has been (or will be) altered.

   a) education

   b) health care

   c) housing

4. The article argues that capitalism causes significant inequality.

   a) What determines the distribution of income in a capitalist economy?

   b) Is this distribution necessary? Why?

   c) Is this distribution just? Explain your definition of "just".

   d) This article argues that the system needs to improve the economic position of low-income groups through social programs. What is the author's reasoning?

   e) Do you agree or disagree? Explain your stance.

5. Consider the market for shoes in the United States. Assume the market is perfectly competitive.

   a) What determines the number of shoes to be produced?

   b) Draw the supply curve for shoes and describe its characteristics.

   c) On the diagram above, add a demand curve for shoes. What determines the shape and position of the demand curve?

d) How is the price and quantity of shoes sold determined?

e) Describe how this sector achieves allocative efficiency.

6. Consider now a socialist (centrally planned) economy that produces shoes.

a) What determines the number of shoes to be produced?

b) Draw the supply curve for shoes and describe its characteristics.

c) On the diagram above, add a demand curve for shoes. What determines the shape and position of the demand curve?

d) How is the price and quantity of shoes sold determined?

e) Is this sector allocatively efficient?

APPENDIX

Video Segments

DEMAND, SUPPLY, AND EQUILIBRIUM

Product markets are in equilibrium when the market price brings the quantity demanded into balance with the quantity supplied. Although equilibrium is the optimal state for both producers and consumers, it can be disturbed by changes in the conditions of supply or demand, leading to a new price-quantity equilibrium. The accompanying video shows how the equilibrium price and quantity of heating oil (and of crude oil and refined oil from which heating oil is derived) was affected by changes in various determinants of demand and supply during a cold northeastern winter.

After studying your text, watching the video, and answering the questions, you should be able to:

◆◆ Recognize the determinants of supply and demand

◆◆ Explain the impact of changes in supply and demand on equilibrium price and quantity

◆◆ Understand that the slopes of the supply and demand curves affect the changes in price and quantity

Preview

◆ Heating oil prices rose in late 1989.

◆ On the face of it, there were numerous suspects to blame, but many had alibis.

◆ The retailer received a higher price, but faced higher costs.

◆ The wholesaler also had stable profit margins.

◆ Crude oil suppliers saw prices rise 15 percent, but had low profits in the recent past.

◆ The oil refiners made windfall profits of 50 cents a gallon due to the appreciation of inventory that was potentially costly to hold.

◆ The real culprit was the unregulated free market.

Heated Up

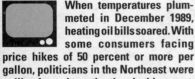 When temperatures plummeted in December 1989, heating oil bills soared. With some consumers facing price hikes of 50 percent or more per gallon, politicians in the Northeast were calling for an investigation. In this report, Paul Solman does his own investigation.

Paul's own winter heating bill is up $275. Part of the increase is due to the extreme cold in December, which caused consumers to burn a third more heating oil than normal. The rest of the increase is due to a higher price for oil. Paul starts his search for the culprit at his own heating oil retailer, Hayes Oil.

From the beginning until the end of December 1989, heating oil in Boston rose from a cost of about $1.00 to $1.50 per gallon. Dan Hayes, the president of Hayes Oil, says that he is not increasing his own profit margin. "We got the same margin at the beginning as we were getting at the end of the month...about 35 cents a gallon." Although he admits to selling more oil, that extra money, he explains, is covering the extra expenses of earlier working hours and operating costs. Drivers are needing to get up earlier so they can wait in long lines at the loading racks.

The retailer, Paul explains, seems to be off the hook. But he provides the next clue as to the true culprit. The drivers are waiting in long lines because the wholesalers are running out of heating oil. Throughout America, fuel oil inventories have been dwindling for years. There may not be enough oil in reserve to get through a long and cold winter.

Paul speaks to the next suspect, the wholesaler, and asks him about these low inventories. The wholesaler's ratio-nale is that you have to watch your cost, and it costs a lot to have a big inventory. "You expose yourself to...market volatility that does exist. You can end up buying big inventories in September, October for the heating oil season and see a much lower price in January. So you cannot risk that, it costs too much." You would have too much oil in a warm winter, and the extra cost of storing all the oil would be passed on to the consumer.

In the recent price hike, typical wholesalers didn't raise their profit margins either. They only added a standard 5 cents a gallon. They can't offer the consumer a break, because the wholesaler has to look at replacement cost—what it would cost him to buy a barrel of oil to replace the barrel he's selling to the retailer. And that price is set by the New York Mercantile Exchange, the next suspect.

Paul visits the Exchange, where buyers and sellers argue over what they think the price of oil is going to be in the future. Joel Faber, one of the key traders of oil futures, defends the speculators on heating oil futures. "The market that we have on the figures is simply a form of price discovery. We are reflecting where the rest of the industry thinks the prices are going to go and what shape the market is in." Paul agrees that, while the commodity exchange seems a likely suspect, the main effect of the Exchange on prices is that it gets them to where they'd be going anyway.

Paul's next suspect is the crude oil supplier. Paul speaks to Kristoffer Maroe, General Manager of Stot Oil, the huge billion dollar Norwegian state oil company. It's the largest crude producer in Europe and a major supplier to the United States. Maroe says they are not gaining huge profits from the price hike, and that crude oil prices are only up 15 percent for the period under discussion. Asked why not forego even that profit, Maroe explains that in recent years the crude oil business has been suffering, and Norway has been in financial trouble because of it.

The last suspect is the oil refiner. Paul returns to the anonymous wholesaler, who also is a small refiner. Asked to justify the windfall profit of as much as 50 cents a gallon, he replies, "Basically the refiner is in a position where he has inventory and if the price goes up sharply that inventory appreciates in value." Can't they give consumers a break? Refiners can't offer the consumers a break because big businesses have to represent their shareholders, and if they can show a profit, they have to take it. In the case of oil hikes, it's especially true because the market will go down just as fast as it went up.

With all the suspects offering alibis, the question still remains, who is the culprit? Paul places the blame on the unregulated free market. It's in business' self-interest to have low inventories. When there is a sudden surge in demand for that inventory, buyers start to bid up the price to get what is left. That extra cost is then passed on to the consumers. The oil companies have to make a business decision not to carry inventory. It's a decision that is definitely not in the public interest. With many consumers unable to meet the cost of their heating bills, Congress is holding hearings to decide how we, as a nation, should soften the effects of the next inevitable price spurt, or if such decisions should be left to the market. ◆ ◆ ◆

QUESTIONS

1. The first suspect was the retailer.

   a) In the retail market for heating oil, who is the consumer and who is the producer?

   b) Draw a diagram of the retail market for heating oil, with the price and quantity of heating oil on the axes. Add a demand curve and a supply curve. Mark the initial equilibrium price and quantity of heating oil traded. Show the effect of the coldest December in a century on the curve(s) and equilibrium. Explain what happened.

   c) The supplier of retail heating oil experienced an increase in his costs of wholesale oil and overtime rates for his drivers, among other things. Show the independent impact of this on the curve(s) and equilibrium on your diagram.

2. The second suspect was the oil wholesaler.

   a) In the wholesale market for heating oil, who demands wholesale oil and who supplies it?

   b) Draw a diagram of the wholesale market for heating oil, with the price and quantity of heating oil on the axes. Show the demand and supply curves and the initial equilibrium price and quantity. Illustrate the impact of the retailers wanting to buy more oil.

   c) The retailer complained that wholesalers had little inventory, so that the price rose significantly relative to quantity. What would have happened to the price level had there been more inventory? On your diagram in 2b draw a different supply curve on which the initial equilibrium lies, but which reflects the greater inventory. Show the implications for the equilibrium wholesale price and quantity of oil traded.

d) Consumer pressure groups are seen in the video arguing for larger inventories. However, the holding of inventories costs money. Amend your second supply curve to reflect inventory costs (which can be seen as a type of resource cost). What happens to the equilibrium price and quantity as a result?

3. The main suspect was the oil refiner.

   a) In the market for refined oil, who demands refined oil and who supplies it?

   b) Why did the demand for refined oil go up appreciably?

   c) Why were the refiners able to make a large windfall profit?

4. A further suspect was the supplier of crude oil.

   a) In the market for crude oil, who is the consumer and who is the producer?

   b) Why did the price of crude oil rise by only 15 percent while the price of refined oil rose so much more?

   c) The crude oil supplier stated that oil producers earn fluctuating profits, unlike when the Organization of Petroleum Exporting Countries (OPEC) was able to reduce production. Draw a diagram of the market for crude oil, with the axes representing the price and quantity of crude oil traded. Add a supply curve and a demand curve, and mark the initial equilibrium price and quantity. Show the effect on equilibrium of a decrease in supply by OPEC.

5. One suggestion made by the crude oil supplier was that consumers buy heating oil storage tanks and purchase oil in the summer.

a) Draw a diagram of the market for heating oil as in question 1, but with a demand curve for oil in the summer and a second demand curve for oil in the winter. Show the equilibrium prices in each season.

b) How would consumers gain according to the crude oil supplier's advice?

c) Under what circumstances would this strategy prove to be worthwhile?

Video 2: Cash in Trash?

Firms are anxious to minimize costs in order to maximize profits and ensure a successful existence free from bankruptcy. Cost minimization requires technological efficiency such that the maximum output is produced from a given set of inputs, and economic efficiency such that the chosen technologically efficient method of producing a given level of output is the least costly.

In perfectly competitive product markets, the equilibrium price and output of the industry is where supply equals demand. The equilibrium output of a representative firm is where marginal cost equals marginal revenue, subject to the shutdown condition whereby price must cover average variable costs for the firm to produce in the short run. The firm's equilibrium price is the market price. Short-run profits are equal to output multiplied by the excess of average revenue over average total cost. Entry in the long run is induced by short-run profits; exit is induced by losses. In long-run equilibrium, entry and exit cause profits to be zero.

The accompanying video focuses on whether costs are minimized by using recycled or virgin materials. It also discusses whether the recycling industry can be profitable.

After studying your text, watching the video, and answering the questions, you should be able to:

◆ ◆ Recognize the components of average total cost and marginal cost

◆ ◆ Determine the equilibrium price, output, and profit of a competitive firm and industry

◆ ◆ Predict the effect of changes in demand and costs on the equilibrium of a competitive industry and representative firm

◆ ◆ Determine whether a firm should shut down in the short run

Preview

◆ Recycling is increasingly popular because landfill space is declining.

◆ Supporters claim that reusing materials is more energy efficient than using virgin supplies.

◆ Recycling may also avoid damaging public relations, as McDonald's found.

◆ Opponents of recycling argue that new resources are often cheaper, resulting in low demand and prices for recycled material.

◆ Given that environmental problems are caused by using virgin resources, some argue that there is a need for the government to induce recycling through the market mechanism.

◆ However, government intervention may not be palatable.

Cash in Trash?

In this report, Paul Solman investigates the economics of recycling, taking the example of New York City which is trying to turn trash into cash. Rather than pack scarce landfills, trash is sold to people who reuse it to make new products. Paul speaks with environmentalist Barry Commoner who says that the only thing that stands in the way of recycling is the social organization. He says that reusing a product like plastic is more energy efficient than making it out of raw stock like petroleum.

Paul also looks at McDonald's' recycling program. In response to public pressure, McDonald's tries to recycle all of its waste into other products; for instance, cardboard boxes are recycled into take-out bags. McDonald's has created its own market for its recycled goods; this is known as "closed loop recycling."

Paul asks whether this loop can be closed in the world at large. Looking at recycled newspaper, Paul discovers that the market is just not there. New York City not only pays for its newspapers to be taken away, it turns out that the papers are not even used in this country. They are shipped to the Far East where they do not have enough trees.

Recycling plastics, as well, is not economical. While it costs $300 per ton to collect the recycled material, it only sells for $10 per ton. In fact, the only recycled product that pays for itself is aluminum, which costs a lot to make from scratch. We see that recycled trash is just piling up around the country. The supply of recycled materials is growing faster than the markets for them.

Paul asks whether or not the government should do what McDonald's has done, and invest in and foster a recycling industry. He speaks with a Harvard professor who suggests a plan whereby the government would require a minimum level of recycling from companies. He thinks the free market creates environmental problems, and that the government needs to harness the market in some way.

Paul notes that another approach is for the government to act as a catalyst, to bring companies together to make recycling efficient and orderly. We see an example of this in Taiwan, where plastic makers have pledged to buy all the recycled plastic to convert to different products. They have managed to close the loop nationally.

Paul concludes that closing the loop nationally in the United States would probably be seen as too much government intervention and that recycling will, for the time being, remain politically popular but expensive. ◆◆◆◆◆◆◆◆

QUESTIONS

1. a) Given that firms are profit maximizers, under what circumstances would they be willing to use recycled materials rather than virgin resources?

    b) Why might it be cheaper to use recycled raw materials than use virgin resources?

2. Recycled aluminum is cheaper than aluminum made from bauxite.

    a) Draw a supply and demand diagram of the aluminum goods industry. Mark the equilibrium price and output. Assuming the market is competitive, also draw a diagram of a representative firm, including its cost curves and its demand curve. Show the firm earning zero profits at the equilibrium price and output level.

    b) What would be the effect on short-run industry price and output and on the firm's price, output, and profits, of using cheaper, recycled, aluminum? Illustrate in your above diagram.

    c) What will happen in the long run?

3. McDonald's restaurants recycle their waste following consumer pressure.

    a) Draw a supply and demand diagram of the fast food industry, showing the equilibrium price and quantity. Also draw a diagram of a representative franchise, including its demand and cost curves, assuming for simplicity that the market is perfectly competitive. Show the franchise in long-run equilibrium.

    b) What was the short-run impact of the demonstrations and consumer boycotts of fast-food restaurants on the equilibria of the industry and the representative franchise? Illustrate your answer in the above diagram.

    c) Why was McDonald's obliged to recycle its waste in the long run?

4. For most raw materials it is cheaper to use virgin supplies.

    a) Why might it be cheaper to use virgin supplies than recycled raw materials?

    b) In the market for used paper, the producers are communities and the consumers are the recycling mills. Draw a supply and demand diagram of the used paper industry, showing the equilibrium price and quantity at low levels. What causes these low equilibrium values? Refer to the determinants of supply and demand.

c) At the side of the above diagram, draw a diagram of a representative community that supplies used paper. Assume there is perfect competition. In marking the equilibrium, show the community sustaining a loss. Under what conditions should it continue to recycle paper in the short run? And in the long run?

5. Montgomery County, Maryland, requires newspapers to use recycled paper.

a) Draw a supply and demand diagram of a competitive newspaper industry, showing its equilibrium price and quantity. Also, in a separate diagram, show the cost and demand curves of a representative newspaper, and its equilibrium price, output, and profits, assuming it is in long-run equilibrium.

b) What happens in the short run to the industry and firm equilibria if recycled paper is more expensive than virgin paper? What happens in the long run?

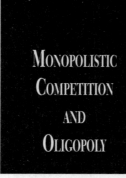

Monopolistic Competition and Oligopoly

Between the extremes of perfect competition and monopoly on the spectrum of competitiveness lie monopolistic competition and oligopoly. Like monopoly, oligopoly is characterized by barriers to entry. However, unlike monopoly, in an oligopolistic market there is more than one firm. The limited number of firms causes price and output decisions to be interdependent. Producers may compete or cooperate. Profits may exist in the long run.

Monopolistic competition is characterized by a large number of consumers and producers and free entry and exit, as in perfect competition. However, in contrast, the product is differentiated, causing the firm's demand curve to be less than perfectly elastic. Profits may be earned in the short run, but in the long run free entry competes profits away, while free exit rids the industry of any losses. Allocative inefficiency exists, and equilibrium output is below that at minimum long-run average cost. However, society may benefit from product variety and advertising.

The accompanying video illustrates monopolistic competition and oligopoly in different segments of the beer industry. It pays particular attention to producers' strategies to maximize profits.

After studying your text, watching the video, and answering the questions, you should be able to:

◆◆ Recognize different market forms

◆◆ Explain why oligopoly persists

◆◆ Explain how monopolistically competitive firms attempt to influence the demand curve for their product

◆◆ Explain the impact of product differentiation and brand loyalty on the firm's demand curve and on equilibrium price, output, and profits

◆◆ Understand the advantages and disadvantages of monopolistic competition

Preview

◆ Competition exists in the market for premium beer.

◆ Samuel Adams lager is a new entrant to the market.

◆ Its producer has attempted to find a market niche.

◆ The product image is one of patriotism.

◆ The beer is also differentiated in terms of appearance, ingredients, taste, and aroma.

◆ It is promoted through beer tasting and denigrating the competition.

◆ Sam Adams lager has increased market share in the premium beer market.

Beer Wars

In this report, Paul Solman presents the business strategy of Jim Koch, president and creator of Samuel Adams Boston Lager. Starting a brewery seemed like a foolhardy idea even to Koch, whose family had been brewers for generations. But Koch's strategy was to find a niche, a distinctive corner of a large market.

Koch began by analyzing the beer industry's recent history. As we see from old television ads, thirty years ago the market was crowded with small regional breweries. By the 1960s, a few companies beat their regional rivals to the mass market—they advertised nationally, were available everywhere, and were cheaper to produce. By 1986, Anheuser Busch alone controlled almost 40 percent of the market.

Koch figured he couldn't compete against efficient giants like these. So he targeted the only growing segment of the American beer market: the imports.

Koch named his beer Samuel Adams Boston Lager, after an American patriot who instigated the American Revolution. "He was the man who, more than anyone else, threw the foreigners out—and on top of it, he was a brewer," Koch explains.

Koch's promotion budget was tiny. He set out to convince bartenders — and their customers — that his beer was better than their foreign favorites. Paul takes us to one of these innovative beer tasting competitions. Since there's no consensus on quality in the beer industry, Koch made his beer noticeably different: Sam Adams is darker, has more body, and is more bitter and more aromatic than the foreign beers.

Less than seven weeks into production, Sam Adams got an unexpected boost in the summer of 1985, when it took first place at the Great American Beer Festival in Denver. Armed with this victory, Koch launched a campaign designed to goad his competitors into a public confrontation.

He charged that the imports had been adulterated for the American market, and that as a result, they couldn't meet German domestic beer standards. When competitors couldn't let these charges go unchallenged, Sam Adams Boston Lager got much needed press.

Whether this particular strategy worked is unknown. But within a year of start-up, Koch had already captured a sizable portion of the elite beer drinking market in Boston. He had found a niche, and positioned Sam Adams as the highest priced, highest quality American alternative to foreign beers. ◆◆◆◆◆◆◆

QUESTIONS

1. a) How would an economist characterize the structure of the market for nonpremium beer? Why?

   b) What barriers to entry exist in the market for nonpremium beer?

2. a) How would an economist characterize the structure of the market for premium beer? Why?

   b) Why is entry into the premium beer market easier than into the nonpremium beer market?

3. Assume that the premium beer market is monopolistically competitive. Jim Koch engaged in a number of different strategies in introducing Samuel Adams lager. Explain carefully the impact of the following strategies on the demand curve.

   a) differentiating the beer from other beers

   b) choosing a heroic and patriotic figure as the name for the beer

   c) heightening awareness of the product through gimmicks and stunts

   d) denigrating the competition

4. a) Apparently Samuel Adams lager is still sustaining a loss. Draw a diagram of the market for the beer, with axes representing the price and the quantity traded. Add the demand curve, the marginal revenue curve, and the marginal and average cost curves. Show the equilibrium price and output and the loss.

b) Assuming the aggressive advertising continues and is successful, what will be the impact on the equilibrium price, output, and profits? Illustrate your answer.

c) Assuming that the beer shows a profit, will it last in the long run? Why or why not?

5. a) What is the advantage of having multiple brands of premium beers?

b) What is the associated disadvantage of having variety?

c) Is society allocating sufficient resources to the production of Samuel Adams lager? Answer in the light of your diagrams above and in terms of what you know about external costs.

LABOR
MARKETS

In competitive labor markets the equilibrium wage rate is determined by the supply of and demand for labor. Labor demand is negatively related to the wage rate. The demand for labor depends on the wage rate, the price of the product, the marginal productivity of labor, and the prices and marginal productivities of other factors. Labor supply is positively related to the wage rate. Labor supply depends on the wage rate, tastes for work versus leisure, other income, and alternative wage rates.

In unionized labor markets collective bargaining overrides the free-market equilibrium wage. The level of employment depends on the demand for labor at the collectively bargained wage. The elasticity of demand for labor determines the power of the union to raise wages without causing significant employment reductions. It depends on the elasticity of product demand, the ratio of labor costs to total costs, and the substitutability of other factors for labor. Unions can also raise wage rates by influencing the supply of and demand for labor. Unions can raise the demand for the products their members make, and can decrease the supply of labor.

The accompanying video shows how some unions increase wages above nonunion wage levels and seek to avoid reductions in employment.

After studying your text, watching the video, and answering the questions, you should be able to:

◆ ◆ Explain the determinants of nonunion wages

◆ ◆ Understand how unions affect wages in different ways

◆ ◆ Recognize the role of the elasticity of demand for labor in determining the employment of unionized workers

Preview

◆ Unions' conventional tactics have been having diminishing success.

◆ New union strategies involve alliances with management.

◆ Union wages are paid if workers picket nonunion firms to encourage patronage at high-cost unionized stores.

◆ Causes of the new cooperation include a distaste for conflict, a loss of local jobs, mutual dependence in the service industry, increasing nonunion competition, and a recognition by the union that labor costs are easiest to control.

◆ The new cooperation has enabled unions to increase membership and unionized firms to benefit at the expense of nonunion firms.

Labor Day

Traditionally, the tactic taken by unions was a confrontation with management, often resulting in picketing and arrests. Today unions are exploring new methods of getting what they want, even if it means working with, and not against, management.

In this report Paul Solman explains that the old ways aren't working as well as they used to. For example, in Maine, union workers found they had been replaced by nonunion workers when they ended their 16-month strike against International Paper Company. It's stories like these that have caused some unions to rethink their "us vs. them" approach, and to explore new strategies.

Paul takes us to Ohio, where a new strategy is paying off for supermarket workers. In northeast Ohio, new non-union grocery stores pose a serious threat to unionized grocery stores and the workers they employ. So labor and management are working together. The deal is that union stores agree to pay union wages, as long as the workers agree to picket these low-wage newcomers. The union is picketing to preserve union jobs and the stores that provide them.

Things have been especially tough for labor in the rust belt. Lots of manufacturing jobs have left town. But a supermarket cannot pack up and relocate. Management's lawyer Bob Duvin realized that they were "married" to the union, and that "...if we didn't learn how to live together, and to strengthen our common interest, we were going to die together."

Speaking for the United Food and Commercial Workers, George Hennigin explains that it is difficult to get people to understand that the employer is not the enemy. The enemy is whoever is competing against your employer, because he/she has the ability to drive your own wages down.

Paul explains the economics of the grocery industry, and how this can happen. A good profit margin in groceries is 1 percent, which means a penny in profits for every dollar in sales. Of the remaining 99 percent, 15 percent goes to labor, and the rest goes to things like rent and utilities. You don't have control over these items, so the only item that you can play with is labor. With a profit margin of only 1 percent, if you can trim labor costs by even a few percentage points, you can do wonders for your bottom line and increase your profits; or you can pass the savings on to consumers by lowering prices and taking business away from the competition.

Several union stores have already been put out of business. To fight this type of competition, union and management have joined forces. ◆◆◆◆◆◆

QUESTIONS

1. a) In the nonunion supermarkets in the video, the wage was $4.50 an hour. In a diagram of the labor market for nonunion supermarket workers, draw axes representing the wage rate and the level of employment. Add the demand and supply curves, and mark the equilibrium wage rate and the associated level of employment.

   b) What might have been the causes of the relatively low level of wages? Explore the reasons for the positions of the supply and demand curves.

2. a) In unionized work places, unions negotiate wage levels above the equilibrium wage. Draw a diagram of the labor market for unionized workers. Show the equilibrium wage as being where the supply and demand curves intersect. Add a horizontal line representing the collectively bargained wage. Also mark the level of employment.

   b) Why does the elasticity of demand for labor make it difficult for unions to raise wage rates above the equilibrium level?

   c) With reference to the video, explain why manufacturing workers have increasingly faced an elastic demand for their labor.

   d) Similarly, explain why supermarket workers in Ohio faced an elastic demand for their labor.

e) Explain how the elasticity of demand for unionized supermarket workers was affected by

- picketing and telepicketing nonunion stores.

- the relative inability of supermarkets to relocate.

- the willingness of management to cooperate with the union rather than to undermine it.

f) What were the implications of the changes in 2e for unionized wages?

3. Unions can also affect wage rates through influencing the demand for their labor.

a) Draw another diagram of the labor market for unionized supermarket workers, with the wage rate and the employment level on the axes. Add a supply curve and a demand curve. Show the equilibrium wage and the collectively bargained wage of $10.50 an hour.

b) How did the UFCW increase the demand for unionized supermarket labor in northern Ohio?

c) Show the effect of the increase in the demand for labor on the levels of wages and employment on your diagram.

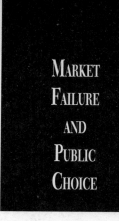

MARKET FAILURE AND PUBLIC CHOICE

When unregulated markets fail to achieve allocative efficiency, there is market failure. A different allocation of resources would increase total production and economic welfare.

One cause of market failure is a public good, where one person's consumption does not reduce the amount available for others and no one can be excluded from consuming the good. There is a role for the government to provide public goods itself. The cost can be covered by taxes.

A second cause of market failure is where economic benefits fall on a third party and are not taken into account by producers. Marginal social benefit is more than marginal private benefit. Allocative efficiency requires that output be increased by introducing subsidies.

The accompanying video focuses on a relocation decision by a company. It shows the implications for tax revenues and therefore public services, as well as for the community in general. It also discusses the issue of whether the government should intervene to prevent the relocation because of the social benefits of the company's continued presence.

After studying your text, watching the video, and answering the questions, you should be able to:

◆◆ Describe the relationship of government taxes and transfers to economic activity

◆◆ Determine the appropriate subsidy required to internalize external benefits

Preview

◆ Stewart Warner is relocating to Texas and Mexico.

◆ Some community leaders, in an effort to save jobs, would like the city to seize the company and resell it to local investors, using the principle of eminent domain.

◆ The cost to the community includes the cost of transfer payments, the loss of tax revenues, the loss of business, individual misfortune, medical problems, and medical costs.

◆ The company is looking at different costs: it can save $17 million and remain competitive by moving.

◆ Whether the community should allow progress to occur, albeit with costs, or intervene in the economy requires a judgment call.

Factory Fight

This news report analyzes the costs of shutting down a factory. Paul Solman takes us to Chicago where the Stewart Warner plant, which makes industrial instruments, is on the verge of closing. It has been bought by a British company, BTR, which wants to move the operation to Texas and Mexico. A group of local investors wants to buy the plant, but BTR won't sell. The community is trying to pass new legislation that would actually allow Chicago to seize the property by eminent domain and sell it to local investors.

Paul explains that eminent domain is a new tactic in the struggle between business and the community. The company views the economics narrowly: maximize profits while cutting losses. But the workers see the cost to the community, a figure that can in fact be calculated.

A local economist performs an analysis of the costs to the community of the plant shutting down. These costs include: unemployment, welfare, food stamps, and Medicaid. Layoffs also lead to less government revenue. Workers no longer pay taxes, and neither do local businesses that dry up because of reduced business.

Paul speaks with a representative of BTR who looks at the situation from an entirely different perspective. He says the company needs to stay competitive. If the company moves, it can pay less to its workers.

Finally, Paul speaks with a Chicago financial reporter about the idea of eminent domain. He thinks this sends a negative signal about the business climate in Chicago: that if people don't like the decision a company makes, the city can seize the assets and sell the business to someone else. In any case, he argues, Stewart Warner is housed in an old factory on land that could be put to better use.

Paul sums up both sides of this argument. On the one hand, business argues that a free market economy must clear out the old and make way for the new; it's the price you have to pay in the difficult process of adapting to a new world. But the community disagrees. They say that the price to society is too high.

In conclusion, Paul states it is a judgment call; that the numbers work out to be about the same. Does the market produce efficiently enough in the long run to justify short term brutality? Or can people manage the economic process more fairly while preserving the dynamism that keeps any economy alive? The answer reflects one's basic beliefs. ◆◆◆◆◆◆◆

QUESTIONS

1. The damage to the community of the relocation included the loss of tax income.

   a) Draw a graph showing the demand for and supply of goods in Illinois. Mark the equilibrium price and quantity in the absence of taxes. Given that there was a sales tax on goods sold in the state, and assuming it was levied on each unit produced, show the equilibrium including the tax. Shade in the area representing tax receipts.

   b) When employees lost their jobs, what happened to income tax receipts?

   c) What happened as a result of unemployment to the demand for goods and services in Illinois? On your diagram show the implications for equilibrium and for sales tax receipts.

2. The relocation was caused by relatively high costs of production in the Chicago area.

   a) Draw a diagram of the Chicago economy with one axis representing price, cost, and benefit in dollar terms, and the other representing the quantity of production. Add curves representing the marginal cost and the marginal private benefit of production by Chicago-area businesses. Mark the private equilibrium price and quantity.

   b) The availability of low-cost facilities in Texas and Mexico increase the opportunity costs of remaining in Chicago. Show the impact of this on the marginal cost curve and on the quantity of production remaining in Chicago.

c) Why might the social benefit of production in Chicago be greater than the private benefit?

d) Draw the marginal social benefit curve on your diagram. Assuming that the marginal cost curve is the same for private producers as for society, mark the socially optimal level of production in Chicago before and after the change in marginal costs.

e) What could the city do to ensure that the socially optimal level of production occurs? Refer to your diagram.

f) Does your analysis indicate that the city should attempt to keep all industry from relocating? Why? Under what circumstances should it intervene? Explain in terms of your diagram.

g) Specifically, ignoring the signal sent to other businesses, should the city use eminent domain to take over the company and use tax dollars to operate the firm? Explain your answer in terms of the principle derived in 2f and illustrate with information from the video.

Video 6: Adding Things Up

The most widely known and used price index is the Consumer Price Index (CPI), developed by the Bureau of Labor Statistics. The CPI measures the average level of price of the customary goods and services (the "market basket") purchased by a typical urban family of four. The prices of thousands of items are recorded. The cost of this market basket of goods and services for a given time period is compared with the cost for a base period. Since the market basket is essentially unchanged, changes in the CPI show price changes — inflation or deflation.

The CPI plays a vital role in the U.S. economy. Social security payments, pensions, and some wages are linked to the CPI. Government policymakers monitor movements in the CPI and base policies to control inflation on the index's change.

For most people the CPI is a number widely reported in the media. The accompanying video provides an in-depth look at the CPI and its weaknesses.

After studying your text, watching the video, and answering the questions, you should be able to:

◆◆ Distinguish a change in the general price level and a change in relative prices

◆◆ Understand how the CPI is calculated

◆◆ Describe the shortcomings of the CPI

◆◆ Recognize how the CPI overstates the actual rate of inflation

◆◆ Calculate a weighted price index

◆◆ Explain the importance of money wage increases

Preview

◆ Data for the Consumer Price Index (CPI) are collected by the Bureau of Labor Statistics (BLS) on a monthly basis.

◆ Prices are checked for a market basket of goods and services representing the budget of an average American.

◆ The basis of the CPI is important because it is used in macroeconomic policymaking and it determines increases in payments such as social security.

◆ Inflation is overstated because the BLS is slower than consumers to find the cheapest goods.

◆ Changes in the market basket to reflect sales and technical progress are limited.

◆ Consumers are unhappy because wages increased at an even slower rate than prices in the 1980s.

Adding Things Up

What is the consumer price index (CPI)? Where do the numbers come from? What is their impact? In this video, Paul Solman seeks to answer these questions by traveling around from store to store with a government worker who looks at changing prices from month to month.

The monthly CPI figure reflects the rate at which prices are rising. It is calculated from data collected by 330 employees of the Bureau of Labor Statistics (BLS) who check prices in stores on a monthly basis. The goods and services surveyed are representative of the budget of the average American. The BLS shoppers are careful to ensure that the product is unchanged, and that comparisons of like with like are being made.

It is vital for the CPI to be correctly calculated. It is used to frame macroeconomic policy. Also it is used to determine increases in payments such as social security.

One criticism of the CPI is that it overstates inflation. The government changes the stores it surveys in order to keep up with consumers who are shopping at discount stores. But we hear from critics who claim that the government switches less quickly than consumers and thus the CPI misses declines in prices that have been occurring for years.

Paul outlines other ways that critics claim the CPI is not keeping pace, and is thus overstating inflation. In particular, changes in the market basket are limited. The index fails to recognize that consumers stock up when items go on sale. It also ignores changes in goods due to technical progress.

Paul speaks with experts who say that the inflation rate, although already low, is really lower than we think. Why aren't people happier about the low inflation rate? Paul explains that we don't experience a rise in inflation but growth in income relative to inflation. We don't notice the slow growth in inflation because wage growth has been slower. ◆◆◆◆◆

QUESTIONS

1. The video shows that the CPI focuses on the average price level, not relative prices.

    a) What is the average price level?

    b) What are relative prices?

    c) Can relative prices change without the average price level rising? Explain your answer.

2. a) Price data are collected for a market basket of goods. How is this market basket determined?

    b) Why is the CPI rarely accurate for any consumer?

    c) Why is the CPI an inaccurate measure of price changes over time?

3. The video shows that the market basket—which represents the spending habits of the average urban American family—is made up of the following types of goods and services:

housing	41%	apparel	6%
food and beverages	18%	entertainment	4%
transportation	18%	other (including education)	7%
medical	6%		

a) How is your basket different from the above? Think about your spending over the last year and write down the proportions of your total expenditure accounted for by each category.

b) Suppose that the increases in the prices of each category over the last year were:

housing	5%	apparel	5%
food and beverages	2%	entertainment	3%
transportation	3%	other	8%
medical	15%		

i) What would have been the rate of inflation for the average urban American family? Show your calculations.

ii) What was the rate of inflation for you? Show your calculations.

4. How would you think the basket would differ for

a) the average urban American family in New York City?

b) the average rural American family?

c) the average childless urban American family?

d) the average retired American family?

e) the average unmarried American mother?

5. If the price index for 1820 was 100, last year it was approximately 2000. Is it therefore correct to say that the cost of living is 20 times greater nowadays than in 1820? Why or why not?

6. The video reports that inflation has been low recently while wages have increased even more slowly.

a) What happens to the value of money during inflation?

b) How might wage increases remedy the consequences?

c) Why might wages have failed to keep up with inflation?

d) Is it likely that all U.S. residents have suffered equally? If not, who might have been the winners and losers? Explain your answer.

Video 7: Boom to Bust

The business cycle goes through four phases: contraction, trough, expansion, and peak. As it proceeds, there are changes in income, unemployment, inflation, and stock prices. The fluctuations in aggregate income are caused by changes in autonomous expenditure—that is, expenditure that is independent of the level of real GDP.

Changes in autonomous expenditure cause bigger changes in equilibrium aggregate expenditure, depending on the size of the autonomous expenditure multiplier. The parameters that determine the size of the multiplier are the marginal and average propensity to consume (or save), import, and tax.

The accompanying video analyzes the business cycle in Massachusetts over the past decade. It illustrates the importance of the multiplier in the determination of the change in equilibrium aggregate income.

After studying your text, watching the video, and answering the questions, you should be able to:

◆ ◆ Recognize the indicators of a boom and a recession

◆ ◆ Understand the economic causes of fluctuations in aggregate income

◆ ◆ Describe the role of the multiplier in the business cycle

◆ ◆ Discuss the factors that impact the size of the multiplier

◆ ◆ Describe the dimensions of a typical recession

Preview

◆ Massachusetts was booming in the early 1980s.

◆ Tourism and defense contracts increased wages, employment, and profits.

◆ The benefits were spread throughout the community as wages were spent.

◆ However, defense cutbacks led to layoffs and lower income and spending.

◆ Local business slumped and lower government revenues prejudiced education and extracurricular activities.

◆ Recessions are generally short, but this one may be longer owing to the large amount of consumer and business debt.

Boom to Bust

In the early 1980s, the saying was "Make it in Massachusetts." That's exactly what many people were doing: starting new business ventures, buying homes and cars, and spreading the wealth around. But by the end of the 1980s, the "Massachusetts Miracle" was over. In a state of recession, it set the pattern for many states across the country. In this report, Paul Solman travels to Southbridge and Sturbridge, Massachusetts, to see how this downward spiral has affected the people there and to explain how it happened.

The Southbridge/Sturbridge area experienced the euphoric upside of the business cycle. It seemed especially well protected against recession since it featured one of New England's most time honored tourist attractions, Old Sturbridge Village. Here, the only problem was finding enough employees to meet their needs. A short drive away, the new Galileo Electro Optics company manufactures fiber optical devices for the military. During the defense buildup of the 1980s, it experienced a doubling of its work force, and a quadrupling of sales.

That money was spread throughout the local community. Money taken in by the companies would get paid out to the employees. The employees would spend the money on food, clothes, and luxuries, stimulating the local economy and causing lots of opportunities for new business. With new businesses, you need advertising. Loren Ghiglione, publisher of a local paper, says that he was so successful, he was able to expand by purchasing new publications.

The problem, Paul points out, is that as businesses became more successful, they took on greater debts. Looking toward a future of growth, they believed that debts incurred now would be financed by that future growth. Consumers did the same thing, and as housing prices skyrocketed, they took on higher mortgages, expecting the value of houses to continue to increase. People forgot that it could all come to an end.

Economists define a recession as when the GNP declines for at least 6 months. Nick Perna, a local bank economist, puts it in more practical terms, "When you see things like home construction, car sales declining, business spending on a new plant and equipment declining, those are all the signs and things and components of a recession."

Paul points out that in the Sturbridge/Southbridge area, these signs are everywhere. When cutbacks in defense spending occurred, Galileo laid off 20 percent of its work force.

When New Englanders saw these signs, they stopped spending on such things as tourist attractions. Sturbridge Village had to cut its staff by 20 percent. The same spiraling process that took Massachusetts up the business cycle has now slipped into reverse and is spiraling the economy back down. ◆ ◆ ◆ ◆ ◆

QUESTIONS

1. In the 1980s, Galileo Electro Optics won government contracts from the Defense Department.

   a) Assume that the company was awarded $100 million in contracts. What was the consequence of this for the area's GDP? Be as precise as you can in your response.

   b) Describe the process that resulted in an increase in the area's GDP.

   c) What factors determined the size of the overall increase in GDP?

2. The decline in the economy of Southbridge/Sturbridge was in part attributable to defense cutbacks.

   a) Suppose that no Galileo employee ever made purchases from the local jewelers, florists, or realtors. Were these enterprises impacted by the loss of defense contracts at Galileo?

   b) How did consumer confidence play a role in the multiplier process?

   c) The video mentions that employment expanded at Old Sturbridge Village in the boom, and affected wage rates. What impact do you think the recession had on wages in the Southbridge/Sturbridge area? Explain your answer.

   d) Why was the local football team affected by the cutbacks at Galileo, Sturbridge, and other enterprises?

3. The video discusses the prospects for a recovery from the recession.

   a) What is the definition of a recession?

   b) What is the average duration of post-World War II recessions?

   c) Why have modern recessions not been as wrenching compared with recessions earlier in the century?

4. a) What measures could the local government of the Sturbridge area take to stimulate the local economy? Justify them in terms of the concepts illustrated in the video.

   b) How successful do you think your suggested measures would be? Why?

Video 8: The Search for the S&L Culprit

Financial intermediaries—such as commercial banks, savings and loans (S&Ls), savings banks, credit unions, and money market mutual funds—take deposits and make loans. S&Ls are important not only because of their influence on the money supply but also because they are a major lender of money to home buyers.

The Federal Deposit Insurance Corporation (FDIC) and the Federal Savings and Loan Insurance Corporation (FSLIC) insure depositors' savings. Some banks are also restricted by state charter as to their asset structure and liquidity. In the 1980s, some S&Ls got into financial difficulty. The cost to the government of bailing out the failed S&Ls was estimated at one half trillion dollars in 1992.

The accompanying video investigates the many causes of the S&L crisis.

After studying your text, watching the video, and answering the questions, you should be able to:

◆◆ Explain the circumstances that led to the S&L failures

◆◆ Discuss the contribution of management, regulators, and politicians to the problem

◆◆ Recognize the cost of bailing out the S&Ls

Preview

- ◆ Many S&Ls are in financial difficulty.
- ◆ Many factors are to blame.
- ◆ Inflation raised deposit rates while mortgage rates were fixed, squeezing profits.
- ◆ Management tried to grow out of its problems by making riskier loans.
- ◆ Politicians contributed to the crisis by raising insurance levels and allowing wider loans.
- ◆ Embezzlement added to S&L losses, but was not a primary cause.
- ◆ Regulators compounded problems by merging weak S&Ls.
- ◆ In a sense, business reporters are to blame because they did not blow the whistle on the S&Ls.
- ◆ The public is also at fault for their expectations of fixed-rate mortgages.

The Search for the S&L Culprit

Savings and Loans across the country are in serious financial trouble, with the government bailing many of them out. In this report, Paul Solman searches for the culprit and explains what caused the crisis.

Paul visits Norwalk, Ohio, and the home of his brother's brother-in-law, Alan Myers. Myers was a loan officer at a local S&L that failed, Home Savings and Loan. When he started, it was local farmers coming to the S&L to deposit their money. When they needed a loan, the S&L could give it to them, at a higher interest rate than the S&L was paying them for their deposit.

Paul introduces us to another brother-in-law, Harold Freeman. Freeman was the junior counsel for the failed bank. Freeman says when he joined the bank, it was experiencing an inflationary spiral. Paul says that the first culprit in this story is inflation.

Paul explains that for decades, S&Ls had paid only 3 percent interest. Bankers called the loan process a "3-6-3" business. When people deposited their money, you paid them 3 percent interest. When they borrowed the money for home mortgages, you charged them 6 percent interest. Why 3-6-3? Because you pay 3, collect 6, and you're on the golf course by 3 in the afternoon.

Due to inflation, banks had to start paying higher interest as depositors became more sophisticated and more options became available. But, they still had the long-term mortgages at the old rates of interest. The S&L developed a way to handle this profit squeeze, which eventually became national policy. Freeman explains that the board of directors decided to expand, to "grow out of their problems." They expanded from one to seven locations. The second culprit, Paul decides, is the bank management, which proposed this idea.

The idea was that the new offices would give out new mortgages, at higher interest rates. But loans at higher rates of interest are almost always riskier loans. Freeman says the bank started to give out speculative loans to home builders. The idea was that once the home was built, it would be sold, and the builder could pay off the mortgage with the money from the sale. But when the homes were built, there was nobody to buy them. So the bank was forced to foreclose, leaving it with bad pieces of property.

But are the bank president and the board of directors really to blame? Freeman defends them, saying they had to do something. And, he says, the money wasn't the bank's, it was the depositors', and the government insures depositors' money.

Bank insurance made sense in the 1930s, when banks were failing, thereby threatening the national economy. Bankers didn't have to worry about the depositors' money, the government did. Normally, the government didn't allow risky loans. But faced with inflation in the 1970s, the government started to allow the loans. In the 1980s, legislation was passed that let S&Ls make loans beyond home mortgages. And because those loans made depositors nervous, the government increased the limit on insured deposits from $40,000 to $100,000. So this new legislation was also to blame.

The next suspect Paul looks at is the crooked banker. Norwalk even had an embezzler at their S&L. The bank's secretary had embezzled $400,000 from the bank. But recent studies Paul consulted indicate that fraud accounted for only 3 percent to 10 percent of the total S&L losses. Most of the losses actually resulted from bad loans, which could have been avoided if the weak S&Ls had been allowed to close. But the government developed the strategy of merging troubled banks.

Home Savings of Norwalk merged with another troubled S&L, Ohio Valley Savings. It was again expanding out of the problem. And again, expanding meant more risk. The bank started to invest in hotels and out-of-state projects. While the returns were greater, the risk was even greater. The federal government had to bail out the loans, and the bank merged with World Savings of California.

Paul ends by saying that along with the bankers and the politicians, business correspondents could be to blame. They could have blown the whistle a long time ago. But, who would have listened, when they could still get low mortgages and high interest rates on deposits? This time, maybe we are all to blame, and all of us will wind up paying the tab. ◆ ◆ ◆ ◆

QUESTIONS

1. a) What services do S&Ls sell?

   b) How do they make a profit?

   c) Why is the interest rate at which borrowers obtain money generally higher than is paid on savings accounts?

2. a) What is the impact of inflation on rates paid to depositors?

   b) What is the impact on fixed-rate mortgages?

   c) What happens to profits as a result?

3. In 1980, Congress reacted to the S&L situation by lifting the interest rate ceilings that previously existed, and allowing wider lending.

   a) Illustrate the results of these steps for interest rates and S&L funds in a diagram of the demand for and supply of S&L funds.

b) How did management expect to grow out of the crisis?

4. a) When a firm goes bankrupt, who generally foots the bill?

b) Why doesn't the government treat S&Ls as just another firm and refuse to bail them out? Answer in terms of the money supply and also in terms of the implications for output and prices.

5. In response to the disadvantages of the traditional 30-year fixed-rate mortgage, the banking industry has attempted to create other mortgage instruments that consumers would desire but which would not have the potential for causing the disaster that the S&Ls experienced. For each of the following, explain the features of the mortgage and the attraction to consumers.

a) adjustable rate mortgages (ARMs) (3-year or 1-year)

b) 7-23 ARMs (fixed for 7 years, variable for 23 years)

STABILIZING THE ECONOMY

The government's stabilization goals are price stability and unemployment at the natural rate. However, there is a tradeoff between inflation and unemployment. As aggregate demand increases, employment increases and unemployment decreases; however, the rise in aggregate demand puts upward pressure on prices.

To achieve these goals, the Fed uses open-market operations and changes in the discount rate to influence aggregate demand. An increase in the money supply lowers interest rates and causes an increase in aggregate demand. However, there is a debate about whether the government should follow fixed-rule or feedback-rule policies. Much depends on whether the policy tools are accurate enough to avoid worsening the economic situation.

The accompanying video explains why and how policymakers attempt to steer a course between inflation and unemployment through nautical and classical metaphors.

After studying your text, watching the video, and answering the questions, you should be able to:

◆◆ Discuss the objectives of a stabilization program

◆◆ Understand the problems and tradeoffs in achieving stabilization objectives

◆◆ Describe the process by which stabilization policies work

◆◆ Discuss the relative merits of fixed-rule and feedback-rule policies

Preview

◆ The Fed has the difficult task of steering a course between inflation and recession.

◆ Inflation causes higher interest rates and the erosion of fixed income, and it is costly to control.

◆ Recession can have far-reaching consequences for economic activity and employment.

◆ The Fed watches economic indicators in deciding how to react.

◆ The idea is to lean against the wind and bring about a soft landing.

Steering the Course

 In this report Paul Solman literally goes to sea with Franco Modigliani and Robert Solow, two leading M.I.T. economists, to illustrate the perils of inflation and recession and show how Federal Reserve Bank Chairman Alan Greenspan must steer a precarious course.

The Federal Reserve Bank manages the nation's money supply, buying and selling government bonds and trying to adjust interest rates. When the Fed stimulates the economy, it risks inflation; when the economy slows, inflation ebbs but recession fears rise.

Greenspan emerges "from his temple and like an oracle makes pronouncements about where the economy is headed." Greenspan suggests the balance or risk may have shifted somewhat away from greater inflation. If inflation is finally at bay, will he now increase the money supply to prevent recession? Observers try to interpret his words and unlock the secrets of the temple.

Paul makes the analogy to the famous passage in the Odyssey that describes Ulysses trying to negotiate a passage between Scylla, the multiheaded sea monster (inflation) and Charybdis, the man-eating whirlpool (recession). The economists explain that like Ulysses, Greenspan is forever navigating treacherous waters. Historically, the greater fear has been the monster of inflation that robs innocent victims of their wealth.

To illustrate this point, Paul stops at a tourist haven, Martha's Vineyard, to examine the cost of inflation. Merchants can't afford the high interest rates that inflation brings. With double-digit mortgage rates, pensioners on fixed incomes have to give up their Vineyard retirement dreams. Once we get into an inflationary spiral, it is very costly to get out. For example, in Argentina and Brazil with 1000 percent inflation, the predominant concern is to control inflation.

When Captain Greenspan feels the boat is getting too close to the Scylla of inflation, he clamps down on the money supply and sets sail in the direction of a slower economy. But then the danger is the Charybdis of recession. A little recession often spirals into a deeper recession that is far-reaching. The complex nature of the economy and the chance of false signals demand that Greenspan cast his net broadly, gathering information on economic activity, financial and foreign exchange markets, and related data.

The economists point out that we can't ignore the Scylla of inflation in order to avoid the Charybdis of recession. The big mistake is to concentrate on only one thing in normal times. It's a sign of success when we are worrying about both things. It's when we are going down the middle that we have to keep looking at either side. Paul explains that Greenspan is simply doing what Fed chairmen always do, leaning against the wind, always trying to steer that narrow course between inflation and recession and hoping for a soft landing. Greenspan has to be very good or very lucky to get it right. ◆

QUESTIONS

1. a) What are the goals of stabilization?

    b) Identify the Fed's major policy instruments for achieving these goals.

2. Six months before the video was produced, the danger was inflation.

    a) Draw a diagram of the U.S. economy, with real GDP and the price level on the axes. Add the aggregate supply curves and the aggregate demand curve, assuming that the economy is in macroeconomic equilibrium with unemployment less than the natural rate.

    b) Suppose that the Fed reduced the supply of money. What would have happened to interest rates in the money market? Why?

    c) What would have been the implications for aggregate demand and/or supply and for macroeconomic equilibrium? Illustrate your answer on your diagram.

3. At the time the video was produced, the danger was a recession.

    a) If you had been the chair of the Fed, how would you have changed the money supply? How would you have achieved this?

b) What would you have expected to have happened to

- interest rates? Why?

- investment? Why?

- aggregate demand and/or supply? Why?

- macroeconomic equilibrium? Why?

c) Draw another diagram of the U.S. economy, with real GDP and the price level on the axes. Add the aggregate supply curves and the aggregate demand curve, assuming that the economy is in macroeconomic equilibrium with unemployment greater than the natural rate. Illustrate on your diagram the impact on macroeconomic equilibrium of the policy you suggest.

4. a) Is the policy described in the video a fixed-rule or a feedback-rule policy? Explain your answer.

b) The video refers to a "crash landing" and a "soft landing." In the context of stabilization policy, describe the meaning of these two terms.

c) Why is it so difficult to "steer the course"? Refer to

- the strengths and certainty of important relationships among the policy instruments and their targets.

- lags in implementation of monetary policy.

- the difficulty of recognizing trends.

- rational expectations.

5. The video discusses the dangers of pursuing a monetary policy that is too tight or too expansive and the difficulty of finding a middle course.

   a) Is there an alternative to an activist role? Explain.

   b) How would this alternative mechanism operate?

   c) Some economists prefer the alternative. Explain their argument.

   d) Do you think their arguments are valid? Under what conditions would their arguments make the alternative more viable?

GROWTH AND DEVELOPMENT

Video 10: Paradise Lost

Developing countries have a relatively low standard of living, caused in part by high birth and death rates and low output per capita. They typically have difficulty accumulating capital, owing to low education levels and a low savings rate. They also tend to have a high level of international debt. Measures proposed for remedying these problems include population control, foreign aid, greater international trade, and devaluation which increases exports and decreases imports.

The accompanying video illustrates the growing pains of developing countries with reference to Jamaica. In particular, it analyzes the conditions imposed on Jamaica by the International Monetary Fund (IMF) in return for loans.

After reading your text, watching the video, and answering the questions, you should be able to:

◆◆ Understand the impediments to economic growth and development

◆◆ Explain the impact of various development strategies

◆◆ Discuss the costs of development strategies

Preview

◆ The Jamaican government has been criticized for borrowing from the IMF because of the conditions imposed.

◆ In return for the IMF helping Jamaica increase its productive potential, Jamaica has to follow four rules.

◆ It has to get the state out of the economy to improve efficiency and profitability, although it causes layoffs.

◆ It must reduce subsidies to pay off debt and put more into the economy, although it worsens poverty.

◆ It has to encourage exports to help pay off debts, but markets are very competitive.

◆ It must discourage imports by devaluation and tariffs, although importers and consumers may be hurt.

489

Paradise Lost

 Jamaica is a test case for the policies of the International Monetary Fund (IMF). Jamaica has borrowed heavily from the IMF, and in accordance with IMF policy, in return must adopt a free market economy, bitter medicine for a country that cares about its poor.

Michael Manley was prime minister of Jamaica in the 1970s. He was a champion of the dispossessed, borrowing heavily from abroad to help the poor of Jamaica. But foreign investors saw a communist threat in Manley and pulled out of Jamaica. With Jamaica's debts mounting, and state-run businesses losing money, Manley was voted out.

The 1980s saw renewed borrowing. This led to an economic boom followed by a crash. Manley was again elected as prime minister in 1989; this time as an avowed capitalist who believed strongly in a market economy.

Paul Solman reports that Jamaica is a good test case for the IMF approach, an approach that is being touted all over the world as a solution to a country's debt problems. Paul examines the basic tenets of the IMF, policies that he refers to as "commandments."

Commandment #1 is to get the state out of the economy. Paul speaks with the owner of a popular tourist spot in Jamaica, Sandals. Under government ownership, Sandals was in debt. Now under private ownership, the resort is turning a handsome profit. The owner feels the free market is the only way. It puts money in people's pockets and teaches them marketable skills.

Commandment #2 is to reduce government subsidies. This has meant taking money away from social services, which is hurting the poor. Though the IMF acknowledges that in the short run this can be painful, it feels it is in Jamaica for the long haul and that eventually fewer government subsidies will mean more money for the state to help pay off its debts.

Commandment #3 is to encourage exports in order to get money in to help pay off Jamaica's debts. To do this, the government has created tax-free zones where exporters receive tax breaks and Jamaicans are employed. We see a t-shirt factory and a data-processing plant that have been opened in a tax-free zone. But Paul notes that, because the IMF is encouraging many other Third World countries to export these same kinds of goods and services, it is questionable whether these businesses will bring prosperity.

Commandment #4 is to discourage imports. This is done by devaluing the Jamaican currency so that imported goods cost more and people will buy fewer of them. Another way to discourage imports is to raise taxes on imports. This has met with much resistance from working class entrepreneurs who have for years traveled abroad to duty-free ports and brought back consumer goods, tax exempt. Manley has taken away this tax exemption, claiming it is hurting many local industries. But it seems Jamaicans would much rather buy foreign goods than products made in their own country.

Paul speaks to a Caribbean scholar who says that Jamaica is swamped by American mass media and the things that Jamaicans want are determined by America. This has led to many Jamaicans migrating to the United States. Paul speaks with a Jamaican in New York who is having trouble making a living. But he plans to stay anyway, because he says there is not much for him back in his own country.

Back in Jamaica, Michael Manley is optimistic that the future promises to be better in Jamaica, that the economy will revive, and the debt will be reduced. ◆

QUESTIONS

1. Jamaica is a relatively poor country and the United States is a rich country.

   a) What accounts for the difference in per capita income between the two countries?

   b) What makes per capita income change?

2. Jamaica is borrowing money from the IMF to fund investment projects.

   a) Draw a diagram of the Jamaican economy, with real GDP and the price level on the axes. Add the aggregate demand and supply curves. Show the economy in macroeconomic equilibrium at more than the natural rate of unemployment.

   b) On your diagram, show what Jamaica hopes will happen to its economy.

   c) What impact is the repayment on the loans having on the aggregate demand and supply curves and on equilibrium? Illustrate your answer.

   d) How does this explain the requirements that exports be increased and imports be reduced?

3. Another requirement is that government subsidies be reduced.

   a) Draw a supply and demand diagram for an industry, with price and quantity on the axes. Show the impact of a subsidy on equilibrium price and quantity. Shade the area representing the subsidy.

b) Who benefits and who loses from the subsidy?

c) Why do you think the IMF objects to such subsidies?

4. a) How would reducing state ownership of industry benefit the economy?

b) Why would private ownership be more successful?

5. In the short run, the IMF's rules impose costs on the Jamaican population. How are the people affected by

a) reduced state ownership?

b) reduced subsidies to industry?

c) greater exports?

d) lower imports?